WINDOWS 2000
PROFESSIONAL

In Record Time

WINDOWS® 2000 PROFESSIONAL

In Record Time™

Peter Dyson
Pat Coleman

SYBEX®

San Francisco • Paris • Düsseldorf • Soest • London

Associate Publisher: Roger Stewart
Contracts and Licensing Manager: Kristine O'Callaghan
Acquisitions & Developmental Editor: Ellen Dendy
Editor: Jeff Gammon
Technical Editor: Michelle Poole
Book Designers: Franz Baumhackl, Patrick Dintino, and
Catalin Dulfu
Graphic Illustrator: Tony Jonick
Electronic Publishing Specialists: Cyndy Johnsen and
Franz Baumhackl
Project Team Leader: Jennifer Durning
Proofreaders: Jennifer Campbell, Nelson Kim, and Dave Nash
Indexer: Nancy Guenther
Cover Designer: Design Site
Cover Photographer: Adri Berger/Tony Stone Images

To the Katy Ya-Ya's—you know who you are.
PC

To Tulsa. My muse and constant companion.
PD

Acknowledgments

Writing a computer book is a collaborative process that often starts out as an idea in the publisher's mind. In this case, the idea for the book and the invitation to write it came from Gary Masters, then Associate Publisher for hardware and operating system books at Sybex and now Director of Special Projects. Besides being the repository of enough ideas to write a thousand books, Gary is a long-time friend and colleague whose interaction in the development cycle is always guaranteed to provide entertainment and inspiration. Thanks, Gary.

Other thanks go to our developmental editor Ellen Dendy, especially for her proactive efforts in helping track the software development process and for providing us with what we needed to write this book. As usual, Kristine O'Callaghan sorted out all the contract details in her always efficient and gracious manner.

Special thanks go to the Sybex editorial and production team, which included Jeff Gammon, Editor; Michelle Poole, Technical Editor; Jennifer Durning, Production Team Leader; Cyndy Johnsen, Electronic Publishing Specialist; and Jennifer Campbell, Nelson Kim, and Dave Nash, Proofreaders.

In addition to our collective gratitude, we each want to thank some people who helped us with all sorts of things. Pat sends special thanks to Bill Hertzing and Sonja Hertzing for technical and moral support in setting up a new network, and she thanks her older son, Miles Pratt, for several long and engaging phone calls concerning everything from getting an old printer to work to where to find the best buy on a network card.

Peter sends special thanks to our mutual friend, Gene Weisskopf, for sharing his experiences in setting up a network using Digital Subscriber Line connections and the unusual security issues involved, and, of course, special thanks to Nancy.

Contents at a Glance

Table of Contents

Introduction

Windows 2000 Professional represents the next step in the progression of Windows desktop operating systems. It is bigger, faster, slicker, more capable, and easier to use than anything that has gone before, and it will help more people get more stuff done.

In thousands of corporations, businesses, and home offices across the world, new networks are constantly being set up; the benefits of sharing files, folders, printers, and other resources are obvious to everyone these days. Many of these new networks will be based on Windows 2000 Professional, both as a workstation attached to a large network and as a server on a smaller, peer-to-peer network. Windows 2000 Professional provides exactly what these networks need: a robust operating system that provides security, stability, and the ability to manage both Internet and intranet connections.

Who Should Read This Book?

Unless you're in the habit of browsing the computer section in your favorite bookstore for hours on end or continually searching the catalogs of all the online bookstores, you've probably picked up this book for a reason. Perhaps your company or organization has decided to upgrade all its workstations to Windows 2000 Professional, or you're in the process of setting it up on your small business or home network. You need to rather quickly figure out how Windows 2000 Professional is different from the system you've been using, and you don't have time to wade through a thousand pages or more.

This book is for you if you are new to networking, if you are upgrading from previous versions of Windows, including Windows 3.1, Windows 95/98, or Windows NT 4 Workstation, or if you are coming to the Windows world from another operating system. Here you will find everything you need to know to manage your Windows 2000 Professional workstation.

We should also point out some assumptions we made about you while writing this book. We assume that you know how to use a mouse and keyboard, that you know how to navigate windows and dialog boxes, and, as you sit down to work with Windows 2000 Professional, that this is not your first time working with a computer. We think you are a rather sophisticated and intelligent computer user who just needs a jump start in using this new operating system.

How This Book Is Organized

Unlike a lot of computer books, this book is organized around what you need to do, not according to the features of Windows 2000 Professional. We don't think that most people need to be able to recite from memory what items are found in Control Panel. Most people do need to know how to change the resolution on their monitor, how to connect to other people on their network, how to print, how to connect to the Internet, and so on. So that's our approach. We thought about how we and others we know work with computers, and then we tailored our topics and the order in which we discuss them accordingly.

Another organizing principle in this book is its lack of theory. The purpose of a book in the In Record Time series is to get you up and running quickly and using even some of the more advanced features of a program. The idea is that you don't necessarily need to know, for example, all the nuances of how TCP/IP (Transmission Control Protocol/Internet Protocol) makes the Internet possible. But you do definitely need to know how to set up Internet Explorer and Outlook Express so that you can quickly and efficiently search the Internet, send and receive mail, and transfer files.

You'll also find that we move rather briskly through the tasks in each skill. We don't tell you about all the various ways you can accomplish a task. We simply point out what we think is the most efficient and most intuitive technique. Here's a brief description of what you'll find in each skill.

Skill 1 Evaluating Windows 2000 Professional

This skill explains the structure of the new Windows 2000 family of operating systems and delineates the differences between Windows 2000 Professional and previous versions of Windows. Don't skip it; it contains a lot of information you can use now and in the future.

Skill 2 Installing and Upgrading to Windows 2000 Professional

Normally, you find installation instructions relegated to an appendix. We put this information right up front, however, because, unlike with some previous versions of Windows, you need to make some informed decisions before and as you install Windows 2000 Professional. Even if you are on a corporate network and installation is out of your hands, take a look at this skill, which helps you understand a lot about how and why your Windows 2000 network operates as it does.

Skill 3 Exploring the Desktop

The Desktop is what you see when you start Windows 2000 Professional. This skill describes and explains each item on the Desktop and shows you how to use it. If you've been using Windows 98, the Windows 2000 Professional Desktop will look familiar, but many items have been relocated and renamed. Turn to this skill for driving instructions.

Skill 4 Managing Files and Folders

As we mentioned earlier, our approach in organizing this book was to try to take you logically through tasks and skills in terms of what you do at your computer every day. Thus, we followed information about the Desktop with information about how you access documents, how you create, move, copy, and rename files and folders, and how you set up your system so that it is organized in a way that lets you find what you want when you need it. We think you need to know this and do some of this before you start personalizing your system, which is the topic of the next skill.

Skill 5 Customizing Your Desktop

The Desktop in Windows 2000 Professional, by default, is set up in a rather sleek, uncluttered fashion, and you will probably want to keep many of these default settings. However, you will, no doubt, want to change others to suit your own special needs and preferences. This skill includes information on how to specify Accessibility options (settings that make Windows 2000 Professional easier to use if you have a visual or aural challenge), how to set up your system to work in your geographical location, how to change your display so that it makes the most of your monitor, and so on.

Skill 6 Setting Object Properties

In Windows 2000 Professional, an object is just about anything on your computer or on your network—a modem, a file, a folder, a shortcut, even another computer—and all objects have properties, which are settings that affect how the object looks and, oftentimes, how it works. The properties for each object are collected together in a special Properties dialog box. Some of these you can change; others are "etched in pixels." This skill explains how you set and work with object properties.

Skill 7 Installing and Running Your Applications

A new operating systems isn't of much value without the applications you use to get your work done. This skill tells you how to add and remove programs and how to work with our old friend the command prompt, and it introduces you to the Registry, which is the database that stores all the configuration settings used on your system.

Skill 8 Printers and Printing

Even though most of us have almost a fatal attraction to the paperless office, we still need to print. This skill includes instruction on setting up a new printer, both local and network, and provides the information you need in order to print exactly what you want and in what format.

Skill 9 Sharing Information between Applications

The idea of sharing information has always been central to the development of the Windows family of operating systems, and, of course, it is the heart and soul of the Internet. In this skill, we start with the basics and then take a look at Net-Meeting, which you can use to share data, collaborate on documents, and conference over the Internet or an intranet.

Skill 10 Using the Windows 2000 Professional Applications

Windows 2000 Professional comes with a number of applications, including Fax, Notepad, WordPad, Address Book, CD Player, Sound Recorder, and so on. In this skill, we quickly show you how to make the most out of each one. By the way, Windows 2000 Professional includes a new game, so check out the Games accessory if you haven't yet done so.

Skill 11 Connecting to the Outside World

Can't get your work done any more if you don't have e-mail or access to the Web? Neither can we. Windows 2000 Professional includes some new Wizards that make it easier to establish and maintain dial-up connections, and this skill explains how to use them. It also shows you how to use Phone Dialer and HyperTerminal.

Skill 12 Web Browsing with Internet Explorer

The latest release of Internet Explorer, version 5, is included with Windows 2000 Professional. It includes some handy new tools such as a greatly improved Search feature and a Radio toolbar. This skill explains these new features and also tells you how to use Internet Explorer to maximize your time on the Web.

Skill 13 Using Outlook Express for E-mail and News

Of all the features of the Internet, intranets, and local area networks, e-mail is the most used and, probably, the most indispensable these days. You can use Outlook Express to send and receive mail, transfer files, read and post to newsgroups, and send a Web page or a link. This skill steps you through all these and a few more tasks.

Skill 14 Getting the Most Out of Windows 2000 Professional

This skill explores several important areas within Windows 2000 Professional, including Computer Management, adding and configuring hardware, and optimizing hard-disk performance. It also looks at configuring multimedia and sound and setting up scanners, cameras, and game controllers. Don't skip this skill if you have any of these devices. In addition, this skill discusses how to manage virtual memory. Carefully using virtual memory allows you to run more programs simultaneously than your system's physical memory would allow.

Skill 15 What to Do when Something Goes Wrong

Windows 2000 Professional is a robust and reliable operating system, but sometimes things do go wrong. In this skill, we take a look at a couple of things you can do to make life easier for Windows and yourself, and then we look at the tools you can use to see what is going on inside your system in more detail. Finally, we look at some of the techniques you can use to rescue a Windows installation.

Skill 16 Setting Up a Small Network

Once upon a time, if you had more than two computers in your office, you might have vaguely considered networking them together to share files, folders, printers, and other resources. These days, networking hardware is so cheap, available, and reliable that you are putting yourself at a distinct disadvantage if you *don't* network your computers. In this skill, we tell you how.

Skill 17 Connecting to a Corporate Network

In this skill, we look at the different ways you can connect a Windows 2000 Professional system to a large corporate network. We also look at how to get the best out of the networked environment, and examine some of the features that make Windows 2000 Professional a great choice for mobile users.

Appendix A Glossary

In most cases, we explain terminology that we think might be unfamiliar in the text. Additionally, though, we've included a rather comprehensive glossary that contains a substantial collection of networking terms as well as terms and concepts specific to Windows 2000 Professional. Check the glossary right away if you need more explanation about something you are reading.

Conventions Used in This Book

The URLs in this book are in a special typeface and look like this:

`http://www.sybex.com`

We have tried not to break a URL across a line; when we have to do so, it breaks after a slash (/) or before a period (.).

Anything you need to type is in boldface. For example, choose Start ➤ Run, and type **clipbrd** in the Open box to open the Clipboard.

In addition, you'll find Notes, Tips, and Warnings:

NOTE A note usually contains some additional or clarifying information.

TIP A tip contains instructions about a quick and easy way to do something or contains a pointer to a helpful tidbit of information.

WARNING A warning is an alert that something can go wrong and what to do to prevent it or to recover from it.

Sidebars are also scattered about. A sidebar normally contains valuable information that is related to the text but not essential to explaining a process.

Evaluating Windows 2000 Professional

- **Understanding the Windows 2000 family of operating systems**

- **Comparing Windows 2000 Professional and Windows 3.1**

- **Comparing Windows 2000 Professional and Windows 95/98**

- **Comparing Windows 2000 Professional and Windows NT Workstation 4**

- **Understanding networks**

Whether or not you adhere to a purist interpretation of when one century ends and another begins, you have to admit that the approach and celebration of the year 2000 engendered a mind-boggling array of turn-of-the-century transitions—everything from revisiting the prognostications of Nostradamus to making sure your VCR will still work on January 1, 2000. And the computer world has taken the opportunity to introduce what many describe as major innovations.

The Windows 2000 operating system is the latest iteration of what in 1981 appeared as a white `A:\` prompt on a black screen. We've now come to expect and assume that our computers and the software they run will become faster and faster, more and more reliable, and easier and easier to use, and, for the most part, we have not been disappointed. Windows 2000 lives up to these expectations.

In this book, we'll take you skill by skill through the steps to get started and to use one variation of Windows 2000: Windows 2000 Professional. Before we do that, though, we'll show you how this family of operating systems is structured, how Windows 2000 relates to previous versions of Windows, and how to use Windows 2000 Professional to work more effectively.

Understanding the Windows 2000 Family

The Windows 2000 platform actually consists of four products that can work either together or separately:

- Windows 2000 Professional
- Windows 2000 Server
- Windows 2000 Advanced Server
- Windows 2000 Data Center

Each product serves a specific purpose and is appropriate for use in particular situations.

Windows 2000 Professional

Windows 2000 Professional—the topic of this book—is the successor to Windows NT Workstation 4 and looks much like Windows 98. You can run Windows 2000 Professional on a stand-alone machine, on a small network, or on a large corporate network. Its features include a new, simplified Desktop, Internet Explorer 5, tight security options, Plug-and-Play support for hardware, and easy-to-use configuration Wizards. Figure 1.1 shows the Desktop in Windows 2000 Professional.

FIGURE 1.1: The Desktop in Windows 2000 Professional

To exploit many features of Windows 2000 Server, which we'll discuss next, Windows 2000 Professional needs to be installed on users' workstations.

 NOTE

In networking, a *workstation* is any personal computer (other than the file server) that is attached to a network. A *server* is any computer that makes access to files, printing, communications, and other services available to users of a network.

Windows 2000 Server

The term *server* can apply to hardware or software. The server machine (hardware) usually has a more advanced processor, more memory, a larger cache, and more disk space than a personal computer used as a workstation. Windows 2000 Server is software that runs on the network server machine.

Windows 2000 Server is the successor to Windows NT Server 4 and was designed to be easier to use, install, and maintain, but it will generally require newer, more powerful computers than Server 4. You can deploy Windows 2000 Server on anything from a small home network to a network of several hundred users.

Table 1.1 compares the hardware requirements for Windows 2000 Server, Windows 2000 Professional, and a few other popular operating systems in use today. Figure 1.2 shows the Desktop for Windows 2000 Server.

TABLE 1.1: Hardware Requirements for Some Current Operating Systems

Operating System	Processor	RAM (in MB)	Hard Disk Space
Windows 98 Second Edition	Required: P166 MMX Recommended: PII-300	Required: 24	Required: 260MB using FAT16; 210MB using FAT32
Windows NT Workstation 4	Required: P166	Required: 16 Recommended: 32	Required: 110MB
Windows 2000 Professional	Required: P166 Recommended: PII-300	Required: 32 Recommended: 64	Required: 2GB, with 650MB of free space
Windows NT Server 4	Required: 486DX Recommended: P166	Required: 16 Recommended: 32	124MB
Windows 2000 Server	Required: P166 Recommended: PII-300	Required: 64 Recommended: 128	Required: 400MB Recommended: 1GB
Novell NetWare 5	Required: P166	Required: 64 Recommended: 256	Required: 500MB Recommended: 1GB
Red Hat Linux 6.1	Required: Intel 386 Recommended: Intel 486	Required: 4 Recommended: 16	Required: 200MB Recommended: 500MB

FIGURE 1.2: The Desktop in Windows 2000 Server

The new features in Windows 2000 Server include the following:

- Upgraded user account and system management
- Active Directory
- Internet and intranet support
- Operating stability
- Processing power
- Internal security
- Kerberos authentication
- Support for a maximum of four processors

HARDWARE AND WINDOWS 2000

Throughout the development cycle of Windows 2000, Microsoft received the support of all the major hardware vendors, including IBM, Compaq, Dell, Data General, Gateway, Hewlett-Packard, and Toshiba. Dell even offered to preinstall beta releases on systems for corporate customers. Thus, hardware compatibility issues should take a back seat when either you or your organization consider upgrading to Windows 2000 and acquiring new hardware.

In addition, Windows 2000 Professional includes drivers for more than 2500 different printers. It's highly likely that you'll find yours there when you want to install a new printer.

For the last word on hardware compatibility, go to www.microsoft.com/ hwtest/hcl, where you'll find information on a variety of equipment vendors, computer systems, and specific peripherals by name and type.

 NOTE   For more information about Windows 2000 Server, see the following excellent reference, from Sybex: *Mastering Windows 2000 Server*.

Windows 2000 Advanced Server

Windows 2000 Advanced Server is for enterprises that use large database applications and online transaction processing (for example, airline reservation systems, banks, and oil companies).

Advanced Server extends the features of Windows 2000 Server to include the following:

- Support for a maximum of eight processors

- A 64GB memory address space for applications

- High-availability clustering (that is, two servers can join in a fail-safe configuration that minimizes downtime)

Windows 2000 Data Center

Windows 2000 Data Center is server software that provides maximum processing power for large-scale enterprise Internet and intranet operations. It supports a maximum of 32 processors.

Comparing Windows 2000 Professional and Other Windows Operating Systems

You can upgrade to Windows 2000 Professional from the following operating systems:

- Windows 3.1
- OS/2
- Windows 95
- Windows 98
- Windows NT 3.51 Workstation
- Windows NT Workstation 4

As you will see in the next skill, how you install Windows 2000 Professional depends on which of these systems is currently installed.

Let's take a look at how Windows 2000 Professional compares with some of the operating systems you might be using now.

Windows 2000 Professional versus Windows 3.1

If your workstation or your network is running Windows 3.1 (and we know for a fact that some companies still are) and you are upgrading to Windows 2000 Professional, you are about to take a giant leap forward. Figure 1.3 shows the screen you see when you first open Windows 3.1. Compare this with the Windows 2000 Professional Desktop shown in Figure 1.1, earlier in this skill. Quite a difference, huh?

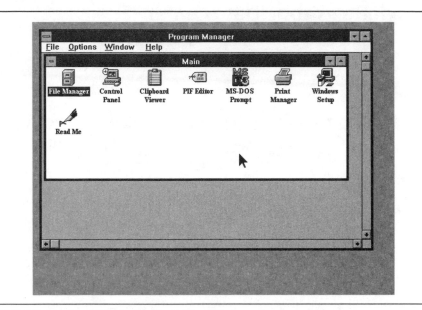

FIGURE 1.3: The Windows 3.1 interface

Here are just a few of the features that are different from Windows 3.1 in Windows 2000 Professional:

Filenames   You are probably painfully aware that in Windows 3.1 filenames can consist of only eight letters plus a three-letter extension. In Windows 2000 Professional, filenames can contain a maximum of 215 characters, including spaces.

Multitasking   As you probably know, multitasking means doing more than one thing at a time (for example, continuing to edit one document while printing another). Theoretically, Windows 3.1 can multitask, but if you're in the habit of trying to do what we just described, you know it doesn't really work. Fortunately, Windows 2000 Professional has true multitasking; you can even download files from the Internet while calculating a large spreadsheet.

Shortcuts   In Windows 3.1, you can accomplish a lot by left-clicking, but you have to click, and click, and click. In Windows 2000 Professional, you can right-click almost anything to display a shortcut menu from which you can immediately select a command.

Program Manager   Windows 2000 Professional replaces Program Manager with a truly graphical Desktop and the Start menu.

File Manager   In Windows 2000 Professional, you use Windows Explorer to manage your files, and directories have been replaced with folders, many of which also have an Explorer-like appearance.

The Internet and E-mail   Windows 2000 Professional includes Outlook Express, an Internet mail and news reader, as well as the Internet Explorer Web browser. No longer do you have to install separate applications for these services.

Windows 2000 Professional versus Windows 95/98

As we mentioned earlier, the Windows 2000 Professional interface has the look and feel of Windows 98, as Windows NT Workstation 4 has the look and feel of Windows 95. Obviously, the differences between Windows 2000 Professional and Windows 95/98 are not in the same league as the differences between Windows 2000 Professional and Windows 3.1, but there are some distinct differences and improvements worth mentioning. Here are just a few:

Security   In Windows 95/98, you can password protect your system and files, but you don't have to. And, anyway, all a user has to do to bypass the Password dialog box is to press Esc. This doesn't work in Windows 2000 Professional; you have to know the password and have rights and privileges to start the system or access any files or programs.

The File System   The file system is the set of principles by which files are stored on your hard drive. Windows 95 uses the FAT16 (file allocation table) file system, which stores files in a database in the boot sector of your hard drive (the place that contains the files crucial to starting up your computer). Consequently, if the boot sector becomes damaged, you can lose data. Windows 98 initially also uses the FAT16 file system, but you can convert to the FAT32 file system, which has compression techniques that let you save considerable hard-disk space. With Windows 2000 Professional, you can elect to use either FAT or NTFS (new technology file system). A number of advantages are associated with using NTFS, including automatic backup of the Master File Table and security controls for files, folders, and programs. For much more information about NTFS, see Skill 2.

Right-Clicking   Although you can gain quick access to commands and tasks by right-clicking in Windows 95/98, you can right-click almost anywhere in Windows 2000 Professional to make something happen.

Streamlined Desktop   One of the first things you'll notice about Windows 2000 Professional is the uncluttered, lean Desktop. Quite an improvement over all the stuff that gets displayed in Windows 95/98 (and an even greater improvement if you have an OEM version of either operating system).

Personalized Start Menu   By default, the Start menu in Windows 2000 Professional always displays the programs you most frequently use and hides those you don't use.

Searching   The Find command has been replaced with the Search command and is accessible from any open folder window.

Active Desktop   In Windows 2000 Professional, you can specify that your Desktop behaves like a Web page. Point to select; click to open. This feature is also available in Windows 98, but not in Windows 95.

Folder Links   Most folder have links to related folders that you can quickly access. For example, from the Printers folder, you can link to Microsoft Support.

Windows 2000 Professional versus Windows NT Workstation 4

Windows 2000 Professional has been described as combining the setup and hardware awareness of Windows 98 with the stability of Windows NT Workstation 4. It has also been described as not just putting a new spin on the interface but as breaking new ground. If you've used NT Workstation 4, you may at first feel as if the new ground is a little shaky; lots of items have been relocated, and some of their names have changed. We'll point these changes out throughout this book, where appropriate. So, to begin with, let's take a brief look here at some differences between Windows 2000 Professional and Windows NT Workstation 4:

Plug and Play   The Hardware Abstraction Layer (HAL) has been removed, and Windows 2000 Professional is fully Plug and Play. The Plug-and-Play agents check to see what hardware is installed and what configuration is needed, and they communicate that information to the operating system.

Start Menu The Start menu is now customizable, displaying the items you use most often. If you don't see a familiar item, click the More button at the bottom of a menu. You can also quickly alphabetize Start menu items and rename them.

Folder Bars The Open and Save As dialog boxes now include an Outlook-like folder bar that you can use to specify a folder quickly.

The Find Command This command has been renamed Search and is available in any open folder window. You can also extend your search to the Internet.

Network Neighborhood This has been renamed My Network Places, and, from this folder, you can create Desktop shortcuts to network shares.

Folder Links Many folders contain links that you can click to quickly open other folders. For example, the My Network Places folder contains links to My Documents and My Computer.

Toolbars Most folders include a toolbar that is similar to the toolbar in Internet Explorer and contains Back and Forward buttons as well as a History button.

My Pictures Folder This new folder is the default repository for image files, just as My Documents is for text files.

Folder Views You can now click the View menu to specify how you want to view the contents of a folder—with large icons or small icons, as a list, or with detailed information.

Favorites Tab The Help program now contains a Favorites tab in which you can store and quickly access Help topics that you frequently look up.

Windows Update Choose Start ➤ Windows Update to connect to an area on Microsoft's Web site, where you can download updates, patches, fixes, device drivers, and add-ons.

Disk Defragmenter With Windows NT 4, you had to purchase a third-party defragmenter tool; it comes with Windows 2000 Professional.

Power Management Power-conserving schemes are available for both desktop and noteboook computers.

Other new features in Windows 2000 Professional include Computer Management, Advanced Configuration and Power Interface (ACPI) power management,

Windows Installer, Safe Mode boot option, interactive troubleshooters, and support for the following:

- FAT32 volumes
- Universal Serial Bus
- Firewire/IEEE 1394 bus
- DVD (digital video disc)
- IrDA (Infrared Data Association)
- Infared connections
- Multiple monitors

APPLICATIONS AND WINDOWS 2000 PROFESSIONAL

When a new operating systems is released, one big question always concerns which applications can run on it. For the latest information about which applications are ready right now, go to www.microsoft.com/windows/professional/deploy/compatible. At the time this book was being finalized, a number of the usual suspects did not yet have products on the list, most notably Corel, Adobe, Lotus, and IBM. At the top of the list of applications that exploit features specific to Windows 2000 Professional was Microsoft Office 2000. (One would certainly hope so!)

You can, however, do your own compatibility testing if you want. Here are the steps:

1. Install and open the application.
2. Verify that the following functions work:
   - Printing
   - Saving files
   - Customizing menus
   - Exporting data
   - Cutting and pasting through the Clipboard
3. Run routine tasks to verify that their stability has not been affected.

Networking and Windows 2000 Professional

While we were writing this book, we were running Windows 2000 Professional on a couple of small networks. We mention this for two reasons. First, you can also run Windows 2000 Professional on a stand-alone system, if you want; all the features are enabled except for those related to networking. Second, because we were working on a network, the figures and graphics in this book reflect that. Nevertheless, everything in this book should work, with very minor differences, whether you are running in stand-alone or network mode.

If you work for a corporation, your computer is probably part of a network, and, furthermore, unless you are the IT manager, you probably have or had no part in the decision about what operating system or systems to run. However, if you have a small business or a busy home office, you may decide while reading this book that a network makes sense for you. A network provides many advantages if you're working with a group of people or simply have multiple computers:

- You can share a printer or printers.

- You can easily share files with others.

- You can back up to another computer if you don't have the space or budget for a zip drive or some other external device.

- You can share an Internet connection.

- And, with Windows 2000 Professional, you can secure your systems and your data.

Thus, you'll find in the last two skills of this book information about how to set up a small network and how to work more effectively on a corporate network.

Now, as promised, we are going to take you step by step through the process of installing and using Windows 2000 Professional.

Are You Up to Speed?

Now you can...

- ☑ understand the family of Windows 2000 operating systems

- ☑ define the differences between Windows 2000 Professional and Windows 3.1, Windows 95/98, and Windows NT Workstation 4

- ☑ decide whether Windows 2000 Professional and a network setup are for you

Installing and Upgrading to Windows 2000 Professional

- Checking hardware compatibility
- Installing Windows 2000 Professional as an upgrade
- Installing Windows 2000 Professional as a new installation
- Running Setup
- Choosing a file system
- Installing Windows 2000 Professional dual boot
- Creating a new user account

If you are on a corporate network that has upgraded to Windows 2000 Professional, you probably don't need the step-by-step instructions in this skill. You will benefit, however, from the information this skill contains about operating systems and file systems; we recommend that you check out the sections concerning those topics.

If you are a current Windows user and are about to install or upgrade to Windows 2000 Professional, this skill is required reading. Installing or upgrading Windows 2000 Professional is very different from installing or upgrading to previous versions of Windows. Although installing Windows 2000 Professional will probably take you half the time of earlier Windows installations, you need to make some informed decisions during the process. Before you dive into Setup, you need to give some thought to how you currently use your system and how you plan to use it in the future. Some of these decisions can be changed once the installation is complete, but others cannot, and you need to make the right choice the first time. We could have hidden this information away in an appendix at the back of the book, but, because some of the issues involved are so fundamental to how you will use Windows 2000 Professional, we decided to put them right at the front of this book.

Before proceeding with your installation, your to-do list needs to include the following:

- Make sure your hardware meets the minimum requirements for Windows 2000 Professional.

- Collect network, workgroup, and domain information from your system administrator if you will be part of a network.

- Back up your current files before upgrading, in case you need to restore your current operating system.

- Turn off or uninstall your virus-protection software. Popular antivirus programs such as McAfee AntiVirus version 3 for Windows NT and IBM's AntiVirus are not compatible with Windows 2000 Professional.

- Decide between upgrading your current operating system and making a completely new installation of Windows 2000 Professional.

- Choose the file system you want to use.

- Read the `Read1st.txt` file on the Windows 2000 Professional CD. This file contains late-breaking information that may affect your installation.

In the sections that follow, we'll go through each of these issues and explain the choices you need to make. Then we'll go through running the Setup program. Finally, we'll create new accounts for each of the people who will use Windows 2000 Professional.

Windows 2000 Professional Hardware Requirements

Before you install Windows 2000 Professional, make sure your computer meets these minimum hardware requirements:

- A 166-megahertz (MHz) Pentium microprocessor. This is an absolute minimum requirement; we suggest a 300MHz Pentium II for a desktop PC and a 233MHz processor in a notebook computer. (This is definitely a case where more is better.)

- At least 32 megabytes (MB) of RAM; 64MB is recommended, and 4 gigabytes (GB) is the maximum. (Again, as with the processor, as far as memory is concerned, more is better.)

- At least a 2GB hard disk with a minimum of 650MB of free space.

- A VGA or higher-resolution monitor.

- Keyboard.

- Mouse or compatible pointing device.

- CD-ROM drive.

- High-density 3.5-inch floppy disk, unless your CD-ROM drive is bootable and supports starting the Setup program from a CD.

For a network installation, you will also need a compatible network adapter card, a connection to the network, and access to the network share that contains the Setup files.

Checking Your Hardware Compatibility

The Windows 2000 Professional Setup program automatically checks your hardware and software and tells you of possible problems. To avoid any conflicts, check that your hardware is on the Hardware Compatibility List (HCL) before you start. You can view the Hardware Compatibility List by opening the Hcl.txt file in the Support folder on the Windows 2000 Professional CD. You will find every category of hardware in this list—everything from audio devices to Universal Serial Bus (USB) hubs, stopping at desktop systems, Small Computer System Interface (SCSI) controllers, and hard disk drives along the way.

> **TIP** If you have Internet access, you can view the latest HCL on the Microsoft Web site at http://www.microsoft.com/hwtest/hcl.

If your hardware isn't listed in the HCL file, the Setup program may not work as expected, and your installation may not be successful. Contact the hardware manufacturer and ask if there's a Windows 2000 driver for the component; remember, you don't need any special drivers for your Plug-and-Play devices.

Collecting Network Information

If your computer is going to connect to a network, you need the following information:

- The name of your computer
- The name of the workgroup or domain you belong to
- A TCP/IP address, if your network doesn't have a Dynamic Host Configuration Protocol (DHCP) server

You also need to decide if your computer will be joining a domain or a workgroup. If you don't know which option to choose or if your computer won't be connected to a network, you should select the workgroup option; you can always join a domain later. Your network administrator can provide you with all this information.

Making a Backup

If you're upgrading from a previous version of Windows, you should back up your current files to a disk, to a tape drive, or to another computer on your network. This is mainly a precaution in case something goes wrong during the installation or you decide to return to your previous operating system at some point in the future. If you are upgrading from Windows 95, 98, or 98 Second Edition, use the Backup program, or if you are upgrading from Windows NT, use the Windows Backup program.

 Windows 2000 Professional Backup does not support the restoration of backup files saved to disk using Windows 98.

Should You Upgrade or Make a New Installation?

You can install Windows 2000 Professional as an upgrade to your existing operating system, or you can install it alongside your current operating system and then use one or the other as you see fit. Let's take a look at the differences.

During an upgrade, Setup replaces your existing Windows files but preserves all your current settings and applications. You can upgrade to Windows 2000 Professional from the following operating systems:

- Windows 95
- Windows 98
- Windows 98 Second Edition
- Windows NT 3.51 Workstation
- Windows NT Workstation 4

During a new installation, Setup installs Windows 2000 Professional in a new folder. For more details, see "Performing a New Installation" later in this section.

 If you're currently using a non-supported operating system, such as Microsoft Windows 3.1 or IBM OS/2, you must perform a new installation. Once the installation is complete, you will have to reinstall all your applications and reset your settings.

You can also use a dual-boot configuration to run both Windows 2000 Professional and another compatible operating system, such as Windows 98, on your computer. In this case, you should install Windows 2000 Professional on a different hard-disk partition than the one used by your current operating system. We'll look at how to make a dual-boot installation in more detail later in this skill.

Running Setup

Whether you make a new installation or perform an upgrade, it's the Setup program that does all the work. Most of the time, Setup is completely automatic, but, from time to time, it pauses to ask you a question or ask you to confirm certain choices, such as time-zone information and other regional settings. Just follow the instructions on the screen.

Then Setup copies all the appropriate files to your hard disk, checks your hardware, and configures your installation. Because Windows 2000 Professional supports Plug and Play, all device-driver selection and loading is completely automatic. Setup also restarts your computer several times during the installation. The whole process takes about an hour or so to complete. The method you use to start Setup depends on several things, including whether you are making a new installation or performing an upgrade. We'll look at all these options in the next few sections.

Performing a New Installation

If your current operating system is not supported, if you want to install Windows 2000 Professional in a dual-boot configuration, or if your computer has a blank hard disk, you need to start your computer using either:

- The Setup boot floppy disks.

- The Windows 2000 Professional CD—if your CD-ROM drive is bootable. Certain CD-ROM drives can boot from the CD and automatically launch Setup.

> **WARNING**   The Setup start-up or boot disks are not the same as the Windows Emergency Repair Disk. See Skill 15 for more information on how to start a damaged system using these Setup boot disks and the Emergency Repair Disk.

To start a new installation using the Setup boot floppy disks, follow these steps:

1. With your computer turned off, insert the Windows 2000 Setup boot Disk 1 into your floppy disk drive.

2. Start your computer. The Setup program starts automatically.

3. Follow the instructions on the screen.

Making Setup Start-up Floppy Disks

If you don't have copies of the Setup start-up or boot disks, you can create them yourself. These floppies are used to start Setup if you can't start Setup from your hard drive or from your CD. Here are the steps:

1. Insert a blank, formatted disk into the floppy disk drive and the Windows 2000 Professional CD into your CD-ROM drive. (You will need four blank, 1.44MB, formatted, 3.5-inch disks, labeled "Setup Disk 1," "Setup Disk 2," and so on.)

2. Click Start, and then click Run.

3. At the prompt, type the following command, replacing the letter d with the letter of your CD-ROM drive and replacing a with the letter of your floppy drive:

    ```
    d:\bootdisk\makeboot.bat a:
    ```

4. Follow the instructions that appear on the screen.

To start a new installation from the CD, follow these steps:

1. Start your computer by running your current operating system, and then insert the Windows 2000 Professional CD into your CD-ROM drive.

2. If Windows automatically detects the CD, click Install Windows 2000. The Setup program then starts.

    If Windows doesn't automatically detect the CD, start Setup from the Run command. In Windows 95, Windows 98, or Windows NT 4, click Start, and then click Run. In Windows NT 3.51 or Windows 3.1, in Program Manager, click File, and then click Run. At the prompt, type the following command, replacing the letter d with the letter of your CD-ROM drive:

    ```
    d:\i386\winnt32.exe
    ```

If you're using Windows 3.1, type the following command at the prompt, replacing the letter d with the letter of your CD-ROM drive:

```
d:\i386\winnt.exe
```

3.   Press the Enter key and follow the instructions on the screen.

Upgrading to Windows 2000 Professional

Upgrading to Windows 2000 Professional is a straightforward process. The Setup program automatically detects your hardware and installs the appropriate drivers, or, if it finds hardware incompatible with Windows 2000 Professional, it creates a report on devices that cannot be upgraded.

TIP   You must uncompress any DriveSpace or DoubleSpace volumes before upgrading to Windows 2000 Professional.

To upgrade to Windows 2000 Professional from Windows 95, Windows 98, or Windows NT Workstation 4, follow these steps:

1.   Start your computer by running your current operating system, and then insert the Windows 2000 Professional CD into your CD-ROM drive.

2.   If Windows automatically detects the CD and asks if you want to upgrade to Windows 2000 Professional, click Yes. Otherwise, click Start, and then click Run. At the prompt, type the following command, replacing the letter d with the letter of your CD-ROM drive:

```
d:\i386\winnt32.exe
```

3.   Press the Enter key.

4.   Follow the instructions on the screen.

WARNING   If you are upgrading from Windows 95 or Windows 98, you may see some of your applications listed in the Upgrade Report window. These applications are those known to have serious problems with the upgrade to Windows 2000 Professional. To prevent problems once the upgrade is complete, you should follow the recommendations given in the Upgrade Report window. See Skill 7 for more information on running your applications under Windows 2000 Professional.

To upgrade to Windows 2000 Professional from Windows NT Workstation 3.51, follow these steps:

1. Start your computer by running your current operating system, and then insert the Windows 2000 Professional CD into your CD-ROM drive.

2. In Program Manager, click File, and then click Run. At the prompt, type the following command, replacing the letter d with the letter of your CD-ROM drive:

   d:\i386\winnt32.exe

3. Press the Enter key.

4. Follow the instructions on the screen.

Choosing a File System

Before you install Windows 2000 Professional, you must decide which file system you want to use. The file system consists of the complete set of organizational elements that allow the operating system to communicate with your hard disk. Windows 2000 Professional supports the NT file system (NTFS) as well as the file allocation table file systems FAT or FAT32. You can only use one file system at a time, so let's take a look at the different options.

NTFS

NTFS is the file system recommended for use with Windows 2000 Professional. NTFS is a high-performance file system that provides the following advantages over the FAT and FAT32 file systems:

- Increased file security controls.

- Better disk compression.

- File encryption.

- Support for large hard disks of up to 2 terabytes (TB), and, as drive size increases, performance does not degrade as it does with FAT.

- Better protection from viruses. Most viruses are written to attack FAT and FAT32 file systems and don't know what to do when they encounter NTFS.

- Long filenames.

NTFS creates backup records of the Master File Table (MFT)—the NTFS version of the FAT file allocation table—so, if the boot sector of your hard disk is damaged by accident, the information can be replaced from one of the backup records. This means you are much less likely to lose data due to disk problems.

MS-DOS, Windows 3.*x*, Windows 95, and Windows 98 do not understand NTFS, so if you're using a dual-boot configuration with Windows 2000 Professional and one of these operating systems, you won't be able to read the files in the NTFS partition from the other operating system on your computer.

FAT and FAT32

FAT32 is an enhanced version of the FAT file system and is used on drives from 512MB to 2TB in size. FAT and FAT32 offer backward compatibility with operating systems other than Windows 2000 Professional. If you are setting up a dual-boot configuration and it is important that you be able to access from MS-DOS, Windows 3.*x*, Windows 95, or Windows 98 the files you create with Windows 2000 Professional, you should consider using FAT or FAT32.

Use FAT if the hard disk partition you want to use with Windows 2000 Professional is smaller than 2GB, and choose FAT32 if the partition is 2GB or larger. In fact, if you choose FAT in the Setup program and the partition is larger than 2GB, Setup automatically formats the partition as FAT32.

A Quick Look at Disk Partitions

Disk partitioning is a way of dividing your hard disk so that each section functions as a separate unit. You can create a partition for several reasons, including to back up data, to organize different kinds of information, or to dual boot another operating system. When you create partitions on a disk, you are dividing the disk into areas that can be formatted by different file systems. A hard disk can contain as many as four partitions. Remember to back up any files in a partition that you plan to reformat, because reformatting the partition destroys any data that it contains.

TIP   The Setup program can make changes to your partitions as you install Windows 2000 Professional, but if you prefer to make the changes yourself before you start the installation, use a program such as PartitionMagic from Power-Quest Corporation. PartitionMagic is very powerful but is very easy to use, and you can see exactly what is happening on the screen in front of you. Call 800-379-2566 or point your Web browser to www.powerquest.com for more information.

Depending on your existing hard disk configuration, you have several partitioning options when installing Windows 2000 Professional:

- If your hard disk is unpartitioned, you can create and size the Windows 2000 Professional partition.

- If the existing partition is large enough, you can install Windows 2000 Professional in that partition. Installing to an existing partition overwrites any data on that partition.

- If the existing partition is too small but you have enough unpartitioned space, you can create a new Windows 2000 Professional partition in that space.

- If the hard disk has an existing partition, you can delete it to create more unpartitioned disk space for the Windows 2000 Professional partition. Deleting an existing partition also erases any data on that partition.

If you're setting up a dual-boot configuration, you must always install Windows 2000 Professional in its own partition. Installing Windows 2000 in the same partition as another operating system will cause Setup to overwrite files required by the original operating system.

TIP   Although Windows 2000 Professional requires a minimum of 500MB of free hard-disk space for installation, using a larger partition gives you the flexibility to add future updates, operating system tools, applications, and other files.

Setting Up a Dual-Boot Configuration

By using a dual-boot configuration on your computer, you can choose between operating systems or even between versions of the same operating system from a menu every time you start your computer. Windows 2000 Professional supports dual-boot configurations with the following operating systems:

- Windows NT 3.51

- Windows NT 4

- Windows 95

- Windows 98

- Windows 98 Second Edition

- Windows 3.*x*

- Windows for Workgroups 3.11

- MS-DOS

- OS/2

To establish a dual-boot configuration, you must install each operating system into a separate partition. During Setup, you can use the Advanced Setup option to select a folder on an unused partition.

> **TIP**   You can also set up a multiboot configuration, where you load more than two operating systems onto one computer.

If you are planning a dual-boot configuration, here are some things to think about before you start:

- Each operating system must be installed on a separate drive or disk partition.

- Before you start to install the second or subsequent operating system, take the time to create an Emergency Repair Disk if you are using Windows NT Workstation or a Start Up disk if you are using Windows 95 or 98. You might need it later.

- Consider using the FAT32 file system for dual-boot configurations. Although using NTFS in a dual boot is certainly supported and offers considerable benefits over FAT32, such a configuration introduces additional operational complexity.

- To set up a dual-boot configuration between MS-DOS or Windows 95 and Windows 2000 Professional, you should install Windows 2000 last; otherwise, important files needed to start Windows 2000 Professional could be overwritten. If you want to dual boot between Windows 98 and Windows 2000 Professional, you can install the operating systems in any order.

- In a dual boot of Windows 2000 Professional with Windows 95 or MS-DOS, the primary hard-disk partition must be formatted as FAT; for a dual boot with Windows 95, OS/2, or Windows 98, the primary partition must be formatted as FAT or FAT32.

- If you're upgrading an NT Workstation dual-boot computer, you can't gain access to NTFS partitions from any operating system other than Windows NT 4 with Service Pack 4 (SP4). Also, if you modify existing files or create new files on the NTFS partition, you can't use those files with any other operating system, including Windows NT 4, with SP4. What this means is that a dual boot with Windows 2000 Professional and any other version of Windows NT is not recommended if the computer uses only NTFS partitions. This is because Windows 2000 Professional supports a new version of NTFS called NTFS 5, which is not compatible with earlier versions of the NT family of operating systems.

- If you install Windows 2000 Professional on a computer that dual boots between IBM's OS/2 and MS-DOS, Windows 2000 Professional Setup configures your system so you dual boot between Windows 2000 Professional and the operating system (either MS-DOS or OS/2) that you used immediately before running Setup. This is due to the way that the OS/2 boot manager works.

- Don't install Windows 2000 Professional on a compressed drive unless the drive was compressed with the NTFS file system compression utility. You don't have to uncompress DriveSpace or DoubleSpace volumes if you plan to dual boot with Windows 95 or Windows 98, but those compressed volumes won't be available to you while you're running Windows 2000 Professional.

- If the dual-boot computer is part of a Windows NT or Windows 2000 Professional domain, each installation of Windows NT Workstation or Windows 2000 Professional must have a different computer name.

- If you're using NTFS and dual booting with Windows NT, you must upgrade to Windows NT 4 with SP4 or later before continuing with the Windows 2000 Professional installation.

Once you have decided whether these issues are likely to be important in your installation, you can proceed with a new Windows 2000 Professional installation on your system.

Choosing Between NTFS and FAT32 on a Dual-Boot System

If you want to install a Windows 2000 Professional dual-boot system with an existing Windows 98 installation, consider your choice of file system carefully. Windows 98 uses FAT32, and Windows 2000 Professional supports FAT, FAT32, and NTFS. To install Windows 2000 dual boot, you must have two separate hard-disk partitions available—one for Windows 98 and one for Windows 2000 Professional.

The Windows 98 partition will be formatted with FAT32 so that much is given and can't be changed, but with Windows 2000 Professional, you can choose the file system to use. If you install FAT32 on the Windows 2000 Professional partition, you will be able to read files from both partitions using both operating systems. In a typical system, you will have Windows 98 on drive C, Windows 2000 Professional on drive D, and your CD-ROM drive will become drive E. But you get none of the performance or security benefits of NTFS.

If you install NTFS on the Windows 2000 Professional partition, things change quite a bit. When you boot Windows 2000 Professional, you will be able to read the FAT32 files from drive C and the NTFS files from drive D. Your CD-ROM drive stays as drive E. But when you boot Windows 98, the NTFS partition that was drive D disappears along with all the files it contains. You can read the files from the FAT32 partition, and this time your CD-ROM drive becomes drive D. The files on drive D have not been deleted, and they are still there on the disk; it's just that Windows 98 can't see them.

So it all comes down to how you will use your system. If it is important that you be able to read all files on all disks from both operating systems, install FAT32 on the Windows 2000 Professional partition. If this is not an important operational consideration, install NTFS on the Windows 2000 Professional partition, and take advantage of the better security and increased performance.

Installing the Add-On Components

The Windows 2000 Professional CD contains several system elements not included as part of the standard installation. To look at or install these programs, insert the Windows 2000 Professional CD into the CD disk drive, and then click Install Add-On Components to start the Windows Components Wizard. Using the Wizard, you can install:

- Internet Information Server (IIS) Web server and associated files. If you upgrade to Windows 2000 Professional from a previous version of Windows NT Workstation, IIS is installed automatically if Personal Web Server was previously installed on NT.

- Management and Monitoring Tools, including Simple Network Management Protocol (SNMP).

- Message Queuing Services.

- Indexing Service.

- Script Debugger for working with client and server scripts written in VBScript or JScript.

- Networking Services, including RIP (Routing Information Protocol) Listener, and additional TCP/IP (Transmission Control Protocol/Internet Protocol) services such as Quote of the Day.

- Other Network File and Print Services, including Print Services for Unix.

Follow the instructions on the screen to install one or more of these optional elements. See Skill 7 for more details on adding and removing Windows 2000 Professional optional components.

TIP   You will also find demo versions of non-Microsoft, third-party software in the Valuadd directory on the Windows 2000 Professional CD.

Creating a New User Account

The password you gave Setup during the installation process gives you access to the Administrator account, but once the installation is complete, you should create user accounts for all the people you expect to use the Windows 2000 Professional system. A user account identifies a user name and password, group membership, and which network resources can be accessed, as well as personal files and folders.

Windows 2000 Professional has two kinds of user accounts: domain user accounts and local user accounts. With a domain user account, you log on to the domain to access network resources. This kind of account is often used with client/server networks; see Skill 17 for more information. With a local user account, you log on to a specific computer to access resources available only on that computer. This kind of account is suitable for use on a peer-to-peer network; see Skill 16 for more information.

To create a new user account, follow these steps:

1. Click Start ➤ Settings ➤ Control Panel to open Control Panel.

2. Click Users and Passwords to open the Users and Passwords dialog box, which is shown in Figure 2.1.

3. Make sure the Users Must Enter a User Name and Password to Use This Computer check box is checked.

4. Click Add to open the Add New User Wizard. Enter a name for the new user, and click Next.

5. Enter and confirm a password for this user. Click Next.

6. Select the level of access for this user. Choose Standard User, and click Finish. We'll look at these different access levels in more detail in Skill 16.

7. Click Apply and then OK to close the Users and Passwords applet.

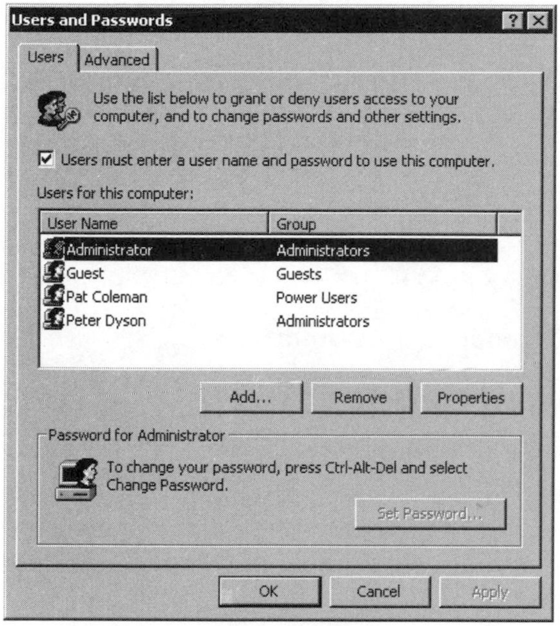

FIGURE 2.1: The Users and Passwords dialog box

Repeat these steps to create an account for each of the people who will be using the system, including one for yourself. Then log off from the Administrator account, and log back on again using your new user account:

1. Click Start ➢ Shut Down, and then select Log Off from the drop-down list. Click OK.

2. Enter your Standard User name and password into the Log On To Windows dialog box.

When you have finished your work, you should choose Start ➢ Shut Down to log off the computer so that other users can log on.

Are You Up to Speed?

Now you can...

- ☑ check hardware compatibility
- ☑ run Setup
- ☑ install Windows 2000 Professional as a new installation, an upgrade, or a dual boot
- ☑ choose a file system
- ☑ create a new user account

SKILL 3

Exploring the Desktop

- Logging on
- Using the Start menu
- Working with the Taskbar
- Using the icons on the Desktop
- Creating shortcuts

If you have been a Windows NT user, the Windows 2000 Professional Desktop will look familiar. However, you will no doubt soon discover that some items have moved to new locations, that there are some new items, and that some items have new names. If you have been a user of Windows 95 or Windows 98 and are upgrading to Windows 2000 Professional, the Desktop will also look familiar. You'll notice right away, however, that it is much less cluttered than the version of Windows you've been using and that you need to right-click to open such essentials as Windows Explorer.

In Windows 2000 Professional, you can view the Desktop using the classic Windows interface or the Active Desktop. In the Active Desktop view, your Desktop looks and works like a Web page. You single-click an item rather than double-clicking to open it. By default, the Windows 2000 Professional Desktop displays in classic view, but files and folders display in Web view. This is a hybrid view and is the setup we used as we wrote this book. You can continue to use this view, or you can change it so that everything is either in the classic view or in Web page view. You can also create some other combination. You do all this using the Folder Options applet in Control Panel, and we'll look at this in detail in the next skill.

In this skill, we'll look at all the parts and pieces of the Desktop in its default classic view and then point you to the particular skills that show you in detail how to use them.

Logging On

Although logging on is a simple process and we discussed it at the end of Skill 2, we're giving it a reprise here—just in case you skipped Skill 2. You need at least two things to log on: your user name and your password. If you are connected to a corporate LAN, you may also need the name of a domain if you're supposed to log on to a domain other than the default. If this is the case, your network administrator will let you know.

Enter your user name and password in the dialog box requesting that information, and click OK. That's really all there is to it, unless you make a typo or you're asked to supply a new password. On corporate networks, most administrators set the system so that user passwords expire every 30 days, and they set password history so that you can't repeat a password until you've used 12 or 13 other passwords. If you think you might not remember the new password, write it down and put it in a safe place—this doesn't mean on a sticky note attached to your computer. Passwords are a vital part of network security, and most organizations have rules about them. Be sure you understand them and implement the policy properly.

TIP   The most common way to mistype your password is to have the Caps Lock key on when it shouldn't be. We have been collectively logging on to networks more years than we want to count, and we still make this mistake. Check the Caps Lock key immediately if your password is not accepted.

Using the Start Menu

If you place your mouse cursor over the Start button, you'll see a screen tip that says "Click here to begin," and so that's how we'll get started exploring the Desktop. If you don't see the Start button (and the Taskbar, which we'll discuss next), move your mouse cursor to the bottom of the screen. Figure 3.1 shows the Desktop before you click the Start button. Your Desktop will look different from the one shown here. For starters, you probably don't have a FullShot99 icon (FullShot99 is the program we used to capture the screens in this book), and you may have other icons for programs that you or your network administrator has installed.

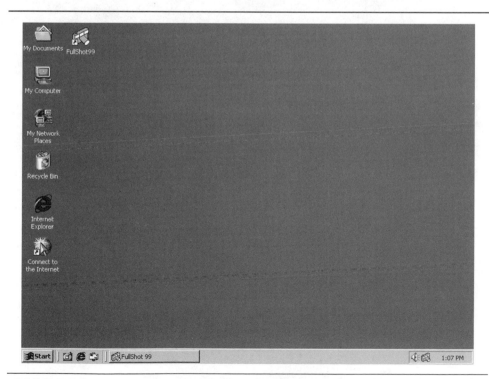

FIGURE 3.1: The Windows 2000 Professional Desktop

Skill 3

Clicking Start

Clicking Start opens the menu shown in Figure 3.2. Let's briefly look at each of these items, starting at the top.

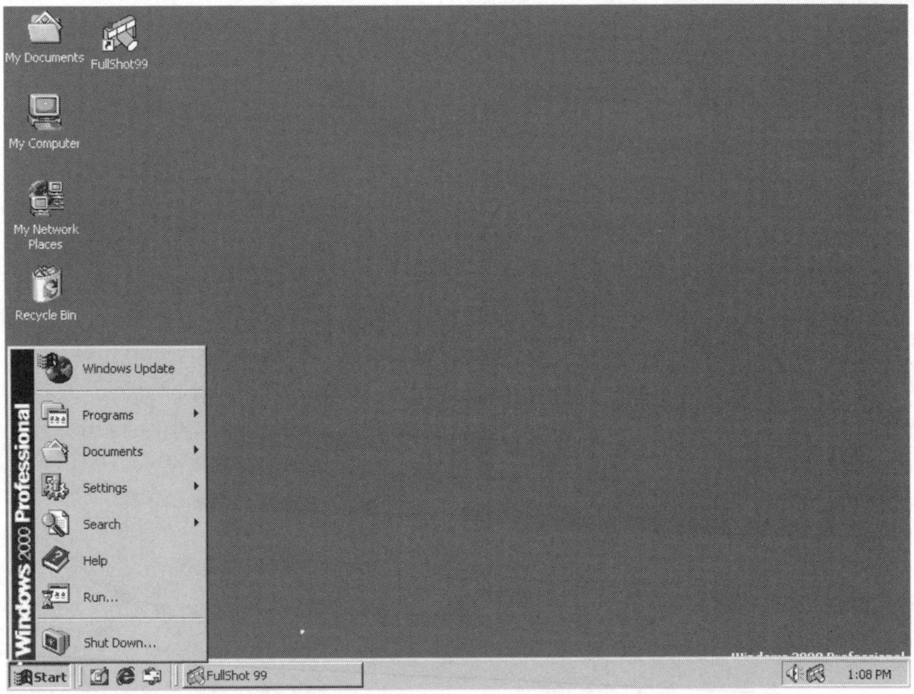

FIGURE 3.2: The items on the Start menu

Windows Update

When you select Windows Update, you'll be connected to the Microsoft Windows Update site (if you are currently connected to the Internet) and see a page similar to that shown in Figure 3.3. Here you can get up-to-date information and news about Windows products, support, and help. If you scroll down the page, you'll find a link that takes you to a page specific to Windows 2000 Professional that contains information about new features and troubleshooting tips.

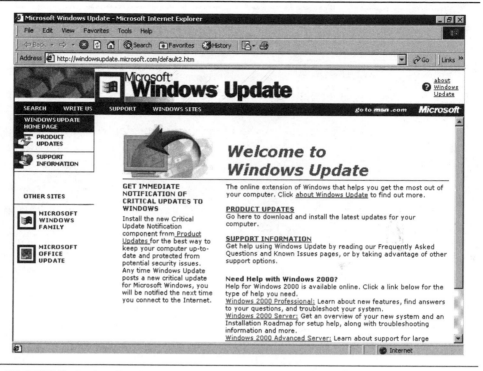

FIGURE 3.3: The Microsoft Windows Update page

Programs

Clicking Programs opens a submenu that contains at least the following items:

Accessories   Contains yet another submenu of programs. Some of these we'll discuss in Skill 10, and others we'll discuss in Skills 14 and 15.

Startup   Contains the names of any programs that you want to start every time you start Windows. To place an item on this menu, drag its icon to the Start button, then to the Programs button, and then drop it on Startup.

Internet Explorer   Opens the Microsoft Internet Explorer Web browser. For all the details, see Skill 12.

Outlook Express   Opens Outlook Express, the mail and news program included with Windows 2000 Professional. See Skill 13 for the details.

NOTE   The Programs menu may contain other items, depending on what you have installed on your system.

By default, Windows 2000 Professional personalizes menus such as the Programs menu. In other words, it places the names of the programs you've most recently used at the top of the list and hides the names of others. To display those that are hidden, click the More button (the double chevron) at the bottom of the menu. If you've used Microsoft Office 2000, you are familiar with how this works. If you prefer static rather than personalized menus, follow these steps:

1. Choose Start ➢ Settings ➢ Taskbar & Start Menu to open the Taskbar and Start Menu Properties dialog box. We'll take a closer look at this dialog box in a later section.

2. On the General tab, click the Use Personalized Menus check box to clear it.

3. Click OK.

Documents

Clicking Documents displays a menu that lists the last 15 documents you've opened as well as your My Documents folder. Clicking My Documents opens that folder in Windows Explorer, and clicking any of the other documents opens those documents. For the most part, this is a quick and easy way to open both a document and the program in which you created it. Some documents, however, do not open in the program in which you created them. For example, an image file will open in Imaging Preview. To change the program in which the document will open, follow these steps:

1. Right-click the document name in the list, choose Open With, and then choose Choose Program to open the Open With dialog box:

2. Select a program from the list and click OK. If you don't see the program you want, click Other, select a program, and click Open. Windows 2000 Professional adds the program to the list. Select it, and click OK.

If you want all like files to open in the same program, click the Always Use This Program to Open These Files check box in the Open With dialog box.

RIGHT-CLICKING IN WINDOWS 2000 PROFESSIONAL

In Windows 2000 Professional, right-clicking almost anywhere produces something helpful. In most cases, right-clicking opens a shortcut menu that contains some fairly standard commands such as Send To, Cut, Copy, Delete, Properties, and so on, as well as some items that are specific to what you right-clicked. In some cases, right-clicking opens a What's This? box that you can click to get help on the item.

If you're ever in doubt, just try it. You can't hurt anything; worst case, you'll get nothing.

We'll talk a lot more about the virtues of right-clicking in Skill 6.

To clear the items in the Documents list, follow these steps:

1. Choose Start ➤ Settings ➤ Taskbar & Start Menu to open the Taskbar and Start Menu Properties dialog box.

2. Click the Advanced tab.

3. Click Clear, and then click OK.

NOTE   Clearing the items in the Documents list does not delete them from your system. It just empties the list and makes room for other, more recent items.

Settings

When you click Settings, you see a menu that contains the following items:

- Control Panel

- Network and Dial-Up Connections

- Printers

- Taskbar & Start Menu

You will return to these items often as you begin to set up and manage your Windows 2000 Professional system, and so you will find information about them throughout this book. Skill 8 discusses printers and printing, Skill 11 discusses dial-up networking, and Skills 16 and 17 discuss the local area network. The applets in Control Panel are discussed in the skills for which they are most appropriate. Here, let's take a brief look at what you'll find when you select one of these items.

Click Control Panel to open the screen shown in Figure 3.4. These items are often referred to as applets, small programs that you use to take care of a specific task such as adding or removing a program from your system, changing the settings in your display, setting up your connections to the Internet, and so on.

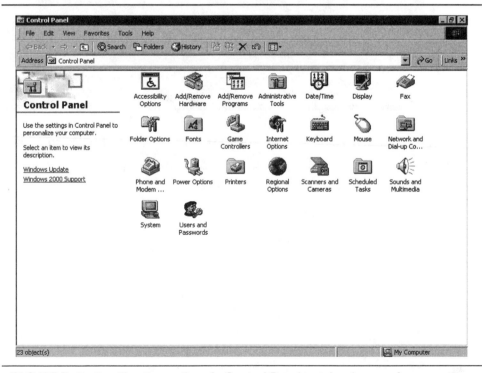

FIGURE 3.4: Use the options in Control Panel to take charge of your system.

Click Network and Dial-Up Connections to open the Network Connection Wizard and create a connection to another computer or a network, to see the status of a local area connection, and to connect to the Internet.

Click Printers to open the Printers dialog box, which you use to add a printer, manage your print queue, check the status of jobs you've sent to the printer, and so on.

Click Taskbar & Start Menu to open the Taskbar and Start Menu Properties dialog box (see Figure 3.5), which we mentioned earlier. You use the options in this dialog box to customize your Desktop. We'll look at this dialog box in more detail in Skill 5.

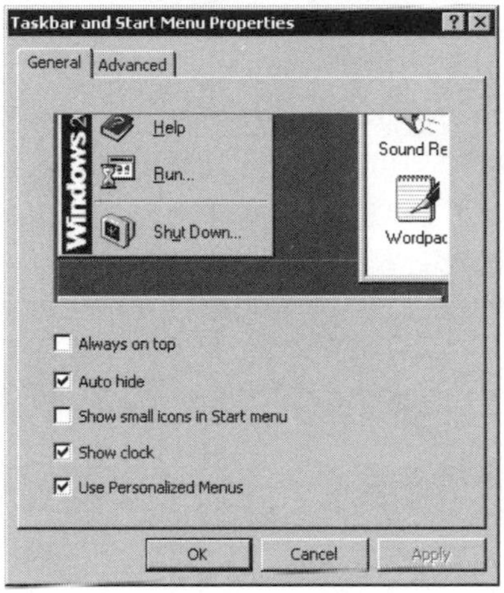

FIGURE 3.5: The Taskbar and Start Menu Properties dialog box

Search

Have you been looking for the Find command? Well, it's not there; Find has metamorphosed into Search, and you can use it to locate files, folders, people, and sites on the Internet. For example, if you want to find a file or a folder, click Start ➤ Search ➤ For Files or Folders. You'll see the Search Results dialog box, as shown in Figure 3.6. When the search is completed, you'll see files and folders matching your criteria in the pane on the right. We'll discuss how to use this dialog box in detail in the next skill.

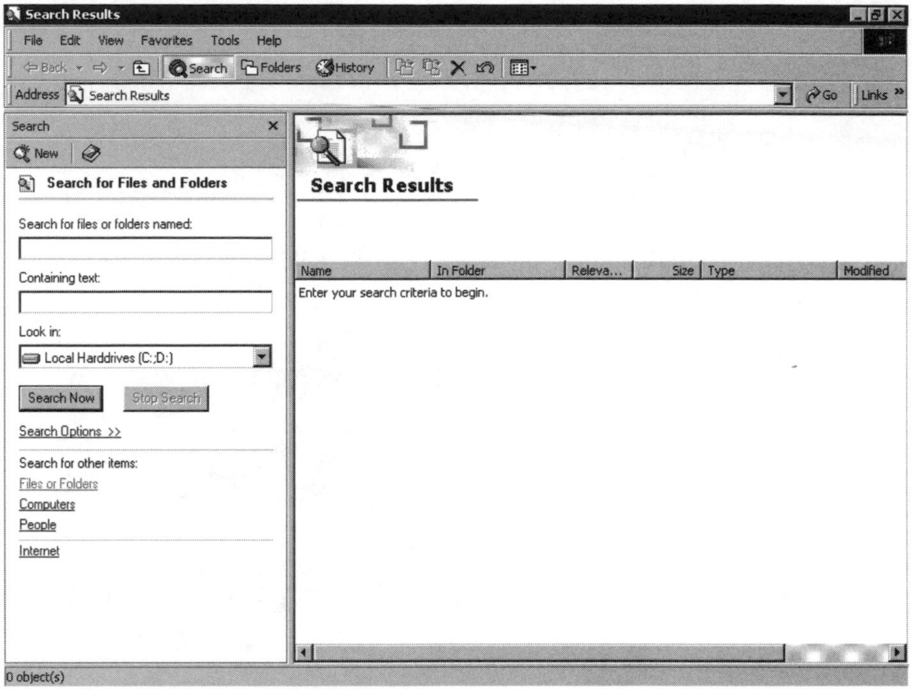

FIGURE 3.6: Use the Search Results dialog box to find files and folders on your local drive or on a network.

Clicking On the Internet opens the Search bar in Internet Explorer. For information on how to use the Search bar, see Skill 12.

Clicking For People opens the Find People dialog box, which you can use to locate people in your Address Book or on Internet search services (if you are connected to the Internet).

Help

Click Help to open the Windows 2000 Professional help system. You'll see the screen shown in Figure 3.7. If you've used Help in Windows applications and in previous versions of Windows, you'll be glad to hear that Windows 2000 Professional Help is really easy to use, and it's fast. Click a tab, click a topic, and then view the information in the right pane.

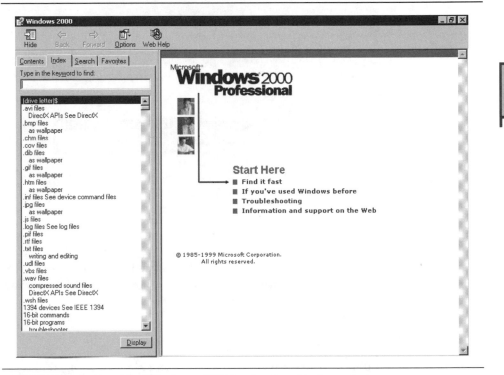

FIGURE 3.7: The Windows 2000 Professional help system

If you're a seasoned user of either Windows 95/98 or NT, be sure to check out the "If You've Used Windows Before" topic under Start Here. As we mentioned at the beginning of this skill, many components have new names and are in new locations. For example, click the first topic in the right pane, Active Desktop. In Windows 98, Active Desktop was on the Settings menu; in Windows 2000 Professional, it's part of Folder Options in Control Panel.

You'll also notice an additional tab, Favorites, which we find particularly useful. With a topic open in the right pane, click the Favorites tab, and then click Add. Now, whenever you want to return to that topic, simply select it from your Favorites list instead of searching for it again.

Run

As you'll find out when you get to Skill 7, you can run applications from several places in Windows 2000 Professional, including the Run dialog box, which opens when you click Run:

In addition to opening a program by typing its name in the Open box, you can open a folder, a document, or an Internet site. Start entering the name of something, and AutoComplete will display a list of items that start with that letter. Select an item, and click OK to open it.

Shut Down

You'll find out soon enough, if you don't already know, that it's to your benefit to shut down Windows 2000 Professional properly. If you don't, the next time you start up, you'll have to wait while Windows 2000 Professional does some file checking and maintenance, and you could even lose some data or some configuration settings.

When you're through with work for the day or ready to head for bed, click Shut Down to open the Shut Down Windows dialog box. You have three choices:

- Log Off

- Shut Down

- Restart

Choose Log Off to end your current session and leave the computer running. Choose Restart to restart the system (for example, when you are working on a dual-boot system and you want to start the other operating system). Windows 2000 Professional will shut down and then restart automatically. Choose Shut Down when you are ready to power down the computer. Windows 2000 Professional will let you know when it's safe to turn off your computer.

Right-Clicking Start

Remember our earlier declaration about how important right-clicking is in Windows 2000 Professional? It starts with the Start button. Right-click the Start button to open a menu that has the following items:

- Open

- Explore

- Search

- Open All Users

- Explore All Users

Open

Click Open to open the Start Menu dialog box, which contains the Programs folder and links to My Documents, My Network Places, and My Computer. We'll discuss these links in the next section.

Explore

Been wondering where Windows Explorer was? Click Explore to open it. As you can see in Figure 3.8, it opens with the Start Menu folder highlighted and its contents in the right pane. When you select another file or folder, its name appears in the title bar. For example, if you select My Computer, the title bar displays My Computer, and the folder contents are displayed in the right pane.

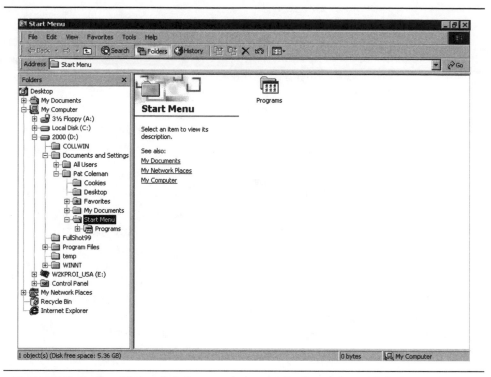

FIGURE 3.8: Right-click Start and choose Explore to open Windows Explorer.

Search

Click Search to open the Search Results dialog box that we discussed earlier.

Open All Users

Click Open All Users to open the Start Menu folder, which shows the Start Menu items (files, folders, and programs) available to any user who logs on to this computer.

Explore All Users

Click Explore All Users to open the Start Menu folder in Windows Explorer, which will show you the Start Menu items available to any user who logs onto this computer.

Working with the Taskbar

By default, the Taskbar contains the Quick Launch toolbar, the Volume icon, and the clock. You can, however, choose to display the Address, Links, and Desktop toolbar, and you can create and add a new toolbar. We'll look at those options in Skill 5. In this section, we'll quickly go over the defaults, which are shown in Figure 3.9, and describe how you use them.

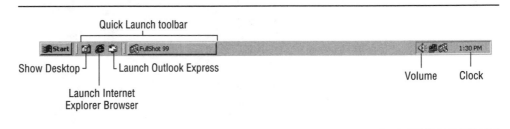

FIGURE 3.9: The Taskbar in Windows 2000 Professional

The Quick Launch Toolbar

As you can see in Figure 3.9, the Quick Launch toolbar is at the left end of the Taskbar. Click an icon once to activate it. You can, of course, open Internet Explorer and Outlook Express in many other ways, but if you are at the Desktop, using the Quick Launch toolbar is quickest.

> **Show Desktop**   If you have multiple windows open and you need to access something on your Desktop, click Show Desktop to minimize all the open windows. For this to work, you need to be able to see the Taskbar. We'll discuss hiding and displaying the Taskbar later in this section.
>
> **Launch Internet Explorer Browser**   Click to open Internet Explorer.
>
> **Launch Outlook Express**   Click to open Outlook Express.

The Rest of the Taskbar

At the right end of the Taskbar are the Volume icon and the clock. Click the Volume icon once to display the volume control slider bar and the Mute check box. If you have speakers and a sound card, you can use this control to quickly adjust the volume. If you want to fine-tune the sound, double-click the Volume icon to open the Volume Control dialog box, as shown in Figure 3.10.

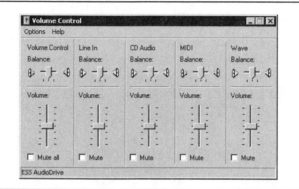

FIGURE 3.10: Use the slider bars in this dialog box to adjust volume and balance and to mute the sound.

To display the current date, place your mouse cursor over the time at the far right end of the Taskbar. To change the date or time, double-click the time to open the Date/Time Properties dialog box.

Hiding and Displaying the Taskbar

As we mentioned earlier, you need to see the Taskbar if you want to use it when you are working with an application or otherwise not at the Desktop. If you set up the Taskbar properties correctly, you can hide the Taskbar when you don't need it and display it when you do. Follow these steps so that the Taskbar will only display when you point to the bottom of the screen (regardless of where you are in Windows 2000 Professional):

1. Right-click the Taskbar, and choose Properties to open the Taskbar and Start Menu Properties dialog box.

2. On the General tab, select both the Always on Top and the Auto Hide check boxes.

3. Click OK.

Using the Icons on the Desktop

The icons you see on your Desktop are actually shortcuts to programs and tools on your computer. We'll take a look at using and creating shortcuts in the last section in this skill, but an important thing to remember about shortcuts is that they are just that—a quick way to open their target (what they point to). They are a representation of the program or tool, not the real McCoy. If you delete a shortcut, you are removing only the representation, not the program or tool itself.

In this section, we'll explore the icons that appear on the Windows 2000 Professional Desktop when you first install the system.

> **TIP** You can rearrange the icons on your Desktop if you want. Simply click an icon, and then drag it to a new location.

My Documents

Clicking the My Documents icon opens the My Documents folder, which contains a My Pictures folder by default and any other files or folders you've created and stored in the My Documents folder. As you can see in Figure 3.11, folders are displayed in Web view. Simply double-click a folder to display its contents. When you click a folder on the right, information about it is displayed on the left, such as its type, size, date, and attributes. (Attributes are explained in Skill 6.) Click the Back or Forward button to move from file view to folder view.

The My Documents folder also contains links to My Network Places and My Computer. Click one of these links to open that folder. To delete the My Documents icon from your Desktop, right-click it and choose Delete. Remember, this doesn't delete the My Documents folder but only its representation on your Desktop.

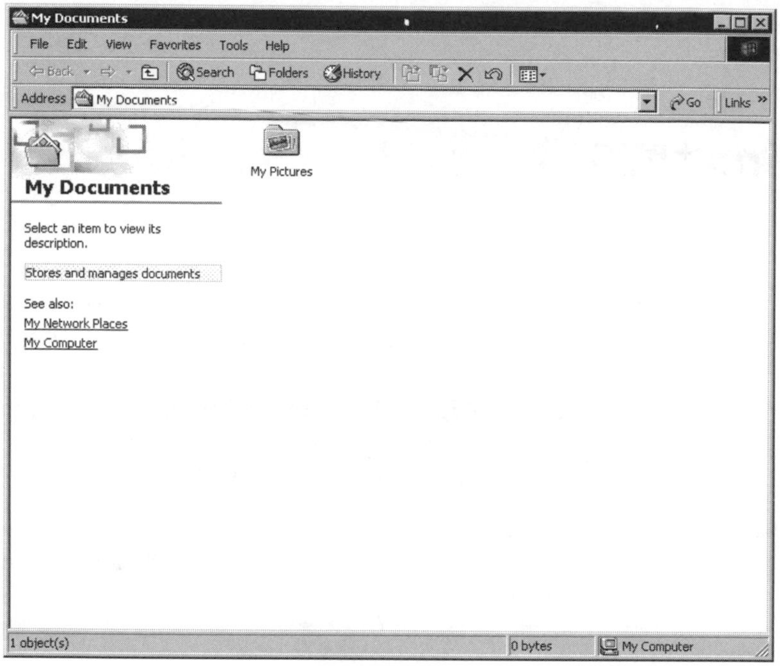

FIGURE 3.11: To open a document stored in your My Documents folder, click the My Documents icon on the Desktop.

RIGHT-CLICKING A DESKTOP ICON

In Windows 2000 Professional, there's no way to get away from the right-click, nor would you want to. Right-clicking any Desktop icon opens a shortcut menu that contains a few common items such as Open, Explore, Search, Rename, and Properties, as well as items specific to the icon. Right-clicking a Desktop icon is often the most efficient and the fastest way to get information you need or to perform a task.

Take the time to right-click each of these icons and check out the options on its shortcut menu.

My Computer

Clicking the My Computer icon opens a window onto your local computer, as shown in Figure 3.12. This is, in a sense, an overview of what you see in Windows Explorer. Click any icon to view its contents. And, just as you did in the My Documents folder, click the Back or Forward button to move between the big picture and the folder or file view. The pane on the left displays usage statistics about the disk you are viewing.

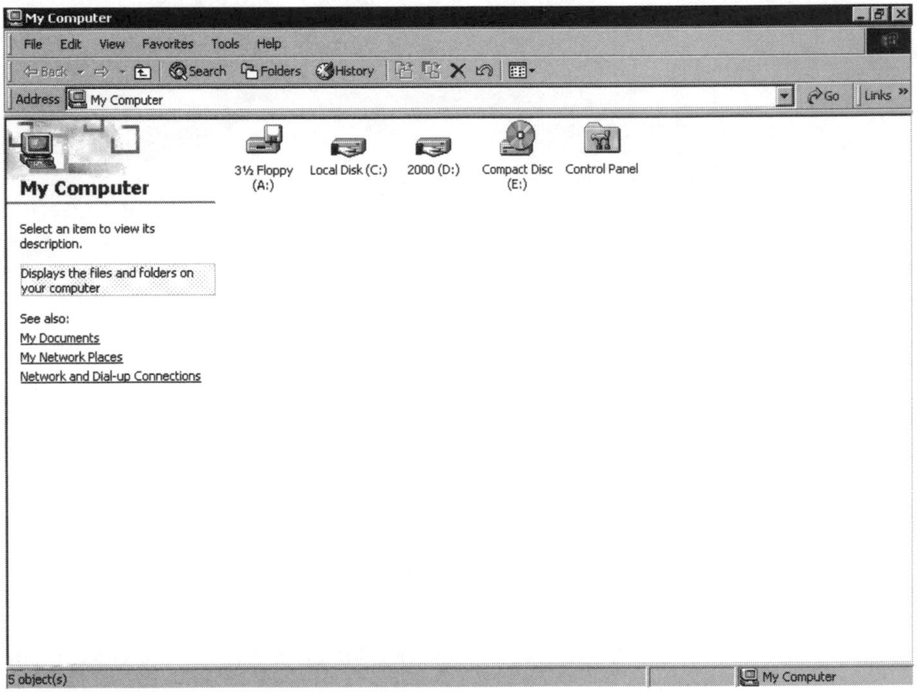

FIGURE 3.12: The My Computer folder contains big-picture information about the configuration of your system.

TIP When you want information about your system or any system component, right-click My Computer, and choose Properties to open the System Properties dialog box.

My Network Places

Clicking My Network Places opens a window onto your local area network. You use the options in the My Network Places folder (see Figure 3.13) to set up and use the network. See Skill 16 for information on how to set up a small network, and see Skill 17 for information on connecting to a corporate network.

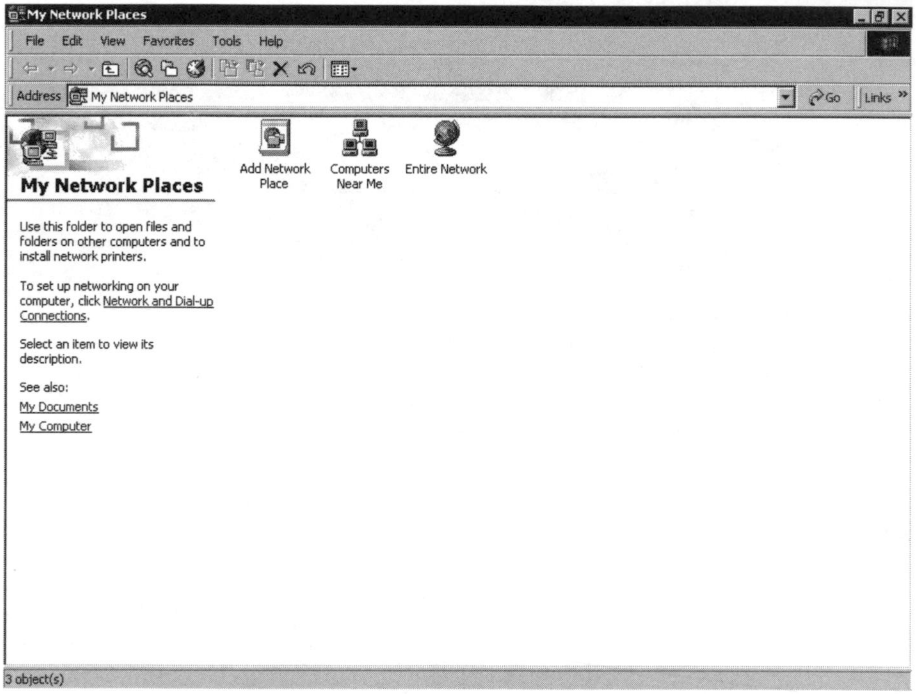

FIGURE 3.13: My Network Places gives you a view of your local area network.

 NOTE In previous versions of Windows, My Network Places was called Network Neighborhood.

Recycle Bin

You probably already know that by default the Recycle Bin is where files and folders go when you delete them from your hard drive. They are not really removed until you empty the Recycle Bin, so up until that point, you can retrieve them. To retrieve a file from the Recycle Bin, follow these steps:

1. Double-click the Recycle Bin to open the Recycle Bin folder.

2. Right-click a file or folder, and choose Restore from the shortcut menu.

To empty the Recycle Bin, right-click it and choose Empty Recycle Bin.

If you want to bypass the Recycle Bin altogether and remove files immediately when you delete them, follow these steps:

1. Right-click the Recycle Bin, and choose Properties from the shortcut menu to open the Recycle Bin Properties dialog box.

2. If necessary, click the Global tab.

3. Check the Do Not Move Files to the Recycle Bin check box.

4. Click OK.

If you have more than one hard drive, you can specify that you want to bypass the Recycle Bin on some drives and not others by selecting the tab for the specific drive rather than the Global tab.

To change the size of the Recycle Bin, move the slider bar in the Recycle Bin Properties dialog box.

NOTE   The Recycle Bin is the only icon on the default Desktop that you cannot rename. Neither can you delete it.

Internet Explorer

Double-click the Internet Explorer icon to open Microsoft Internet Explorer. As you know, you can do the same thing by single-clicking the Internet Explorer icon on the Quick Launch toolbar. See Skill 12 for information about Internet Explorer.

Connect to the Internet

Click Connect to the Internet to start the Internet Connection Wizard and sign up for a new Internet account, transfer an existing account, or set up an Internet connection through your local area network. See Skill 11 for how to use this Wizard and for a lot of other information about how to connect to the Internet and other computers.

Creating Shortcuts

As we've been looking at the icons on the default Desktop, you've been using shortcuts, and we also mentioned earlier how to move shortcuts around on the Desktop. Because shortcuts are so handy, let's briefly look at how to create them.

When you install an application, the installation process itself will often place a shortcut to it on the Desktop. If it doesn't, you can create one. Follow these steps:

1. Choose Start ➤ Programs.

2. Click the name of the application in the menu, and drag it to the Desktop.

That's all there is to it if you can see the item for which you want to create a shortcut. If you can't see it, follow these steps:

1. Right-click the Desktop, and choose New ➤ Shortcut to open the Create Shortcut dialog box:

2. Enter the name of the file or folder, or click Browse to locate it.

3. Click Next to open the Select a Title for the Program dialog box.

4. Accept the name that Windows 2000 Professional suggests, or type a new name in the text box.

5. Click Finish.

The shortcut will appear on your Desktop.

To Rename a shortcut, right-click it, choose Rename from the shortcut menu, type the new name, and then click outside the name box on the Desktop.

You can also change the icon of some shortcuts. Follow these steps:

1. Right-click the icon, and choose Properties from the shortcut menu to open the Properties dialog box for that icon.

2. Click the Change Icon button to open the Change Icon dialog box:

3. Select an icon, and click OK.

WINDOWS LOGO KEY SHORTCUTS

If you bought your computer recently, you have a Windows logo key on the keyboard. You can use it in combination with other keys to display essential dialog boxes quickly.

- Press Windows+R to open the Run dialog box.
- Press Windows+M to minimize all open windows to the Taskbar.
- Press Windows+D to minimize or restore all open windows.
- Press Windows+F to open the Search Results dialog box.
- Press Windows+Ctrl+F to open the Search Results – Computers dialog box.
- Press Windows+E to open the My Computer folder.
- Press Windows+U to open the Utility Manager dialog box.
- Press Windows+F1 to open Windows 2000 Help.

Are You Up to Speed?

Now you can...

- ☑ log on
- ☑ use the items on the Start menu
- ☑ right-click the Start menu to access additional items
- ☑ work with the items on the Taskbar and the Quick Launch toolbar
- ☑ hide and display the Taskbar
- ☑ use the icons on the Desktop
- ☑ right-click icons and the Desktop to perform specific tasks
- ☑ use, create, and customize shortcuts

SKILL 4

Managing Files and Folders

- Using Windows Explorer
- Selecting files and folders
- Creating, saving, and sharing files and folders
- Copying and moving files and folders
- Renaming files and folders
- Deleting files and folders
- Finding files and folders
- Keeping files current with Synchronization Manager
- Understanding and using the Folder Options folder
- Formatting and copying floppy disks

Although we both work from our home offices now, we spent several years in the corporate world, and our guess is that many of you work in a company or an organization outside your home. Traveling from office to office or even cubicle to cubicle can be a trip into myriad personal styles. Some people decorate their workspace with family photos, mementos, and other objects d'art, while others give no clue that they have a life after work. Some offices are obsessively neat, and others look as if a Texas tornado has just ripped through. We once had a manager whose desk was piled so high with file folders, papers, musical scores, and other documents that we had to walk around it to see him, and he was well over six feet tall.

We tend to think that how you organize your physical office probably influences how you organize your computer. Some people use photos of their pets or pithy personal aphorisms as screen savers, and others prefer a blank screen. Regardless of your personal style, however, you'll quickly run into trouble if you don't impose some sense of organization on the files and folders on your system. You need to recognize the names you give them, you need to know where or how to find them, and you need to be able to manipulate them in whatever ways your work requires.

In this skill, we'll look at what you need to know about files and folders in Windows 2000 Professional, and we'll start with the essential tool, Explorer.

> **NOTE**   Everything in this skill applies equally, whether you're using FAT16, FAT32, or NTFS. If you're using the NTFS file system and want information about file compression and file encryption, see Skill 6. File and folder security in NTFS are covered in Skill 16.

Using Explorer

Whether you're coming to Windows 2000 Professional via Windows NT or Windows 95/98, you'll find that Explorer has a new look. As you can see in Figure 4.1, the Menu bar, toolbar, and Address bar are borrowed from Internet Explorer. And, as we mentioned in Skill 3, folders are in Web view by default. In addition, the title bar displays the name of the selected folder rather than the words *Exploring – folder name*. We think this new version of Explorer is also easier to use than previous versions.

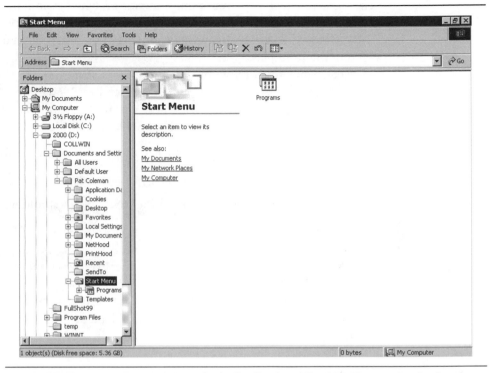

FIGURE 4.1: The Windows 2000 Professional Explorer has a new look.

NOTE If you have any questions about how the Menu bar, toolbar, or Address bar work, see the descriptions of these items in Skill 12.

From the Desktop, you can start Explorer in several ways:

- Right-click Start, and select Explore.

- Choose Start ➢ Programs ➢ Accessories ➢ Windows Explorer.

- Right-click My Documents, My Computer, My Network Places, or Recycle Bin, and choose Explore.

The view in which Explorer opens depends on which commands you used. For example, if you open it from the Start menu, the Start Menu folder is selected, the title bar displays Start Menu, and the contents of the Start Menu folder are displayed in the right pane.

You'll also encounter Explorer-like windows in several other places in Windows 2000 Professional (for example, the Search Results window, My Computer, and My Documents). Regardless of where you find an Explorer-like window, you can use the following techniques to display files and folders:

- In the Folders pane, select a folder to display its content in the right pane.

- In the Folders pane, click the plus (+) sign to display a list of what it contains.

- In the right pane, double-click a folder to display subfolders or files.

To flip between folder view and subfolder view or between file view and folder view, click the Back and Forward buttons.

If you can't see all the items in the hierarchical Folders pane, drag the horizontal scroll bar to the right or drag the vertical scroll bar up or down.

In this section, we have rather quickly covered Explorer basics. As we discuss the other tasks related to managing files, we'll look at the other ways you can use Explorer to navigate and organize your system.

Opening Files and Folders

To open any file or folder, simply double-click it in the right pane of Explorer. As we discussed in Skill 3, it will usually open in the program in which it was created or in the program you specified in the Open With dialog box. Here's a quick way to specify that all files of a certain type open in the program you specify:

1. Double-click the folder or subfolders until you see all the files in that folder.

2. Choose Edit ➢ Select All to select all the folders.

3. Right-click a file, and choose Open With from the shortcut menu to open the Open With dialog box.

4. Select the program you want, and click OK.

For more detail about the Open With dialog box, see Skill 3.

To open a file on another computer on your network, follow these steps:

1. Open My Network Places, and then click the icon for that computer.

2. Keep clicking folders until you find the file you want.

> **NOTE**   For information about using a local area network, see Skill 16.

Creating a Folder

You can create a folder either from the Desktop or from Explorer. To create a folder from the Desktop, follow these steps:

1. Right-click an empty space on the Desktop, and choose New ➤ Folder from the shortcut menu.

2. Type a name for the folder, and then click outside it.

This new folder will be stored in the Desktop subfolder in your user name folder on your hard drive.

To create a folder inside another folder in Explorer, follow these steps:

1. Select the folder.

2. Choose File ➤ New ➤ Folder.

3. Type a name for the folder, and click outside it.

If you're trying to set up a common-sense system for organizing files and folders, it's probably a good idea to create folders in Explorer so that you can see the relationships. You can, however, easily move a folder that you create on the Desktop, as you'll see shortly.

> **NOTE**   If you're working on a corporate network, your network administrator may have specified naming conventions as well as where you are to create and store your files and folders.

NAMING FILES AND FOLDERS

Unless you are coming to Windows 2000 Professional straight from Windows 3.*x* or MS-DOS, you already know that you are no longer limited to the 8.3 filenaming convention. Filenames can contain a maximum of 215 characters and can contain spaces, commas, semicolons, equal signs (=), and square brackets ([ ]). Filenames can be in uppercase and lowercase letters.

But don't get carried away. In Explorer, 215 characters is the equivalent of a rather longish paragraph, and you'll be hard-pressed to display it easily on the screen.

Be sure, though, to give files and folders names that you will easily recognize several months hence when, for instance, you're trying to clean up your hard drive or when you need to send someone the monthly sales report for April of last year.

Creating a File

You can create a file in three ways:

- From the Desktop
- From Explorer
- From within an application

To create a file from the Desktop, follow these steps:

1. Right-click an empty space on the Desktop, and choose New.

2. From the submenu, select the type of file you want to create.

3. Type a name for the file, and then click outside on the Desktop. This file is stored in the Desktop folder in your user name folder.

To create a file from within Explorer, follow these steps:

1. Open the folder that will contain the new file (whether it's on your local hard drive or the network).

2. Right-click in a blank space in the right pane of Explorer.

3. Choose New, and then, from the submenu, select a file type.

4. Type a name for the file, and then click outside it in a blank space.

You'll probably most often create a new file from within an application. For purposes of example, here are the steps for creating a new file in Notepad:

1. Choose Start ➤ Programs ➤ Accessories ➤ Notepad to open Notepad:

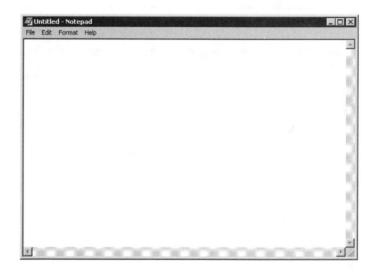

2. Choose File ➤ Save As to open the Save As dialog box:

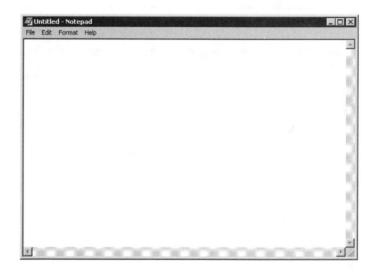

3. Select a folder in which you want to save the document.

4. Enter a name in the File Name box.

5. Click Save.

NOTE   To save a file the first time, choose File ➢ Save As. To save it again later after you've edited it, choose File ➢ Save to save it without changing its name. Choose File ➢ Save As to save it under a new name.

UNDERSTANDING FILE TYPES

Regardless of how you create or save a file, Windows gives it an extension that identifies its type. When you create a file from the Desktop or Explorer, you select a type from the shortcut menu's submenu. For example, selecting Rich Text Format creates a file that has the .RTF extension, and selecting Bitmap Image creates a file that has the .BMP extension. To see a file's extension in Explorer, choose View ➢ Details.

Sharing Files and Folders

If you are on a network and want to share your drives, folders, or files with another computer, right-click the resource in Explorer, and choose Sharing from the shortcut menu to open the Properties dialog box for that resource. You use this dialog box to set up sharing, permissions, and so on. For information about how to do this, see Skill 16.

Copying and Moving Files and Folders

You can copy or move a file or a folder in four ways:

- By dragging and dropping with the right mouse button
- By dragging and dropping with the left mouse button
- By copying and pasting or cutting and pasting
- By using the Send To command

Which method you use depends on your personal preference and, to some extent, on the circumstances. When you can see both the source and the destination, dragging and dropping is easiest.

To copy or move a file or folder using the right mouse button, follow these steps:

1. Locate the file or folder in Explorer.

2. Right-click it, and then drag it to its destination.

3. Release the mouse button, and then choose Copy Here or Move Here.

If you change your mind en route, press Escape.

To copy a file when the source and destination are on different drives, left-click the file, and drag it to its new location. If you use the left mouse button to drag and drop and the source and destination are on the same hard drive, the file is moved rather than copied. To move a file when the source and destination are on different drives, click the file with the left mouse button, and hold down Shift while you drag the file.

To copy or move a file using the Cut, Copy, and Paste commands, follow these steps:

1. Right-click the source file, and choose Cut or Copy from the shortcut menu.

2. Right-click the destination folder, and choose Paste from the shortcut menu.

Another way to copy a file to a new location, such as a floppy disk or another hard disk, is to right-click the file and choose the Send To command on the shortcut

Skill 4

menu. If the shortcut menu doesn't include a destination you want to use regularly, you can add it. Follow these steps:

1. In Explorer, locate your user name folder, and then locate the Send To folder within it.

TIP   If you don't see the Send To folder, choose Tools ➢ Folder Options to open the Folder Options folder, and click the View tab. In Advanced Settings, scroll down, click the Show Hidden Files and Folders option, and then click OK. We'll look at the Folder Options dialog box in detail later in this skill.

2. Select the Send To folder, and then choose File ➢ New ➢ Shortcut to open the Create Shortcut dialog box:

3. Enter the name of the shortcut you want to add, or click Browse to find it.
4. Click Next.
5. Type a new name for the shortcut if you want, and then click Finish.

Renaming Files and Folders

You can easily rename a file or a folder in two ways:

- Left-click twice (wait about a second between clicks) the name of the file or folder, and enter a new name in the highlighted box.
- Right-click the name of a folder, choose Rename from the shortcut menu, and then type a new name.

If you change your mind about the new name, you can click Undo, or you can re-rename the file or folder.

Deleting Files and Folders

You can delete a file or a folder in three ways:

- In Explorer, right-click the name of the file or folder, and then choose Delete from the shortcut menu.

- In Explorer, left-click the name of the file or folder, and then press Delete or click the Delete button on the toolbar.

- If the Recycle Bin is visible on the Desktop, click the name of the file or folder, and drag it to the Recycle Bin.

 TIP   To bypass the Recycle Bin, hold down Shift when choosing or pressing Delete.

To restore a file you've sent to the Recycle Bin, follow these steps:

1. Double-click the Recycle Bin to open the Recycle Bin dialog box.

2. Right-click the file, and choose Restore from the shortcut menu.

The file is restored to its original location.

WARNING   You cannot use the Undo command to retrieve a file that you delete from the Recycle Bin.

Finding Files and Folders

As we mentioned in Skill 3, the Find command that you used in previous versions of Windows is now called Search, and the Search Results dialog box is similar to the Internet Explorer window. If you can't remember where you stored a file or what you named it, you can try to locate it in a couple of ways. You can scroll endlessly through Explorer, or you can right-click a drive and choose Search from the shortcut menu. In the Search Results dialog box, shown in Figure 4.2, you can search for the filename, and you can search for a file containing the contents you specify.

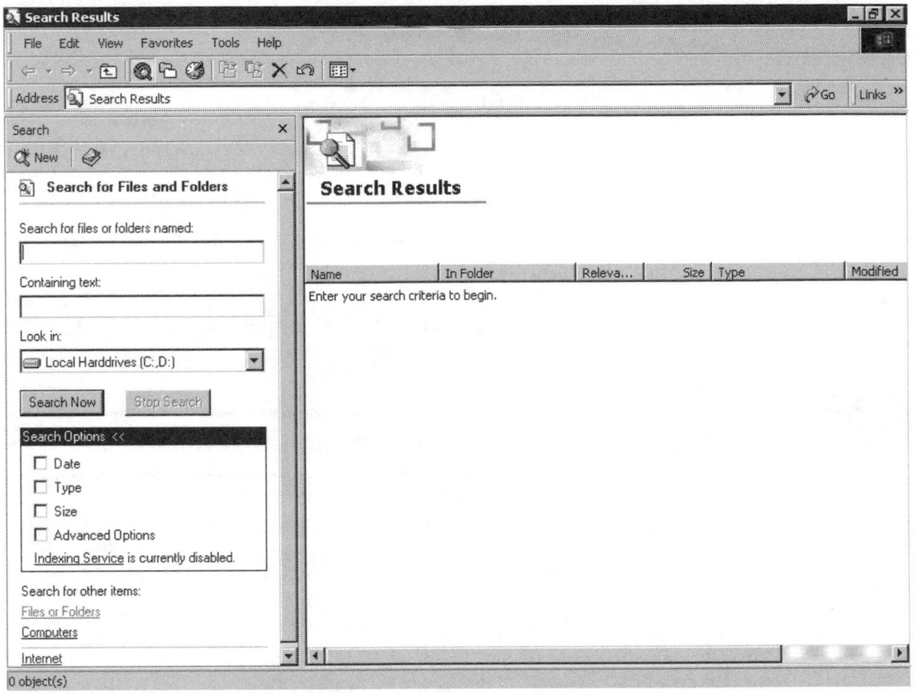

FIGURE 4.2: Use the Search Results dialog box to find files and folders.

To find a file if you know its name or even part of its name, follow these steps:

1. Choose Start ➤ Search ➤ For Files and Folders to open the Search Results dialog box.

2. In the Search for Files or Folders Named box, enter your search term.

3. Click Search Now.

All files matching the criteria you entered are displayed in the right pane. If you want to search on file contents, enter your text in the Containing Text box.

TIP

You can also use the wildcard characters * and ? when you're searching. The asterisk represents one or more characters, and the question mark represents a single character. For example, *.doc will find all files that have the .DOC extension; chap? will find *chaps* and *chap1* but not chapter.

Sometimes you may not remember the filename or part of the filename, but you do remember when you created or last edited the file. To search for a file by date, click Search Options, click the Date check box, and enter your criteria. You can also use Search Options to locate a file by its type or size.

In the Search Options submenu, click the Advanced Options check box to specify subfolders to search or to specify that the search is case sensitive.

Skill 4

INDEXING SERVICE

In the Search Results dialog box, you will also see a link to Indexing Service. When you click it, you'll see the Indexing Service Settings dialog box:

Indexing Service Settings	☒
When Indexing Service is enabled, the files on your computer are indexed and maintained so you can perform faster searches. Indexing Service also provides greater search capabilities. For more information, click Help.	OK
	Cancel
Status: Indexing Service is currently disabled.	Advanced
Do you want to enable Indexing Service?	Help
○ Yes, enable Indexing Service and run when my computer is idle.	
● No, do not enable Indexing Service	

Indexing Service, which is not enabled by default, is a program that reads through files and extracts the text and properties and places them in an index. Searching the index is much faster and can be more powerful than searching all the files themselves.

If you are on a corporate network, see your network administrator for information about enabling or using Indexing Service. For in-depth information about how Indexing Service works, click the Advanced button in the Indexing Service Settings dialog box, and then, in the Indexing Service dialog box, choose Action ➢ Help.

Keeping Files Current with Synchronization Manager

Whether you are working with files on a local area network or on the Internet, you can choose to work with them offline. To enable offline viewing, in My Computer or My Network Places, right-click the file and select Make Available Offline from the shortcut menu.

To synchronize this file with the one on your network or on the Internet, right-click the file, and choose Synchronize from the shortcut menu. You can also specify that offline files are synchronized when you log on to your computer or log off or at a scheduled time. To set this up, select the file, and then follow these steps:

1. In Explorer, choose Tools ≻ Synchronize to open the Items to Synchronize dialog box:

2. Click the check box for the file you want so synchronize, and then click Setup to open the Synchronization Settings dialog box:

3. If you want to update the file when you log on or off, select the Logon/Logoff tab, and select options.

4. If you want to update the file when your computer is idle (for example, while you're at lunch), select the On Idle tab, and then select the file.

5. To establish another synchronization schedule, select the Scheduled tab, and click Add to start the Scheduled Synchronization Wizard. Follow the onscreen instructions.

Understanding and Using Folder Options

We mentioned in Skill 3 that, by default, the Windows 2000 Professional user interface is a hybrid—that is, the Desktop uses the classic Windows interface, and folders display in Web view. In Skill 5, we'll look at how to customize your Desktop, and in this section we'll look at how to set the display for files and folders, using the Folder Options dialog box.

To open the Folder Options dialog box, choose Start ➤ Settings ➤ Control Panel, and then click the Folder Options icon. You'll see the dialog box shown in Figure 4.3, which opens at the General tab.

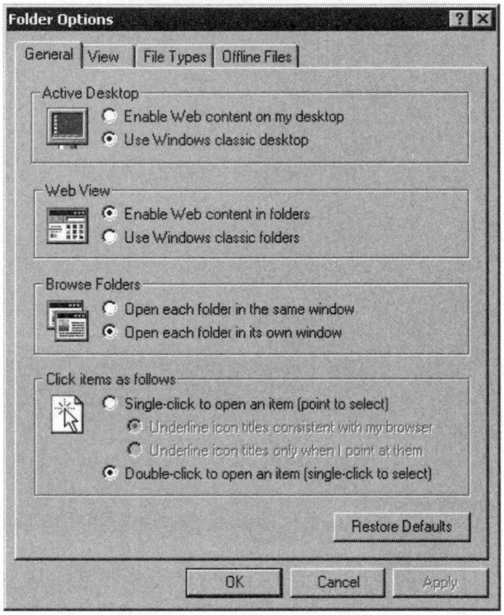

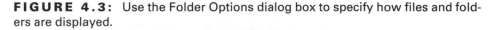

FIGURE 4.3: Use the Folder Options dialog box to specify how files and folders are displayed.

As you can see, in the Web View section, Enable Web Content in Folders is selected. Figure 4.4 shows Control Panel in Web View. Figure 4.5 shows Control Panel as it is displayed when you choose Use Windows Classic Folders. Regardless of which view you choose, Control Panel works the same, as is the case with My Computer, My Network Places, Explorer, and so on. Which view you use is simply a matter of personal preference and, perhaps, the size of your monitor.

FIGURE 4.4: Control Panel in Web view

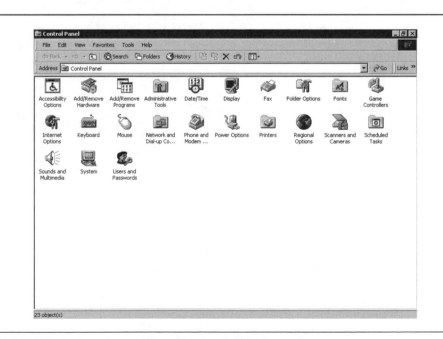

FIGURE 4.5: Control Panel in classic Windows view

In the Browse Folders section, you can choose to open each folder in the same window or in its own window. Click each of these options to see how this setting affects the display (notice that the icon in this section changes).

In the next section, you can specify whether you want to single-click, as you do on the Web, or double-click to open items.

Select the View tab, as shown in Figure 4.6, to specify how and which folders are displayed. Earlier in this skill, we used this tab to tell Windows 2000 Professional to display hidden files in Explorer. In the Advanced Settings section, use the scroll bar to check out the other options. If you have already made some changes and want to display all folders as they were when you installed Windows 2000 Professional, click Reset All Folders. If you have made changes to the Advanced Settings and want to restore this area as it was when you installed Windows 2000 Professional, click Restore Defaults.

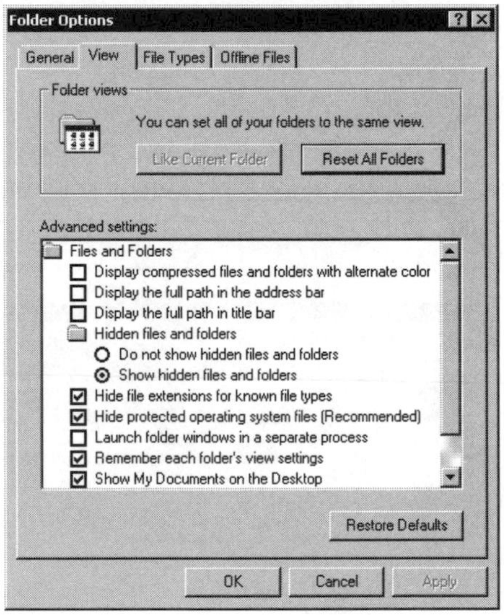

FIGURE 4.6: Specify which files to display and how in the Advanced Settings section of the View tab.

Select the File Types tab to display the screen shown in Figure 4.7. Here you see a list of filename extensions, their associated file types, and applications that are registered with Windows 2000 Professional. (For information about the Registry, see Skill 7.) You can add, delete, and change items on this list, but we strongly recommend that you leave this list alone unless you really know what you are doing, have a good reason for doing it, and/or have spoken with your network administrator if you are on a network.

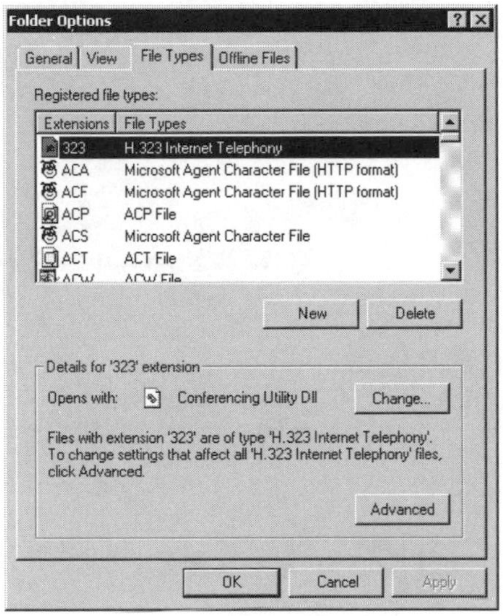

FIGURE 4.7: The File Types tab in the Folder Options dialog box.

Select the Offline Files tab, as shown in Figure 4.8, to enable or disable the use of offline files and reminders and to specify some synchronization options such as whether to update files before logging off.

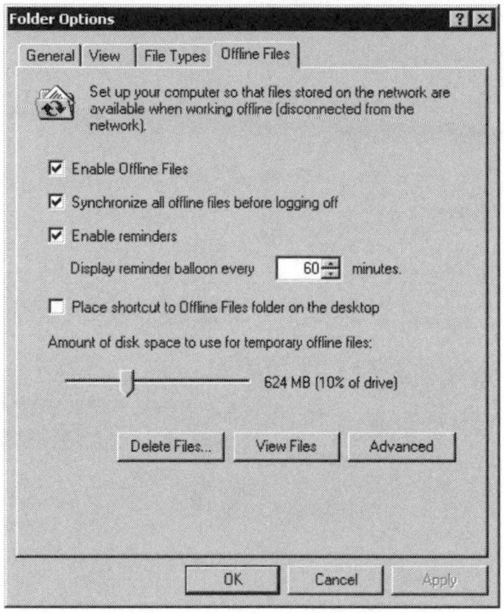

FIGURE 4.8: You can enable and disable offline viewing in the Offline Files tab of the Folder Options dialog box.

Handling Floppy Disks

Whether you work on a stand-alone system, you're connected to a local area network, or you live and breathe via the Internet, you probably also use sneakernet from time to time. On a sneakernet, you copy files to a floppy and schlepp the disk over to a co-worker. Some of you may think this is tantamount to programming with a pen and quill, but since it's still a fact of life, let's complete this skill by looking at how you format and copy a floppy.

Formatting a Floppy Disk

Unless you buy formatted disks, you must format a disk before you can store information on it. Formatting a disk that already contains files deletes those files. Follow these steps to format a floppy:

1.   Insert a disk in your floppy drive.

2. In Explorer, scroll up in the Folder pane until you see the icon for the floppy, and then right-click it.

3. Choose Format from the shortcut menu to open the Format *drive letter* dialog box:

4. Ensure that the correct options are selected, and then click Start. A bar at the bottom of the dialog box will indicate the progress of the format.

5. When Windows 2000 Professional says Format Complete, click OK, and close the Format dialog box.

Copying a Floppy Disk

To copy a floppy disk, follow these steps:

1. In Explorer, scroll up in the Folder pane until you can see the icon for the floppy drive, and right-click it.

2. In the shortcut menu, choose Copy Disk to open the Copy Disk dialog box:

3. When prompted, place the disk you want to copy in the floppy drive, and click OK.

N) NOTE   If you have more than one floppy drive, you can specify the From and To disks. We know, if you're on a network, you may be lucky to have one floppy drive, much less two. For security purposes, network computers often have no floppy drive.

4. When Windows 2000 Professional has finished reading the source disk, it will ask you to insert the destination disk. Do so, and click OK.

5. When the copy is completed, click Close.

Are You Up to Speed?

Now you can...

- ☑ use Explorer
- ☑ open files and folders
- ☑ create files and folders
- ☑ share files and folders
- ☑ copy and move files and folders
- ☑ rename files and folders
- ☑ delete files and folders
- ☑ find files and folders
- ☑ synchronize files and folders
- ☑ use the Folder Options dialog box
- ☑ format and copy a floppy disk

SKILL 5

Customizing Your Desktop

- Opening Control Panel
- Setting up your Active Desktop
- Making Windows 2000 Professional more accessible
- Customizing the keyboard
- Adjusting your mouse
- Changing the display
- Establishing your regional settings
- Adjusting the date and time
- Personalizing the Start menu

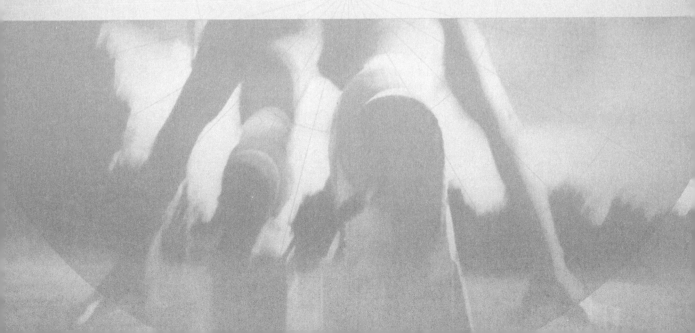

We've already mentioned a few times in the first four skills of this book that you can customize your Desktop, and we've taken a couple of quick looks at the instrument you use to do this: Control Panel. The items in Control Panel are variously referred to as applets, folders, icons, tools, and so on. Clicking one of them usually opens a dialog box or another folder in which you can choose options that specify how that particular item will work. For example, if you are left-handed, you can configure your mouse so that the buttons are reversed, and if you move from Bellingham, Washington, to Athens, Greece, you can change the time zone.

The changes you make using Control Panel are stored in the Registry, the central database that contains all the configuration settings used on your system. Every time you change an option in an applet, that change is reflected in the Registry. It stays in effect until you change it again and is reloaded every time you start Windows 2000 Professional. In Skill 7, you'll learn a bit more about the Registry. What we want to stress here, however, is that you don't need to use the Registry to customize your system. In fact, you shouldn't; always use Control Panel instead.

In this skill, we are going to look at the items you'll use to customize your Desktop. You'll find information on the rest of the Control Panel items in other skills:

- For information on Folder Options, see Skill 4.

- For information on the Add/Remove Programs applet and Scheduled Tasks, see Skill 7.

- For information on Printers and Fonts, see Skill 8.

- For information on Internet Options, Network and Dial-up Connections, and Phone and Modem Options, see Skill 11.

- For information on the System folder, the Add/Remove Hardware applet, Scanners and Cameras, Game Controllers, and Sounds and Multimedia, see Skill 14.

- For information on Administrative Tools and Users and Passwords, see Skill 16.

If you've been using other versions of Windows, you probably already know basically how you want to set up your system. If something isn't where you expect it to be, check the index of this book or take a look at the "If You've Used Windows Before" topic in Help. If you're new to Windows or to NT technology, on which Windows 2000 Professional is based, you probably want to become familiar with the default interface before you start changing it.

In addition, if you're on a corporate network, you may need permission to adjust certain items, and you'll find that you need to be logged on as Administrator to tinker with others. Your organization may even have published policies about this. In any event, check with your network administrator.

Now, with all that said, let's open Control Panel, look quickly at how you change the Active Desktop settings, and then check out some other important ways you can set up your system to work the way you want.

Opening Control Panel

Choose Start ➤ Settings ➤ Control Panel to open Control Panel, as shown in Figure 5.1. As we mentioned in earlier skills, Control Panel opens in Web view by default. To open any item, simply click it. To create a shortcut on the Desktop for a Control Panel item, right-click the item and choose Create Shortcut. For more information on creating shortcuts, look back at Skill 3.

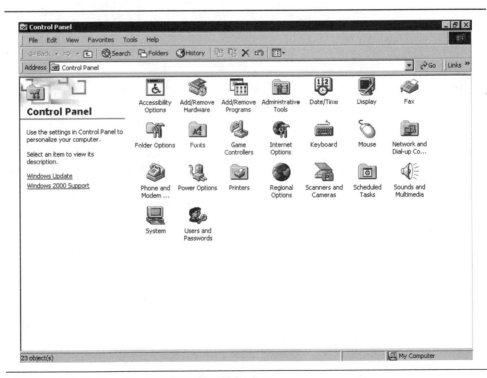

FIGURE 5.1: Control Panel in Web view

Setting Up the Active Desktop

Folder Options

As we've mentioned, the default user interface for Windows 2000 Professional is somewhat of a hybrid. It employs the classic Desktop but uses Web view for folders. To change this arrangement, open the Folder Options dialog box, as shown in Figure 5.2. In Skill 4, we discussed the portions of the General tab that concern folders; here we'll simply look at the options for the Desktop.

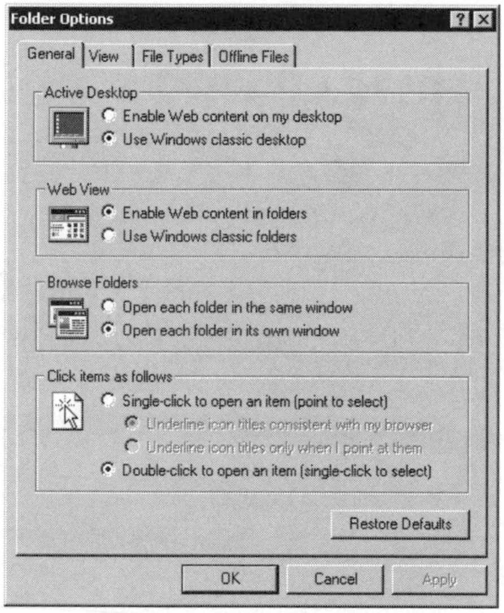

FIGURE 5.2: The General tab of the Folder Options dialog box

To use the Web view instead of the classic Desktop, click Enable Web Content on My Desktop in the Active Desktop section. If you want to open files and folders with a single click instead of a double click, click those options in the Click Items As Follows section. When you're done, click OK.

Making Windows 2000 Professional More Accessible

In the last several years, we have seen many marvelous advances in accessibility technology. Speech recognition systems, alternative keyboards, and adaptive devices for people with spinal cord injuries are but a few of the developments that enable people with physical challenges to improve the quality of their lives by using the computer. Enhancing the accessibility options was key in the development of Windows 2000 Professional. Nevertheless, the current tools provide only a minimal level of functionality for users with special needs.

Most physically impaired users will need special programs and devices. For a list of these and some very helpful information, check out Microsoft's Accessibility Web site at www.microsoft.com/enable/?RLD=185.

You set up some of the accessibility options in Windows 2000 Professional through the Accessibility Options dialog box; others you can access by choosing Start ➢ Programs ➢ Accessories ➢ Accessibility. In this section, we'll look first at the Accessibility Options dialog box and then look at the features available through the Accessibility accessory, including the Accessibility Wizard.

> **NOTE**   You need Administrator privileges in order to customize some of these features.

Specifying Accessibility Options

Accessibility Options

To open the Accessibility Options dialog box, click its icon in Control Panel. In this dialog box, you can set keyboard, sound, display, mouse, and administrative options. Figure 5.3 shows the Accessibility Options dialog box open at the Keyboard tab:

- Click Use StickyKeys if you have trouble pressing two keys simultaneously, such as Ctrl+Alt.

- Click Use FilterKeys if you want brief or repeated keystrokes to be ignored.

- Click Use ToggleKeys if you want to hear a high-pitched sound when you press Caps Lock, Scroll Lock, or Num Lock and to hear a low-pitched sound when you turn off these keys.

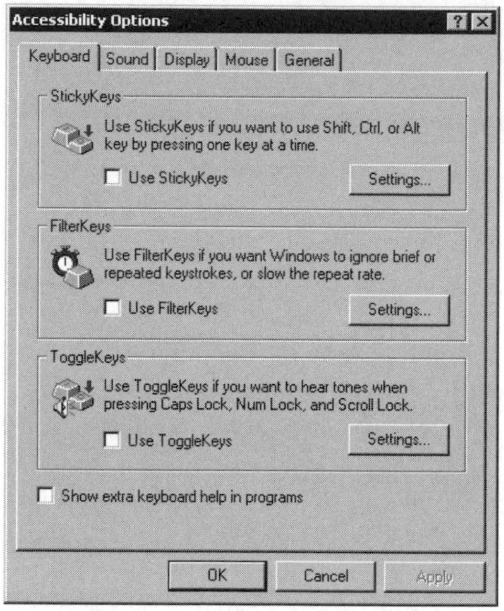

FIGURE 5.3:   To set keyboard options, you can use this tab, the Keyboard applet, and the Accessibility Wizard.

Here are the features available in the other tabs:

Sound   Click Use SoundSentry if you want a visual cue when your system generates a sound. Click Use ShowSounds if you want to display captions for speech and sounds.

Display   Click Use High Contrast and then Settings to specify that Windows 2000 Professional use black-and-white or a custom color scheme instead of the standard color scheme. You might consider enabling this feature if you are color-blind.

Mouse   Click Use MouseKeys to control the mouse pointer with the keys on the numeric keypad.

General   Use this tab to set a time after which accessibility features are turned off, to tell Windows 2000 Professional that you want a message or sound when turning a feature on or off, to enable an alternative mouse or keyboard device, and to select administrative options.

Using the Accessibility Accessories

The Accessibility accessories include the Narrator, the Accessibility Wizard, the Magnifier, the On-Screen Keyboard, and the Utility Manager. Let's start with the Narrator, which is new in Windows 2000 Professional.

Running Narrator

To start the Narrator, whose name is Sam, by the way, choose Start ➢ Programs ➢ Accessories ➢ Accessibility ➢ Narrator. You'll see the Narrator dialog box, as shown in Figure 5.4. Click the check boxes that apply to what you want the Narrator to do, and then click the Minimize button. Now when you open a dialog box, point to an item, or type something, the Narrator will read it to you. To specify the speed at which Sam reads, his volume, or pitch, click the Voice button to open the Voice Settings dialog box. To turn off the Narrator, click the Exit button in the Narrator dialog box.

N **NOTE**   You'll need a sound board, speakers, and text-to-speech program capability to get the benefit of the spoken word.

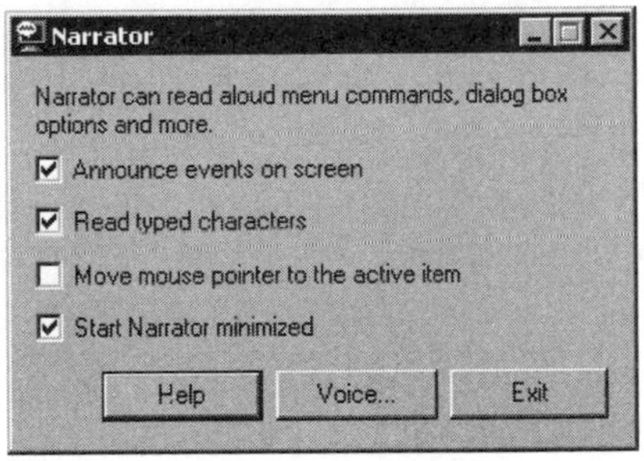

FIGURE 5.4: The Narrator can read items that are displayed on the screen.

Using the Accessibility Wizard

To start the Accessibility Wizard, choose Start ➢ Programs ➢ Accessories ➢ Accessibility ➢ Accessibility Wizard. At the opening screen, click Next. Now, follow the onscreen instructions to customize such features as text size, display size, options for vision, hearing, and mobility, and the size and color of the mouse cursor. Figure 5.5 shows the screen on which you can configure your mouse to work with either your left hand or your right hand. When you've set all the options you want, click Finish.

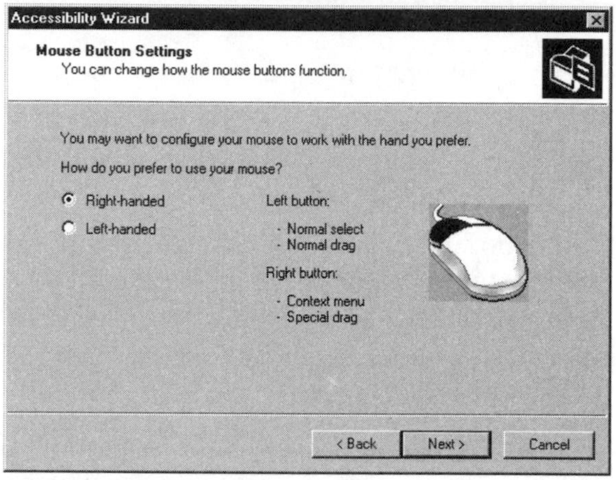

FIGURE 5.5: Use the Accessibility Wizard to configure the mouse for left-hand or right-hand use.

You can also use the Accessibility Wizard to set up Magnifier, and that's what we'll look at next.

Using Magnifier

Magnifier is a utility that displays a magnified portion of your screen in a separate window. To set up Magnifier, follow these steps:

1. Open the Accessibility Wizard, and on the second screen, select Use Microsoft Magnifier, and Large Title and Menus, and click Next.

2. Set the options you want in the Magnifier dialog box, which is shown in Figure 5.6. You can set Magnifier to follow the mouse, the keyboard focus, or text editing.

To return to regular view, click the Close button.

NOTE   When Magnifier is running, you must make selections in the magnified portion of the screen.

To start Magnifier, choose Start ➤ Programs ➤ Accessories ➤ Accessibility ➤ Magnifier.

FIGURE 5.6: The Magnifier dialog box

Using the Onscreen Keyboard

If you aren't a good typist or if you have a physical disability that makes typing difficult, you can display the keyboard on the screen and use the mouse to type. To see how this works, follow these steps:

1. Choose Start ➤ Programs ➤ Accessories ➤ Notepad to open Notepad.

2. Maximize Notepad.

3. Choose Start ➤ Programs ➤ Accessories ➤ Accessibility ➤ On-Screen Keyboard. Now your screen looks like the one in Figure 5.7.

FIGURE 5.7: Use the mouse to type on your onscreen keyboard.

4. Click they keys with your mouse to enter text in Notepad. You can alternate between "typing" on the keyboard and choosing commands from the menu in Notepad.

5. When you're finished, click Close to close both Notepad and the keyboard.

> **TIP** If you can't see the portion of the screen you want to use, click the title bar of the keyboard and move it.

Using Utility Manager

You use Utility Manager to start and stop Narrator and Magnifier and to specify that either starts when Windows 2000 Professional starts or when you start Utility

Manager. To open Utility Manager, choose Start ≻ Programs ≻ Accessories ≻ Accessibility ≻ Utility Manager.

Customizing the Keyboard

Keyboard

When you install Windows 2000 Professional, the installation routine recognizes the keyboard installed on your computer system and identifies the keyboard on the Hardware tab in the Keyboard Properties dialog box. Therefore, you normally don't have to fiddle with the keyboard settings. You can, however, use the Keyboard applet to adjust the repeat rate and the cursor blink rate if you want to, and if you need to use more than one language, you can specify the keyboard layout for other languages.

When you select Keyboard in Control Panel, you'll see the dialog box shown in Figure 5.8. The Speed tab contains the following options:

Repeat Delay   Determines the time that passes before a character repeats after you press the key.

Repeat Rate   Determines the speed at which a character repeats when you press and hold down a key.

Cursor Blink Rate   Determines the blinking speed of the cursor.

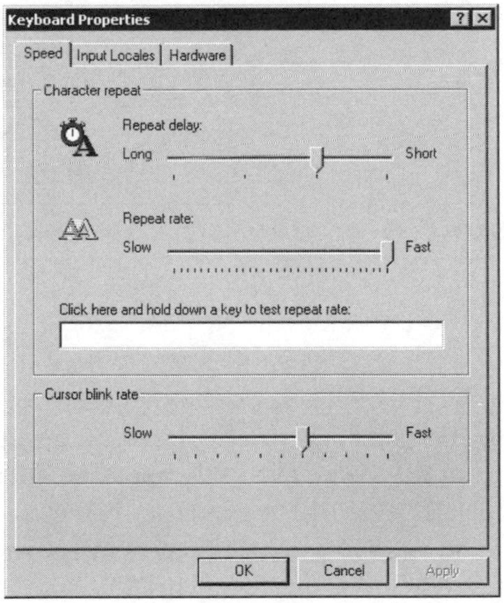

Skill 5

FIGURE 5.8: Use the Keyboard applet to adjust keyboard settings.

Use the settings on the Input Locales tab to set up the keyboard for multiple languages and to specify how the Caps Lock key is turned off (you can either press Caps Lock again or press Shift).

Adjusting Your Mouse

Mouse

We mentioned earlier that you can make some mouse adjustments using the Accessibility Wizard. You can make others in the Mouse Properties dialog box, which is displayed when you select the Mouse icon in Control Panel. Figure 5.9 shows the Mouse Properties dialog box open at the Buttons tab.

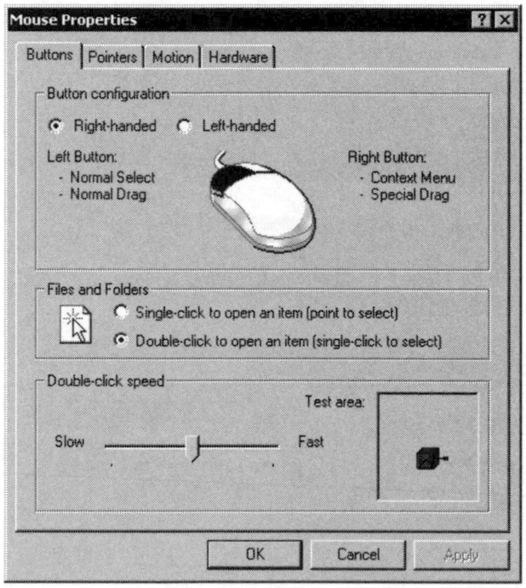

FIGURE 5.9: Use this dialog box to configure your mouse.

In the Buttons tab, you can configure your mouse for the right or left hand, specify whether to open files and folders with a single or a double click, and adjust the double-click speed of your mouse.

In the Pointers tab, you can choose a design scheme for the pointers on your system, and you can even select specific alternate icons for certain pointers. For fun, click the down arrow in the Scheme box to display a list of design schemes. Select Dinosaur to see how your pointers would appear. (None of your choices are etched in stone until you click OK, and then, of course, you can always change them back.) To display a collection of alternate icons, click the Browse button to open the Browse dialog box, as shown in Figure 5.10. If you look closely, you'll see that you can even choose a banana for a pointer!

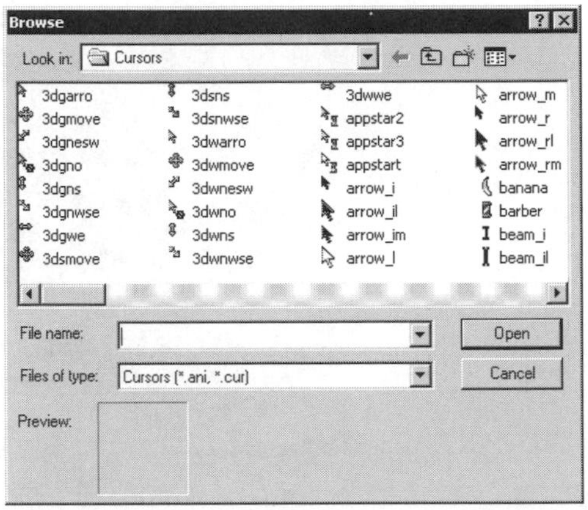

FIGURE 5.10: Move the slider bar to see all your choices.

In the Motion tab, you can adjust the speed of your pointer and specify that the pointer always moves automatically to the default button in a dialog box. The Hardware tab identifies your mouse as it was recognized during installation.

Changing the Display

Display

If you're the type of person who likes to make a personal statement with your computer system, you can access a bag of tricks by opening the Display applet. Among other things, you can use the Display Properties dialog box to configure a spiffy background for your Desktop, compose a message to be used as a marquee screen saver, play around with the Windows 2000 Professional color scheme, and change the resolution at which your monitor displays.

To open this dialog box, you can double-click Display in Control Panel, or you can right-click the Desktop and choose Properties. You'll see the screen shown in Figure 5.11.

TIP If you want to change some settings on only one tab in the Display Properties dialog box, click OK after you make your modifications. If you want to change settings in more than one tab, select the options in the tab, and click Apply. When you've finished making changes in all the tabs or all the tabs you need, click OK.

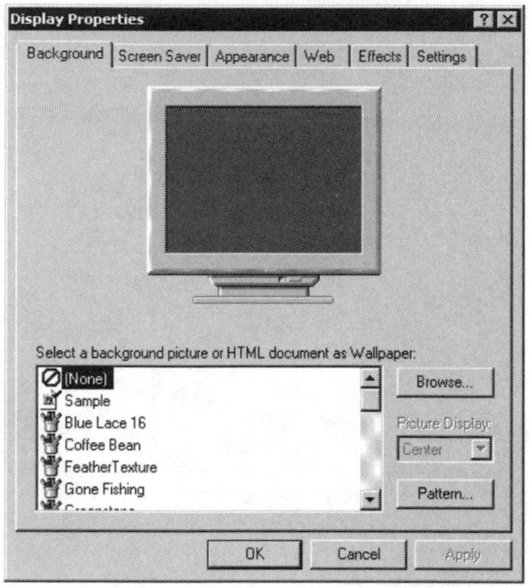

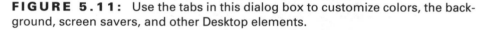

FIGURE 5.11: Use the tabs in this dialog box to customize colors, the background, screen savers, and other Desktop elements.

Customizing the Desktop Background

You have a lot of options when it comes to setting the background, or wallpaper, for your Desktop:

- You can choose None, as we have done in the screens in this book.

- You can select one of the backgrounds in the list box in the Background tab.

- You can browse your local computer, your local area network, or the Web to find a background.

When you choose one of the backgrounds in the list box, a preview is displayed on the monitor in this tab. You can choose to center the background, tile it, or stretch it. If you choose Center, you can click Pattern to select a pattern to fill any leftover space. Some wallpaper can only be displayed if Active Desktop is enabled. When this is the case, you'll be asked if you want to do this.

TIP   To use a graphic you find on the Web as wallpaper, right-click it, and choose Set As Wallpaper.

Choosing a Screen Saver

Use the Screen Saver tab, as shown in Figure 5.12, to select a screen saver, set a password for it if you want, and specify the idle time before the screen saver starts. If you select a screen saver that can be modified in some way, you can click the Settings button to set it up.

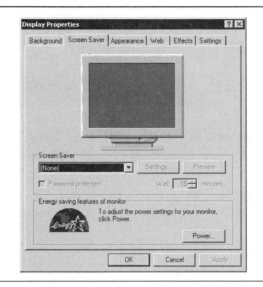

FIGURE 5.12: Specify and configure a screen saver on this tab.

Adjusting the Power Settings

You can also manage the power settings for your computer in the Screen Saver tab. To do so, click Power to open the Power Options Properties dialog box, which has the following tabs:

Power Schemes   Select a scheme that corresponds to your situation, and then specify when or whether to turn off your monitor and hard disks.

Advanced   Click the Always Show Icon on the Taskbar check box if you want to display a power icon in the status area of the Taskbar. You can then click the icon to change your power settings.

Hibernate   Hibernation turns off your monitor and hard drive, saves data to your hard drive, and then turns off your computer. Hibernation is not enabled by default. Click the Enable Hibernate Support check box if you want this option.

APM   To conserve power, you can enable Advanced Power Management by clicking the check box on this tab.

UPS   If you have an uninterruptible power supply, you can configure it using the settings on this tab.

Changing the Appearance of Windows Elements

In this book, we have used the Windows Standard color scheme for elements such as title bars, dialog boxes, menus, and so on, but you can get pretty wild and crazy in this area if you're so inclined. To take a look at the options, select the Appearance tab, which is shown in Figure 5.13, and click the down arrow in the Scheme box. You can use the other options in this tab to color particular items and to change the display font.

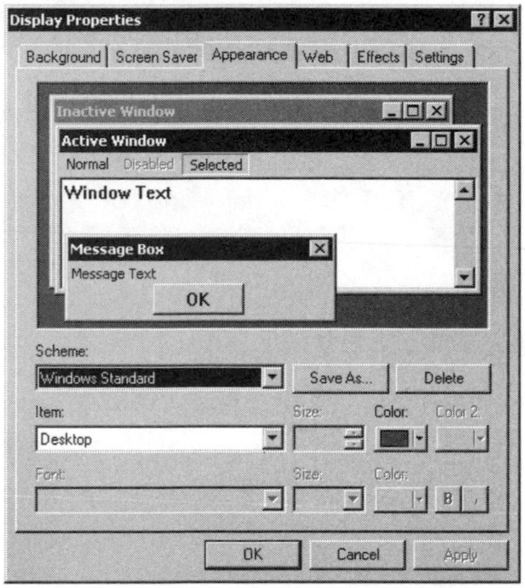

FIGURE 5.13:   Changing the color of Windows elements

Enabling Web Content on Your Desktop

Earlier in this skill, we mentioned how you can enable the Active Desktop in the Folders Options folder and in the Screen Saver tab in the Desktop Properties dialog box. You can also do so by using the Web tab and clicking the Show Web Content on My Active Desktop check box, which is shown in Figure 5.14. To add new items, live Web content, or pictures, click New to open the New Active Desktop Item dialog box. Click Visit Gallery to go to a Microsoft Web site that contains new items you can use on the Desktop. To add a picture or an HTML document, type its URL in the Location box or click Browse to find it.

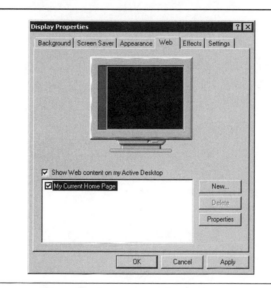

FIGURE 5.14: In this tab, you can enable Web content on the Desktop.

Changing Desktop Icons and Effects

If you're bored with or just plain don't like the default icons on your Desktop, you can change them in the Effects tab of the Display Properties dialog box (see

Figure 5.15). In the Desktop Icons section, select an icon, and click Change Icon to see the possible alternatives. To modify the visual effects, click a check box in the Visual Effects section.

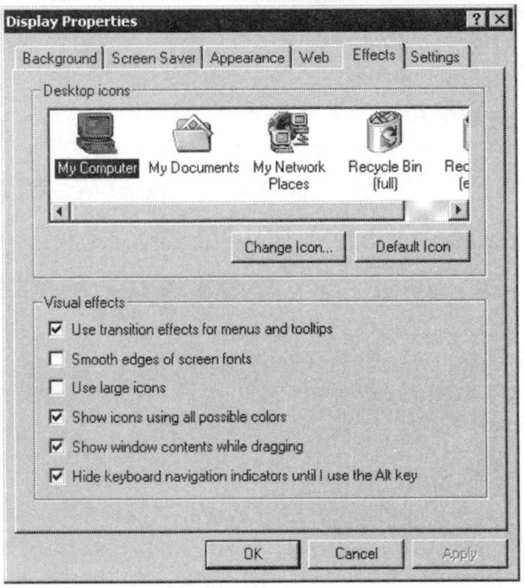

FIGURE 5.15:   Modify icons and effects in this tab.

Modifying the Display of Colors and Resolution

Perhaps nothing changes the appearance of your display as much as changing the options in the Settings tab, which is shown in Figure 5.16. If you click the down arrow in the Colors box, you'll see a list of the color settings available on your system. The maximum number of colors that you can display are determined by your monitor and your display adapter. The screenshots in this book were captured with 256 colors because file size was important. A High Color setting displays more than 65,000 colors, and a True Color setting displays more than 16 million colors.

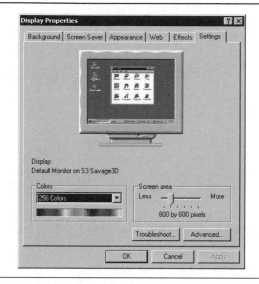

FIGURE 5.16: The Settings tab in the Display Properties dialog box

In the Screen Area of this tab, you can change resolution. Resolution is the number of pixels (dots) on the screen and the number of colors that can be displayed at the same time. As strange as it may seem, the higher the resolution, the smaller elements appear on the screen. For example, a resolution of 640 × 480 pixels will display larger icons on the Desktop than a resolution of 800 × 600. But at a lower resolution, you probably won't be able to see all the elements of a Web page, for example. Here are some common settings and the monitors on which they are best used:

640 × 480   A standard VGA display. On a 15-inch monitor, this is quite readable for most people.

800 × 600   A typical super VGA display. On a 15-inch monitor, this is quite small, but it's quite readable on a 17-inch monitor.

1024 × 768   The upper limits of super VGA. If you have good eyesight, it's readable on a 17-inch monitor.

1280 × 1024   For large monitors. Not really readable on a 17-inch monitor.

To change the font size display, click the Advanced button to open the Properties dialog box for your monitor. In the top half of the General tab, select a font size.

When you change the display settings, you often need to restart your computer; if you don't, some programs may not operate properly. By default, however, Windows 2000 Professional is set up so that the new settings apply without restarting.

If you want to change this, select one of the options in the Compatibility section of the Properties dialog box.

The other tabs in the Properties dialog box contain information about your display adapter and your monitor, troubleshooting tips for working with your graphics hardware, and options for setting color profiles.

> **NOTE** In previous versions of Windows, the General tab on the Properties dialog box for your monitor contained an option you could select to place a settings icon on the Taskbar. If you changed resolutions frequently, this was a big time saver. Unfortunately, this option is not available in Windows 2000 Professional.

Establishing Your Regional Settings

Regional
Options

By default, Windows 2000 Professional installs so that it is set up for U.S. English, the decimal numbering system, the U.S. measurement system, the U.S. currency system, a time format of h:mm:ss tt (*tt* is A.M. or P.M.), and the standard form of writing dates in the United States (10/30/99, October 30, 1999). To change any of these, open the Regional Options applet, as shown in Figure 5.17. First, select the locale on the General tab, and then modify the settings accordingly in the other tabs.

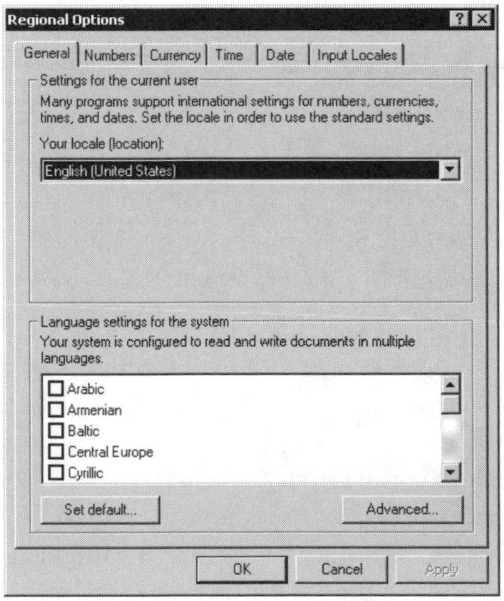

FIGURE 5.17: Modify the system for date and time, currency, numbers, and so on in the Regional Options dialog box.

Adjusting the Date and Time

Date/Time

You adjust the format for the date and time in the Regional Options dialog box, as you have just seen, but you actually change the date and time in the Date/Time Properties dialog box, as shown in Figure 5.18. You can open this dialog box by clicking the Date/Time icon in Control Panel or by right-clicking the time in the Taskbar and choosing Adjust Date/Time from the shortcut menu.

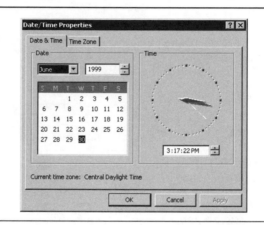

FIGURE 5.18:   Change the date or time in this dialog box.

> **NOTE**   You must be logged on as Administrator to change the date and time, which are very important settings on a local area network.

Personalizing the Start Menu

To add, remove, and re-sort items on the Start menu, you use the Taskbar and Start Menu Properties dialog box. To open it, right-click the Taskbar, and choose Properties from the shortcut menu. Select the Advanced tab, as shown in Figure 5.19, to display your options.

FIGURE 5.19: Customize the Start menu by using the options on the Advanced tab.

To add an item to the Start menu, follow these steps:

1. On the Advanced tab, click Add to open the Create Shortcut dialog box.

2. Enter the location of the item or click Browse to find it, and then click Next.

3. Select Start Menu, and then click Next.

4. Type a name for the item, and then click Finish.

To remove an item from the Start menu, click the Remove button to open the Remove Shortcuts/Folders dialog box, select the item, and click Remove. To rearrange items on the Programs menu so that they are in default order, click Re-sort.

To add an item in the Start Menu Settings section of the Advanced tab, click it, and then click OK.

Are You Up to Speed?

Now you can...

- ☑ enable the Active Desktop
- ☑ make Windows 2000 more accessible
- ☑ customize the keyboard
- ☑ adjust your mouse
- ☑ choose your own wallpaper
- ☑ adjust the power settings
- ☑ change the appearance of Windows elements
- ☑ modify Desktop icons and effects
- ☑ specify colors and the resolution for your display
- ☑ change regional settings
- ☑ adjust the date and time
- ☑ personalize the Start menu

Skill 5

SKILL 6

Setting Object Properties

- Right-clicking in Windows 2000 Professional
- Using Property dialog boxes
- Changing file properties
- Compressing and encrypting files with NTFS
- Changing folder properties
- Using My Computer property settings

In Skills 4 and 5, we looked at how to manage files and folders and how to customize your Desktop. We clicked our way through some of the Control Panel applets, and when working with files, we sometimes right-clicked. In this skill, we are going to take right-clicking even further and will look at how you can use a right-click to get stuff done faster. We'll start with a quick review of right-clicking, and then we'll take a look at Property dialog boxes and file properties. We'll examine how to compress and encrypt files and folders in NTFS and then close this skill with a look at folder properties and the settings you will find associated with My Computer.

Right-Clicking in Windows 2000 Professional

When you right-click an object in Windows 2000 Professional, a shortcut menu opens containing options that relate to the type of object you are working with. Sometimes the same options are available from the conventional menus, but using a right-click can be faster and more convenient.

NOTE   For all of this discussion, we are assuming that you have not switched the mouse button functions by changing the settings in Control Panel. If you have, you will have to switch this discussion too. And if you don't use a mouse but use some other type of pointing device, such as a trackball, you'll have to find the equivalent right-click button; consult the Help files that come with the pointing device for more information.

There are many places you can right-click in the Windows 2000 Professional interface, and you can right-click inside many of today's applications too. For example, Microsoft Word, Excel, and the other Office 2000 applications all support context-sensitive right-clicking, as do many of the Windows 2000 Professional accessory programs and system utilities. When you right-click a spreadsheet cell, the options contained in the shortcut menu will be different from those in the shortcut menu of text or a graphic in Word.

The thing to remember is that right-clicking can do no harm; so if you don't know whether an item will open a shortcut menu, try it and see. If it does, the menu will open; if it doesn't, nothing will happen. Just remember that you can close any Windows 2000 Professional shortcut menu by clicking somewhere else or by pressing the Esc key on the keyboard. Many of these menus will also have some standard entries, such as Cut, Copy, Paste, Open, Print, and Rename.

> **TIP** Many of today's keyboards have a right-click or menu key located between the Windows key and the right-hand Ctrl key; you can press it to trigger a right-click for the currently highlighted object. If you are a touch typist, using this key will be faster than moving your hand to the mouse, moving the mouse pointer, and clicking the right button.

Here's a quick review of what happens when you right-click certain common objects:

- Right-click the Desktop and you will see the menu we covered in Skill 5, which is used to customize your Desktop.

- Right-click the Start button to open a menu that contains Open, Explore, and Search options, as well as two entries relating to users.

- Right-click a blank part of the Taskbar to open a menu you can use to manage any windows open on the Desktop, run the Task Manager, or look at the Taskbar properties. We'll be looking at properties in more detail later in this skill.

- Right-click a program icon on the Taskbar. This opens the application's System menu, just as if you had right-clicked the application window's title bar or clicked the System button. Use the selections it contains to resize the application window or to close the application.

- Right-click a file and the menu contains lots of options, including opening the file with its associated application program. Depending on the file type, you will also see Open With, which allows you to specify the program you want to use to open this file.

- Right-click a folder and the menu you see is very similar to the one for a file. If you choose Open, you will see the contents of the folder.

- Right-click a printer in the Printers folder to set a printer as the default printer or, if you are on a network, to work offline.

Skill 6

For example, if you right-click the My Computer icon on the Desktop, you'll see this menu:

```
Open
Explore
Search...
Manage

Map Network Drive...
Disconnect Network Drive...

Create Shortcut
Rename

Properties
```

And if you right-click the Taskbar, this is what you'll see:

```
Toolbars                    ▶

Adjust Date/Time
Cascade Windows
Tile Windows Horizontally
Tile Windows Vertically

Minimize All Windows

Task Manager...

Properties
```

Many Windows 2000 Professional objects, such as My Network Places, My Computer, printers, and folders, have the shortcut menu item Explore, which opens the item in an Explorer two-pane format, with the object in the left pane of the window and its contents in the right pane. The contents will vary according to the object and can include other computers on the network, disk drives, files, folders, and even print jobs being processed by your printer.

TIP Certain items, such as fax modems, hard disks, and printers, have a Sharing selection in their shortcut menus, so you can specify how each item is shared with other users on the network.

Certain applications will add their own entries to a shortcut menu. For example, the file-compression program WinZip adds the menu selection Add to Zip so you can select files to add to an archive.

Using Property Dialog Boxes

All objects in Windows 2000 Professional—from modems, folders, files, and shortcuts to other computers on the network—have properties, or settings, that affect how the object looks and, oftentimes, how the object operates. These properties are collected together and displayed on one or more tabs in a special dialog box called a Property dialog box. When you install a new printer or set up your modem, for instance, the Wizard that walks you through the configuration steps collects all the information together and places that information in the appropriate Property dialog box.

The very last item in many of the shortcut menus that we looked at in the preceding section is the Properties selection, which gives you fast and easy access to these Property dialog boxes. You can also get to an item's properties through the Control Panel, and many dialog boxes have a Properties button that performs the same function. Once a Property dialog box is open, you can not only display the current settings but can also change them. Some Property dialog boxes have a single tab with just a few settings, while others may have multiple tabs; it all depends on the complexity of the object you are working with.

> **TIP** To open an object's Property dialog box from the keyboard, highlight the object, and press Alt+Enter.

Changing File Properties

Right-click a document file and choose Properties to open the file's Properties dialog box, as Figure 6.1 shows. The document file in Figure 6.1 is a Microsoft Office document created by Word, and you'll see that there are several tabs, because Word keeps its property information in several locations; files created by other applications may display a dialog box with just a single tab.

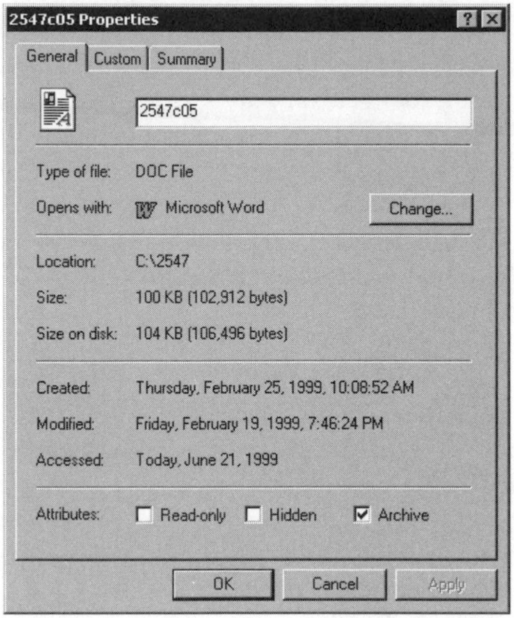

FIGURE 6.1: A Property dialog box for a Word document file on the FAT32 file system

The information shown on the General tab includes the document type and the name of the application associated with this file type, its location and size, as well as the create, last modified, and last accessed dates.

The document shown in Figure 6.1 is on a hard disk formatted with FAT32 and includes these three attribute check boxes:

Read-Only   Set this attribute to prevent anyone from doing anything to this file other than reading it.

Hidden   Check this box to hide the file. It will function as normal, but you won't be able to see it in the Explorer or other programs.

Archive   A check in this box indicates that the document has not been backed up since it was created or last modified.

The Custom tab lets you create your own properties to attach to this file, and the Summary tab details the document title, subject, author, and other details, such as page and character count and the revision number.

The Property dialog box for the same Word file created on a hard disk formatted with NTFS is shown in Figure 6.2. Now there are four tabs: General, Custom, Summary, and a new one called Security.

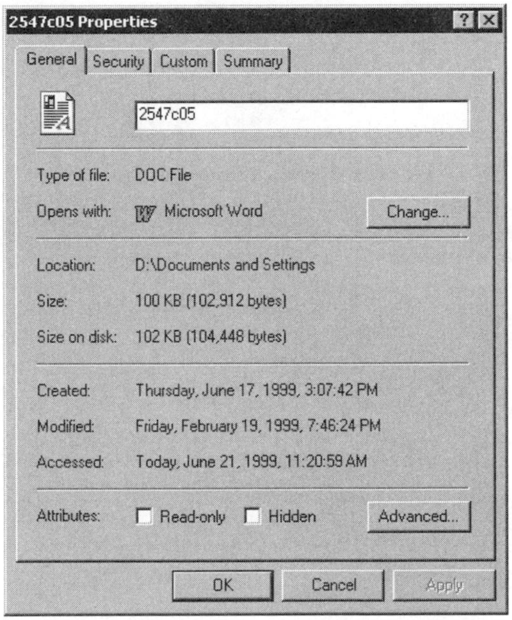

2547c05 Properties   ? X

General | Security | Custom | Summary |

2547c05

Type of file: DOC File

Opens with: Microsoft Word   Change...

Location: D:\Documents and Settings

Size: 100 KB (102,912 bytes)

Size on disk: 102 KB (104,448 bytes)

Created: Thursday, June 17, 1999, 3:07:42 PM

Modified: Friday, February 19, 1999, 7:46:24 PM

Accessed: Today, June 21, 1999, 11:20:59 AM

Attributes: ☐ Read-only   ☐ Hidden   Advanced...

OK   Cancel   Apply

FIGURE 6.2: A Properties dialog box for a Word document file on the NTFS file system

The General tab contains the same information as under FAT32, except this time only two attributes, Read-only and Hidden, are shown.

NOTE   We'll deal with the settings on the Security tab in Skill 16.

Compressing and Encrypting Files with NTFS

Using NTFS allows you to take advantage of advanced file-system features not present on a FAT or a FAT32 drive, such as file compression and encryption. Right-click a file on an NTFS disk, choose Properties, and click the Advanced button on the General tab to open the Advanced Attributes dialog box, which is shown in Figure 6.3. The attributes shown here are only available with NTFS. They are not available if you are using FAT32; the Advanced button will not even be present.

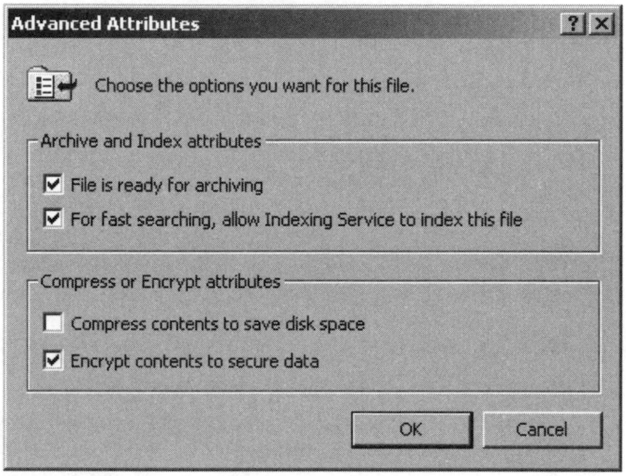

FIGURE 6.3: The Advanced Attributes dialog box

At the top of the Advanced Attributes dialog box, you will see two check boxes:

File Is Ready for Archiving   Specifies whether the file has been changed or modified since it was last backed up.

For Fast Searching, Allow Indexing Service to Index This File   Specifies whether the contents of the file should be indexed to allow for faster searching. Once the contents are indexed, you can search for text within the file as well as for properties, such as the create date or other attributes. We looked at indexing and how to use the Indexing Service in detail in Skill 4.

At the bottom of the Advanced Attributes dialog box, you will see two more check boxes:

Compress Contents to Save Disk Space   Check this box to compress the file so that it occupies less space on your NTFS hard disk. Files are compressed by about one-third, so a 200MB file shrinks down to 135MB. This is a great way to keep large files that you only need to access occasionally. The next time you use the file, it is automatically uncompressed; you don't have to do anything special. There are certain types of files that you shouldn't compress, however. For example, most multimedia and graphics files are already stored using their own compression scheme, and there is no point in compressing a database file since the added overhead of decompressing the file for each transaction you run could seriously affect performance. If you compress a file, you cannot encrypt it.

Encrypt Contents to Secure Data   Check this box to encrypt the file so that others cannot read it; only the user who encrypted the file can open it. If you encrypt a single file, you are asked if you also want to encrypt the folder containing the file. Once the file is encrypted, you can open and change the file just as you would normally; you don't have to decrypt the file before you can use it. Mobile users can encrypt important files so that if their computer is stolen the thief cannot access those files. If you encrypt a file, you cannot compress it, and you can't encrypt Windows 2000 Professional system files.

The Windows 2000 Professional Encrypting File System (EFS) forms the basis for encrypting files on NTFS hard disks. Before you rush off and encrypt all your files though, here are some operational points to consider:

- If you are part of a network, remember that encrypted files cannot be shared, and files opened over the network will be decrypted before they are transmitted.

- When you move or copy an encrypted file to a non-NTFS disk, the file is decrypted.

- Any user with Delete permission can delete an encrypted file or folder, so encryption is not protection against accidental deletion.

- Use Cut and Paste to move a file into an encrypted folder; if you use drag-and-drop, the file will not automatically be encrypted.

- If you use applications that create temporary files, such as Microsoft Word, encrypt at the folder level so that these temporary files are encrypted automatically. If you just encrypt a single important document, the Word temporary files will not be encrypted. You should also encrypt the Temp folder on your hard disk for this same reason.

Changing Folder Properties

Many of the properties we looked at in the last section also apply to folders. Figure 6.4 shows the Property dialog box for a folder on an NTFS volume.

To change folder properties, right-click the folder, select Properties, choose the General tab, and then click the Advanced button to open the Advanced Attributes dialog box for this folder, where you can compress or encrypt the folder. Again, as with files, these are mutually exclusive choices, you must choose one or the other. When you apply compression or encryption at the folder level, you are asked if you want the change to apply to all subfolders as well.

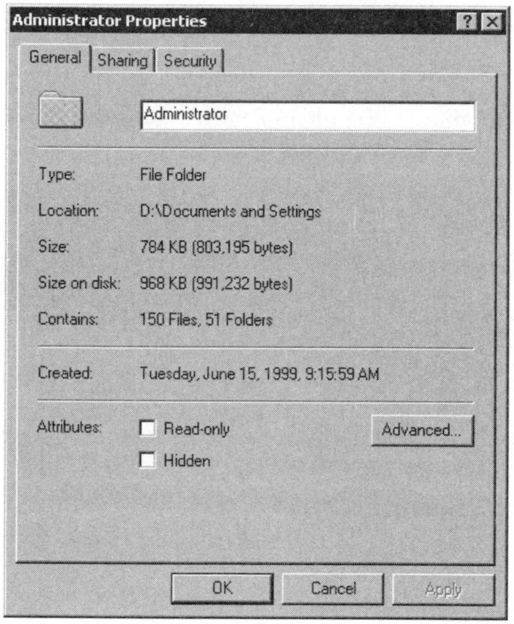

FIGURE 6.4: A Property dialog box for an NTFS folder

If you add or copy a file into a compressed folder, the file is compressed automatically by Windows 2000 Professional. If you move a file from another NTFS drive into a compressed folder, the file is compressed automatically. However, if you move a file from a folder on the same NTFS drive into a compressed folder, the file stays in its original state, either compressed or uncompressed.

To display a compressed file or folder in a different color, follow these steps:

1. Choose Start ➢ Settings ➢ Control Panel to open Control Panel.

2. Open the Folder Options applet.

3. Select the View tab.

4. In Advanced Settings, check the Display Compressed Files and Folders with Alternate Color check box.

5. Click OK to close the Folder Options applet.

> **TIP** You can also encrypt or decrypt a file or folder from the command prompt using the cipher command. Type **Cipher /?** at a command prompt for more information. And for more on using the command prompt, see Skill 7.

My Computer Property Settings

Once the Windows 2000 Professional installation is complete, you will see a number of icons arranged down the left side of the Desktop, depending on the options you or your system administrator chose for your system. One of these icons is My Computer, which gives you access to some of the most important sets of properties in Windows 2000 Professional. Right-click the My Computer icon, and choose Properties to open the dialog box shown in Figure 6.5. Click the General tab to bring it to the front.

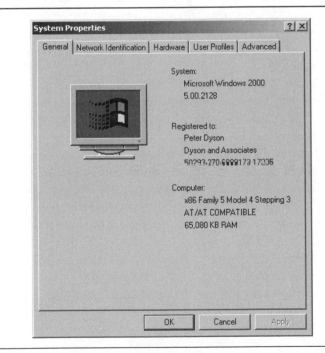

FIGURE 6.5: The Properties dialog box for My Computer open at the General tab

The General tab lists detailed information about your computer, including the processor and the amount of memory installed. When someone asks you a technical question about your system, this is likely the place to find the answer.

The Network Identification tab details the information that identifies your computer to others on the network. Click Network ID to open the Network Identification Wizard, which guides you through making the changes, or click Properties to change the name of your computer or to change your workgroup or domain membership; consult your system administrator before making any changes here.

The Hardware tab gives you access to the Hardware Wizard, which is used to install or remove hardware components from your system, and the Device Manager, which is used to adjust hardware configuration. (We'll look at both of these elements in Skill 14.) Hardware Profiles is the place you go to create different hardware configurations. You can create additional profiles to enable or disable certain hardware devices on your system. Once you have two or more hardware profiles, you will be prompted to choose one of them when Windows 2000 Professional starts. You can also create different hardware profiles for different users.

The User Profiles tab lets you save different Desktop configurations, which can be associated with different users. You can also create a roaming profile that provides your Desktop appearance to every computer on your network, so, no matter where you log on to the network, you will always have your own configuration available.

The Advanced tab, shown in Figure 6.6, contains three sets of options: Performance, Environment Variables, and Startup and Recovery.

The Performance options control how your computer responds to applications versus background system services, allowing you to set the system responsiveness and look at and change the computer's virtual memory settings. It's best to leave these alone and let Windows 2000 Professional manage virtual memory automatically, unless you really know what you are doing.

The Environment Variables options let you tweak system variables, such as the system path—something you might want to change from time to time.

The Startup and Recovery options let you choose a different operating system to load on restart, assuming that you installed Windows 2000 Professional as a dual-boot system. You can also specify what you want Windows 2000 Professional to do when it encounters a serious system error, such as a system halt. For example, you can specify that if the system stops Windows 2000 Professional will log the event to the system log, send an alert, or reboot automatically.

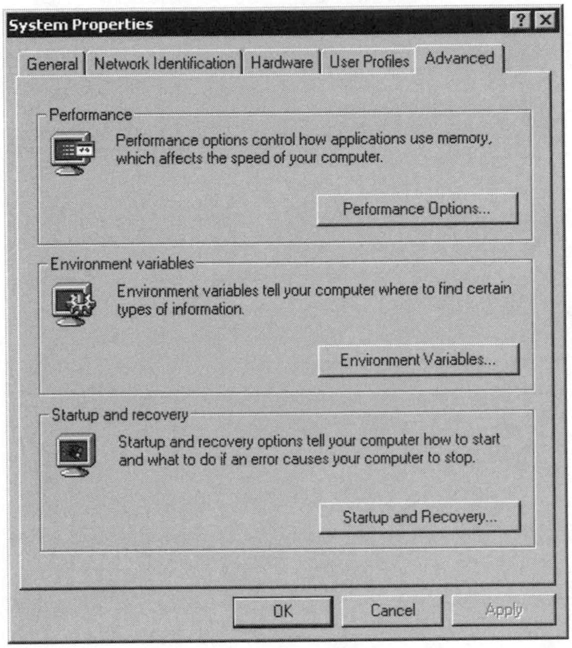

FIGURE 6.6: The Properties dialog box for My Computer open at the Advanced tab

Are You Up to Speed?

Now you can...

- ☑ right-click in Windows 2000 Professional
- ☑ use the right-click menu to open Property dialog boxes
- ☑ change file properties
- ☑ compress files with NTFS
- ☑ encrypt files with NTFS
- ☑ change folder properties
- ☑ examine My Computer settings

SKILL 7

Installing and Running Your Applications

- Running programs from the Start menu
- Running programs from Explorer
- Running programs from Search
- Running programs from a document
- Starting programs automatically
- Using the Run command
- Working from the Command Prompt
- Using the Add/Remove Programs applet
- Understanding the Windows 2000 Professional Registry
- Scheduling programs

The reason you installed Windows 2000 Professional in the first place was to have a secure, stable platform upon which to run your applications, right? And as you might expect with Windows 2000 Professional, you can start an application in several ways, and you can manage that application in several ways once it is running. In this skill, we'll look at all the ways you can do these things. We'll also explain how to add and remove applications and Windows 2000 Professional components, and we'll take a quick look at the Registry and explain how it plays a central role in application configuration. Finally, we'll explain how you can make Windows 2000 Professional run your applications at specific times.

Running Programs from the Start Menu

As its name suggests, you can use the Start button to begin anything in Windows 2000 Professional. To start an application previously installed on your system for your use, follow these steps:

1. Click the Start button to open the Start menu.

2. Click Programs. Along with some application names, your Programs menu will likely include several folders for different categories of programs, such as Accessories and a folder for startup programs that run automatically when you start Windows 2000 Professional; more on this in a later section in this skill.

3. Choose the program group that includes the application you want to start.

4. Click the program you want to start from the selections listed in the submenu.

The next thing you see on the screen will be the application starting to run, unless the program has been configured to run minimized, which is something we'll be looking at in a later section. Windows 2000 Professional also provides keyboard alternatives to using the mouse:

- To open the Start menu from the keyboard, press Ctrl+Esc, or press the Windows key if your keyboard has one.

- To move around inside the menus, use the cursor movement keys (sometimes called the arrow keys) to highlight the entry you are interested in, and then press Enter to launch it.

But Will My Old Applications Run on Windows 2000 Professional?

The answer to that question is that it all depends. Almost all MS-DOS and Windows 3.x applications bypass certain portions of the operating system and manipulate the computer hardware directly, and that is something that violates Windows 2000 Professional system security. So they won't run. Even some Windows 95 programs will not run properly under Windows 2000 Professional, and if you run a proprietary in-house application, consult your system administrator for more information on how to proceed.

New applications, particularly those that display the Certified for Windows 2000 logo, certainly will run, and you can be sure that certified applications have passed a stringent battery of tests and are capable of taking advantage of all the operating system services built into Windows 2000 Professional.

If you are concerned about whether your favorite application will run on Windows 2000 Professional, or is, as they say, Windows 2000 Professional compliant, check the constantly updated catalog of Windows 2000–ready products at www.microsoft.com/windows2000/ready. You can search through a database by product name, product category, or company name to find the application you are interested in.

Skill 7

Running Programs from Explorer

Another way to start an application is to click its name or icon in a folder or in the Explorer window. Alternatively, you can right-click the icon and choose the Open command from the shortcut menu, or select the item and press the Enter key. This also applies to the other Explorer-type windows in Windows 2000 Professional such as My Computer and My Documents, and you can open any application you are authorized to use from My Network Places. Figure 7.1 shows the contents of a Microsoft Office folder open in Explorer; click the Microsoft Word icon to start the application running.

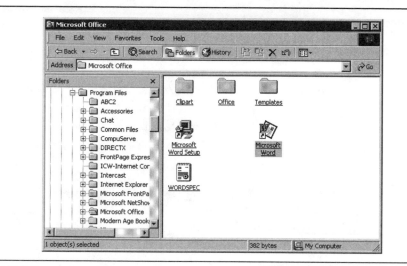

FIGURE 7.1:   Click the Microsoft Word icon to run the application.

> **TIP**   See Skill 3 for details of how to add your own shortcuts to the Start menu.

Running Programs from Search

Another window that works like the Explorer is the Search Results window, and you can launch applications from it in a similar way. Search is particularly useful for applications that do not appear in any of the Start button Program submenus but are located somewhere on your hard disk or on the network. Follow these steps:

1. Click Start, choose Search, and then choose For Files and Folders. Alternatively, right-click the Start button, and choose Search.

2. Enter the name of the file you want to locate in the Search for Files or Folders Named field. You can use the * wildcard character to search for files with

similar names. And if you don't know the name of the file you are looking for, you can locate all the executable files (in other words, all the program files) by entering ***.exe**.

3. Use the drop-down list from the Look In field to select the drive you want to search; you can search any drive attached to your computer, including floppies and CD-ROMs as well as mapped network drives.

4. Click the Search Now button to start the search. You can wait until the search completes, or if you spot the file you are looking for, click Stop Search.

Once the search is complete, the Search Results window lists all the files that match your search criteria. The example shown in Figure 7.2 shows all the files on drive D: with the filename extension of .EXE. To run one of the programs listed, highlight it and choose File ➢ Open, or right-click the program and choose Open, or just double-click the program name.

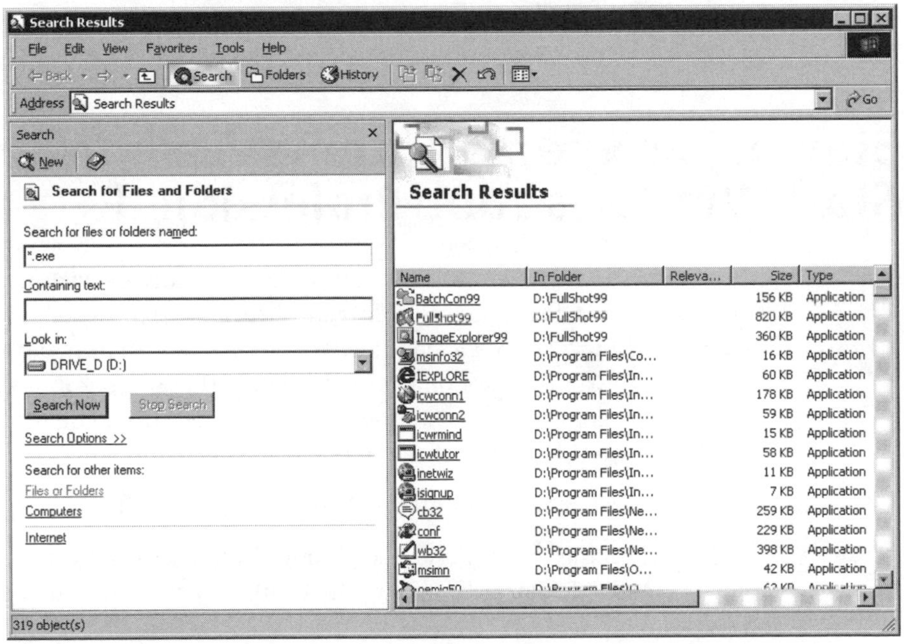

FIGURE 7.2: A list of files displayed in the Search Results window

Running Programs from a Document

As you go about your day-to-day work, opening applications and creating documents, Windows 2000 Professional keeps track of your 15 most-recently-used documents and makes these documents available from the Documents menu on the Start menu. To open one of these documents and open the parent application at the same time, choose Start ➤ Documents, and then choose the name of the document you want to work with. The application starts running and opens the appropriate document on the Desktop.

The Documents submenu can only ever hold a maximum of 15 documents; as you continue to work, new items replace the least-recently-used items. If you start a new project and realize that all the documents on your menu are now out of date, follow these steps to clear the entire menu and start over:

1. Choose Start ➤ Settings ➤ Taskbar & Start Menu.

2. In the Taskbar and Start Menu Properties dialog box, click the Advanced tab to bring it to the front.

3. Click the Clear button, and click OK to close the dialog box.

Starting Programs Automatically When You Start Windows 2000 Professional

You can also make applications start automatically every time you start Windows 2000 Professional by adding applications to a special folder called the Startup folder. Everyone has at least one program that they use on a regular basis (a word processor or a spreadsheet, perhaps), so you may as well have your most commonly used programs start every time you start up your computer. To do this, follow these steps:

1. Choose Start ➤ Settings ➤ Taskbar & Start Menu.

2. When the Taskbar and Start Menu Properties dialog box opens, click the Advanced tab to bring it to the front, and click the Advanced button.

3. In the Start Menu folder, find the shortcut to the program you want to have start automatically when you start Windows 2000 Professional, and drag it to your Startup folder.

4. The next time you start Windows 2000 Professional, this application will be started automatically.

In Figure 7.3, you can see an application called FullShot99 within Peter Dyson's Startup folder.

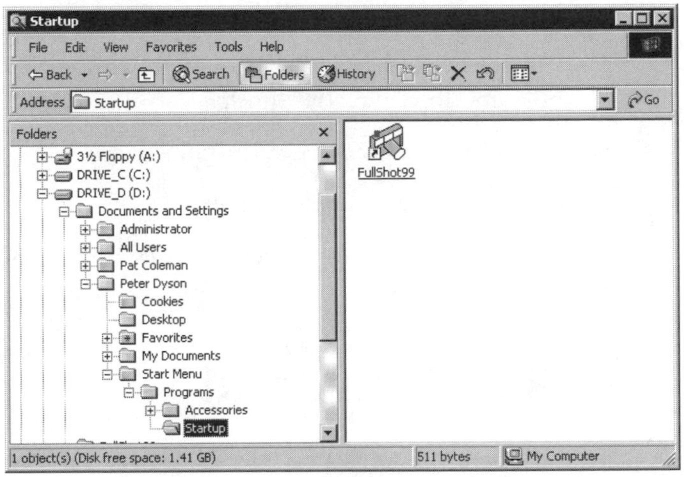

FIGURE 7.3: The Startup folder contains FullShot99.

Running Programs Minimized

You can also specify that any application you use is run minimized so that it appears as a button on the toolbar rather than as an open window on the Desktop. By setting the Run Minimized option in an application's Properties dialog box, every time you run the application, it will automatically run minimized.

Automatically running a program minimized can be a very useful way to start a program that you know you will need but that you don't want to run at start-up.

And if you have a collection of applications in your Startup folder, you can configure them to run minimized so that they don't take up space on your Desktop.

To make any application run minimized, follow these steps:

1. Choose Start ➤ Settings ➤ Taskbar & Start Menu to open the Taskbar and Start Menu Properties dialog box.

2. Click the Advanced tab to bring it to the front, and click the Advanced button to open the Start Menu folder.

3. Find the shortcut to the application you want to start minimized in the Start Menu folder, and select it.

4. Choose File ➤ Properties to open the Properties dialog box for that application, and then click the Shortcut tab.

5. In the Run list box, select Minimized.

6. Click OK to close the dialog box.

The next time you start this application, it will start as a minimized button on the Taskbar; simply click the button to open a full-sized window.

Using the Run Command

The Start menu contains a very useful Run command that you can use to launch programs, to open folders, to connect to shared computers, and even to open Web sites. The Run command is most useful when:

- The program you want to run is not available on your Programs menu or as an icon on the Desktop.

- You want to rerun or reopen a recently used program, document, or folder.

- The program you want to run requires one or more command-line parameters.

As Figure 7.4 shows, the Open field in the Run dialog box presents as a default the name of the program or document you last opened; to rerun this item, just click OK. Better still is the fact that the Open field is really a drop-down list; click the arrow to the right to see a list of your most-recently-used Run commands. Just select the one you want from the list, and click OK. You can also connect to the Internet or to a corporate intranet using Run. For example, to reach the Sybex Web site, type **www.sybex.com** into the Open field and click OK.

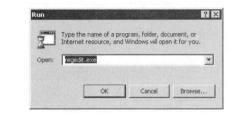

FIGURE 7.4: Use the Run command to launch programs that don't appear in your Programs menu.

Working from the Command Prompt

Windows 2000 Professional also contains a command prompt you can use to start programs and run utility programs. To open a Command Prompt window, choose Start ➣ Programs ➣ Accessories ➣ Command Prompt, or choose the Run command from the Start menu, enter **cmd** in the Open box, and click OK. To close the Command Prompt window, type **exit** and press Enter, or click the Close button. Figure 7.5 shows a Command Prompt window.

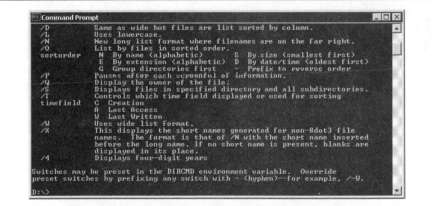

FIGURE 7.5: A Command Prompt window open on the Desktop

Skill 7

TIP When using a command prompt, you can get simplified help for utilities and commands by typing the command name followed by **/?**. For example, to see help information on the directory command, type **dir /?**.

To open another Command Prompt window, type **start** or **start cmd** at the command prompt. If you want to customize the appearance of the Command Prompt window, click the window's Control menu icon to open the shortcut menu, and select Properties. You can change the font, colors, cursor size, and other options used in the window.

Adding and Removing Programs

So far in this skill, we have looked at how you can run application programs from various places in Windows 2000 Professional. In this section, we'll look at how you can add new programs and Windows components as well as how to remove them from your system if you find that they are underused and just taking up space.

In the past, every application provided its own Setup program, so each application had to manage installation and removal. Quite often, applications installed an older version of a file over a newer version, causing an apparently unrelated application to stop working. Some programs provided an installation program but no way to uninstall the package if you decided you didn't want to use it any more. All that has changed with the Windows 2000 Professional Installer service. The Installer service manages all aspects of application installation and removal as well as installation of updates and the separate configuration of components of larger packages such as the Office 2000 suite.

And the best thing about the Installer service is that you don't have to know anything about it at all. The Add/Remove Programs applet in Control Panel helps you to manage programs on your system and guides you through the process of installing new or removing existing programs and optional Windows 2000 Professional system components.

WARNING You can only install programs written for Windows with Add/Remove Programs.

To start Add/Remove Programs, choose Start ➤ Settings ➤ Control Panel, and then select the Add/Remove programs applet. The opening screen is shown in Figure 7.6 and includes three options down the left side of the window: Change or Remove Programs, Add New Programs, and Add/Remove Windows Components. We'll begin with Add New Programs.

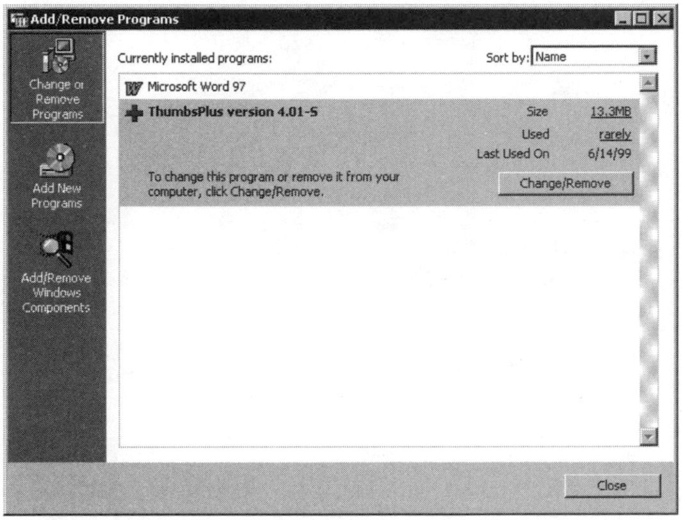

FIGURE 7.6: Add/Remove Programs applet opening screen

Adding New Programs

Click the Add New Programs button on the left side of the Add/Remove Programs window, and you will see the screen shown in Figure 7.7. If you want to add a new program using floppy disks or a CD, click the CD or Floppy button. If you want to connect to Microsoft's Windows Update Web site and download new Windows 2000 Professional features, device drivers, and other updates over the Internet, click the Windows Update button. A Wizard then guides you through the remaining installation and configuration steps; just follow the instructions on the screen.

TIP   You can also click Start ➤ Windows Update to connect to the Windows Update Web site.

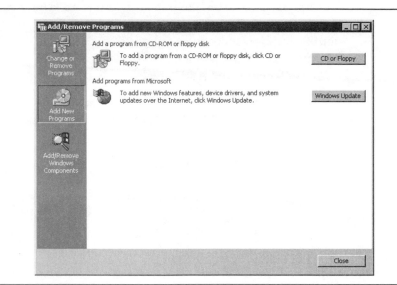

FIGURE 7.7: Adding a new program from CD or floppy disk

If you are connected to a network, any programs you are authorized to install over the network are listed at the bottom of the Add New Programs window. If your system administrator has organized several types of applications into different groups, you can select a different option in Category to find the program you want to install. Select the program or programs you want to install, and click Add. Follow the instructions on the screen.

Changing or Removing Programs

You can also use Add/Remove programs to change existing installations of large software packages such as Microsoft Office 2000 and to remove programs you no longer use. Click the Change or Remove Programs button on the left side of the Add/Remove Programs main window, and you will see a list of the applications currently installed on your system displayed to the right. You can sort these programs by name, size, date last used, or frequency of use to get an idea of how useful or important they are to the way you work. To remove or change one of the applications, select it in the main window, click the Change/Remove button, and follow the instructions on the screen.

Using Add/Remove Programs is the only safe way to remove installed applications and to be completely certain that all the appropriate files have been removed and that all the appropriate Registry entries have been changed as required. We look at the Windows 2000 Professional Registry in the next section and discuss why the Registry is so important.

Adding and Removing Windows Components

As we saw in Skill 2, the Windows 2000 Professional CD contains several optional components that you can install if you need to use them. By using Add/Remove Programs, you can fine-tune your selection of these optional elements, adding or removing them as appropriate.

Make sure your Windows 2000 Professional CD is in your CD-ROM drive, and then click the Add/Remove Windows Components button to the left of the main window. The Windows Components Wizard opens to guide you through the installation, configuration, or removal of these optional components. See Skill 2 for more details on these optional components.

Looking at the Registry

In the last section, we mentioned the Windows 2000 Professional Registry and that it is important to the normal operation of the system. In this section, we'll look at the Registry in a bit more detail. Simply put, the Registry is just a database that contains all the configuration settings used on your system. Everything, from users and accounts to applications programs and the kinds of documents they create, to property settings for your Desktop, to printers, modems, and other hardware, have entries in the Registry.

Registry entries are updated automatically by Windows 2000 Professional operating system services when they receive a request from one of the Control Panel applets, so most of the time you don't need to worry about the Registry. However, there are a couple of warnings that we need to get out of the way before we go too much further in this discussion. So here they are.

WARNING Be absolutely sure you know what you are doing before you change anything in the Registry. Making a mistake can turn your system into a boat anchor (in other words, render it completely unusable).

WARNING   Any changes you make in the Registry are made immediately, and there is no undo function in the Registry Editor. You only get one chance, and it's got to be right the first time.

With these warnings in mind, it is OK just to *look* at the contents of the Registry, and we use the Registry Editor to do that. To open the Registry Editor, choose Start ➢ Run, and then type **regedit** in the Open box. The Registry Editor presents the information contained in the Registry in a hierarchical structure, as Figure 7.8 shows.

```
Registry Editor                                                        _ □ ×
Registry  Edit  View  Favorites  Help
□ 🖳 My Computer                     │ Name              Type          Data
  ⊞ 📁 HKEY_CLASSES_ROOT            │ 📄(Default)        REG_SZ        (value not set)
  ⊟ 📁 HKEY_CURRENT_USER            │ 🔢Directory Name   REG_DWORD     0x5c7214d2 (1550980306)
    ⊞ 📁 AppEvents                  │ 📄User ID          REG_SZ        {5C7214D2-1DF0-11D3-BD0E-9F34DDDD7D43}
      📁 Console                    │ 📄Username         REG_SZ        Main Identity
    ⊞ 📁 Control Panel
      📁 Environment
    ⊞ 📁 EUDC
    ⊟ 📁 Identities
      ⊟ 📁 {5C7214D2-1DF0-11D3-BD0E-9F
        ⊞ 📁 Software
    ⊞ 📁 Keyboard Layout
    ⊞ 📁 Printers
    ⊞ 📁 Software
      📁 UNICODE Program Groups
      📁 Volatile Environment
  ⊞ 📁 HKEY_LOCAL_MACHINE
  ⊞ 📁 HKEY_USERS
  ⊞ 📁 HKEY_CURRENT_CONFIG
◄                          ►  ◄                                        ►
My Computer\HKEY_CURRENT_USER\Identities\{5C7214D2-1DF0-11D3-BD0E-9F34DDDD7D43}
```

FIGURE 7.8: The Registry Editor presents Registry information in a hierarchical structure.

In the left pane of the Registry Editor, you will see these subtrees:

HKEY_CLASSES_ROOT   Contains information on file-association data and about OLE; see Skill 9 for more on OLE.

HKEY_CURRENT_USER   Contains information about the user currently logged on to this computer.

HKEY_LOCAL_MACHINE   Stores information about the hardware available on your computer, as well as device drivers, device settings, and hardware profiles.

HKEY_USERS   Stores information about users and their preferences, along with network and Desktop settings.

HKEY_CURRENT_CONFIG   Contains information about the currently active hardware configuration.

Below these subtrees, you will see keys represented as folder icons in the left pane of the Registry Editor window. These keys contain values, and these values are displayed in the right pane. Each value has three parts: a name, a data type, and some sort of associated value. This data can be of several types, including binary, hexadecimal, or text. You navigate your way up and down the Registry Editor's left pane in the same way you navigate folders displayed in Explorer.

To change a value's data, double-click the value; a dialog box opens to receive the new data. To add a value, first select the appropriate key, choose Edit ➢ New, and then choose whether the new data will be in the form of a string value or one of the other data types. There is also a Find command available from the Edit menu you can use to locate specific keys in the Registry database.

In this skill so far, we have talked about all the different ways that you can run your favorite applications, but wouldn't it be neat if you could start running programs while away from your computer? Well, you can if you use the Task Scheduler, which is explained in the next section.

Scheduling Tasks

Windows 2000 Professional contains a Task Scheduler, which is a program you can use to run selected applications at specific times—daily, weekly, or even monthly—without any input from you or involvement on your part. The Task Scheduler starts running in the background every time you start Windows 2000 Professional; it just sits there until it is time to run one of your selected tasks, and then it moves into action.

Certain tasks are well suited to unattended automatic operation, such as making a tape backup or running hard-disk utilities. You can run these programs while you work, but it often makes more sense to run them when your system is turned on but is not too busy, such as at lunch time, when you are attending a regularly scheduled company meeting, or during the night.

You can open the Task Scheduler in several ways:

- Double-click the Task Scheduler icon on the Taskbar if the Task Scheduler is already running.

- Open the Scheduled Tasks folder in Control Panel.

- Choose Start ➤ Programs ➤ Accessories ➤ System Tools ➤ Scheduled Tasks.

The main Task Scheduler window opens as shown in Figure 7.9, listing any currently scheduled tasks along with information about when they will run next and when they were run last.

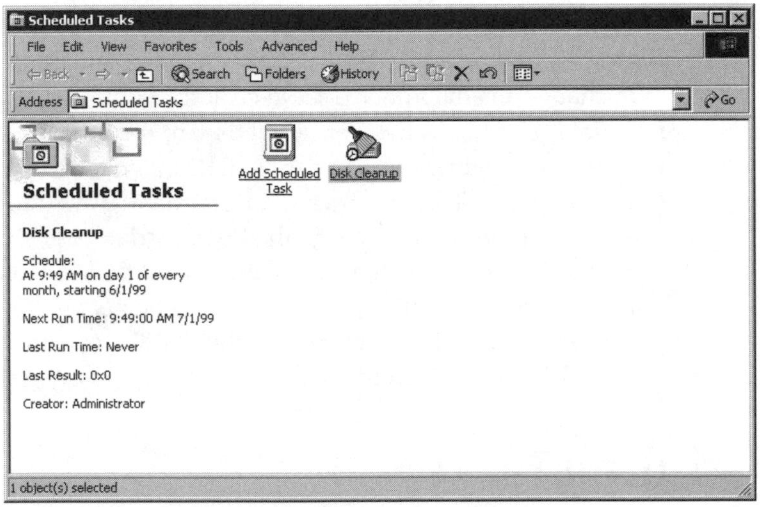

FIGURE 7.9: The Scheduled Tasks main window lists currently scheduled tasks.

Adding a New Scheduled Task

To add a new scheduled task, follow these steps:

1. Open the Scheduled Tasks folder in Control Panel, or double-click the Task Scheduler icon on the Taskbar to open Task Scheduler.

2. Click Add Scheduled Task to open the Scheduled Task Wizard.

3. The Wizard presents a list of programs you can run unattended; click Browse to look for more. Make a selection, and then click Next.

4. Select the frequency at which you want the program to run, and click Next.

5. Select the time and day when you want the program to run, and click Next.

6. Enter a user name and password; the program you have chosen will run as though started by that user. Click Next.

7. The Wizard confirms the task name and tells you when the task will run next. Click Finish to add this task to your Windows schedule.

Modifying an Existing Scheduled Task

To modify an existing task, right-click the task, and then choose Properties from the pop-up menu. The dialog box contains the following tabs:

Task   Changes the name of the program you want to schedule.

Schedule   Changes when the program is run.

Settings   Customizes the task configuration.

Security   Specifies the security for the task.

To halt a scheduled task that is currently executing, right-click to open the shortcut menu, and then select End Task; to resume the task, right-click, and choose Run. To remove a task, right-click it, and select Delete from the pop-up menu.

Using the Advanced Menu

The Task Scheduler Advanced menu includes the following options:

Stop Using Task Scheduler   Turns the Task Scheduler application off and halts all scheduled tasks. Task Scheduler will not start automatically the next time you start Windows. This menu selection changes into Start Using Task Scheduler so that you can use it to restart operations.

Pause Task Scheduler   Temporarily stops the Task Scheduler. This menu item changes into Continue Task Scheduler so that you can restart operations. Any tasks that were due to run during the time Task Scheduler was paused will not run until their next scheduled time.

Notify Me of Missed Tasks   Informs you of any scheduled tasks that did not run.

AT Service Account   Specifies the account used for the Task Scheduler. In previous versions of Windows NT software, the Task Scheduler was known as the AT command.

View Log   Opens the Task Scheduler log file in a Notepad window.

Skill 7

Are You Up to Speed?

Now you can...

- ☑ run programs from the Start menu
- ☑ run programs from Explorer
- ☑ run programs from Search
- ☑ run programs from a document
- ☑ start programs automatically every time you start Windows 2000 Professional
- ☑ run programs minimized
- ☑ use the Run command
- ☑ work from the Command Prompt window
- ☑ add programs
- ☑ remove programs
- ☑ explore the Registry
- ☑ use regedit
- ☑ schedule tasks to run at a specific time

SKILL 8

Printers and Printing

- Installing local and network printers
- Printing from Windows
- Printing from an application
- Printing to a file
- Managing the print queue
- Customizing printer properties
- Working with fonts

We have a friend who is bound and determined to have a paperless office. He's on the road a lot and has office space at corporate headquarters and at home. Two things really set off this Type-A guy, however: not being able to get on e-mail and not being able to print. No matter how much we may strive to work electronically, Hewlett Packard and the rest of the printer manufacturers are thriving.

Installing and using printers becomes easier and easier with each new generation of equipment, which, by the way, continues to decrease in cost and size and increase in output speed and number of features. In addition, each new version of Windows includes tools that make installing a printer easier and faster. In this skill, we will go step by step through the process of installing both a network and a local printer, and then we'll discuss how to establish the settings that are most appropriate for how and what you print.

TIP   When you buy or acquire a new printer, put the manual somewhere where you can find it. Each printer or series of printers has idiosyncrasies, such as how you change the cartridge and the type of cartridge to use, and you'll need to follow the manufacturer's advice about these things.

Adding Printers

If you have a stand-alone system and upgraded to Windows 2000 Professional, you may not have to install your printer; the installation routine should have recognized it, as it did your keyboard, mouse, monitor, and so on. If you did a clean install on a new machine or a new partition on your hard drive, however, you will need to install your printer. If you're on a corporate network, your network administrator has, no doubt, done this for you, and you can skip to the "Printing Documents" section of this skill.

Obviously, if you've just bought a new printer or are connecting to a different printer, you'll need to install it. Installing involves more than simply plugging in the printer. Installing is a matter of giving Windows 2000 Professional the information it needs so that it knows how to use your printer.

Before we get down to business, though, we need to define a couple of terms. A *local* printer is one that is physically attached to your computer by a cable. A *network* printer is a printer that is attached to another computer on your network; that computer becomes a *print server,* and you access it via the network, just as you access other network resources.

To install either a local printer or a network printer, you use the Printers folder. Let's start by looking at how to install a local printer.

Installing a Local Printer

You can open the Printers folder, which is shown in Figure 8.1, in two ways:

- Choose Start ➢ Settings ➢ Control Panel, and then click the Printers icon.
- Choose Start ➢ Settings ➢ Printers.

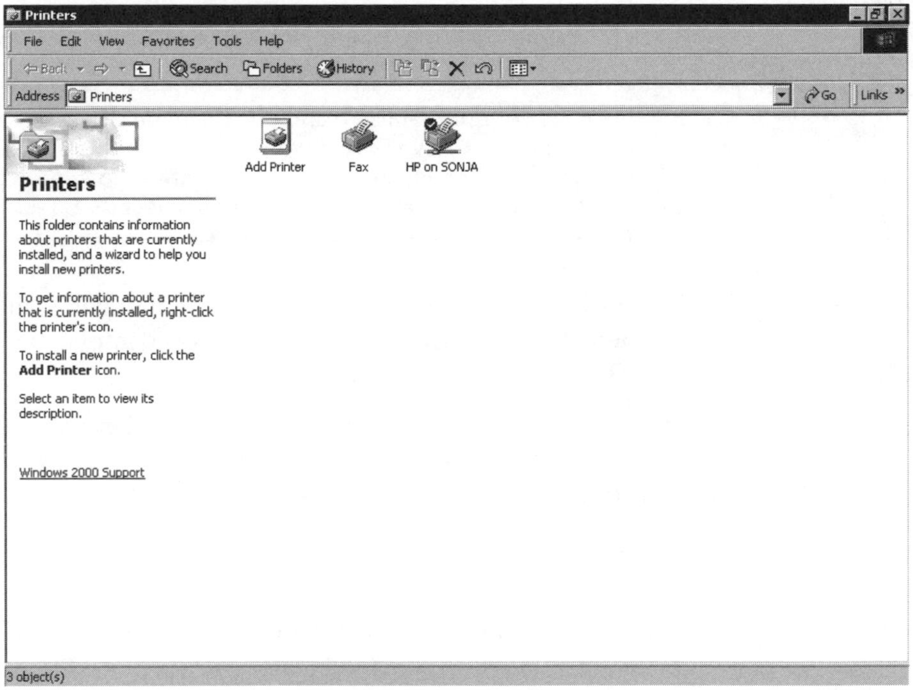

FIGURE 8.1: Use the Printers folder to add, remove, and configure printers.

To add a new printer to your system, first be sure that the printer cable is securely connected to both the printer and to your computer. Also, be sure you've followed any setup instructions that came with the printer. Now, turn on the printer, click Add Printer to open the Add Printer Wizard, which is shown in Figure 8.2, and follow these steps:

1. At the Welcome screen, click Next.

2. Click Local Printer. If you want Windows 2000 Professional to find and install your printer, leave the Automatically Detect and Install My Plug and Play Printer check box checked. Otherwise, click this check box to clear it, and click Next.

3. Select the printer port to use (most likely, LPT1, which is selected by default), and click Next.

4. Select the manufacturer and model of your printer, and click Next.

NOTE   If you don't see your printer listed and you have the CD or floppy disk that came with your printer, click Have Disk. If you don't see your printer listed and no disk came with your printer, check your printer manual to see if your printer emulates (imitates) a printer that is on the list, and select that one.

5. Supply a name for your printer, choose whether you want this printer to be the default printer (the one that Windows and applications automatically print to), and then click Next.

6. If you're on a network and you want others to be able to use your printer, click Share As, and provide a share name. Otherwise, leave Do Not Share This Printer selected, and click Next.

7. If you want to print a test page (always a good idea), select that option, and click Next.

8. Click Finish, and Windows 2000 Professional will copy the driver for your printer. You'll see an icon for the new printer in the Printers folder.

FIGURE 8.2: To install a printer, you use the Add Printer Wizard.

WHAT TO DO IF YOUR TEST PAGE DOESN'T PRINT

Most of the time, installing a printer is a straightforward process, but if your test page didn't print or didn't print correctly, the first thing to do is click No in the dialog box that asks about this. You'll be presented with a list of troubleshooting steps, which you'll also find in the Troubleshooting section of Help.

If you work through these and you still can't print, make sure your printer is on the Hardware Compatibility List, which you'll find at www.microsoft.com.

If your printer is on the list, locate your printer manual, and look for a telephone number for technical support. We know from personal experience that sometimes even the printer driver on the CD or disk that comes with your printer may not be the correct one. (A printer driver, by the way, is a program that controls or regulates the printer.) If the correct driver is not installed, the printer won't work or won't work properly. In the worst case, you may have to acquire the appropriate driver from the manufacturer.

Skill 8

To delete a printer from the Printers folder, right-click it, and choose Delete from the shortcut menu. To rename a printer, right-click it, choose Rename, type a new name in the box, and then click outside the box. To set a different printer as the default, right-click the printer, and choose Set As Default Printer from the shortcut menu. To create a shortcut to this printer on the Desktop, right-click it, and choose Create Shortcut from the shortcut menu.

Installing a Network Printer

Before you can install a network printer, you or someone else must do the following:

1. Physically connect the printer to the network cable or to a computer on the network. (To connect the printer to the network cable, the printer must have a network interface card installed.)

2. Install the printer on a computer on the network.

3. Set the printer up as a shared printer.

4. Get the network up and running.

5. Turn on the printer.

NOTE   See Skill 16 for information about how to set up a small network, and see Skill 17 for information about connecting to a corporate network.

When all that's been taken care of, you're ready to start your installation. Follow these steps:

1. Choose Start ➤ Settings ➤ Printers to open the Printers folder.

2. Click the Add Printer icon to start the Add Printer Wizard.

3. At the Welcome screen, click Next.

4. Select the Network Printer option, and click Next.

5. Enter the name of the network printer you want to use. If you don't know the name, click Next to open a screen that displays the resources available on your network (this may take a few seconds, depending on the speed of your network). When you find the printer, click it, and then click Next.

6. If you want to set this printer as the default, click Yes. (Remember, you can always do this later by right-clicking this printer in the Printers folder and selecting Set As Default Printer.) Click Next to continue.

7. Click Finish to copy the driver and print a test page.

To remove a network printer from the Printers folder, to rename it, to set it as the default printer, or to create a shortcut to it on the Desktop, right-click it and choose the appropriate command from the shortcut menu.

SHARING A NETWORK PRINTER

Before you can install and use a network printer, that printer must be shared. And, if you have a printer that you want others on the network to be able to use, you must share it. To share a printer, follow these steps:

1. In the Printers folder, right-click the printer, and choose Sharing from the shortcut menu to open the Properties dialog box for that printer:

continued▶

Skill 8

2. Click the Shared As option button.

3. Accept the name that is generated, or enter a new one.

4. Click the General tab if you want to enter a comment about this printer.

5. Click OK.

The icon of this printer in the Printers folder will now have a hand under it to indicate that it is shared.

Printing Documents

After you add a printer, either local or network, you're ready to print, and you can do so either from the Desktop or from an application. Regardless of where you print from, Windows 2000 Professional is actually handling the process. The print spooler program accepts the document and holds it on disk or in memory until the printer is free, and then the printer prints it.

If you want to print an existing document, the quickest way is to print from the Desktop.

Printing from the Desktop

You can print from the Desktop in a couple of ways:

- By using drag-and-drop
- By right-clicking the document

Using Drag-and-Drop to Print

To print with drag-and-drop, you need a shortcut to your printer on the Desktop, and you need an open folder that contains the file. In other words, you need to be able to see both the printer icon and the file name or icon. Simply click the file, and drag it onto the printer icon. Windows 2000 Professional opens the file in the program in which the document was created or in the program you've associated with the file by using the Open With command, and then it prints the file. Figure 8.3 shows a file being dragged to the printer on the Desktop.

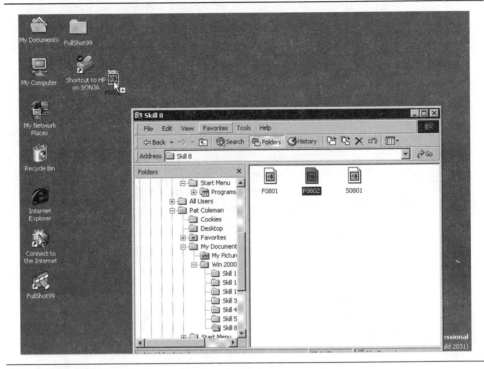

FIGURE 8.3: Printing with drag-and-drop

When you print in this manner, you use the default options in the Print dialog box, which we'll look at in the upcoming "Printing from an Application" section. The entire file is printed, only one copy is printed, the printed output is in portrait orientation (vertical), and the default paper tray is used. You have no opportunity to modify these settings.

Right-Clicking to Print

To print using the right-click method in Windows, open a folder that contains the file you want to print, right-click the file, and select Print from the shortcut menu. In a flash, the program associated with the file opens, and the document prints. Just as when you drag and drop to print, the default settings in the Print dialog box are used.

Printing from an Application

If you want more control over how your document is printed, such as the orientation of the paper, the number of copies, and so on, you'll want to print from the application. You can usually print in a couple of ways in an application:

- By clicking the Print button on the toolbar
- By choosing File ➤ Print

 If you click the Print button, usually the document is immediately spooled to the printer, and you have no opportunity to specify the number of copies, exactly what you want to print, and so on. Choosing File ➤ Print opens the Print dialog box, which is shown in Figure 8.4, in which you can specify the options that control what is printed and how. The specific options you see in the Print dialog box depend on your printer. For example, if your printer can print both in color and in black-and-white, you'll see both those options.

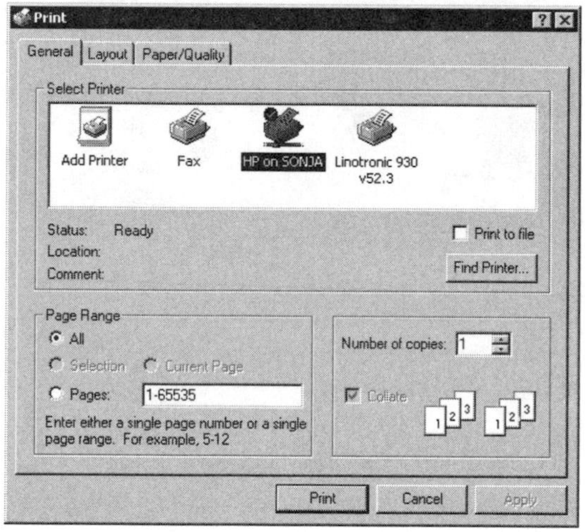

FIGURE 8.4: Specify printing options in the Print dialog box.

NOTE The steps are the same whether you are printing on a local printer or a network printer. But remember, the options in the Print dialog box will vary depending on the printer.

To see how this works, let's walk through the steps to print a document from WordPad, one of the applications that comes with Windows 2000 Professional (we'll look at WordPad in more detail in Skill 10). Follow these steps:

1. Choose Start ➤ Programs ➤ Accessories ➤ WordPad.

2. Open an existing document, or create a new one.

3. Choose File ➤ Save As, and save the document if it is new (it's usually prudent to save before you print).

4. Choose File ➤ Print to open the Print dialog box at the General tab, which you can see in Figure 8.4.

5. In the Select Printer area, click the printer you want to use. If you place the mouse cursor over the printer icon, you'll see a ScreenTip that displays its status—whether it's ready to print or if documents are waiting in the print queue. (We'll look at how you manage the print queue later in this skill.)

6. In the Page Range area, choose whether to print the entire file, only a selection, the current page, or selected pages. To print a selection, you need to select it first and then open the Print dialog box.

7. In the Number of Copies box, select the copies to print. When you print more than one copy, they are collated by default. If, for some reason, you don't want them collated, clear the Collate check box.

8. To specify that your document print in landscape mode (horizontally) rather than portrait (vertically), click the Layout tab, which is shown in Figure 8.5.

Skill 8

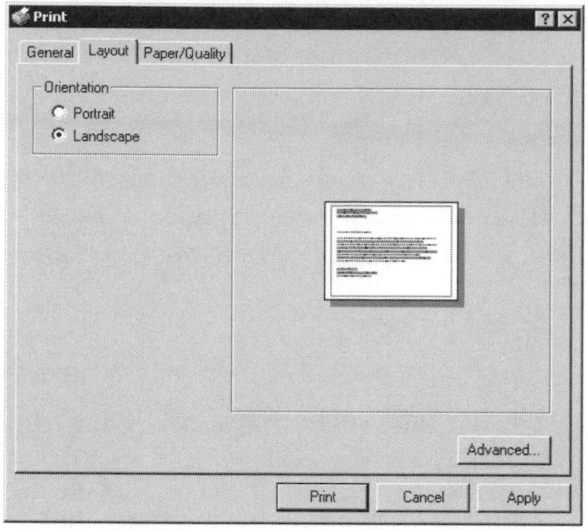

FIGURE 8.5: Click Landscape if you want to print horizontally instead of vertically.

9. To specify the paper source, the kind of paper, the print quality, and the color (if you have a color printer), click the Paper/Quality tab, and select the appropriate options.

10. Click Print.

> **TIP** To see how your printed document will look before you actually print it, click the Print Preview button or choose File ➢ Print Preview.

Printing to a File

Printing to a file is not necessarily something that most people do every day, but, on occasion, it's a handy thing to know about. When you print to a file, you save on disk the codes and data that are normally sent to the printer. In our work, we sometimes need to supply the publisher with a file that has been saved to disk so that it can be printed on their printer. When you want to do this, you can even install on your hard drive a printer that isn't physically installed on your system or the network, and then print the file to that printer.

To print to a file, follow these steps:

1. Choose File ➢ Print to open the Print dialog box.

2. Select the printer, and then click Print to File.

3. Click Print.

4. Enter a name for the file in the Print to File dialog box, and click OK.

By default, these files are stored in your My Documents folder.

Managing the Printing Process

If you've ever meant to print a short paragraph from a file but forgot to click the Selection option and ended up printing an 80-page document instead, you know how important it is to be able to stop the printing process. And if you've ever sent something to the printer and then waited and waited in vain for the document to print, you know you need a way to find out what's going on. To halt printing, to check the status of a document you've sent to the printer, or to clear all documents out of the print queue, you use the printer window that opens when you double-click the printer in the Printers folder. Figure 8.6 shows the printer window for one of the printers on our network.

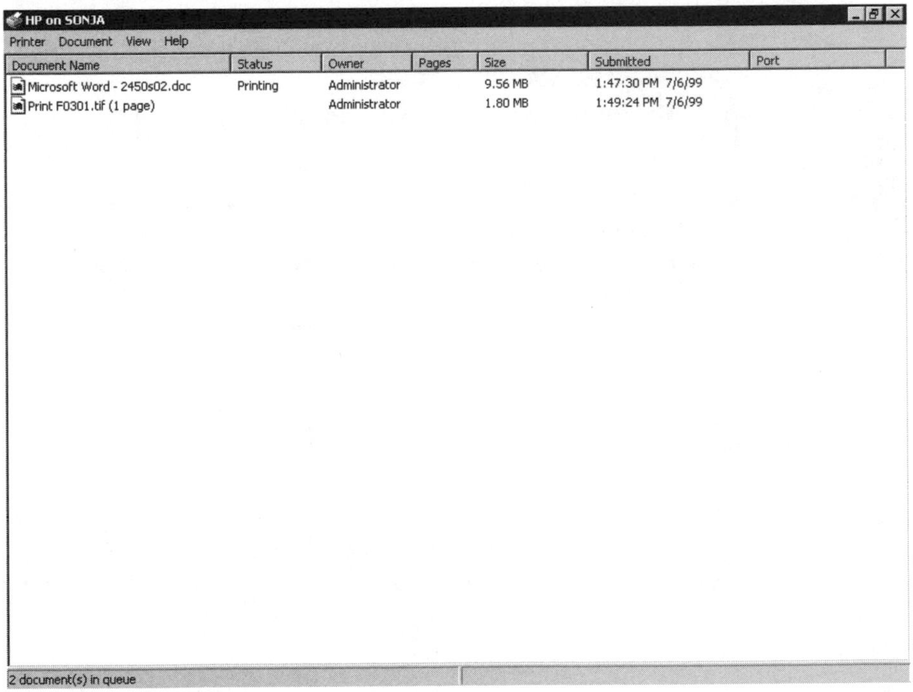

Document Name	Status	Owner	Pages	Size	Submitted	Port
Microsoft Word - 2450s02.doc	Printing	Administrator		9.56 MB	1:47:30 PM 7/6/99	
Print F0301.tif (1 page)		Administrator		1.80 MB	1:49:24 PM 7/6/99	

2 document(s) in queue

FIGURE 8.6: Status information is displayed in a printer window.

Skill 8

You'll need to maximize this window and drag the horizontal scroll bar to see all the information it contains:

Document Name   The name of the document and the total number of pages.

Status   Whether the document is printing, paused, or being deleted.

Owner   The name of the person who sent the document to the printer.

Pages   The number of pages currently printed.

Size   The size of the document in bytes.

Submitted   The time the document was sent to the printer.

Port   The printer port being used.

Once you know what's happening or about to happen in the print queue, you can take charge of it:

- To cancel the printing of a document, right-click the document in the print queue, and choose Cancel from the shortcut menu.

- To cancel the printing of all documents in the print queue, choose Printer ➤ Cancel All Documents.

- To temporarily halt the printing of a single document, right-click the document, and choose Pause.

- To resume the printing of a document you have paused, right-click the document, and choose Resume.

NOTE   When you choose Pause or Cancel, the printing probably won't stop right away. Whatever has already been spooled to the printer's buffer must print before the printing stops.

Customizing the Printer's Properties

As we discussed in Skill 6, all objects in Windows 2000 Professional have properties (or settings) that affect how the object looks and, oftentimes, how the object works. The printer is an object and, thus, has properties, and you can set those properties to specify a number of preferences about your printer, including the following:

- The paper source
- The print quality
- Whether the printer will be shared
- When the printer will be available
- Whether documents will be spooled to the printer or printed directly

The settings that appear in the Properties dialog box on your system depend, to some extent, on your printer. They also depend on whether you are looking at the properties for a local printer or a network printer. In some cases, the Properties dialog box will display the eight tabs shown in Figure 8.7. In other cases, you may see fewer tabs.

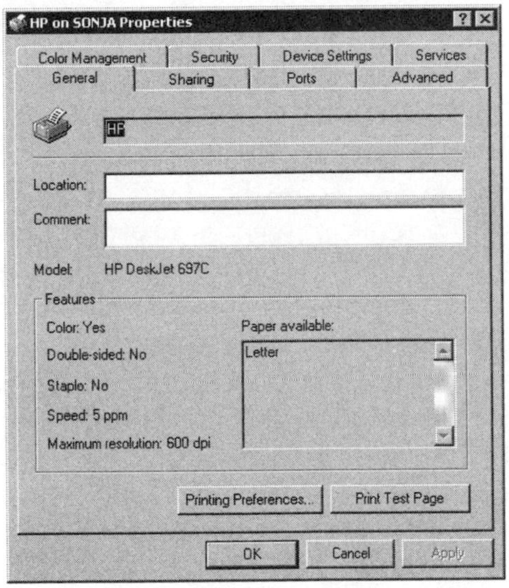

FIGURE 8.7: The printer Properties dialog box

NOTE   You can change the printer settings only if you have the permission to do so. See Skill 16 for more about rights and permissions.

To open the Properties dialog box for a printer, right-click its icon in the Printers folder, and then click Properties. You will notice that some of the items on the short-cut menu take you directly to a portion of the Properties dialog box. For example, you can click Sharing to display the Sharing tab.

In this section, we'll look at each of the tabs in the printer Properties dialog box and describe some of their typical settings.

NOTE   The settings you specify in the printer Properties dialog box become the default settings for that printer. You can, of course, change them at any time.

The General Tab

On the General tab, which is shown in Figure 8.7, you can change only a couple of fields: Location and Comment. For a network printer, you might use the Location box to describe where the printer is situated (for example, third-floor printer room), and you can use the Comments box to say something pertinent about the printer (for instance, "Legal-size paper only").

To specify layout (portrait or landscape), paper source, print quality, and color, click the Printing Preferences button to open the Printing Preferences dialog box. In this dialog box, click the Advanced button to open the Advanced Options dialog box, which contains a description of a number of printer features and in which you can also change the paper size. Back in the General tab, you can click Print Test Page to do just that.

The Sharing Tab

If you want to share your printer with other users on your network, click the Sharing tab, which is shown in Figure 8.8. As we mentioned earlier in the "Installing a Network Printer" section, click the Shared As option button, and then enter a name for the printer. If you will be sharing this printer with people running versions of Windows other than Windows 2000 Professional, click the Additional Drivers button to open the Additional Drivers dialog box. You'll see a list of systems. Click a system so that users on that system can automatically download the driver when they connect to your printer.

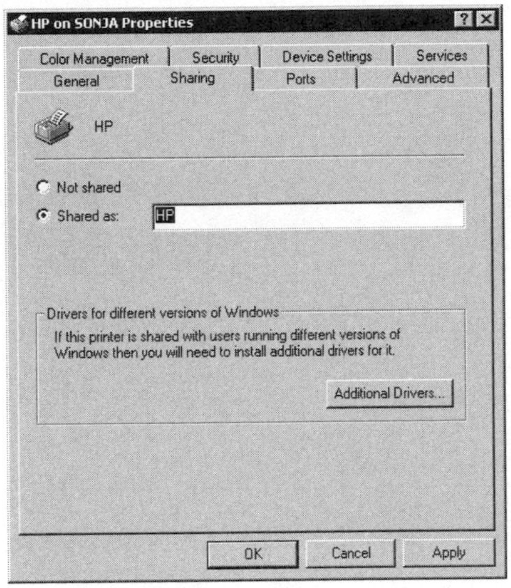

FIGURE 8.8: The Sharing tab

The Ports Tab

You normally don't need to be messing around with the settings in the Ports tab, which is shown in Figure 8.9, and, indeed, if you are on a corporate network, you shouldn't (in addition, you probably don't have permission). On this tab, you'll see a list of ports on your computer, and you'll see buttons to add, delete, and configure ports. Adding and deleting a port is relatively easy; retrieving a deleted port is not. Unless you have permission *and* know exactly what you're doing, don't fiddle with the options on this page.

Skill 8

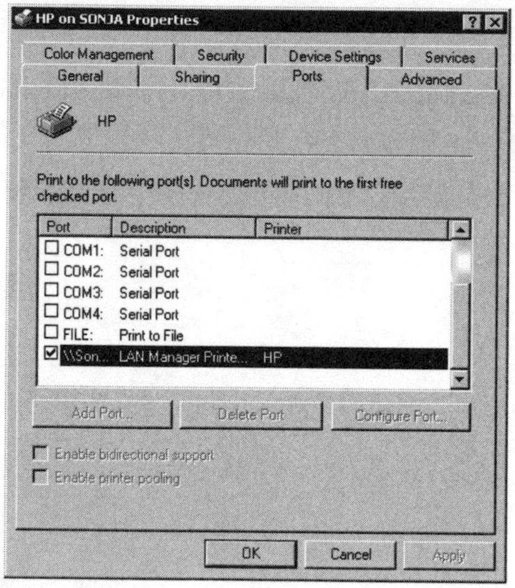

FIGURE 8.9: The Ports tab

The Advanced Tab

You can use the Advanced tab to set a number of options such as the following:

- When the printer is available for use
- The priority of the printing document (1 is the lowest; 99 is the highest)
- The printer driver name
- Whether documents will be spooled to the printer
- To check for mismatched documents (a document whose setup doesn't match the printer setup)
- To store printed documents so that they can be printed from the print queue rather than being spooled again

The Enable Advanced Printing Features is enabled by default. This means that certain features such as page order and pages per sheet are available, depending on your printer.

Clicking Printer Defaults displays the dialog box in which you can specify the layout, paper size, and printing quality. This is the same dialog box you see when you click Printing Preferences in the General tab. Figure 8.10 shows the Advanced tab.

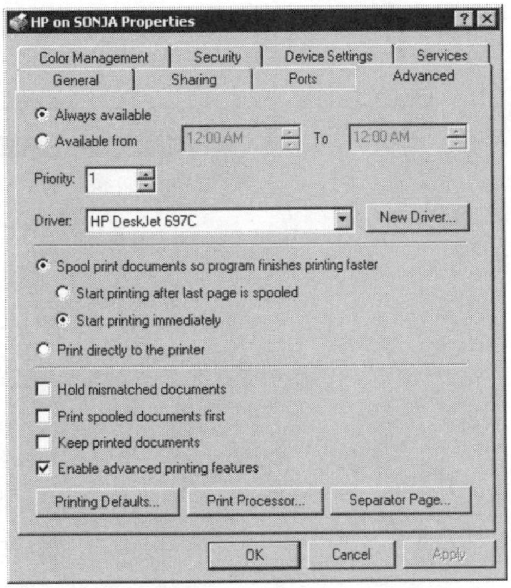

FIGURE 8.10: The Advanced tab

One other handy option on the Advanced tab is the Separator Page button. A separator page identifies the beginning of a document. When several print jobs are being sent to a network printer, a separator page makes it easy for users to locate their particular documents. To specify a separator page, follow these steps:

1. Click Separator Page to open the Separator Page dialog box.

Skill 8

2. In the Separator Page box, enter a filename for the page you want to use, or click Browse to locate one. You'll find some already-existing separator pages in the System 32 folder.

3. Click OK.

The Services Tab

Whether you have the Services tab and its contents depends on your printer. As you can see in Figure 8.11, we can use the options on this page to align or clean the print cartridges on our Hewlett Packard DeskJet.

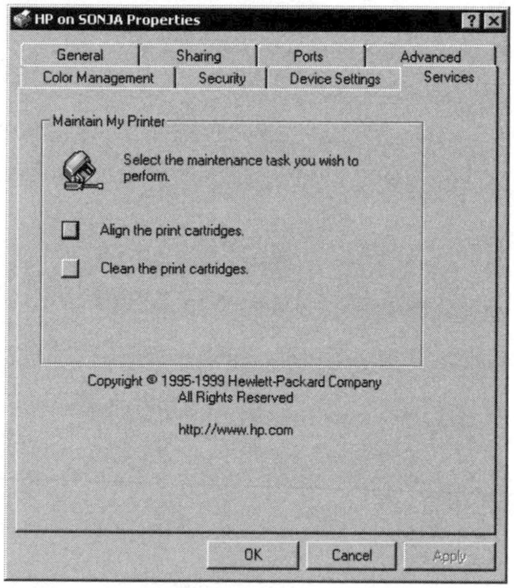

FIGURE 8.11: The Services tab

The Device Settings Tab

If your printer has more that one paper tray, you can use the options on this tab, which is shown in Figure 8.12, to specify which size paper is printed from which tray. You can then select a tray when you print from applications.

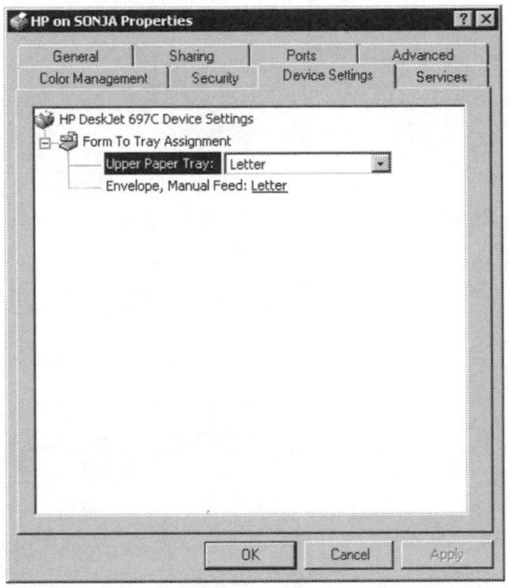

FIGURE 8.12: The Device Settings tab

The Security Tab

If you have the appropriate permissions, you can assign printer permissions on the Security tab, which is shown in Figure 8.13. For more about permissions, see Skill 16.

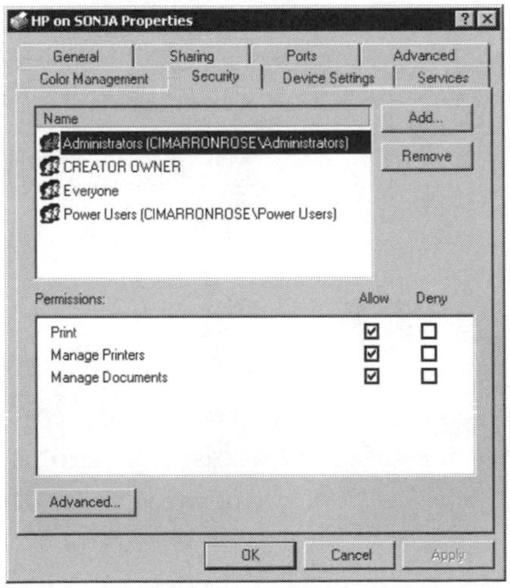

FIGURE 8.13: The Security tab

Skill 8

The Color Management Tab

When you install a new scanner, printer, or monitor, Windows 2000 Professional automatically installs a color profile that is used when colors are scanned, printed, or displayed. For most desktop systems, this profile is sufficient and is selected by default in the Color Management tab, as you can see in Figure 8.14. Graphic artists and those doing complicated color desktop publishing, however, may want to specify a color profile in order to better control the color quality on the printer, scanner, or monitor. To add a color profile, click the Add button, and then select a profile from the list in the Add Profile Association dialog box.

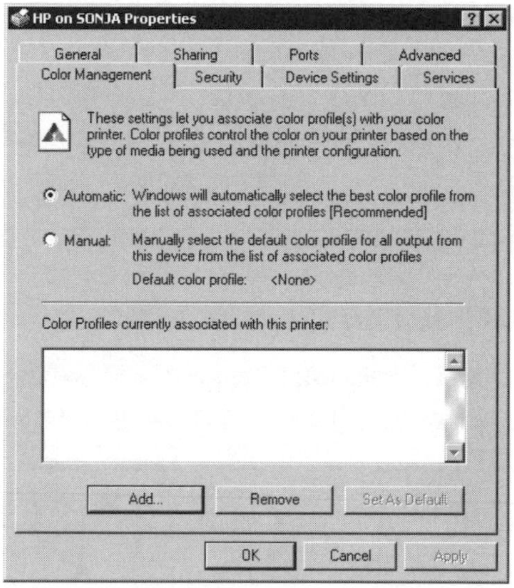

FIGURE 8.14: The Color Management tab

Understanding Fonts

Before we complete our discussion of printers and printing, we need to take a quick look at fonts. In Windows 2000 Professional, a font is the name of a type-face, and a font can have size, which is usually described in points, and a style, such as bold or italic. Most fonts are TrueType fonts; that is, their printed output is identical to what you see on the screen.

> **NOTE**   A point is 1/72 inch.

Some fonts are not TrueType fonts, however, and they are identified with this symbol. They are not scalable and, thus, look really bad at larger point sizes.

To see the fonts installed on your system, click the Fonts icon in Control Panel to open the Fonts folder, which is shown in Figure 8.15. To see what an individual font looks like at several sizes, double-click a font. Figure 8.16 shows representative sizes of the Comic Sans MS font and displays some information about this font. To see printed output of a particular font , simply click the Print button, which is shown in Figure 8.16.

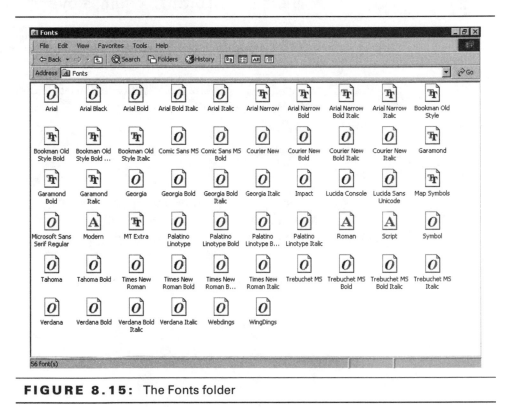

FIGURE 8.15: The Fonts folder

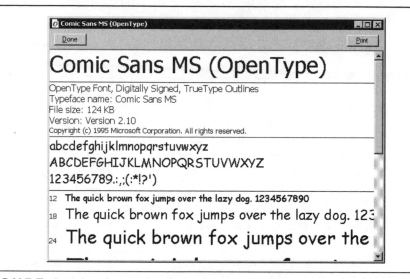

FIGURE 8.16: A sample of what's available in the Comic Sans MS font

If you are overwhelmed by the number and type of fonts shown in the Fonts folder, choose View ➤ Hide Variations (Bold, Italic, etc.). To see a list of fonts that are similar, follow these steps:

1. In the Fonts folder, choose View ➤ List Fonts by Similarity.

2. In the List Fonts by Similarity To drop-down list, select a font.

You'll see a list of font names, in order from the most similar to the least similar.

Although Windows 2000 Professional comes with a great many fonts installed, you may well want to install other fonts for particular purposes. Follow these steps:

1. In the Fonts folder, choose File ➤ Install New Font to open the Add Fonts dialog box:

2. Select the drive and the folder containing the font.

3. Click OK.

By default, fonts are installed into the Fonts folder.

Are You Up to Speed?

Now you can...

☑ **install a local printer**

☑ **install a network printer**

☑ **print from Windows**

☑ **print from an application**

☑ **print to a file**

☑ **manage the print queue**

☑ **customize printer properties**

☑ **work with fonts**

Skill 8

SKILL 9

Sharing Information between Applications

- Using the Clipboard
- Working with the ClipBook Viewer
- Embedding and linking objects
- Communicating and sharing with NetMeeting

Unless you are brand-new to the Windows environment, you have probably used the Cut, Copy, and Paste commands, and you may have even embedded and linked objects—all without knowing you were using Object Linking and Embedding (OLE). In this skill, we'll quickly go over the steps for these tasks and take a look at the underlying structure that makes OLE work.

You will probably find that a couple of the topics in this skill are new to you. In Windows 2000 Professional, the ClipBook Viewer has replaced the Clipboard Viewer, and it includes some features that were not previously available in Clipboard Viewer. (The ClipBook Viewer, however, has been around in previous versions of NT.)

Another topic that you may not be familiar with is NetMeeting, although it has been included with Internet Explorer since version 4. It is now an integrated part of Windows, and you can use it to share and collaborate on applications, video and audio conference, chat over the Internet, transfer files, and finger-chat over the Internet. You'll find in Skill 11 that you can use Phone Dialer to do some of these things, but, in our opinion, using NetMeeting is much more convenient.

The idea of sharing information has always been central to the development of the Windows family of operating systems, and, of course, it is the heart and soul of the Internet. In this skill, we'll start with the basics and then have some fun with NetMeeting, which, by the way, has a new interface in Windows 2000 Professional.

Using the Clipboard

The Clipboard is an area in memory that serves as the temporary storehouse for an item that you cut or copy. When you paste an item, a copy stays on the Clipboard until you cut or copy another item, close Windows 2000 Professional, or intentionally clear the Clipboard. Thus, you can paste the same item multiple times.

How much you can store on the Clipboard depends on the available memory. You don't normally need to be concerned about this unless you are cutting and pasting very large files such as graphics, video, and sound.

> **NOTE** When you cut an item, you actually remove it from the source document and place it in the destination document. When you copy an item, it remains in the source document, and a duplicate is placed in the destination document.

Windows 2000 Professional includes the ClipBook Viewer, a utility that you can use to save and share items that you place on the Clipboard. After we look at the various ways you can use the Clipboard in Windows applications, we'll take a look at the ClipBook Viewer.

Copying, Cutting, and Pasting in Windows Applications

You can cut, copy, and paste as follows:

- Within a document
- Between documents in the same application
- Between documents in different applications
- Between applications in different versions of Windows
- Between applications running on other computers on a local network
- Between a site on the Web and an application on your local drive or a network drive

Regardless of the source and destination, the process is the same. Here are the steps:

1. Open the source document, and select what you want to cut or copy.
2. Choose Edit ➢ Cut (or press Ctrl+X) or Edit ➢ Copy (or press Ctrl+C). The item is now stored on the Clipboard.

Skill 9

3. Open the destination document, and place the insertion point where you want the item.

4. Choose Edit ➢ Paste (or press Ctrl+V).

You choose Edit ➢ Paste Special if you want to link or embed an object within a document, and we'll look at that in the "Understanding OLE" section, later in this skill.

Figure 9.1 show a selection that's being copied from the Sybex Web site, and Figure 9.2 shows that selection copied into WordPad.

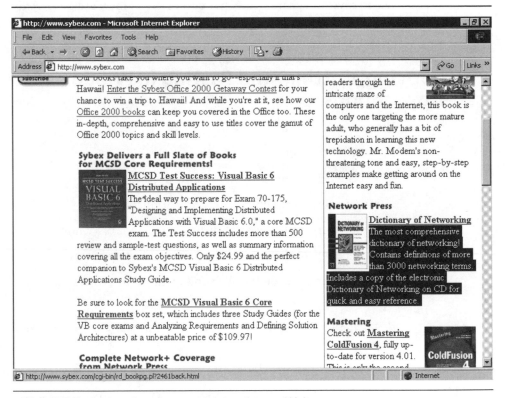

FIGURE 9.1: Copying a selection from a Web page

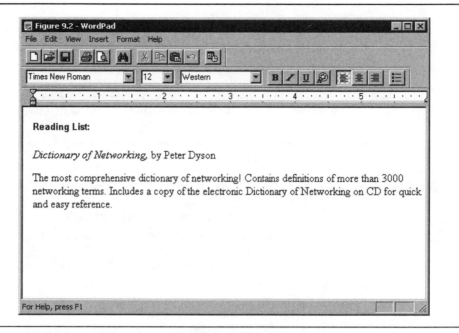

FIGURE 9.2: Pasting the selection into WordPad

You can also use drag-and-drop to cut, copy, and paste, and you can right-click a selection to use the shortcut menu for these tasks. To use drag-and-drop, follow these steps:

1. Open both the source document and the destination document so that both are visible on the Desktop.

2. Select what you want to cut or copy, right-click the selection, drag it to the destination document, and release the mouse button.

3. From the shortcut menu that appears, choose Move Here, or choose Copy Here.

To use right-click, follow these steps:

1. Select the source item, and right-click to open the shortcut menu.

Skill 9

2. Choose Cut or Copy.

3. Open the destination document, place the insertion point where you want the item, and right-click.

4. From the shortcut menu, choose Paste.

NOTE   See the section "Working with the ClipBook Viewer," later in this skill, for information on how to clear the Clipboard.

Capturing Screens with the Clipboard

If you ever create documentation, training materials, or promotional materials about software, you may find it quite handy to capture screens with the Clipboard. If you do a lot of this, you'll want to use a professional program such as Collage or FullShot99, especially if you need to edit the image. You can, however, capture a full screen or a window and save it using the Clipboard. Follow these steps:

1. Open the window or screen that you want to capture.

2. Press Alt+Print Screen to capture the entire screen, or press Ctrl+Alt+Print Screen to capture only the open window.

3. To save the image as a file, choose Start ➢ Programs ➢ Accessories ➢ Paint.

4. In Paint, press Ctrl+V to open the image.

5. Choose File ➢ Save As to open the Save As dialog box.

6. Select a folder in which to save the file, enter a name for the file in the File Name box, and choose the type in which you want to save it from the drop-down Save As Type box. You have the following options:

    - 256 Color Bitmap (*.bmp, *.dib)

    - Monochrome Bitmap (*.bmp, *.dib)

    - 16 Color Bitmap (*.bmp, *.dib)

    - 24-bit Bitmap (*.bmp, *.dib)

7. Click Save.

The file is now saved as a separate document, and you can insert it in your document. For example, to insert the screen capture into a Microsoft Word document, follow these steps:

1. Open the destination document in Word.

2. Choose Insert ➢ Picture ➢ From File to open the Insert Picture dialog box.

3. Select the file, and click Insert.

You can now save the image as part of the destination document. If you do so, the image will reside both in that document and as a separate file in the folder where you originally saved it.

You can also copy the image from the Clipboard directly into a destination document if you want. In that case, the image is not saved as a separate file but as part of the document in which you place it.

Figure 9.3 shows a screen capture inserted in a Word document.

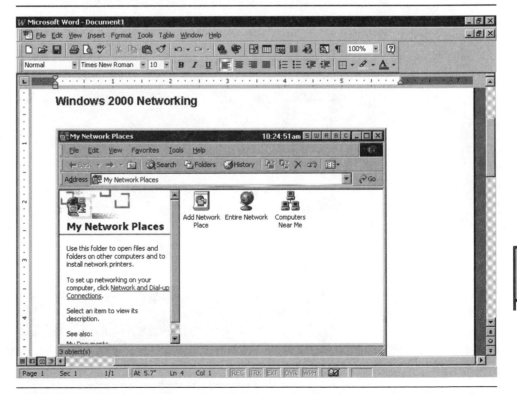

FIGURE 9.3: Even if you don't have a professional program, you can easily capture screens using the Clipboard.

Working with the ClipBook Viewer

As we mentioned in the introduction to this skill, the Clipboard Viewer in previous versions of Windows has been replaced with the ClipBook Viewer. Using the ClipBook Viewer provides several advantages over the Clipboard Viewer:

- You can save what is on the Clipboard as a page and reuse it at a later time. In fact, you can save as many as 127 pages.

- You can give a page a descriptive name of as many as 47 characters.

- You can share pages with others on your network.

Starting the ClipBook Viewer

To start the ClipBook Viewer, follow these steps:

1. Choose Start ➤ Run to open the Run dialog box.

2. In the Open box, type **clipbrd,** and click OK.

You'll see the screen shown in Figure 9.4.

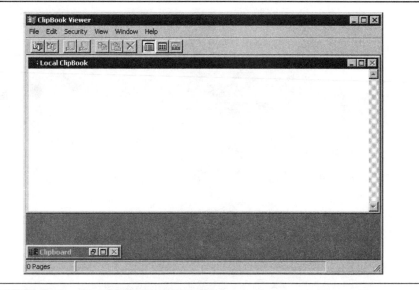

FIGURE 9.4: The ClipBook Viewer

Pasting an Item into the ClipBook

To use the ClipBook, you paste items from the Clipboard into pages. Here are the steps:

1. Cut or copy something to the Clipboard.

2. Open the ClipBook Viewer.

3. Choose Edit ➢ Paste to open the Paste dialog box:

```
┌─────────────────────────────────────────────────┐
│ Paste                                    ? X      │
│                                                   │
│   Page Name  [                    ]    ┌── OK ──┐ │
│                                        └────────┘ │
│                  □ Share Item Now      ┌─Cancel─┐ │
│                                        └────────┘ │
└─────────────────────────────────────────────────┘
```

4. In the Page Name box, enter a name for the page, and click OK.

You'll now see the item in Thumbnail view in the Local ClipBook. You can also view it on the Clipboard. To change the view, choose View ➢ Table of Contents to display an alphabetic list of your pages. To display the contents of a page, choose View ➢ Full Page.

Copying an Item from the ClipBook

To copy an item from the ClipBook into an application, follow these steps:

1. Open ClipBook Viewer.

2. In the Local ClipBook, click the page you want to copy.

3. Choose Edit ➢ Copy.

4. Open the document in the application to which you want to copy the item.

5. Place the insertion point where you want the item.

6. Choose Edit ➢ Paste.

Sharing ClipBook Pages

If you are on a local area network, you can share ClipBook pages with other users who also have ClipBook Viewer installed. Follow these steps:

1. In the Local ClipBook, click the page you want to share.

2. Choose File ➢ Share to open the Share ClipBook Page dialog box.

3. To start the program with which the page was created when a user inserted the page in a document, click the Start Application on Connect check box. To also run the program minimized, also click the Run Minimized check box.

4. If you want to ensure that users can't edit or delete the page, click the Permissions button to open the ClipBook Page Permissions dialog box.

5. After you set the permissions, click OK twice.

NOTE   For information about rights and permissions, see Skill 16.

Clearing the Clipboard

To clear the contents of the Clipboard, follow these steps:

1. Open the ClipBook Viewer.

2. Click the Clipboard window.

3. Choose Edit ➢ Delete, and then click Yes.

Understanding OLE

When you use the Clipboard to insert an item from a document in one application into a document in another application, you are inserting a static element. For example, if you insert an Excel worksheet or a portion of a worksheet into a Word document, the worksheet is not updated in Word when you update it in Excel. In addition, you cannot edit the worksheet in Word.

Most of the time, this is probably what you want. However, in some cases it is really helpful to insert a copy of a document that changes whenever it's edited in the originating application; it can also be useful to be able to edit the source document right inside the destination document. For example, you are working on a report that contains the next quarter's budget, which is in a state of flux. The report is created in Word, and the budget worksheet is being created in Excel. You have a couple of choices here:

- Insert a new copy of the worksheet every time it is updated.

- Insert a link to the worksheet so that changes to it are reflected in the Word document.

Obviously, the most efficient choice is to link to the worksheet. The technology that makes this possible is OLE (object linking and embedding), which has been available in the Windows family of operating systems since Windows 3.1. OLE allows you to create *compound* documents that contain linked or embedded *objects.*

A compound document is simply one that consists of portions created in different applications. For example, our report might contain text created in Word, the budget worksheet created in Excel, and a company logo created in Paint. An object is the portion of the document that you either link or embed, and it can be text, graphics, sound, or video.

To use OLE, all the programs involved must support it. How can you tell if this is the case? If the Paste Special item is not present on the Edit menu, the program does not support linking and embedding. You'll see why this is important in the next section.

Before we get down to the nuts and bolts of linking and embedding, though, we need to define both these terms and explain the differences between them. When you *link* an object to a document, the document contains only a link to the object. To change the object, you edit the original file. Any such changes are reflected in the linked object.

When you *embed* an object in a document, the document contains a copy of the object. Any changes made to the original object are not reflected in the document unless the embedded object is updated. Embedding an object is rather similar to inserting a static element via the Clipboard; the difference is that you can click an embedded object to edit it in the application in which it was created.

Whether you link or embed an object depends on the situation. If it's important for the document to be current at all times, link the object. Otherwise, you can embed the object. Now, let's walk through the steps for doing both and take a look at how you edit an object.

Embedding Objects

To embed an object, follow these steps:

1. Open the application that contains the information you want to embed, and select the information.

2. Choose Edit ➢ Copy.

3. Open the document that will contain the embedded object.

4. Place the insertion point where you want the object, and then choose Edit ➢ Paste Special to open the Paste Special dialog box:

5. Click Paste, and select the format you want to use.

6. Click OK.

To edit an embedded object, follow these steps:

1. Open the document that contains the object.

2. Double-click the object to open it in an editing window that displays the tools and menus of the application in which the object was created.

3. Edit the object, and then click outside it.

Figure 9.5 shows an embedded object ready for editing.

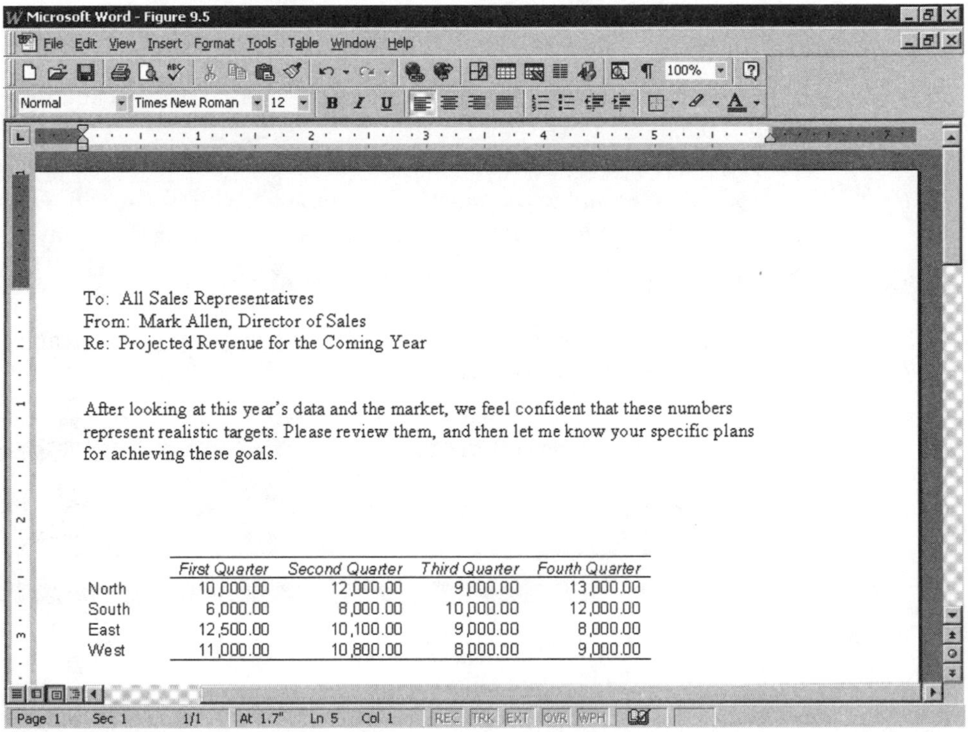

```
W Microsoft Word - Figure 9.5                                              _ |8| X|
File  Edit  View  Insert  Format  Tools  Table  Window  Help              _ |8| X|
```

```
        First Quarter   Second Quarter   Third Quarter   Fourth Quarter
North     10,000.00       12,000.00        9,000.00        13,000.00
South      6,000.00        8,000.00       10,000.00        12,000.00
East      12,500.00       10,100.00        9,000.00         8,000.00
West      11,000.00       10,800.00        8,000.00         9,000.00
```

To: All Sales Representatives
From: Mark Allen, Director of Sales
Re: Projected Revenue for the Coming Year

After looking at this year's data and the market, we feel confident that these numbers represent realistic targets. Please review them, and then let me know your specific plans for achieving these goals.

FIGURE 9.5: This Excel worksheet is ready for editing in a Word document.

TIP To view an embedded object in Word, you need to be in Page Layout view.

Skill 9

Linking Objects

To link an object, follow these steps:

1. Open the application that contains the information you want to link, and select the information.

2. Choose Edit ➤ Copy.

3. Open the document that will contain the embedded object.

4. Choose Edit ➤ Paste Special to open the Paste Special dialog box.

5. Click Paste Link, and select a format for the object.

6. If you want to display a copy of the object in the document, click Float over Text. If you want to display an icon instead, click Display As Icon.

7. Click OK.

Figure 9.6 shows a Word document with an icon that indicates an Excel worksheet is linked to the document.

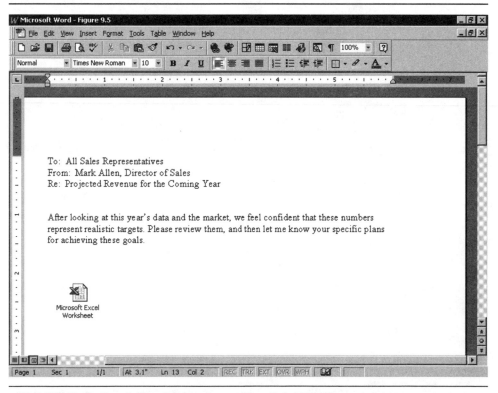

FIGURE 9.6: A Word document with a linked Excel worksheet

To edit a linked object, follow these steps:

1. Open the document that contains the link.

2. Double-click the link (whether it floats on the page or is an icon) to open the originating application and the document that contains the information that was linked and make your changes.

3. Save the file, and then close the application. Changes are reflected in the linked object.

Communicating and Sharing with NetMeeting

NetMeeting is an application that you can use to do the following:

- Chat with someone over the Internet, via a telephone or by typing on the screen
- Audio conference
- Video conference
- Share applications
- Collaborate on documents
- Transfer files
- Draw on the whiteboard

Obviously, you need the proper equipment to do some of these, and, as we look at the individual features of NetMeeting, we'll point that out.

Starting NetMeeting

Before you can use NetMeeting for the first time, you need to configure it a bit and give it some information about yourself. You do this with a Wizard that starts up the first time you open NetMeeting (choose Start ➤ Programs ➤ Accessories ➤ Communications ➤ NetMeeting). After you complete the setup, NetMeeting places a shortcut to itself on your Desktop so that you need only to click the shortcut to start the program.

Let's go quickly through the steps you need to take before you can work (and have fun) with NetMeeting. The first screen presents an overview of NetMeeting. Take a look at it, click Next, and then follow these steps:

1. In the boxes provided, enter at least your first name, your last name, and your e-mail address, and then click Next.

2. If you want to log on to a directory server whenever you start NetMeeting, click Log On to a Directory Server When NetMeeting Starts. If you don't want your name to appear in the directory listing for that server, click Do Not List My Name in the Directory. Click Next.

NOTE Directory servers are maintained by organizations or companies and provide a list of people who are logged on to the server and have chosen to display their names. If you are connected to the Internet and log on to a directory server, you can click a name in the list to connect to that person. We'll look at exactly how this works in a later section in this skill and also talk about why you might or might not want to display your name.

3. In the next screen, specify your modem speed or connection mode, and then click Next.

4. If you want quick access to NetMeeting, leave the options selected in this screen so that you display a shortcut to NetMeeting on your Desktop and an icon on the Quick Launch bar. Click Next to start the Audio Tuning Wizard, and then click Next again.

5. If you have sound equipment (speakers and a sound card), click the Test button to sample the volume, and then change it as necessary.

6. If you have a microphone, speak into it to ensure that the record volume is correct. Click Next.

7. Click Finish.

You're now ready to start using NetMeeting, which is shown in Figure 9.7.

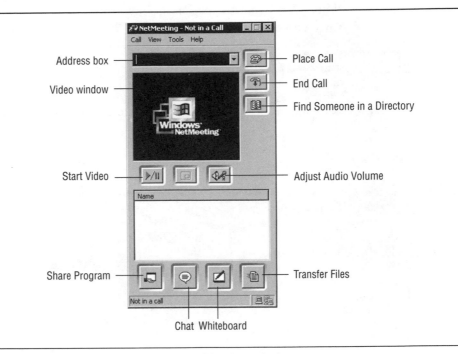

Address box

Video window

Start Video

Share Program

Place Call

End Call

Find Someone in a Directory

Adjust Audio Volume

Transfer Files

Chat Whiteboard

FIGURE 9.7: The opening NetMeeting window

Making a Call

When you make a call in NetMeeting, you can use an e-mail address, an IP address, a network address, or a modem phone number for the person you are calling. The only requirement is that both people must be running NetMeeting.

When you make the connection, you can communicate in several ways, depending on your equipment:

- If both people have microphones, sound cards, and speakers, you can talk just as you would over the telephone.

- If both people have microphones, sound cards, speakers, video cards, and video cameras, you can talk and be seen on the screen.

- If you don't have any of this equipment or just prefer it, you can communicate via the Chat application.

NOTE You can see video even if you don't have a camera, and you can hear another person who is using a microphone if you have speakers. Video runs in the Video window.

To make a call, follow these steps:

1. Click the Place Call button to open the Place a Call dialog box:

Place A Call
Enter the address of the person to call.
To: 123.456.789.0
Using: Automatic
☐ Require security for this call (data only)
Call Cancel

2. In the To box, enter the address (an IP address, an e-mail address, a modem phone number, or the name of the computer).

3. Click Call.

FINDING AN IP ADDRESS

An IP (Internet Protocol) address is a unique number that identifies your computer on the Internet, for example, 209.254.117.155. The first three parts of this number refer to your ISP (Internet Service Provider), and the last three digits refer to your computer. Unless you have a permanent connection to the Internet such as your ISP has, each time you log on you are assigned a different IP address. As we've mentioned, using an IP address is one way to connect through NetMeeting with others who are on the Internet.

continued ▶

To find out what your current IP address is, follow these steps:

1. Choose Start ➤ Run.
2. In the Open box, type **ipconfig** to open the IP Configuration dialog box.

Now you can share your IP address with someone who wants to call you. We've done this via e-mail before, and it works great. If the person you want to call is not running Windows 2000 but Windows 95/98 instead, he or she can type **winipcfg** to find out his or her IP address. Remember, though, every time you disconnect from the Internet or lose your connection, you lose that IP address. You'll get another one when you connect again.

Using the Chat Application

If you've visited chat rooms on the Web, you know how to use chat. What you type appears on the screen for you and others to see. Figure 9.8 shows the Chat window. To open Chat, click the Chat button in the main NetMeeting window.

To use Chat, you need to know only the following:

- Click in the Message box, type, and press Enter to send your words of wisdom.

- If the session involves more than one person, click the down arrow in the Send To box to specify whether to send your chat lines to an individual or to the whole group.

- To save the contents of a Chat session, choose File ➤ Save As.

- To end a session, close the Chat window.

TIP   To customize the format of the Chat window, such as the fonts used and the display of information, choose View ➤ Options.

Skill 9

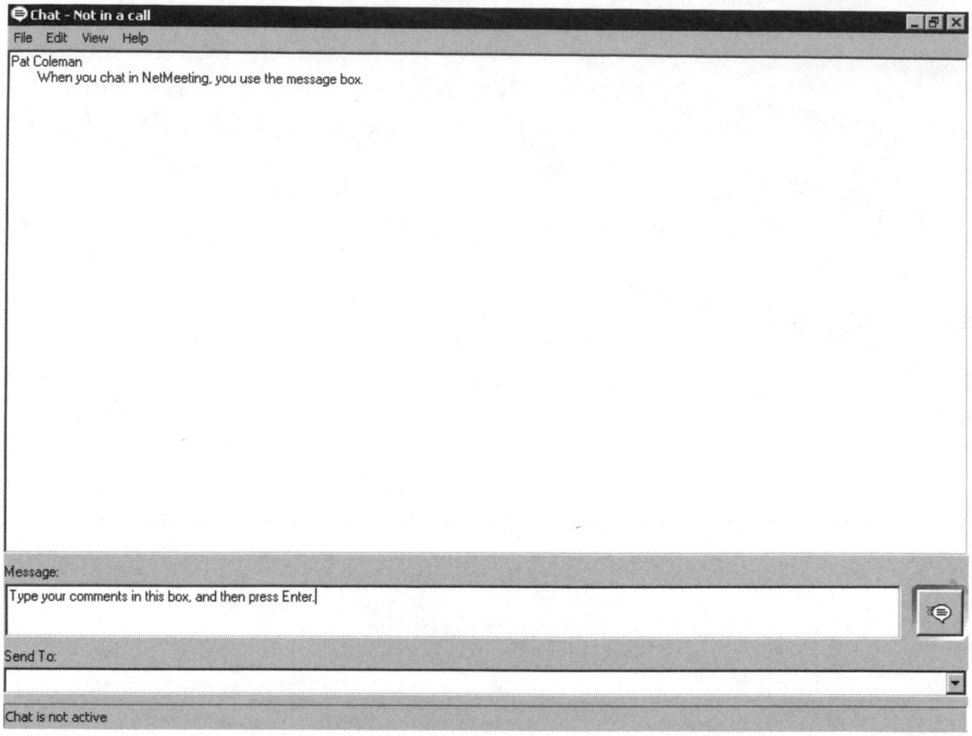

FIGURE 9.8: Chatting in NetMeeting

Using Directory Servers

As we mentioned earlier, a directory server is a service maintained by an organization or a company, and when you connect to it, you can see the names, e-mail addresses, and so on of all the others who are logged on and have chosen to display their names. You can also see whether they are available for video and audio transmission.

By default, NetMeeting points you to the Microsoft Internet Directory service. To log on to it, choose Call ➤ Directory, which opens the Find Someone dialog box, as shown in Figure 9.9. To communicate with someone on the list, click the name. NetMeeting locates the computer of the person and displays a message that someone is calling. If the other person accepts the call, you are connected and ready to interact.

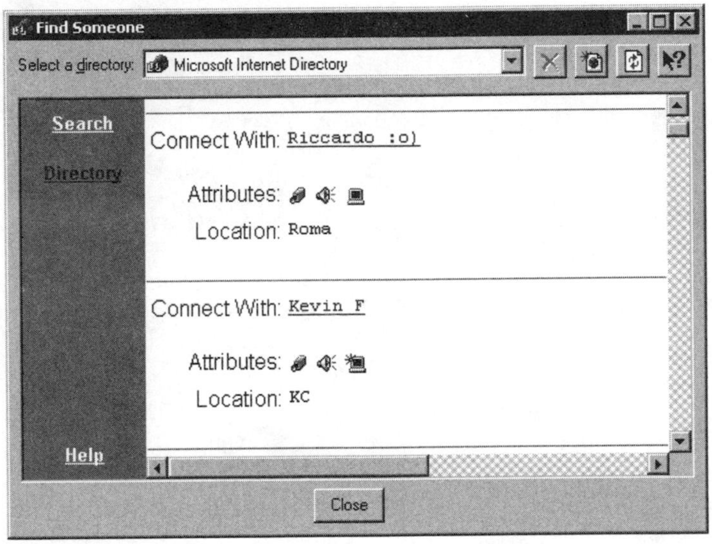

FIGURE 9.9: Logging on to a directory server with NetMeeting

Hosting a Meeting

You can also use NetMeeting to hold a meeting. To set this up, choose Call ➤ Host Meeting to open the Host a Meeting dialog box, as shown in Figure 9.10. Specify the parameters for the meeting, such as whether only you can place or accept calls, share applications, and so on, and then click OK. Now others can call you or you can call others. The meeting lasts until you end it (or until you or the others lose their connections).

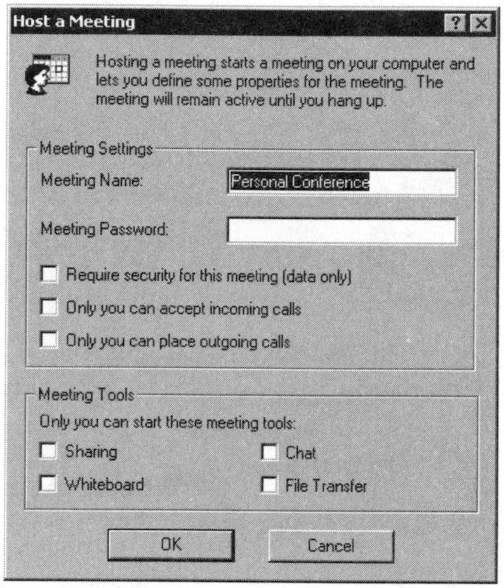

FIGURE 9.10: Setting the guidelines for a meeting

Using Video

When you are receiving or sending video, images are displayed in the video window. To set up video transmissions, choose Tools ➤ Options to open the Options dialog box, and click the Video tab, which is shown in Figure 9.11. You can specify when to send and receive video, the size of the image, its quality (do you want speed or clarity?), and the properties of your camera.

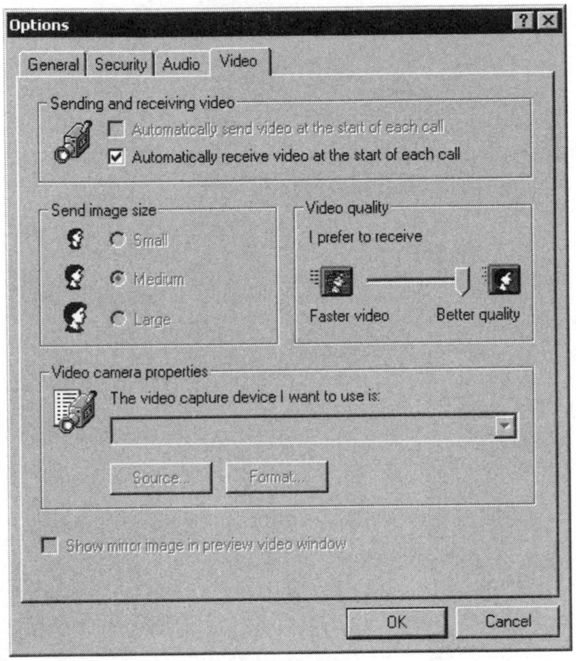

FIGURE 9.11: Setting up video transmission

Sharing Applications

While you are in a call or in a meeting, you can share documents and applications. To do so, open the program you want to share, and then click the Share Program button to open the Sharing dialog box, as shown in Figure 9.12. Specify the program to share and who will control it, and then click Close. Others will now be able to see and interact with you and your application.

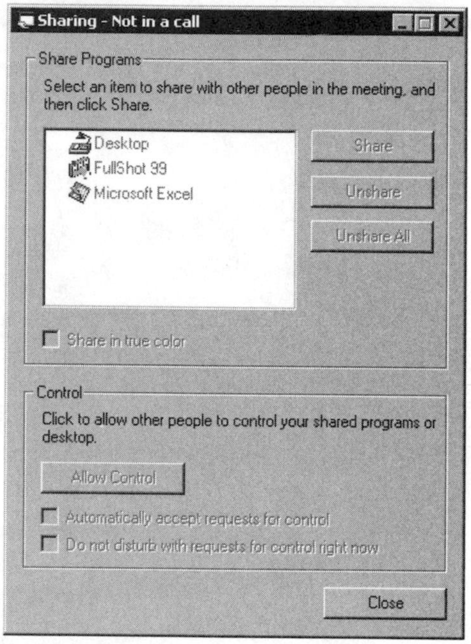

FIGURE 9.12:   Getting ready to share an application

 NOTE   To share the Whiteboard, click the Whiteboard button.

Transferring Files

Whenever you are in a call, you can transfer files. Simply click the Transfer Files button to open the File Transfer dialog box, and follow these steps:

1. Click Add File to select the file to send.

2. Click the name of the person to whom you want to send the file.

3. Click Send All.

To receive a file, click Accept. Received files are stored in the Received File folder in the NetMeeting folder, unless you specify otherwise.

Are You Up to Speed?

Now you can...

- ☑ cut, copy, and paste using the Clipboard
- ☑ capture screens
- ☑ store items in the ClipBook
- ☑ share items in the ClipBook
- ☑ embed objects
- ☑ link objects
- ☑ use NetMeeting to make a call
- ☑ use NetMeeting to share applications and collaborate on them
- ☑ transfer files with NetMeeting
- ☑ chat over the Internet

Skill 9

SKILL 10

Using the Windows 2000 Professional Applications

- Listening to sounds, watching movies, and recording
- Playing games
- Keeping track of your contacts
- Using Calculator
- Using Notepad
- Using WordPad
- Drawing with Paint
- Working with images
- Using your computer as a fax machine

To access the applications that are included with Windows 2000 Professional, you choose Start ➢ Programs ➢ Accessories. The Accessories menu includes a number of items that are standard issue with Windows, such as Games and Notepad. If you haven't noticed, however, the Accessories menu now contains Windows Explorer and a few other relocated items.

We look at some of these programs in other skills:

- Skill 5 discusses the Accessibility applet.

- Skill 9 discusses NetMeeting.

- Skill 11 discusses HyperTerminal, Phone Dialer, Internet Connection Wizard, and Network and Dial-Up Connections.

- Skill 14 discusses System Tools.

- Skill 12 discusses Synchronize.

In this skill, we'll take a look at the rest of the items on the Accessories menu. You may find that you frequently use some of these and never use others. Nevertheless, after working through this skill, you'll know where to find an applet when you need it, and you'll know how to use it. Let's begin by looking at how you can use your computer as a media player and as a recorder.

Listening to Sounds, Watching Movies, and Recording

Whether you ever do so or not, you probably know that you can play audio CDs from your CD drive, watch movies using the Windows Media Player, and, if you have the proper equipment, make sound recordings.

Playing Audio CDs

Playing an audio CD is probably the easiest thing you'll ever do with your computer: just put the CD in the drive and close it. In a second or two, CD Player will display on your screen. In Windows 2000 Professional, CD Player has a sleek, new look. As you can see in Figure 10.1, it resembles the CD player you might have in your car and even has some of the same buttons and dials.

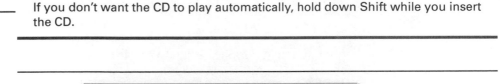

TIP

If you don't want the CD to play automatically, hold down Shift while you insert the CD.

FIGURE 10.1: You use the Windows 2000 Professional CD Player in much the same way you use any CD player.

Before we get into how you actually use CD Player, we need to explore one new feature. When you put a new CD in the drive, in a second or two, before the music starts, you'll see the following dialog box:

To download information about the artist, title, and tracks, click one of the option buttons. As the music begins to play, CD Player looks at a site on the Internet for this data (if you are connected to the Internet). If it can't find it, you'll see the message "The album was not found on the Internet."

By default, CD Player searches the Tunes.com site. You can, instead, search another site: Music Boulevard. To do so, follow these steps:

1. In CD Player, click Internet.

2. Choose Internet Music Sites ➢ Go to Music Boulevard.

This information is stored in the Album Information database. To display it, click Options, choose Preferences, and click the Playlist tab.

Now let's look at the controls in CD Player. Table 10.1 shows what each one does.

TABLE 10.1: The CD Player Controls

Control	What It Does
Pause	Stops the CD. When you click Pause, this control then becomes the Start button.
Stop	Halts the playing of the CD. To start it again, click the Pause button until it becomes the Start button, and then click again.
Eject	Opens the CD-ROM drive.
Scan Back	Moves backward through the current track bit by bit.
Scan Forward	Moves forward through the current track bit by bit.
Previous Track	Plays the previous track.
Next Track	Plays the next track.
Mode	Opens a menu of playing modes, including Standard, Random, Repeat Track, Repeat All, and Preview. Selecting Preview plays a snippet from the beginning of each track.
Volume Control	Adjusts the volume. With the hand that appears, click and drag the little red button to raise or lower the volume.
Mute	Silences the music. This works just like the Mute button on your TV remote control. The CD continues to play, but you can't hear it.

In this section, we haven't covered everything you'd ever want to know about CD Player, but it's enough to get you started. One way to get the hang of it is to experiment. You can also open CD Player, click the Options button, and choose CD Player Help.

TIP You can also manually open CD Player. To do so, choose Start ➢ Programs ➢ Accessories ➢ Entertainment ➢ CD Player.

Adjusting the Volume

In the last section, you saw how to adjust the volume on CD Player by turning the "knob." You can also adjust the volume of the current sound by left-clicking the Volume icon in the system tray. You'll see a slider bar like this:

To adjust the volume of the CD Player as well as other sounds, use the Volume Control dialog box, as shown in Figure 10.2. To open the Volume Control dialog box, right-click the Volume icon, and choose Open Volume Controls from the shortcut menu, or choose Start ➤ Programs ➤ Accessories ➤ Entertainment ➤ Volume Control.

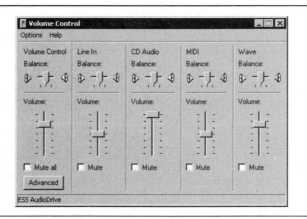

FIGURE 10.2: What you see in the Volume Control dialog box depends on which sound devices are installed on your computer.

The features you see in the Volume Control dialog box depend on the sound devices you have on your computer. For example, if you have a microphone, you'll see a control for it; if you don't have a microphone, you won't. Thus, you may see some or all these devices or more:

- Volume Control is the master switch. It controls the volume and balance of all sounds coming out of your computer.

Skill 10

- Line In controls volume and balance for an audio tap, an FM tuner, or a similar device.

- CD Audio controls the volume and balance for an audio CD you play in your CD-ROM drive.

- MIDI, pronounced "middy," is an acronym for Musical Instrument Digital Interface, which is the format in which synthesized sounds are stored on your computer. Use the MIDI control to adjust their volume and balance.

- Wave sets the volume and balance for playing .WAV files. (The sounds that accompany many Windows actions, such as exiting Windows, are .WAV files. If you'd rather not hear them, click the Mute button in the Wave control.

To adjust the volume or balance of any control, move its slider. If you want to make even finer adjustments to your audio, click the Advanced button to open the Advanced Controls for Volume Control dialog box.

Recording Sounds

If you have all the necessary equipment, you can make your own voice recordings or record from another sound source. To make voice recordings, you need a microphone and a sound card. To record sounds from another device such as an audio CD or a stereo receiver, you'll need a Line In connector to your sound card.

To open Sound Recorder, which is shown in Figure 10.3, choose Start ➤ Programs ➤ Accessories ➤ Entertainment ➤ Sound Recorder.

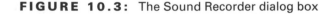

FIGURE 10.3: The Sound Recorder dialog box

Use the buttons at the bottom of the Sound Recorder dialog box to control recording and playback:

- Seek to Start moves to the beginning of a sound file.
- Seek to End moves to the end of a sound file.
- Play starts the playback of a recording.
- Stop ends playing or recording.
- Record begins the recording process.

To make a voice recording, follow these steps:

1. Open Sound Recorder.
2. Choose File ➢ New.
3. Turn on your microphone.
4. Choose File ➢ Properties to open the Properties for Sound dialog box.
5. In the Choose From drop-down list, select Recording Formats, and click Convert Now to open the Sound Selection dialog box.
6. In the Name drop-down list, select a recording quality—CD, radio, or telephone.
7. Click OK twice.
8. Click the Record button, and speak into the microphone.
9. When you're finished, click Stop.
10. Choose File ➢ Save As to save your recording as a file.

Using Windows Media Player

You use Windows Media Player to play audio, video, and mixed-media files that you find on the Internet or that are stored on your local area network or your own system. When you open one of these files, Media Player starts automatically, behind the scenes. Before we get into the nuts and bolts of how Media Player works, let's take a look at what it does. Follow these steps:

1. Connect to the Internet, and open Internet Explorer.

2. Go to www.hipclips.com.

3. Select a clip.

In a small window on the left, the clip loads and plays. And that's all there is to it.

NOTE Your Internet viewing and listening experience will be more satisfying if you have at least a 56Kbps connection.

Now let's take a look at Media Player itself. To open Media Player, choose Start ≻ Programs ≻ Accessories ≻ Entertainment ≻ Windows Media Player, or choose Start ≻ Run, type **mplayer2** in the Open box, and press Enter. You'll see the screen shown in Figure 10.4.

TIP If you know the name of the file you want to play, you can also type it in the Open box (for example, **mplayer2 http://webserver/directory/filename**).

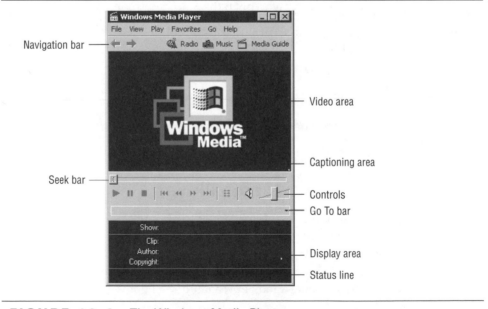

FIGURE 10.4: The Windows Media Player

Depending on the type of media file you are playing, you'll see the following components in the Windows Media Player:

Navigation bar   Click the Forward and Back buttons to open a file you played earlier in the current session; click Web Events to go to WindowsMedia.com, which contains a number of links to media files that you can play and download.

Video area   The video you are viewing displays in this area.

Captioning area   If the file you are playing provides it, this area displays closed-captioning. (Choose View ➤ Captions.)

Seek bar   If the content of the file you are playing makes the Seek bar available, you can drag the slider bar to play a specific section of the clip.

Controls   The controls in Media Player correspond to those on your audio CD player, and you use them in exactly the same way.

Go To bar   Click the down arrow to display a list of markers in the file, if the file provides it. Click a marker to play the section of the file associated with the marker.

Display area   If the file provides it, this area displays the show title, clip title, author, and copyright notice.

Status line   This area displays icons for sound and closed captioning and the following information for the current playing file:

- Connecting
- Buffering
- Playing
- Paused
- Reception quality
- Time elapsed
- Total time

Most of the time, the files you access with Media Player will be those you find on the Internet. You need to know that these files are in streaming media format, which means that as the file is transmitted to your computer it begins playing before all of it is stored in memory. As the file plays, Media Player stores the rest in memory. If you have a slow connection, the play may be jerky at first.

Skill 10

You'll need the very latest version of Media Player to play some files, and you can download it by choosing Go ➢ Windows Media Player Home Page.

Before we, of necessity, leave this all-too-brief discussion of Media Player, we need to take a look at the types of files you can play with it:

> **Microsoft Windows Media Formats**   These files have the extensions .AVI, .ASF, .ASX, .RMI, and .WAV.
>
> **Moving Pictures Experts Group (MPEG)**   These files have the extensions .MPG, .MPEG, .M1V, .MP2, .MPA, and .MPE.
>
> **Musical Instrument Digital Interface (MIDI)**   These files have the extensions .MID and .RMI.
>
> **Apple QuickTime®, Macintosh® AIFF Resource**   These files have the extensions .QT, .AIF, .AIFC, .AIFF, and .MOV.
>
> **Unix Formats**   These files have the extensions .AU and .SND.

 TIP   For much more information about Media Player, including how to customize it, choose Help in Media Player.

Playing Games

And now we come to what many consider an essential life skill: playing computer games. A stroll down the games aisle of any software emporium will be enough to convince you, if you aren't already convinced, of the enormous popularity of computer games. In addition, you can download games from many Web sites.

Your easiest access to games, however, is through the Games item on the Accessories menu in Windows 2000 Professional (choose Start ➢ Programs ➢ Accessories ➢ Games). In previous versions, Windows included four games: Hearts, Solitaire, FreeCell, and Minesweeper. In Windows 2000 Professional, Hearts has been replaced with Pinball.

In this section, we're going to take a brief look at each of these games and show you their interfaces. We won't get into step-by-step instructions for a couple of reasons. First, you probably already know how to play most of them, and, second, if you don't, all you need to do is open the game and choose Help. Let's start with the old favorite and one of the world's greatest time-wasters, Solitaire.

Solitaire

Solitaire is the American name given to a number of card games that can be played by one person. The English name for the game is Patience. When you open the game, the first hand is dealt for you, as Figure 10.5 shows. To deal a new game after you complete one, choose Game ➤ Deal. To turn over cards from the deck, click the deck; to move a card or a stack of cards, drag it.

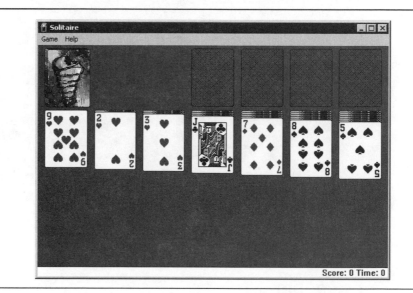

FIGURE 10.5: You can choose from among 12 decks when playing Solitaire.

FreeCell

Unlike Solitaire, it is believed (though not proven) that it is possible to win every game of FreeCell. Like Solitaire, in FreeCell you lay out a tableau of cards and then attempt to arrange them in their respective suits. The object is to move all the cards to the home cells, stacked by suits in order from ace through king. To start a game, choose Game ➤ New Game. Figure 10.6 shows a freshly dealt hand of FreeCell.

Free cells   Home cells

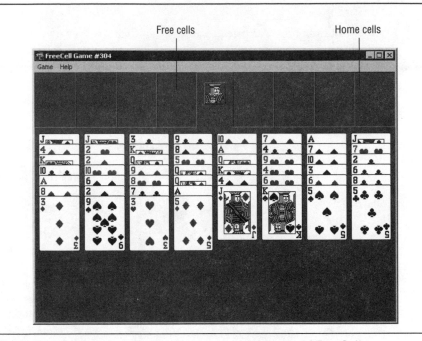

FIGURE 10.6: In theory, you can win every game of FreeCell.

Minesweeper

Minesweeper has to do with deduction and logic. The object is to uncover all the squares in a minefield that don't contain mines and to mark the squares that do contain mines as quickly as possible. (We prefer not to think about any real-world analogy to this game.) Figure 10.7 shows the opening grid of Minesweeper.

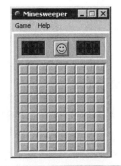

FIGURE 10.7: Click a square to uncover it.

Pinball

Space Cadet 3D Pinball is the electronic version of the pinball machines found in the typical arcade. Unlike the other three Windows games, Pinball is played with the keyboard. The object is to launch the ball and earn lots of points by hitting bumpers, targets, and flags. You begin each game with three balls and at the rank of Cadet. Figure 10.8 shows a game in progress. Even if you aren't a pinball wizard, open and start this game just to hear the great sound effects (unless you're at work, of course).

FIGURE 10.8: A game of Pinball in progress

And that's a very quick trip through the game scene in Windows 2000 Professional. Now, let's get back to business.

Keeping Track of Your Contacts

Although Address Book is a great time-saver when you're composing e-mail since it can automatically store the e-mail address of anyone to whom you reply, you can use Address Book to store much more than e-mail addresses. If you want, it can become the central repository of all the information you need to keep about your contacts, including:

- Home and business addresses

- Phone, fax, pager, and mobile numbers

- Web page addresses

- Job-related data

- Personal info such as spouse's name, children's names, anniversaries, and birthdays

- Conferencing connections

- Digital IDs

In Skill 13, we'll look at how you use Address Book with Outlook Express, and in this skill we'll look at how you can set up Address Book to get the most out of it.

Opening Address Book

You can open Address Book in the following ways:

- Choose Start ➤ Programs ➤ Accessories ➤ Address Book.

- In Outlook Express, click Addresses on the toolbar in the main window.

- When composing a message in Outlook Express, click the To or Cc icon in the New Message window.

Figure 10.9 shows the Address Book window, empty and waiting to be filled with contact information.

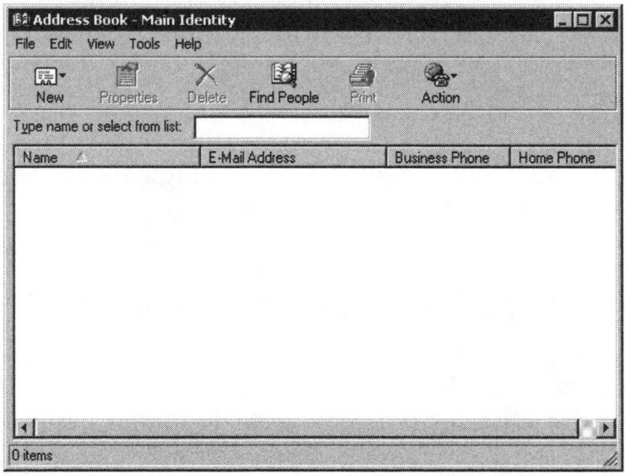

FIGURE 10.9: The main Address Book window

Adding a New Contact

To add information for a new contact, follow these steps:

1. In Address Book, click the New icon, and then choose New Contact to open the Properties dialog box:

2. Fill in as much or as little information as you want on the tabs, which include Name, Home, Business, Personal, Other, NetMeeting, and Digital IDs.

3. When you're finished, click OK.

Now you'll see your new contact's information in the main window.

Adding a New Group

You can also set up a group, or distribution list, in Address Book, which lets you send the same message or file to a number of people without entering all their e-mail addresses. Follow these steps:

1. Click the New icon, and then choose New Group to open the Properties dialog box.

2. In the Group Name box, type a name for the group.

3. Click Select Members to open the Select Group Members dialog box.

Skill 10

4. Select a Name from the Name list, and click the Select button for the names you want to add to the group. (You can use all the usual Windows selecting techniques.)

5. Click OK.

The group name now appears in boldface in the Name list in the main window.

Once you have collected some information in your Address Book, you can sort the list in a number of ways: by name, e-mail address, business phone, home phone, first name, last name, and so on. To do so, choose View ≻ Sort By, and then select a sorting style from the list.

Locating People

You can also use Address Book to locate people in the various directory services. Follow these steps:

1. In the main window, click Find People to open the Find People dialog box.

2. Click the Look In down arrow to display the list of services you can search.

3. Select a service, and then fill in the information you know about this person.

4. Click Find Now.

Printing Your Address Book

If you ever need or want to, you can print your Address Book. Simply click the Print icon to open the Print dialog box. You can print in three formats:

- Memo, which prints all the information you have stored for selected contacts.

- Business Card, which prints the information from Address Book that you would typically find on a business card

- Phone List, which prints all phone numbers you have stored for the selected contact

Creating a Map

To display a map for a specific address, connect to the Internet, and follow these steps:

1. In the main Address Book window, right-click a name, and choose Properties from the shortcut menu to open the Properties dialog box for that person.

2. Click either the Home or Business tab, whichever contains the address you want to map.

3. Click View Map.

You'll see something similar to Figure 10.10.

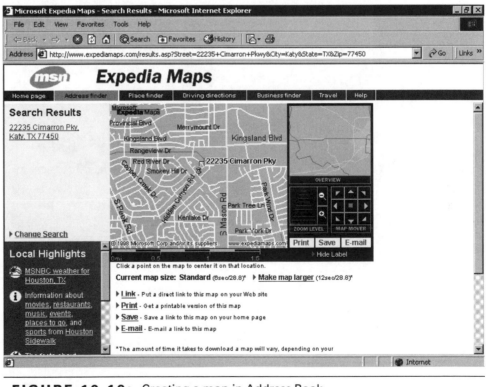

FIGURE 10.10:   Creating a map in Address Book

IMPORTING AND EXPORTING AN ADDRESS BOOK

If you have an address book in any of the following, you can import it into the Windows 2000 Professional Address Book:

- Eudora Pro or Light Address Book (through version 3)
- LDIF – LDAP Data Interchange Format
- Microsoft Exchange Personal Address Book
- Microsoft Internet Mail for Windows 3.1 Address Book
- Netscape Address Book (version 2 or 3)
- Netscape Communicator Address Book (version 4)
- Text File (Comma Separated Values)

To import an address book, follow these steps:

1. In the Address Book main window, choose File ➢ Import, and then select either Address Book (WAB) or Other Address Book.
2. Select the file.
3. Click Import.

You can also export a Windows 2000 Professional Address Book that you create to any of the following:

- Other Windows Address Book files
- Microsoft Exchange Personal Address Book
- Text File (Comma Separated Values)

To export your Address Book, follow the earlier steps for importing, but choose Export instead.

Doing Math

Calculator is simply an on-screen version of the handheld variety, and, essentially, you use it in the same way. It's available in two versions: Standard and

Scientific. When you open Calculator (choose Start ➤ Programs ➤ Accessories ➤ Calculator), it displays in the version last used. Figure 10.11 shows Calculator open in Standard view. To change the view, choose View, and then select Standard or Scientific. If you want results displayed with comma separators, choose View ➤ Digit Grouping.

FIGURE 10.11: Calculator in Standard view

In Standard and Scientific view, Calculator has the following keys:

- * represents the multiplication sign (×) and / represents the division sign (÷).

- Backspace erases a single digit.

- CE clears the last entry. You can also press Delete to do the same thing.

- C clears the calculation altogether. You can also press Esc to do the same thing.

- MC clears a number from Calculator's memory.

- MR recalls a number from Calculator's memory.

- MS stores a number in Calculator's memory and removes what was already there.

- M+ adds a number to the number in Calculator's memory.

In Standard view, Calculator also has the following keys:

- sqrt calculates the square root of a number.

- % lets you add, subtract, divide, and multiply a number by a percentage.

- 1/x is the Inverse key. You use it to divide 1 by a value.

Skill 10

Using the Standard Calculator

To add, subtract, multiply, divide, and perform any other standard arithmetic operations, follow these steps:

TIP You can select Calculator's buttons with the mouse, with the numbers at the top of the keyboard, or with the numeric keypad. To use the numeric keypad, press Num Lock.

1. Enter the first number in the calculation.

2. Click the operator key.

3. Enter the next number.

4. Click = to get the result.

Using the Scientific Calculator

Figure 10.12 shows Calculator in Scientific view. You use this view to calculate logarithms, to convert values to other number systems, and to perform statistical calculations.

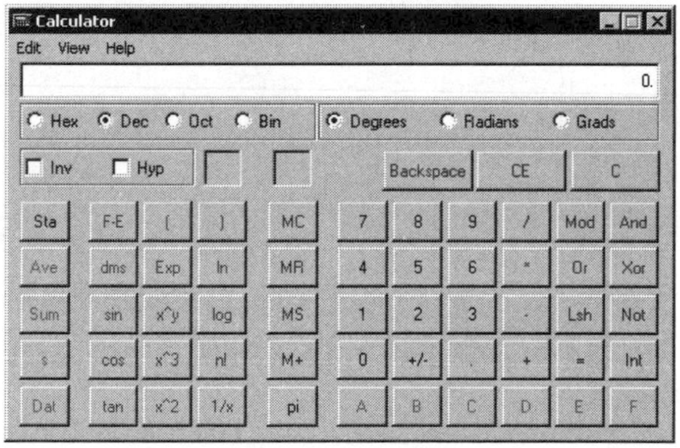

FIGURE 10.12: Calculator in Scientific view

To perform a scientific calculation, follow these steps:

1.   Click an option button to select a number system:

    - Hex (hexadecimal)

    - Dec (decimal)

    - Oct (octal)

    - Bin (binary)

2.   Enter the first number, and then click an operator.

3.   Click = to display the result.

To perform a statistical calculation, follow these steps:

1.   Click Sta to open the Statistics Box:

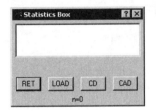

2.   Click Dat to enter the data.

3.   Continue to enter numbers, clicking Dat after each.

4.   Click Sta to once again display the Statistics Box, and click RET to return to Calculator.

5.   Click the statistics function you want.

The Statistics Box contains the following buttons:

    - RET closes the Statistics Box.

    - LOAD displays the number selected in the Statistics Box in Calculator's display area.

- CD removes the selected number.
- CAD clears the Statistics Box.

Creating Text Documents

Windows 2000 Professional includes a couple of word-processing programs: Notepad and WordPad. Notepad is a simple text editor, and WordPad is a simple word processor. Which you use depends on the task at hand, but you will, no doubt, use a full-fledged, fully featured word-processing program, such as Microsoft Word, most of the time when you create large, complicated documents.

In this section, we'll take a look at both Notepad and WordPad and discuss how to put each to its best use.

Using Notepad

As we just pointed out, Notepad is a simple text editor, which means that you can use it to view and edit only .TXT files. Such files are pure text and contain only basic formatting. Normally, you use Notepad to display the contents of the Clipboard, program files, ReadMe files, and your autoexec.bat and config.sys files.

In previous versions, Notepad could not open any file that was larger than 64KB; if you attempted to do so, you received a message asking if you'd rather open the file in WordPad instead. With Windows 2000 Professional, this has changed. Notepad can now load at least a 7MB file. And this is good news for those who like to create Web pages by handcoding HTML rather than using an HTML editor such as Microsoft FrontPage.

When you use Notepad to create HTML documents, there is no way that you can accidentally save special formatting. Special characters inserted in an HTML document may not appear when the page is opened in a Web browser, and, in addition, they can even produce errors.

When you open a Web page in Internet Explorer and choose View ➤ Source, the HTML document opens in Notepad. Figure 10.13 shows the underlying source for a Web page open as an HTML document in Notepad.

Now, let's take a brief look at how to use Notepad to enter text.

```
www.sybex[1] - Notepad                                                    _ 8 X
File  Edit  Format  Help
<HTML>
<HEAD>
        <TITLE>Welcome to Sybex, Inc. - Quality Computer Books</TITLE>
        <META NAME="keywords" CONTENT="Sybex, Sybex Inc., Sybex
computer book publisher, computer books, books, book, publishers,
computer, computers, computing, how-to books, how to books, reference
books, certification, MCSE, MCSD, MOUS, CCNA, CCNP, Cisco
certification, Novell certification, CompTIA certification, study
guides, test success, exam notes, computer games, video games, game
books, programming, internet, database, web design, network,
networking, mastering, network press, strategies & secrets, strategies
and secrets, ultimate strategy guide, developer's handbook, expert
guide, complete, no experience required, office 2000, windows,
Pokemon, 24seven">
<META NAME="Description" CONTENT="Sybex Inc. is an independent
publisher of quality computer books that has been publishing books for
over 20 years in the United States and Europe.">
<META NAME="copyright" CONTENT="&copy; 1999 Sybex Inc.">
</HEAD>
<BODY BGCOLOR="#FFFFFF" BACKGROUND="/images/bg.gif" TOPMARGIN=8
LEFTMARGIN=8 LINK=#003399 ALINK=#CCCC00 VLINK=#660000>
<!--Top Banner-->
<TABLE CELLSPACING=0 CELLPADDING=0 BORDER=0 WIDTH=590>
<TR>
        <TD ALIGN=CENTER VALIGN=TOP WIDTH=85>
        <A NAME="top"><IMG SRC="/images/top_banner/logo.gif" WIDTH=59
HEIGHT=59 BORDER=0 ALT="Sybex, Inc." ALIGN=TOP></A>
        </TD>
        <TD ALIGN=LEFT VALIGN=TOP WIDTH=505 COLSPAN=2>
        <IMG SRC="/images/top_banner/header_sybex.gif" WIDTH=457
HEIGHT=34 BORDER=0 ALT="Sybex, Inc. - Quality Computer Books"
ALIGN=TOP><BR><IMG SRC="/images/top_banner/top_curve.gif" WIDTH=16
HEIGHT=20 BORDER=0 ALT="curve" ALIGN=TOP><A
HREF="/catalog/index.shtml"><IMG
```

FIGURE 10.13: You can safely view and edit HTML documents in Notepad.

Creating a Document in Notepad

To begin a document in Notepad, simply open Notepad (choose Start ➤ Programs ➤ Accessories ➤ Notepad) and start typing. To start a new paragraph, press Enter. To delete the preceding character, press Backspace. To delete several characters, a sentence, a paragraph, and so on, select the text by dragging the mouse over it, and press Delete.

Also new to this version of Notepad (which is version 5) is the Format menu. After you enter text, select it, choose Format ➤ Font to open the Font dialog box, and choose a font, style (Regular, Italic, Bold, Bold Italic), and size for your text.

If you are creating a document of several pages and want to insert headers and footers on the printed pages, follow these steps:

1. Choose File ➤ Page Setup to open the Page Setup dialog box.

2. In the Header and Footer boxes, enter the character and letter combination shown in Table 10.2 that corresponds to the information you want.

TABLE 10.2: Entering Header and Footer Information

To Do This	Type This
Insert the filename	&f
Insert the date	&d
Insert the time	&t
Insert page numbers	&p
Left-align the header or footer	&l
Center the header or footer	&c
Right-align the header or footer	&r

3. Ensure that the paper size, orientation, and margins are the way you want them, and click OK.

NOTE   For information about printing in Windows 2000 Professional, see Skill 8.

If you've used previous versions of Notepad, you may have noticed that the menu bar no longer contains the Search menu. Find and Replace commands have been relocated on the Edit menu. The Edit menu now also contains a Go To command. To go to a specific line of text, choose Edit ➤ Go To to open the Goto Line dialog box, enter a line number, and click OK.

Opening and Saving a File in Notepad

To open a file in Notepad, choose File ➤ Open to display the standard Windows Open dialog box, select the file, and click Open.

To save a file you just created in Notepad, choose File ➤ Save As to open the standard Windows Save As dialog box, locate the folder in which you want to store the document, give the file a name, and choose Save.

To save a file you've saved before, choose File ➤ Save.

Using WordPad

To open Word Pad, choose Start ➤ Programs ➤ Accessories ➤ WordPad. If you've used other Windows word processors, this screen, which is shown in Figure 10.14, will look familiar. Figure 10.14 contains labels for the buttons on the standard toolbar, and Table 10.3 explains what these buttons do.

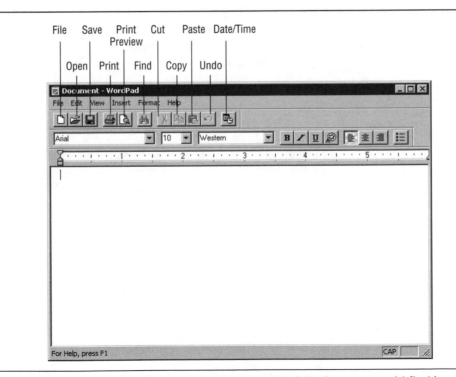

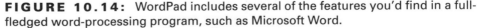

FIGURE 10.14: WordPad includes several of the features you'd find in a full-fledged word-processing program, such as Microsoft Word.

TABLE 10.3: The Toolbar Buttons in WordPad

Button	What It Does
New	Opens a new, blank document
Open	Opens an existing document
Save	Saves your document
Print	Prints your document
Print Preview	Displays on-screen what your printed document will look like
Find	Searches for text you specify
Cut	Moves your selection to the Clipboard
Copy	Duplicates your selection on the Clipboard
Paste	Inserts the contents of the Clipboard at the insertion point
Undo	Reverses your last action
Date/Time	Inserts the current date and time

As we pointed out, Notepad provides only minimal, basic formatting. Word-Pad, on the other hand, provides a great many formatting features, including bullets and the ability to format text in colors. To format, you can use the commands on the Format menu, or you can use the Format bar:

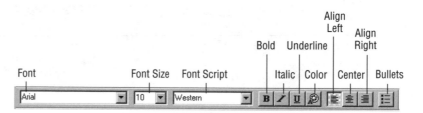

Table 10.4 describes what the Format buttons do. If you don't see the Format bar on your screen, choose View ➤ Format Bar.

TABLE 10.4: The Buttons on the Format Bar

Button	What It Does
Font	Displays a drop-down list of fonts you can use for the current text selection.
Font Size	Displays a drop-down list of font point sizes you can use for the current text selection.
Font Script	Displays a drop-down list of eight non-Western alphabets you can use if your keyboard and system are set up to do so.
Bold	Boldfaces the current text selection.
Italic	Italicizes the current text selection.
Underline	Underlines the current text selection.
Color	Displays a list box of colors you can use to color the current text selection.
Align Left	Left-aligns the current text selection.
Center	Centers the current text selection horizontally.
Align Right	Right-aligns the current text selection.
Bullets	Turns the selected paragraphs into a list of bullet points; click the Bullets tool again to return to regular text formatting.

Creating a Document with WordPad

You create a basic document in WordPad much as you would in Notepad, but you have a great many more options for formatting and for choosing formats in which to save your documents. (Interestingly enough, you can't insert headers and footers in WordPad documents.) To create a document, follow these general steps:

1. Choose File ➤ New to open the New dialog box, and select a type for your document. The choices are:

    - Word 6 Document
    - Rich Text Document
    - Text Document
    - Unicode Text Document

Skill 10

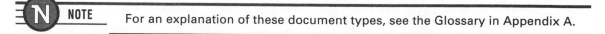

NOTE For an explanation of these document types, see the Glossary in Appendix A.

2. Click OK.

3. When WordPad asks if you want to save changes to this document, click Yes to open the Save As dialog box.

4. Select a folder in which to save the document, type the name for the document in the File Name box, and click Save.

5. Enter your text, and format it using the tools on the Toolbar and the Format bar.

6. When you're finished, choose File ➢ Save to save the document.

You can now print your document if you need to distribute it that way, or you can send it as an e-mail attachment, as you'll see in the next section.

Sending a WordPad Document As an E-mail Attachment

You will see in Skill 13 how to attach a file to an e-mail message. In WordPad, you do the opposite: you create the file and then compose the message. Here are the steps:

1. After you create and save a document, choose File ➢ Send to display the New Message window in Outlook Express. The Attach line includes the document name.

2. Fill in the To and Subject lines, type your message, and click Send. A copy of your message is placed in your Outbox in Outlook Express.

3. If you want to send the message immediately, connect to the Internet, open Outlook Express, and click Send and Receive.

TIP You can insert any of a number of objects in a WordPad document, including another WordPad document, a Word document, a bitmap image, a video clip, clip art, and a wave sound. To do so, choose Insert ➢ Object, and make a selection in the Insert Object dialog box.

Drawing with Paint

Paint is an application you can use to develop and edit graphic images: diagrams, logos, scanned photographs, original art, and so on. You can even set one of your creations as Desktop wallpaper. To open Paint, choose Start ➤ Programs ➤ Accessories ➤ Paint. You'll see the screen shown in Figure 10.15.

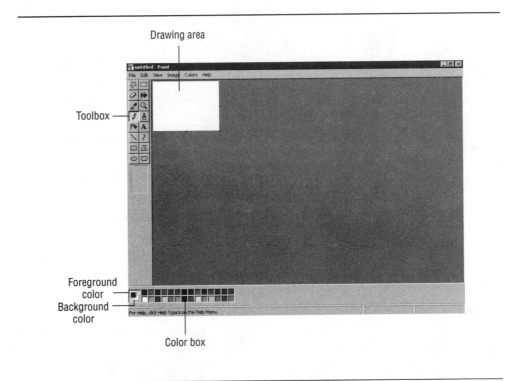

Drawing area

Toolbox

Foreground color
Background color

Color box

FIGURE 10.15: You can use Paint to create and edit graphic images.

To work with or create an image in Paint, you use the tools in the Toolbox, some of which are the electronic equivalents of the utensils you'd use on paper or canvas. Table 10.5 describes what each tool does.

Skill 10

TABLE 10.5: The Paint Tools

Tool	Name	What It Does
	Free-Form Select	Selects an irregularly shaped area of the image.
	Select	Selects a rectangular-shaped area of the image.
	Eraser/Color Eraser	Removes an area of the image as you move the eraser over it.
	Fill with Color	Fills an area with the color you selected.
	Pick Color	Selects the color of an object you click.
	Magnifier	Enlarges the area you select.
	Pencil	Draws a freehand line one pixel wide.
	Brush	Draws lines of different shapes and widths.
	Airbrush	Draws using an airbrush of the size you select.
	Text	Inserts text into an image.
	Line	Draws a straight line. Hold down Shift to create a really straight line.
	Curve	Draws a curved line.
	Rectangle	Draws a rectangle. Choose Rectangle, and hold down Shift to draw a square.
	Polygon	Draws a figure of straight lines connecting at any angle.
	Ellipse	Draws an ellipse. Choose Ellipse and hold down Shift to draw a circle.
	Rounded Rectangle	Draws a rectangle that has curved corners.

To erase your most recent squiggle, choose Edit ≻ Undo, or press Ctrl+Z. To get rid of everything in the Drawing area and start over fresh, choose Edit ≻ Select All, and press Delete.

If you've never worked with Paint before, you'll find that it takes some practice to become comfortable with the drawing tools and to achieve the result you expect. Follow these steps to create a simple image:

1. Choose File ≻ New.

2. Optionally, choose Image ≻ Attributes to open the Attributes dialog box in which you can specify the size and shape of your picture, the unit of measure, color or black-and-white, and so on. Click OK when you're done.

3. Click a drawing tool to select it.

4. Choose a line width, brush shape, or rectangle type from the Toolbox.

5. Click a color in the color box to select a foreground color.

6. Right-click a color in the color box to select a background color.

7. When you're finished, choose File ≻ Save As to save your drawing.

By default, Paint saves your drawing in the number of colors set in the Settings tab of the Display Properties dialog box. To change this, click the down arrow in the Save As Type box, and select another type. You can save a Paint drawing in the following graphic formats:

- 256 Color Bitmap (*.bmp, *.dib)

- Monochrome Bitmap (*.bmp, *.dib)

- 16 Color Bitmap (*.bmp, *.dib)

- 24-bit Bitmap (*.bmp, *.dib)

Displaying and Editing Digital Images

The Imaging application is not new to Windows 2000 Professional, and you may have used it in a previous version of Windows without realizing it. For example, unless you've associated another program with graphic files, clicking a graphic in Windows Explorer opens it in Imaging Preview. But you can use Imaging for much more than quickly displaying a graphic.

If you have a scanner or a digital camera, you can send images you capture with those devices directly to the Imaging application, in which you can resize them, change their colors, annotate them, change their file type, print them, send them as e-mail, and so on. An image can be any photograph, text, or drawing that is digitized.

NOTE   You also use Imaging to view and print received and sent faxes, as you will see in the last section in this skill.

To open the Imaging application, choose Start ➤ Programs ➤ Accessories ➤ Imaging. Figure 10.16 shows a sample image open in Imaging.

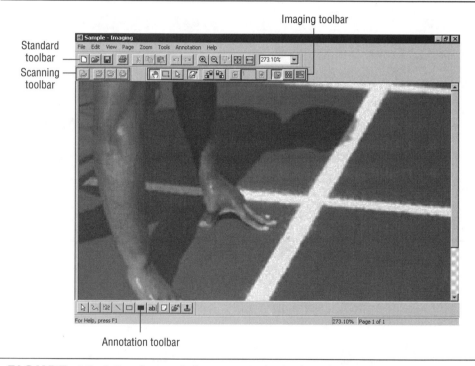

FIGURE 10.16: A sample image open in the Imaging application

To capture or manipulate images, you use the tools on the Standard, Imaging, Annotation, and Scanning toolbars. Table 10.6 describes the tools on the Standard toolbar, Table 10.7 describes the tools on the Imaging toolbar, and Table 10.8 describes the tools on the Annotation toolbar. You'll notice that some of the tools on the Annotation toolbar are similar to those in Paint. If you have a scanner, you can use the tools on the Scanning toolbar to scan a new image, insert a scanned page, append a scanned page, and rescan a page.

TABLE 10.6: The Tools on the Standard Toolbar

Tool	Name	What It Does
	New Blank Document	Creates a new, blank document
	Open	Opens an existing document
	Save	Saves the active document
	Print	Prints the active document
	Cut	Cuts the selection and places it on the Clipboard
	Copy	Copies the selection and places it on the Clipboard
	Paste	Inserts the Clipboard contents in the upper left corner of the window
	Undo	Reverses the last action
	Redo	Redoes the last action that was undone
	Zoom In	Zooms the image to twice its current size
	Zoom Out	Zooms the image to half its current size
	Zoom to Selection	Zooms in on the current selection
	Best Fit	Displays the image to include the entire page in the window
	Fit to Width	Displays the image to fit the width of the window
273.10%	Zoom	Selects a predefined zoom factor

Skill 10

TABLE 10.7: The Tools on the Imaging Toolbar

Tool	Name	What It Does
	Drag	Selects the dragging tool
	Select Image	Selects the Image Selection tool
	Annotation Selection	Selects the Annotation Selection tool
	Annotation Toolbar	Displays or hides the Annotation toolbar
	Rotate Left	Rotates the current page 90 degrees to the left
	Rotate Right	Rotates the current page 90 degrees to the right
	Previous Page	Displays the previous page of the document, if there is one
	Page	Displays the page you specify
	Next Page	Displays the next page of the document, if there is one
	One Page View	Displays the document one page at a time
	Thumbnail view	Displays the pages of the document as thumbnails (little pictures)
	Page and Thumbnails View	Displays the active page and thumbnails

TABLE 10.8: The Tools on the Annotation Toolbar

Tool	Name	What It Does
	Annotation Selection	Selects the Annotation Selection tool
	Freehand Line	Selects the Freehand Line annotation tool
	Highlighter	Selects the Highlighter annotation tool
	Straight Line	Selects the Straight Line annotation tool
	Hollow Rectangle	Selects the Hollow Rectangle annotation tool
	Filled Rectangle	Selects the Filled Rectangle annotation tool
	Text	Selects the Text annotation tool
	Attach-a-Note	Selects the Attach-a-Note annotation tool
	Text from File	Selects the Text from File annotation tool
	Rubber Stamp	Select the Rubber Stamp annotation tool

Many of the items on the menus in Imaging duplicate tools found on the various toolbars, and the menus also include such standard Windows commands as File ➢ Save As and File ➢ Open. Some menu items are, however, specific to the Imaging application. Table 10.9 lists and explains those.

Skill 10

TABLE 10.9: Menu Items Specific to Imaging

Menu	Command	What It Does
File	New	Opens the New Blank Document dialog box, in which you can choose a file type, color, compression ratio, resolution, and size
	Color Management	Opens the Color Management dialog box, in which you can specify the color profiles in which pictures appear on your monitor or in print
View	Scale to Gray	Displays black-and-white images as grayscale images
Tools	General Options	Opens the General Options dialog box, in which you can specify how you want to view documents
	Scan Options	Opens the Scan Options dialog box, in which you can specify how to compress scanned images in terms of quality and size
	Thumbnail Size	Opens the Thumbnail Size dialog box, in which you can specify the size at which thumbnails display on the screen
Annotation	Make Annotations Permanent	Burns the annotations into the image so that they are no longer treated separately but as part of the image

Using Your Computer As a Fax Machine

If you have a fax modem, you can send and receive faxes with the Fax accessory. These days, most modems have fax and data capabilities. If you don't know whether your modem has fax capabilities, choose Start ➢ Settings ➢ Printers to open the Printers folder. If you have an icon for a fax printer, your modem has fax capabilities. Windows 2000 Professional detects this when you install the operating system and installs the fax service and the associated fax printer.

 NOTE   You cannot share a fax printer with others on your network.

Sending a Fax

You can fax a document from within any Windows program that contains a Print command. For purposes of example, let's fax a document from WordPad and assume that this is your first time to fax a document in Windows 2000 Professional. Follow these steps:

1. Choose Start ➤ Programs ➤ Accessories ➤ WordPad to open WordPad.

2. Open an existing document, or create a new one.

3. Choose File ➤ Print to open the Print dialog box.

4. Select the Fax icon, and then click the Fax Options tab.

5. Click Print to start the Send Fax Wizard.

6. At the Welcome screen, click Next.

7. Enter the information that will be included in all your cover pages.

8. In the Fax Properties dialog box, click the Status Monitor tab to specify how you want to be notified when you send or receive a fax. Click OK to open the Recipient and Dialing Information screen of the Send Fax Wizard.

9. Fill in the name and fax number, or select these items from your Address Book if they are stored there. Click Next to open the Preparing the Cover Page screen.

10. Add any additional comments or information that you want to include on your cover page, and click Next to specify when to send the fax.

11. Click Finish.

You'll see the Fax Monitor open on your screen, in which you can track the progress of your fax transmission.

Skill 10

Receiving a Fax

Before you can receive a fax, you must set up your fax service to do so. In order to do this, you need to be logged in with Administrator privileges. Follow these steps:

1. Choose Start ≻ Programs ≻ Accessories ≻ Communications ≻ Fax ≻ Fax Service Management to open the Fax Service Management dialog box:

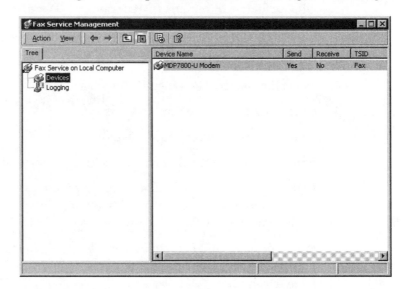

2. In the Tree column, click Devices to display the name of your fax modem.

3. In the Receive column, right-click No, and choose Receive from the shortcut menu so that Yes is displayed in the Receive column.

4. Close the Fax Service Management dialog box.

Now, when you receive a fax, you'll be notified in whatever way you specified in the Monitor tab of the Fax Properties dialog box. Faxes are stored in the My Faxes folder.

To print a fax that you've either sent or received, follow these steps:

1. In either the Received Faxes or the Sent Faxes folder in the My Faxes folder, double-click the fax you want to print to open it in Imaging.

2. Choose File ➤ Print.

Are You Up to Speed?

Now you can...

☑ **use your computer to play sounds, watch movies, and record**

☑ **play games**

☑ **keep track of your contacts**

☑ **use Calculator**

☑ **create documents in Notepad and WordPad**

☑ **draw with Paint**

☑ **work with images**

☑ **send and receive faxes**

Connecting to the Outside World

- Setting phone and modem options
- Using the Phone Dialer
- Connecting with HyperTerminal
- Using the Internet Connection Wizard
- Setting Internet Explorer options

In recent years, the expansion of the Internet has been nothing short of astonishing; everyone wants to connect. Whether your main use is sending and receiving e-mail or browsing the World Wide Web, the first thing you have to do is make sure your modem is configured correctly, and we'll look at that in the first part of this skill. Then we'll go on to look at the Phone Dialer and cover how you can use HyperTerminal to connect to non-Internet online services such as bulletin boards or the book catalog at your local library. Finally, we'll describe how you can use the Internet Connection Wizard to set up a connection to your local Internet Service Provider (ISP), and take a look at some of the options you can choose when configuring the Internet Explorer Web browser. First, let's check out that modem.

Setting Phone and Modem Options in Control Panel

Before you can use your modem to connect to the outside world, you must make sure it is configured correctly, and you do that using the Phone and Modem Options applet in Control Panel. Windows 2000 Professional can detect most of today's modems automatically, but you still have to specify certain dialing information. Here are the steps to follow when installing a modem for the first time:

1. Choose Start ➤ Settings ➤ Control Panel ➤ Phone and Modem Options.

2. In the Location Information dialog box, confirm the name of the country you are in, the area code, any prefix you have to dial to get an outside line, and whether you use tone or pulse dialing. Click OK.

3. The Phone and Modem Options dialog box opens, displaying three tabs—Dialing Rules, Modems, and Advanced—as Figure 11.1 shows.

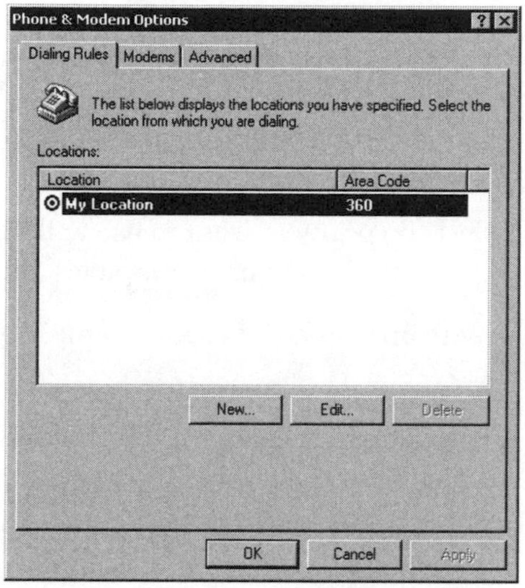

FIGURE 11.1: The Phone and Modem Options dialog box

Adding a New Modem

The Modems tab is the one you use to add or remove a modem or edit the properties of your modem. When the tab is first displayed, it contains the names of the modems currently installed on your computer. To add a new modem, follow these steps:

1. Click the Modems tab to bring it to the front, and click Add.

2. Windows 2000 Professional will automatically locate your modem, but if you would rather choose the manufacturer and model from a list yourself, check the Don't Detect My Modem box. If you use an external modem, make sure it is attached to your computer and that it is turned on. Click Next.

3. If your modem was automatically detected, follow the instructions on the screen. If Windows 2000 Professional could not find your modem or you elected to choose it from a list, select the manufacturer from the list in the left pane and the specific model from the list in the right pane. If your modem does not appear in the list or if you have an installation disk, click Have Disk. Click Next.

4. Select the port you want to use with this modem. Click Next, and Windows 2000 Professional completes the installation.

Two more buttons are available on the Modems tab:

Remove   Deletes the current modem settings from your computer.

Properties   Displays the Communications Port Properties dialog box, which has these tabs:

General   Allows you to see the port used for the modem, and to control the speaker volume and the maximum modem speed to use.

Diagnostics   Allows you to test your modem using standard modem commands, and to control the logging of session information to a log file.

Advanced   Gives access to extra settings, including additional modem-initialization commands. Click the Port Settings button to open the Advanced Settings dialog box, where you can set levels for both the receive and the transmit buffers; use lower levels if you are having connection problems, and use higher levels to boost performance. Click the Change Default Preferences button to open the Default Preferences dialog box, where you can establish error control, flow control, and other hardware settings.

Using the Advanced and Dialing Properties Tabs

As we previously mentioned, there are two more tabs in the Phone and Modem Options dialog box:

Advanced   Lists the telephony drivers installed on your system, and includes Add, Remove, and Configure buttons.

Dialing Rules Specifies how your calls are actually made, including the rules for using the area code when dialing, how to dial an outside line, and how to turn off call-waiting services. You can also specify a calling card for use with long-distance calls.

Now that your modem is configured properly, let's take a look at some of the ways you can use it. We'll start with the Phone Dialer.

Using the Phone Dialer

In previous versions of Windows, Phone Dialer was a simple application that you could use to place outgoing telephone calls through your modem—if you used the same phone line for voice and data. Whether this was easier than picking up the phone and dialing the number is an issue we won't get into here, but you could use your computer as a telephone if you had a modem, a microphone, a sound card, and speakers.

In Windows 2000 Professional, Phone Dialer has been enhanced. In addition to using it to make voice calls, you can now use it to make video calls and conference calls and to connect to an Internet directory. To open Phone Dialer, choose Start ➢ Programs ➢ Accessories ➢ Communications ➢ Phone Dialer. You'll see the dialog box shown in Figure 11.2.

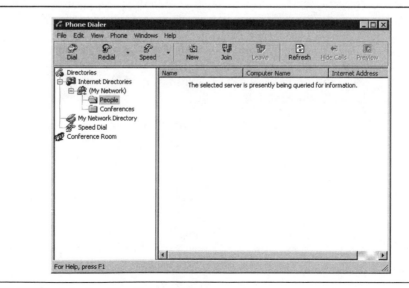

FIGURE 11.2: The Phone Dialer

Placing a Call

To place a simple phone call, follow these steps:

1. Open Phone Dialer, and click Dial to open the Dial dialog box.

2. Click the Phone Call option button, and enter the phone number in the text box.

3. Click Place Call.

That's really all there is to it. If you want to add the number to your speed dial list, click Add Number to Speed Dial List. To add a number to the list manually, choose Edit ➤ Add to Speed Dial List.

 NOTE   To receive a call, Phone Dialer must be running.

Connecting to an Internet directory or placing a video call involves a few more steps, and we'll go through those in the next sections.

Configuring Phone Dialer to Link to a Directory

An Internet directory is a listing of people and conferences that can receive Internet calls. The directory can be on your local server or on the Internet. Before you can connect to an Internet directory, you need to add the name of the server to the list on your system. To add a directory and connect to it, follow these steps:

1. In Phone Dialer, choose Edit ➤ Add Directory to open the Add Directory Server dialog box.

2. Enter the server name in the Directory Name box, and click Add.

3. The name now appears in the directories list, and you can click it to access the server.

Configuring Phone Dialer for Video Calls

To fully participate in a video call, you need speakers and a camera installed on your PC. If you do not have a camera, you can view and hear the other participant, but that person cannot see you. For each video call you want to make, follow these steps:

1. In Phone Dialer, choose Edit ➤ Options to open the Options dialog box.

2. Click the Audio/Video tab, select the line to use, and click the Video Playback check box.

3. Click OK.

TIP   You can also make conference calls using Phone Dialer, but conferencing is much more convenient with NetMeeting, which is described in Skill 9.

Connecting with HyperTerminal

HyperTerminal is a utility program you can use to connect to another computer, perhaps one that uses a different operating system such as Unix, or to an information service such as the book catalog at your local library, or to a bulletin board. You can use this type of connection to download or transfer files.

TIP   HyperTerminal is a class of program known as terminal emulation software. In other words, it pretends to be a terminal attached to the remote computer. HyperTerminal is not a Web browser and cannot access Web sites on the Internet. For that particular task, see the description of how to use Internet Explorer in Skill 12.

Creating a New HyperTerminal Connection

To create the phone numbers and specifics for initiating a HyperTerminal connection, follow these steps:

1. Choose Start ➤ Programs ➤ Accessories ➤ Communications ➤ HyperTerminal to open the Connection Description dialog box in the foreground and the HyperTerminal window in the background.

2. In the Name box, enter the descriptive name you want to assign to this connection, and then choose one of the icons from the selection displayed at the bottom of the dialog box. Click OK to open the Connect To dialog box.

3. Verify the country and area code, type the telephone number you want to use with this connection, and confirm your modem type. Click OK to open the Connect dialog box.

4. Check the phone number for this connection, and if it is incorrect, click Modify to change it. To look at or change any of the settings associated with the phone line or with dialing, click Dialing Properties.

5. When you are ready to make the connection, click Dial. You will be connected to the other computer, and a named window for the connection will open. If you do not want to dial now, click Cancel, and the named window for the connection will be displayed, as shown in Figure 11.3.

The next thing that you see in the window will depend on the service or computer you have connected to; you may be asked to select a terminal type, to enter a password, or to make a selection from a menu. When you are finished, use the appropriate command to log off the remote computer before you close the HyperTerminal window.

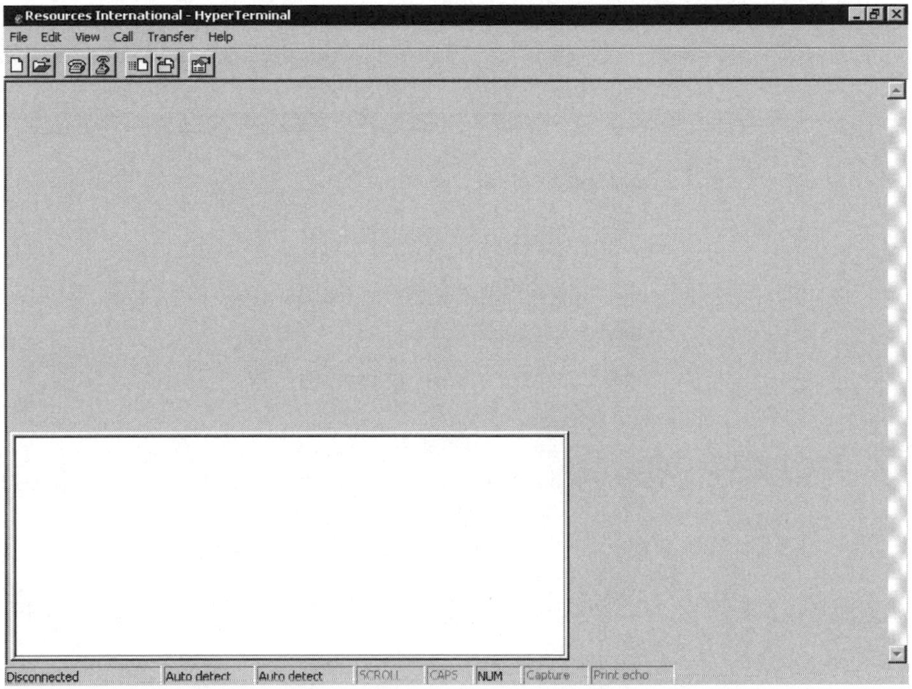

FIGURE 11.3: The main HyperTerminal window

Sending and Receiving Files

While using HyperTerminal, you can send and receive files and capture what you see on your screen to your printer. To send a file, follow these steps:

1. Choose Transfer ➢ Send File to open the Send File dialog box.

2. Enter the name of the file in the Filename box, or click Browse to locate it.

3. In the Protocol box, accept the protocol that HyperTerminal suggests, or click the down arrow to select another protocol from the list.

NOTE   If you know the specific protocol for the system to which you are connected, select that protocol. If you don't know the protocol, stick with Zmodem, which is a generic, commonly used protocol.

4.   Click Send.

To receive a file, follow these steps:

1.   Choose Transfer ➤ Receive File to open the Receive File dialog box.

2.   Indicate where the received file should be stored, and specify the protocol if necessary.

3.   Click Receive.

To capture what you see on your screen to the printer, choose Transfer ➤ Capture to Printer.

Using the Internet Connection Wizard

In times past, setting up a connection to the Internet used to be quite a complex operation, but that is no longer the case. The Internet Connection Wizard walks you through the steps of setting up your Internet connection. All you need is an account with an Internet Service Provider and your credit card number, and you're all set. You can start the Internet Connection Wizard in several ways:

- Click the Connect to the Internet icon on the Desktop. Once you set up your Internet connection, this icon will disappear from the Desktop.

- Choose Start ➤ Programs ➤ Accessories ➤ Communications, and then select Internet Connection Wizard.

- From the Windows 2000 Professional Help system, choose Using the Internet Connection Wizard topic.

- Choose Start ➤ Settings ➤ Control Panel ➤ Internet Options to open the Internet Properties dialog box, select the Connections tab, and click the Setup button.

- In Internet Explorer, choose Tools ➤ Internet Options to open the Internet Options dialog box, select the Connection tab, and click the Setup button.

No matter which method you use, the opening dialog box shown in Figure 11.4 gives you three choices:

I Want to Sign Up for a New Internet Account. (My Telephone Line Is Connected to My Modem.)   Select this option if you do not already have an account. The Wizard takes you through the steps of finding an ISP and starting an account and sets up the dial-up link for you.

I Want to Transfer My Existing Internet Account to This Computer. (My Telephone Line Is Connected to My Modem.)   Establishes a connection to an existing Internet account. Select this option to set up a connection to your existing Internet account or to revise the settings for your current account.

I Want to Set Up My Internet Connection Manually, or I Want to Connect through a Local Area Network (LAN).   Allows you to set up your account configuration manually.

Click Tutorial to learn more about the Internet, or click Cancel if you want to close the Internet Connection Wizard without setting up your account.

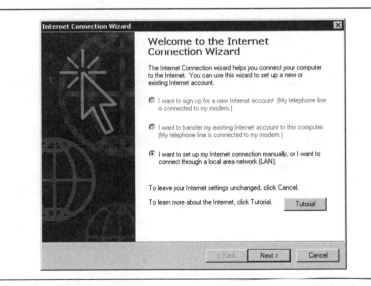

FIGURE 11.4: The Internet Connection Wizard opening dialog box

Creating a New Connection to the Internet

To create a new dial-up connection to the Internet, start the Internet Connection Wizard, and then follow these steps:

1. In the opening dialog box, choose the first option to select an ISP and set up a new Internet account, and then click Next.

2. The Wizard dials out on your modem, connects to the Microsoft Internet Referral Service, and downloads information on ISPs. Not all the ISPs available in your area will be listed here; most of those listed are actually nationwide services.

3. Select one of the ISPs, and click Next. The information shown in the next two dialog boxes depends on which of the ISPs you chose in the last step.

4. Enter your name, address, and phone number in the next dialog box. This information is used for billing purposes only and is only sent to the ISP you selected. Click Next.

5. Choose a billing option from those shown on the screen, and click Next.

6. Choose a method of payment, enter the details of your credit card, and click Next.

7. The Internet Connection Wizard connects to the ISP, selects a user ID and password, and completes the configuration of your Internet connection. Follow the prompts on the screen to complete your setup.

Setting Up Your Connection to the Internet Manually

You don't have to use the ISPs listed by the Microsoft Internet Referral Service. If you want to use an ISP whose name is not listed by the Internet Connection Wizard—perhaps a local ISP known for offering a particularly good service or an ISP recommended by a friend—choose the third option on the Internet Connection Wizard opening dialog box, and follow these steps:

1. Phone the ISP you have chosen, and ask for a dial-up account that will give you e-mail and Internet access; some ISPs also assign space on their systems so you can create a small Web site of your own. The ISP will send you details of the servers they operate, including the names of the mail and

news servers; you will need that information to complete the steps outlined below.

2. Start the Internet Connection Wizard, and in the opening dialog box, select the third option to set up a connection manually.

3. Choose the method you want to use to connect to the Internet. Most people will check the I Connect through a Phone Line and a Modem option. Click Next.

4. In the next dialog box, enter the phone number to dial to make the connection to your ISP.

5. In the next dialog box, enter your user name and password information. These will be provided by your ISP, and remember to enter them in the same case, either uppercase or lowercase, as specified by your ISP. Click Next.

6. Enter the name you want to use for this connection; choose something easy to remember. Click Next.

7. You'll then be asked if you want to set up an Internet e-mail account; click Yes and then Next to specify whether you want to use an existing account or create a new one. If you opt to continue using an existing account, you will be asked to confirm your e-mail account settings; if you establish a new account, you will have to enter this information from scratch. Click Next.

8. Finally, click the Finish button to complete the configuration, close the Wizard, and connect to the Internet.

Setting Internet Explorer Options

Now that we've configured a connection to an Internet Service Provider, we can take a look at how to configure Internet Explorer so that it works most efficiently; we'll cover the details of actually using Internet Explorer in Skill 12. In Windows 2000 Professional, you can view or change the configuration options relating to the Internet Explorer in two ways:

- Choose Internet Options in the Control Panel.

- Choose Tools ➢ Internet Options from within Internet Explorer.

If you open Internet Options in the Control Panel, the dialog box you see is called Internet Properties. If you open Internet Explorer and choose Tools ➤ Internet Options, this same dialog box is now called Internet Options. The tabs are the same, and the functions these tabs perform are the same; just the dialog box name is different.

We'll use Control Panel. Choose Start ➤ Settings ➤ Control Panel ➤ Internet Options, and you'll see the Internet Properties dialog box open on your screen. This dialog box has six tabs, and in the next few sections, we'll review the most important configuration choices you can make on each of these tabs. We'll start with the General tab.

Configuring the General Tab

The Internet Properties dialog box General tab shown in Figure 11.5 contains these groups of settings:

Home Page   Lets you choose which Web page opens each time you connect to the Internet. A home page is the first Web page you see when you start Internet Explorer. Click Use Current to make the current page your home page (if you are online to the Internet), click Use Default to return to the default setting, and click Use Blank to start each Internet session with a blank screen. To use a different Web page as your home page, type the URL in the Address box.

Temporary Internet Files   Lets you manage those Web pages that are stored on your hard disk for fast offline access. If these files are occupying too much hard-disk space, click the Delete Files button to remove them. To control how these files are stored on your hard disk, click Settings to open the Settings dialog box. Click the option that applies to when you want Internet Explorer to check for newer versions of these stored Web pages. You can use the slider to specify how much hard-disk space is given over to these temporary Internet files. Click Move Folder if you want to use a different folder to hold your temporary Internet files; you must remember to restart your computer after making this change so that the new folder is used in place of the default. Click View Files to open an Explorer window listing all the Web and graphics files in the folder, or click View Objects to open an Explorer window listing all the other Web-related files such as ActiveX controls and Java-related files.

History   Contains a list of the links you have visited so that you can return to them quickly and easily using the History button on the Internet Explorer toolbar. You can specify the number of days you want to keep pages in the History folder; if you are running low on hard-disk space, consider reducing this number. To delete all the information currently in the History folder, click the Clear History button.

Colors   Lets you choose which colors are used as background, links, and text on those Web pages for which the original author did not specify colors. By default, the Use Windows Colors option is selected.

> **TIP**   You can always change the Windows colors. In Control Panel, click Display, and then select the Appearance tab.

Fonts   Lets you specify the font style and text size to use on those Web pages for which the original author did not make a specification.

Languages   Lets you choose the character set to use on those Web pages that offer content in more than one language. English is rapidly becoming the most common language in use on the Internet, so you may not use this option often.

Accessibility   Lets you choose how certain information is displayed in Internet Explorer, including font styles, colors, and text size. You can also specify that your own style sheet is used.

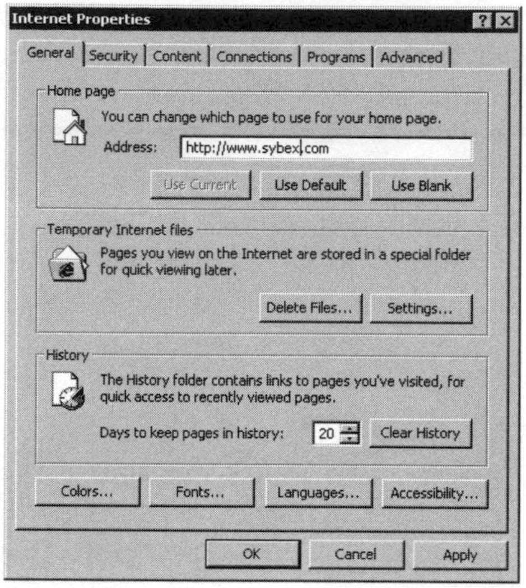

FIGURE 11.5: The General tab in the Internet Properties dialog box

Looking at the Security Tab

The Security tab shown in Figure 11.6 lets you specify the overall security level for each of four zones. Each zone has its own default security restrictions that tell Internet Explorer how to manage dynamic Web page content such as ActiveX controls and Java applets. The zones are:

Internet Sites you visit that are not in one of the other categories; default security is set to Medium.

Local Intranet Sites you can access on your corporate intranet; default security is set to Medium-Low.

Trusted Sites Web sites you have a high degree of confidence will not send you potentially damaging content; default security is set to Low.

Restricted Sites Sites that you visit but do not trust; default security is set to High.

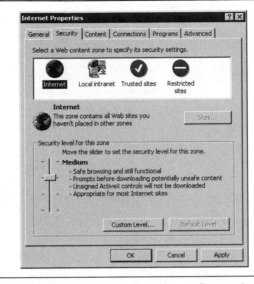

FIGURE 11.6: The Security tab in the Internet Properties dialog box

To change the current security level of a zone, just move the slider to the new security level you want to use:

High   Excludes any content capable of damaging your system. Cookies are disabled, and so some Web sites will not work as you might expect. This is the most secure setting.

Medium   Opens a warning dialog box in Internet Explorer before running ActiveX or Java applets on your system. This is a moderately secure setting that is good for everyday use.

Medium-Low   Same as Medium but without the prompts.

Low   Does not issue any warning but runs the ActiveX or Java applet automatically. This is the least secure setting.

Click the Custom Level button to create your own settings in the Security Settings dialog box, which is shown in Figure 11.7. You can individually configure how you want to manage certain categories, such as ActiveX controls and plug-ins, Java applets, scripting, file and font downloads, and user authentication.

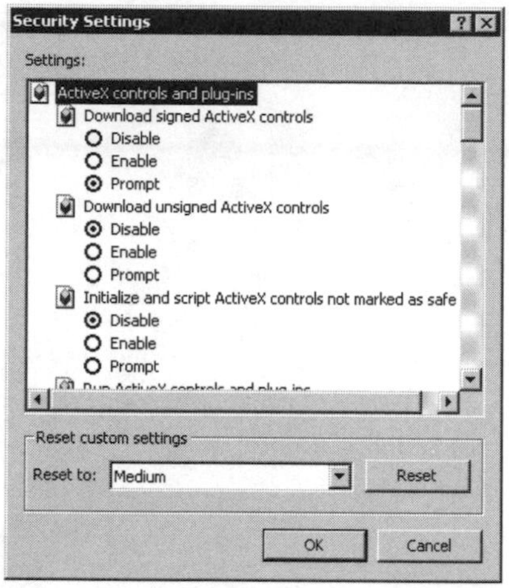

FIGURE 11.7: The Security Settings dialog box

Using the Content Tab

The Content tab, which is shown in Figure 11.8, contains settings you can use to restrict access to sites and specify how you want to manage digital certificates:

Content Adviser   Lets you control access to certain sites on the Internet and is particularly useful if children have access to the computer. Click Settings to establish a password, and then click OK to open the Content Advisor dialog box. Use the tabs in this dialog box to establish the level of content you will allow users to view:

Ratings   Lets you use a set of ratings developed by the Recreational Software Advisory Council (RSAC) for language, nudity, sex, and violence. Select one of these categories, and then adjust the slider to specify the level of content you will allow.

Approved Sites   Lets you create lists of sites that are always viewable or always restricted regardless of how they are rated.

General   Specifies whether people using this computer can view material that has not been rated; users may see some objectionable material if the Web site has not used the RSAC rating system. You can also opt to have the Supervisor enter a password so that users can view Web pages that may contain objectionable material. You can click the Change Password button to change the Supervisor password; remember that you have to know the current Supervisor password before you can change it.

Advanced   Lets you look at or modify the list of organizations providing ratings services.

Certificates   Lets you manage digital certificates used with certain client authentication servers. Click Certificates to view the personal digital certificates installed on this system, or click Publishers to designate a particular software publisher as a trustworthy publisher. This means that Windows 2000 Professional applications can download, install, and use software from these agencies without asking for your permission first.

Personal Information   Lets you look at or change the settings for Windows AutoComplete and your own personal profile. Click AutoComplete to change the way that this feature works within Windows 2000 Professional, or click My Profile to review the information sent to any Web sites that request information about you when you visit their site.

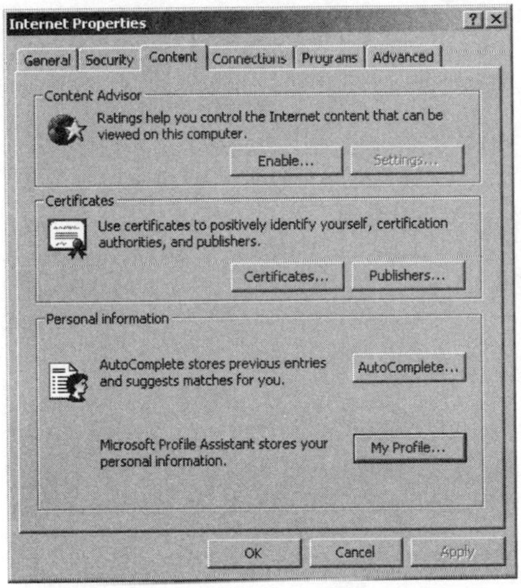

FIGURE 11.8: The Content tab in the Internet Properties dialog box

Setting up the Connections Tab

The Connections tab, which is shown in Figure 11.9, allows you to specify how your system connects to the Internet. Click the Setup button to run the Internet Connection Wizard and set up a connection to an Internet Service Provider. (See the Internet Connection Wizard section earlier in this skill for complete details.) If you use a modem, click the Settings button to open the My Connection Settings dialog box, where you can specify all aspects of the phone connection to your ISP.

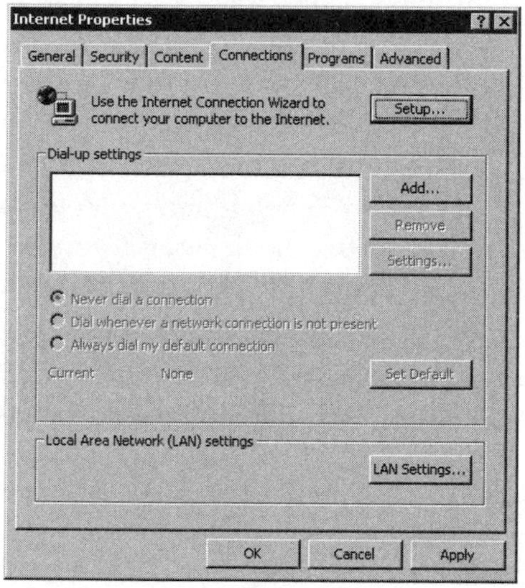

FIGURE 11.9: The Connections tab in the Internet Properties dialog box

Looking at the Programs Tab

The Programs tab, which is shown in Figure 11.10, lets you set your default program choices for HTML editor, e-mail, newsgroup reader, Internet call, calendar, and contact list.

Finally, you can specify that Internet Explorer check to see if it is configured as the default browser on your system each time it starts running.

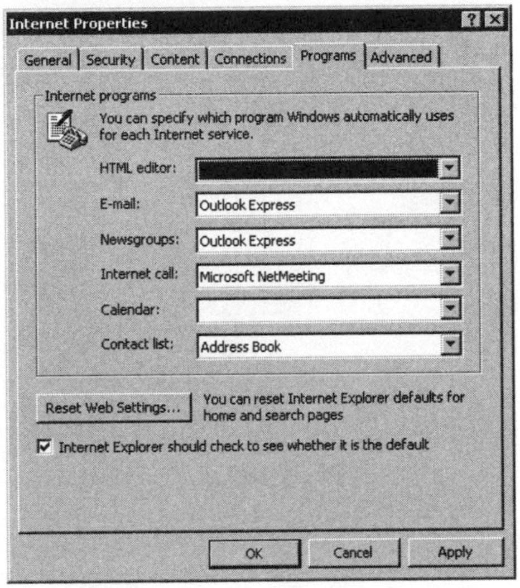

FIGURE 11.10: The Programs tab in the Internet Properties dialog box

Configuring the Advanced Tab

The Advanced tab, which is shown in Figure 11.11, lets you look at or change a number of settings that control much of Internet Explorer's behavior, including accessibility, browsing, multimedia, security, the Java environment, printing and searching, the Internet Explorer toolbar, and how HTTP 1.1 settings are interpreted. Click a check box to turn an option on; clear the check box to turn the option off.

Changes you make here stay in effect until you change them again, until you download an automatic configuration file, or until you click the Restore Defaults button, which returns the settings on the Advanced tab to their original values.

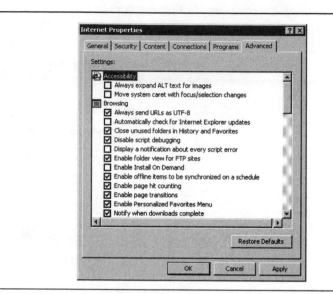

FIGURE 11.11: The Advanced tab in the Internet Properties dialog box

Are You Up to Speed?

Now you can...

- ☑ set up Phone and Modem Options
- ☑ use the Phone Dialer
- ☑ connect with HyperTerminal
- ☑ use the Internet Connection Wizard
- ☑ connect to the Internet
- ☑ set Internet Explorer options

SKILL 12

Web Browsing with Internet Explorer

- Starting Internet Explorer
- Touring Internet Explorer
- Moving around the Web
- Finding exactly what you want on the Internet
- Customizing Internet Explorer

Obviously, the most important thing about Internet Explorer is not the program itself but all the resources you can access using it. And, to be completely honest about it, Internet Explorer is so easy to use that you hardly need a how-to book, a manual, or even this skill. If you know how to open any Windows 2000 Professional program, you know how to open Internet Explorer, and you can start browsing immediately by simply clicking links.

Thus, in this skill we're going to move briskly through the tasks you most commonly perform with Internet Explorer. As we proceed, we'll point out some new features of version 5 and show you how to expand on what comes naturally. For example, you probably know that you can access an Internet resource by typing its URL in the Address bar. That's rather easy in the case of something such as `www.microsoft.com`, but what about `http://finance.yahoo.com/q?s=msft+ brka+csco+ald+mmm+sci+lhsp+yhoo&d-v1`? In this skill, you'll see that in Internet Explorer you have at least a half-dozen ways to access a lengthy URL such as this without ever typing it.

The good news is that as the cost of personal computers continues to drop, browsers such as Internet Explorer become easier to use and more powerful. The only bad news is that most of us usually don't have enough hours in the day even to skim the surface of the abundance of the Internet. You can, however, use the skills you acquire here to streamline your activities and make more efficient use of your time.

Starting Internet Explorer

Unless you've been hiding in a cave and forgot to take along your cell phone, TV, or laptop, you've heard about the integration of Windows and Internet Explorer. Nowhere is this more apparent than in the myriad ways in which you can start Internet Explorer.

When you first start Internet Explorer after installing Windows 2000 Professional, you'll see the start page shown in Figure 12.1. Later in this skill, you'll see how to specify any page you want as your start page. In the next section, we'll identify and discuss the components of the Internet Explorer interface.

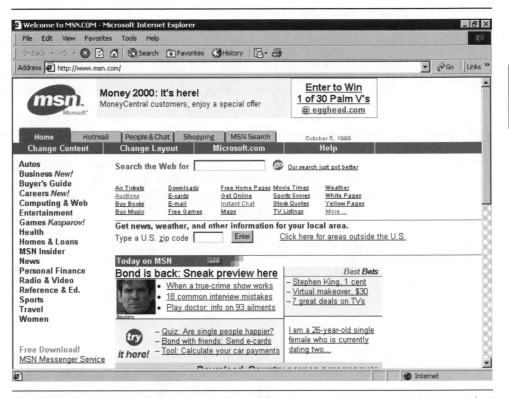

FIGURE 12.1: You can retain the page at www.msn.com as your start page or select any other page that suits your fancy or interests.

From the Desktop

From the Desktop, you can start Internet Explorer in three ways:

- Click the Launch Internet Explorer Browser button on the Quick Launch toolbar.

- Double-click the Internet Explorer shortcut.

- Choose Start ➤ Programs ➤ Internet Explorer.

From a Hyperlink

You can also start Internet Explorer from any document in any Windows application that includes a hyperlink if Internet Explorer is your default browser. For example, if you receive an e-mail that includes a URL in the body of the message, simply click the URL to open Internet Explorer at that page. A hyperlink can be text or an image, and it is usually underlined and in a color that is different from normal text.

> **NOTE** If you have only one browser, Internet Explorer, installed, it is your default browser. If you have more than one browser installed, you'll need to specify one as the default. For information on how to do this, see Skill 11.

From Windows Explorer

In Windows Explorer, HTML files are indicated by the Internet Explorer icon, and when you click such a file, it opens in Internet Explorer.

You can also open any file on your hard drive, a floppy, or your network by choosing File ➢ Open. If it is not an HTML file, it will open in its associated program.

A LOOK BEHIND THE SCENES: VIEWING HTML PAGES

HTML is the abbreviation for HyperText Markup Language, the programming language that is used to create Web pages. HTML uses tags to tell the browser how to display the page on the screen. Tags are enclosed in angle brackets, and most come in pairs. For example, the <H1> tag defines a first-level heading, like this:

```
<H1>This is a level 1 heading.</H1>
```

An HTML file is really just a plain text file that can be created with a text editor such as Notepad or with a program such as Microsoft FrontPage. To view the HTML behind any page you open in Internet Explorer, choose View ➢ Source. The file is displayed in Notepad and looks similar to the following example.

continued ▶

```
www.sybex[1] - Notepad                                                    _ | 8 | X |
File  Edit  Format  Help
<HTML>
<HEAD>
          <TITLE>Welcome to Sybex, Inc. - Quality Computer Books</TITLE>
          <META NAME="keywords" CONTENT="Sybex, Sybex Inc., Sybex
computer book publisher, computer books, books, book, publishers,
computer, computers, computing, how-to books, how to books, reference
books, certification, MCSE, MCSD, MOUS, CCNA, CCNP, Cisco
certification, Novell certification, CompTIA certification, study
guides, test success, exam notes, computer games, video games, game
books, programming, internet, database, web design, network,
networking, mastering, network press, strategies & secrets, strategies
and secrets, ultimate strategy guide, developer's handbook, expert
guide, complete, no experience required, office 2000, windows,
Pokemon, 24seven">
<META NAME="Description" CONTENT="Sybex Inc. is an independent
publisher of quality computer books that has been publishing books for
over 20 years in the United States and Europe.">
<META NAME="copyright" CONTENT="&copy; 1999 Sybex Inc.">
</HEAD>
<BODY BGCOLOR="#FFFFFF" BACKGROUND="/images/bg.gif" TOPMARGIN=8
LEFTMARGIN=8 LINK=#003399 ALINK=#CCCC00 VLINK=#660000>
<!--Top Banner-->
<TABLE CELLSPACING=0 CELLPADDING=0 BORDER=0 WIDTH=590>
<TR>
          <TD ALIGN=CENTER VALIGN=TOP WIDTH=85>
          <A NAME="top"><IMG SRC="/images/top_banner/logo.gif" WIDTH=59
HEIGHT=59 BORDER=0 ALT="Sybex, Inc." ALIGN=TOP></A>
          </TD>
          <TD ALIGN=LEFT VALIGN=TOP WIDTH=505 COLSPAN=2>
          <IMG SRC="/images/top_banner/header_sybex.gif" WIDTH=457
HEIGHT=34 BORDER=0 ALT="Sybex, Inc. - Quality Computer Books"
ALIGN=TOP><BR><IMG SRC="/images/top_banner/top_curve.gif" WIDTH=16
HEIGHT=20 BORDER=0 ALT="curve" ALIGN=TOP><A
HREF="/catalog/index.shtml"><IMG
```

To return to Internet Explorer and the page displayed in the browser, click the Close button in Notepad.

If you're interested in learning more about HTML and creating Web pages, check out the following Sybex titles: *Mastering FrontPage 98* (or *Mastering FrontPage 2000*), and *Mastering HTML 4, Second Edition*.

Getting Help

You have at your fingertips several ways to get help with Internet Explorer. For starters, choose Help ➤ Contents and Index. As in Windows Help, enter a word or phrase to search for a topic. If you want to search the Web for help, click the Web Help button, and then click Support Online in the right pane. If you're connected to the Internet, you'll go to the Microsoft Product Support Services page at www.microsoft.com/support/.

If you're new to Internet Explorer, choose Help ➤ Tour. Click any hyperlink to get information about that topic. If you're new to Internet Explorer but have used Netscape Navigator, choose Help ➤ For Netscape Users to access a list of tips and corresponding terminology.

A Quick Tour of Internet Explorer

The Internet Explorer window has much in common with other Windows application windows: vertical and horizontal scrollbars display as necessary, you can size various portions of the window by clicking and dragging, and you can display a ToolTip by placing the mouse cursor over an item. In the upper-right corner are the Minimize, Restore, and Close buttons.

In this section, we'll look briefly at the components of the Internet Explorer window, and in later sections we'll look at some specific components that you can use to enrich and supplement your browsing experience. Figure 12.2 is your components roadmap.

Here is a general description of each component:

Title bar   Displays the name of the current Web page or other file that is displayed in the Internet Explorer window.

Menu bar   Contains a set of menus, some of which contain the same items that appear on that menu in other Windows programs.

Standard toolbar   Contains several buttons that correspond to items on the Menu bar, as well as navigation buttons such as Back, Forward, and Home.

Address bar   Contains a drop-down box in which you can enter or select the resource you want to access.

Links bar   Contains a short list of preselected hyperlinks. You can add to this list.

Activity Indicator   Is animated when Internet Explorer is sending or receiving data.

Main window   Displays the resource—Web page, document file, image, and so on—that you most recently accessed.

Status bar   Displays information about the current state of Internet Explorer.

- When you choose a menu command, the status bar displays a description of what it does.

- When you point to a hyperlink, the status bar displays its URL.

- When you click a hyperlink to open another page, the status bar displays a series of messages related to the progress of that process.

Security zone   Displays the security zone currently active. For information about Internet Security and selecting security zones, see Skill 11.

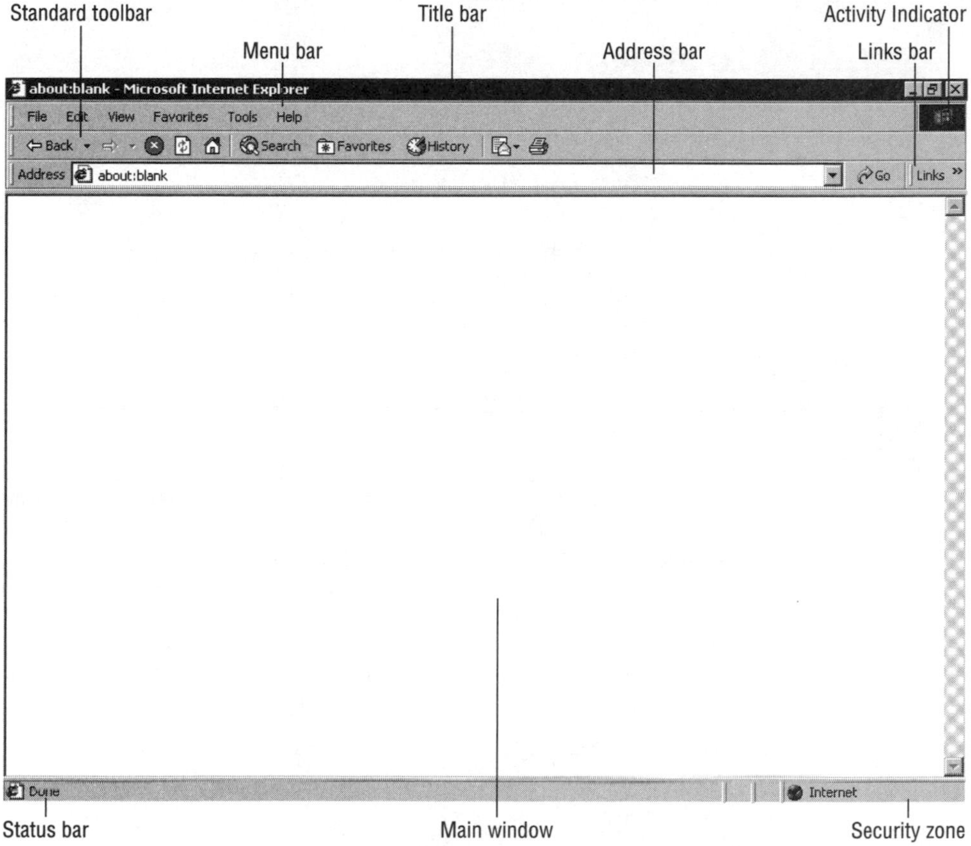

FIGURE 12.2: Many Internet Explorer window components are similar to those in other Windows applications.

Moving around the Web

To even begin to describe what you'll find on the Web these days is an exercise in futility. What was suspect a year ago is commonplace today, and what appears today to be well in the future may be up and running tomorrow. You can buy and sell almost any commodity, search the world's vast storehouse of information, play Blackjack, chat with somebody on another continent, witness the birth of a baby, locate a lost relative, book a cruise, scout new business opportunities—the list is indeed endless. And, as the saying goes, one thing leads to another.

The items on the Internet Explorer toolbars are your best friends in this quest, and in this section we'll take a look at their typical and not-necessarily-so-typical uses.

Going to Specific Sites

You know, of course, that you can enter a URL in the Address bar and press Enter to go to that site. You are probably also aware that you can click the down arrow at the right of the Address bar, select a URL from the list, and press Enter. (You can click Go instead of pressing Enter if you want.) And you may have noticed that on occasion when you start to type an address, it sort of finishes itself for you. That's the AutoComplete feature at work. If the address is the one you want, simply press Enter and you're on your way to that page. If you wanted another site, just continue typing.

> **TIP** AutoComplete also comes to your aid in just about any other field you fill in on a Web page—stock quotes, search queries, passwords, and so on. You can often click a drop-down list and make a selection. This information is encrypted and stored on your computer and is not accessible to Web sites, so you needn't be concerned about security when you use AutoComplete.

Internet Explorer assumes that when you enter a URL in the Address bar you want to go to a Web page or some other HTML document. Therefore, whether you enter `http://www.sybex.com` or `www.sybex.com`, you'll reach the Sybex Web site. If you want to access another type of resource, such as an FTP archive, a Telnet host, or a Gopher server, you'll need to enter the full URL, for example, `ftp://ftp.archive.edu`.

> **TIP** If you want to edit only part of an address that's already displayed in the Address bar, place the cursor in the Address bar, hold down Ctrl, and press the right or left arrow to jump forward or backward to the next separator character (\\\ . , ? or +).

You can also run a program from the Address bar. Simply type its path (for example, `C:\Program Files\FrontPage Express.exe`), and press Enter. To find a file using the Address bar, enter the drive letter (for example, **D:**), and press Enter. Internet Explorer opens a window similar to that shown in Figure 12.3.

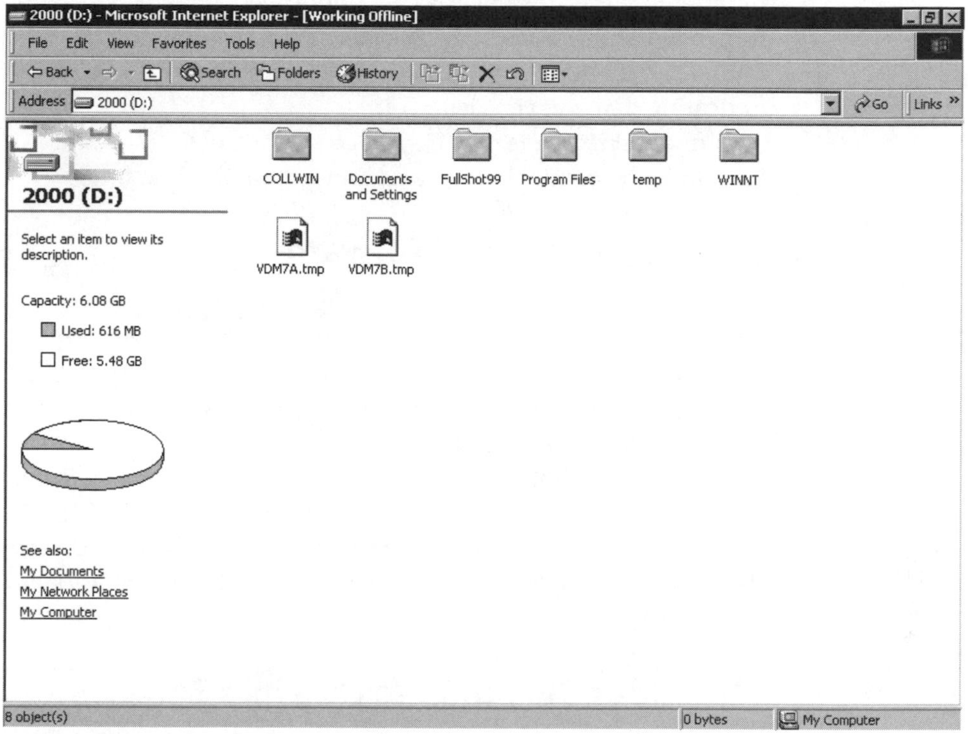

FIGURE 12.3: Finding a file with Internet Explorer

In addition, you can search from the Address bar. Enter the word or phrase you want to find, and click the Search button. We'll look at searching in detail later in this skill in the section "Finding Exactly What You Want on the Internet."

Using and Managing Links

The term *link* is short for hyperlink, which is a term, a phrase, an image, or a symbol that forms a connection with another resource that can reside on your local computer, your local network, or the Internet. You may also hear these connections referred to as hot links, hypertext links, or hypermedia. They all mean the same thing, and clicking one takes you to that resource. Links are the heart and soul of the Internet, and in the incipient days of browser development gave rise to ponderous discussions about the linear structure of books, film, and speech vs. the nonlinear format of the World Wide Web.

Today, we seldom discuss links; we just take them for granted and click. In Internet Explorer, textual links are underlined and are usually in a different color from normal text. After you click such a link to jump to that resource and then return to the page on which the link resides, the link will be in yet another color, indicating that you've "visited" it.

To find out if an image or a symbol is a link, place the mouse pointer over it. If it's a link, the pointer becomes a hand with a pointing finger.

Moving Backward and Forward

In the past, you could easily get lost following links. You still can lose your way when you're just mindlessly surfing the Net, but Internet Explorer provides several tools that can help you retrace your steps, starting with the drop-down list in the Address bar, as we discussed in the previous section. Perhaps even handier are the Back and Forward buttons.

Click the Back button to return to the page you just visited. Click the down arrow next to the Back button to select from the last four pages you visited.

Click the Forward button to return to the page you visited before you clicked the Back button. Click the down arrow next to the Forward button to select from the last few pages you visited.

Adding Your Own Links to the Links Bar

Another way to keep track of links that you follow and want to revisit is to add them to the Links bar. When you first install Windows 2000 Professional, the Links bar contains the following:

- Customize Links, which takes you to a Microsoft page that gives you information on how to add, remove, and rearrange items on the Links bar

- Free Hotmail, which takes you to a page where you can sign up for a Hotmail e-mail account

- Windows, which takes you to the Microsoft Windows site

To add a link, simply drag it from the Web page to the Links bar. To remove a link, right-click it, and choose Delete from the shortcut menu. To rearrange items on the Links bar, click the item, and then drag it to a new location.

Another quick and easy way to keep track of pages you want to revisit is to add them to your Favorites list, and we'll look at how to do that in the following section.

Keeping Track of Your Favorite Sites

As we've mentioned, Internet Explorer provides several devices you can use to prevent getting lost in cyberspace, and a particularly handy one is the Favorites bar. To open it, click the Favorites button on the Standard toolbar, or choose Favorites from the Menu bar. Figure 12.4 shows the screen you'll see if you click the Favorites button, and Figure 12.5 shows the Favorites menu.

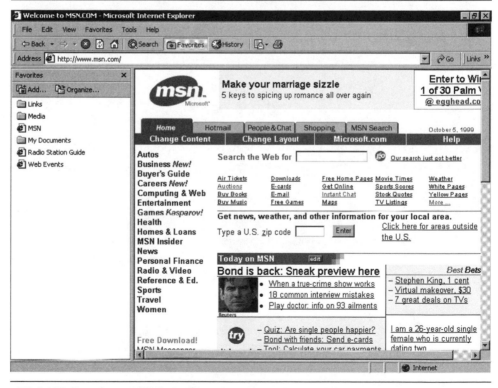

FIGURE 12.4: Click the Favorites button to open the Favorites bar.

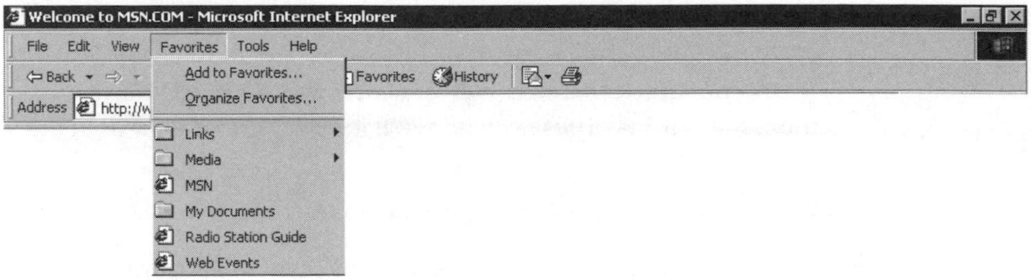

FIGURE 12.5: Choose the Favorites menu to see this drop-down list.

Adding a Site to Your Favorites List

Clicking a Favorites item takes you to that resource. Initially you'll see the following items on the Favorites menu or in the Favorites bar:

- Links, which opens the same list that you see on the Links bar

- Media, which contains links that take you to a variety of sites such as Disney, ESPN Sports, MSNBC, and the Windows Media Showcase, a page where you can search for online audio and video

- MSN, which takes you to the msn.com home page

- My Documents, which takes you to your My Documents folder.

- Radio Station Guide, which takes you to a page where you can click a button to hear a radio webcast from stations such as the BBC and CNN

- Web Events, which takes you to the WindowsMedia.com page, where you can access audio and video headlines, check the weather forecast and your horoscope, get stock quotes, and so on

NOTE   On some Web pages, you will see a suggestion that you "bookmark" this page. Netscape and some other Web browsers refer to a list of sites that you want to revisit as a bookmark list rather than as a Favorites list.

To add a site to your Favorites list, follow these steps:

1. Go to the site you want to add.

2. Click Favorites to open the Favorites bar.

3. Click Add to open the Add Favorite dialog box:

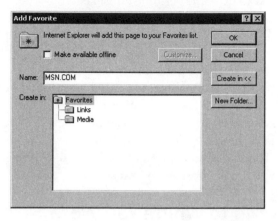

4. If you want to place this page in your top-level Favorites menu, click OK. If you want to add it to an existing folder, click Create In, select a folder, and click OK. If you want to create a new folder for this item, click New Folder, enter a name for the folder, and click OK.

5. In the Add Favorite dialog box, Internet Explorer provides a name for this Favorite site. To give the site another name in your Favorites list, replace the default name with the name you want.

6. Click OK.

You can also add items to your Favorites list in some other ways:

- Right-click a link, and choose Add to Favorites from the shortcut menu.

- Right-click the current page outside a link, and choose Add to Favorites from the shortcut menu to add that page.

- Drag and drop a link on a Web page to the Favorites button on the Standard toolbar.

Maintaining Your Favorites List

You'll find out soon enough that your Favorites list will grow quickly, and before too long the titles that seemed patently clear when you added the site to the list will, unfortunately, be meaningless. In addition, you may no longer really care what's happening on the Learn2.com site. To keep your list manageable, you need to do some periodic housekeeping, weeding out what you don't want and rearranging or retitling what you do keep so that it is meaningful.

Deleting a site from your Favorites list is simple: right-click it in the list, and choose Delete from the shortcut menu. You might, however, want to get in the habit of following the link before you right-click—just in case the site is more important than you remembered and you want to keep it in the list.

To move an item to another place in the list or to another folder, simply click and drag it. To create a new folder, click Organize to open the Organize Favorites dialog box, and click Create Folder.

To rename an item, right-click it and choose Rename from the shortcut menu. Type the new name, and press Enter.

Returning to Where You Were

Yet another way to keep track of where you've been and to quickly revisit sites of interest is the History list. To display it, click the History button on the Standard toolbar. You'll open the History bar, which will look similar to that in Figure 12.6. Simply click a link to go to that page. Click a folder to see pages in that site that have links in the History list. To specify how many days you want to keep links in the History list, choose Tools ≻ Internet Options, and on the General tab change the number in the Days to Keep Pages in History box.

You can display the items in the History list by date, by site, by most visited, and by the order in which you visited sites today. Click the View down arrow to choose an order. If you want to search for something on the history list, click Search, enter a word or a phrase, and click Search Now.

To delete an item from the History list, right-click it, and choose Delete from the shortcut menu. To clear the History list completely, click the Clear History button on the General tab of the Internet Options dialog box.

TIP   If you want really quick access to a Web site, create a shortcut to it on the Desktop. Right-click in an empty area of the page, and choose Create Shortcut. You'll see a message that the shortcut will be placed on your Desktop. Now all you need to do to open Internet Explorer and connect to that page is to double-click the shortcut.

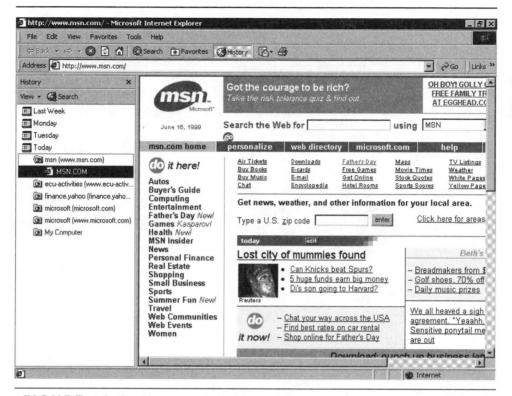

FIGURE 12.6: You can use the History bar to see where you went today and in previous days and weeks.

Reading Mail and News and Sharing Pages

If you hear the You've Got Mail beep as you're exploring the Internet, you can quickly open your Inbox in Outlook Express by clicking the Mail button on the Standard toolbar and choosing Read Mail. To check a newsgroup, click the Mail button, and choose Read News. To compose an e-mail message, click the Mail button, and choose New Message to open the New Message window.

To send a link, follow these steps:

1. Open the page.

2. Click the Mail button, and choose Send a Link. The New Message window opens with the link in the body of the message and the site title in the Subject and Attach lines.

3. Address your message, compose your message, and click Send.

If your recipient is connected to the Internet and has a Web browser, he or she merely needs to click the link in the message to open that page.

To send the page itself, follow these same steps but choose Send Page. The current page you are viewing appears in the body of the message, as you can see in Figure 12.7.

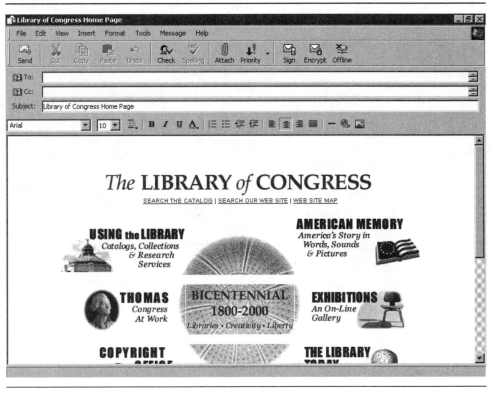

FIGURE 12.7: Sending a Web page in the body of an e-mail message

Before you willy-nilly include Web pages in your e-mail, be sure that your recipient's e-mail program can handle HTML messages. For more information about e-mail and HTML, see Skill 13.

Tuning in a Webcast

If you've used previous versions of Internet Explorer, you'll find something new on the menu when you choose View ➤ Toolbars—the Radio toolbar, which is shown in Figure 12.8. Windows Radio is a feature that gives you direct access to radio stations throughout the United States and around the world through the Internet.

Skill 12

Radio toolbar

FIGURE 12.8: To tune in to music or news of your choice, use the Radio toolbar.

To select a station, click the Radio Stations button, and choose Radio Station Guide to open the WindowsMedia.com site. Click a button to listen to a webcast. The station's home page loads while the station is being found. To adjust the volume, move the slider on the Volume Control. To turn the radio off, click the Stop button on the Radio toolbar.

The quality of your listening experience will depend on your speakers, your system, and the speed at which you are connected. An Internet access speed of at least 56Kbps is recommended.

Saving and Printing Web Pages

If you always want to see the most current version of a Web page, you probably want to place a link to it on the Links bar or the Favorites bar. However, in some cases, you'll want to save it to your local hard drive or to a drive on your network. For example, we recently wanted easy access to a rather long U.S. government document. In this case, the document had been written and distributed over the Internet and was not going to change. It was what it was, so we saved it to our local network so that we could get to it quickly without being connected to the Internet.

Saving the Current Page

In Internet Explorer, you can save the current page in several formats:

- As a complete Web page, including all graphics, frames, and style sheets

- As a snapshot, which includes all the information needed to display the page (if you have Outlook Express 5 or later)

- As text in HTML format

- As plain text in ASCII format

To save the current page, follow these steps:

1. Choose File ➤ Save As to open the Save Web Page dialog box:

2. Select a folder in which to save the page, and in the File Name box enter a name if you want something different from that which Internet Explorer proposes.

3. In the Save As Type drop-down box, select the format in which you want the page saved. Your choices are:

    - Web Page, complete (*.htm,*.html)
    - Web Archive, single file (*.mht)
    - Web Page, HTML only (*.htm,*.html)
    - Text File (*.txt)

4. Click Save.

You can also save a Web page without opening it if its link is displayed. Follow these steps:

1. Right-click the link, and choose Save Target As from the shortcut menu. You'll see a dialog box that shows you that the page is being downloaded.

2. In the Save As dialog box, select a folder, and specify a filename.

3. Click Save.

> **NOTE** When you save a target, the only file type available is Microsoft HTML Document 5.0. If you want one of the other file types, you'll need to open the page and follow the steps for saving information on the current page.

Saving Portions of a Page

You can also save only a portion of text from a Web page or an image. To save a portion of text to use in another document, select the text, and then press Ctrl+C. Open the other document, place the insertion point where you want the text, and press Ctrl+V.

To save an image, follow these steps:

1. Right-click the image, and choose Save Picture As from the shortcut menu to open the Save Picture dialog box.

2. Select a folder, a filename, and a type, and click Save.

To save an image as wallpaper, right-click the image and choose Set As Wallpaper from the shortcut menu. To specify how you want the wallpaper displayed, right-click the image on the Desktop, choose Properties to open the Display Properties dialog box, and select an option in the Picture Display drop-down box.

Printing the Current Page

If you want to quickly print the current page, simply click the Print button on the Standard toolbar. If, however, you want more control over what's printed and how, choose File ➤ Print to open the Print dialog box, as shown in Figure 12.9.

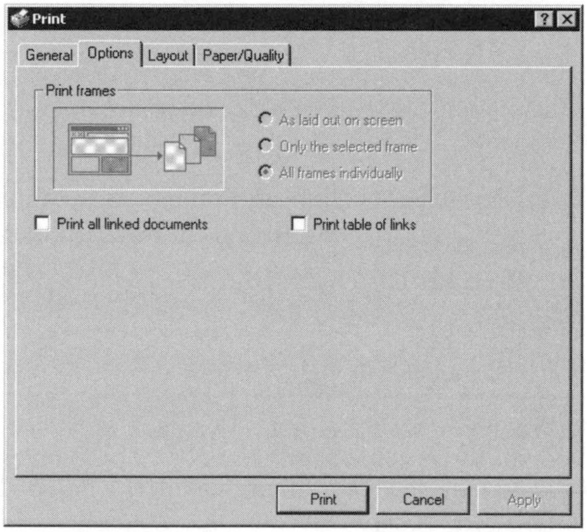

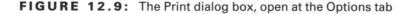

FIGURE 12.9: The Print dialog box, open at the Options tab

For the most part, this is your standard Windows Print dialog box. (For details about printers and printing in Windows 2000 Professional, see Skill 8.) The difference is the Options tab, which you can use to specify how frames and links are printed and is shown in Figure 12.9. Here are the specifics:

- Select the As Laid Out on Screen option in the Print Frames section to print the Web page exactly as it is displayed on your screen.

- Select the Only the Selected Frame option to print only a frame you have previously selected. (To select a frame, click inside it in an empty space—in other words, not on a link.)

- Select the All Frames Individually option if you want to print each frame on a separate sheet of paper.

- Select the Print All Linked Documents option if you want to print the pages that are linked to the current page as well. (Be sure you really want to do this; you could need lots of paper.)

- Select the Print Table of Links option if you want to print a table that lists the links for the page at the end of the document.

When you have all your options selected, click the Print button on any tab to print the document.

To print the target of any link, right-click the link, and choose Print Target from the shortcut menu to open the Print dialog box.

TIP   By default, Windows does not print the background colors and background images of Web pages. First, the printed output could be illegible, and, second, unless you have a rather powerful printer, spooling and printing could be really slow. If, for whatever reason, you want or need to print the background, choose Tools ➢ Internet Options to open the Internet Options dialog box. Click the Advanced tab, scroll down to the Printing section, check the Print Background Colors and Images check box, and click OK.

Working Offline

As we mentioned earlier in this skill, if you want to view Web pages when you aren't connected to the Internet, and their currentness is not important, you can simply save them to your local hard drive. If their currentness is important, you can choose to "work offline."

To make the current page available for offline viewing, follow these steps:

1. Right-click in an empty spot on the page, and choose Add to Favorites to open the Add Favorite dialog box.

2. Click the Make Available Offline check box.

3. If you want to view only certain content offline, click the Customize button to start the Offline Favorite Wizard. Follow the onscreen instructions. You can also establish a schedule for updating the page using this Wizard. Click Finish when you're done.

4. Before you close your connection to the Internet, choose Tools ➤ Synchro-
    nize to ensure that you have the most up-to-date content for the page you
    want to view offline.

To view pages offline, choose File ➤ Work Offline, and in the Favorites bar
select the page you want.

> **TIP** In the previous version of Internet Explorer, offline viewing was called
> "subscribing."

Finding Exactly What You Want on the Internet

The serendipitous experience of clicking and following hyperlinks may suffice
while you're polishing off your lunch of tuna sandwich and chips or filling the
occasional lazy, rainy afternoon, but most of the time when you connect to the
Internet, you have something specific in mind that you want to do or find.
Regardless of what you're looking for—information about a topic, an e-mail or a
mailing address, a business, a Web page, and so on—the way to find it is to use a
search service. *Search service* is a relatively new term for what we referred to in the
past as a search engine, a program that can search a file, a database, or the Internet for keywords and retrieve documents in which those keywords are found.

Examples of search services that you may have used include Yahoo!, Excite,
InfoSeek, AltaVista, and Lycos. To search with one of these services, you go to the
site (for example, `http://www.yahoo.com`); optionally, select a category, enter a
keyword or phrase, and click Search (or some similar button). Although these
search services are very efficient, you are accessing only one of them at a time.

In Internet Explorer 5, you can use the Search Assistant to search several services simultaneously. Let's do a simple search to see how this works.

Performing a Simple Search

If you've read any of the pre-release publicity about Microsoft Office 2000 or the
Windows family of operating systems, you may have seen that all these programs

contain support for the euro symbol (€). You may also have been wondering why this is important. Let's search the Internet for the answer. Follow these steps:

1. In Internet Explorer, click the Search button on the Standard toolbar to open the Search bar:

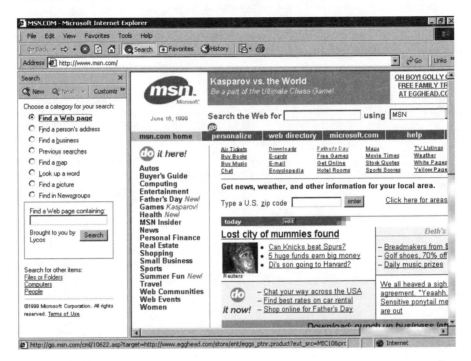

TIP If you don't see all the categories shown here, click More.

2. In the Find a Web Page Containing box, type **euro symbol.**

3. Click Search.

Skill 12

4. Scroll down the Search bar, and you'll see something similar to the following:

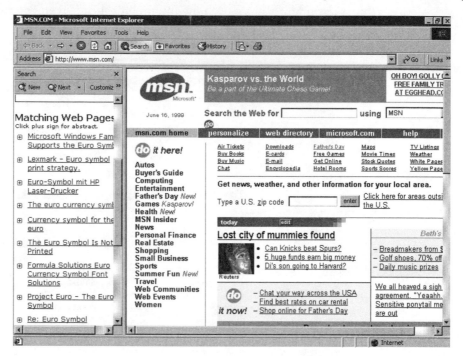

5. Click the Euro Currency Symbol link, and you'll see the page shown in Figure 12.10 in the pane on the right.

If you peruse this page, you'll find out that the euro symbol is the name of the single currency of the European Union. It was officially designated on January 1, 1999, and will be in common use in the form of coins and bills by 2002. In Windows programs, the symbol is available in the Times New Roman, Arial, and Courier New fonts.

TIP If you want to find Web pages similar to the current page, choose Tools ➤ Show Related Links. A list of links is displayed in the Search bar.

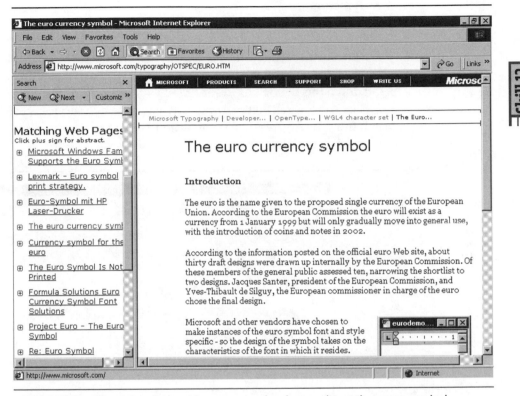

FIGURE 12.10: Everything you need to know about the euro symbol

Power Searching

In the Search bar, you can specify to search for any of the following by selecting that option:

- A Web page
- A person's address
- A business
- Previous searches
- A map
- A word

- A picture

- A word or phrase in a newsgroup

You can further refine your searches in the Customize Search Settings dialog box (click the Customize button in the Search bar), which is shown in Figure 12.11. Scroll down this dialog box to survey all your options. At the bottom of this dialog box, click Autosearch Settings to specify which search service is used when you search from the Address bar. If you want to return to the default set of search options, click the Reset button.

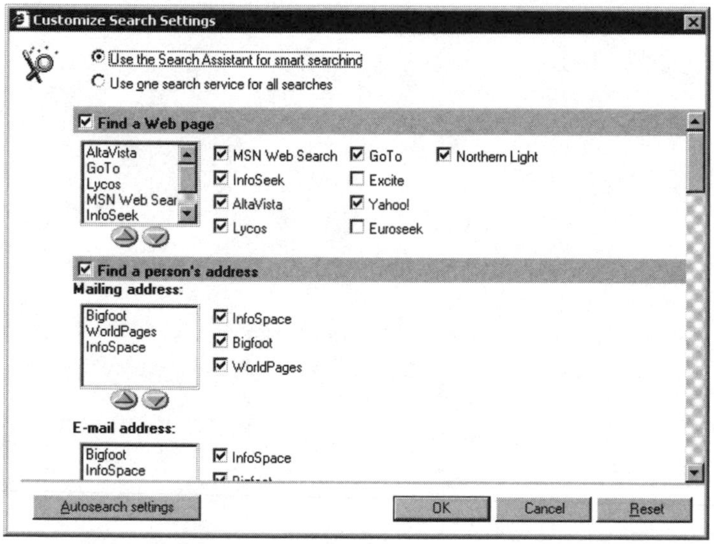

FIGURE 12.11: Refine your searches in the Customize Search Settings dialog box.

Customizing Internet Explorer

You can personalize the way you connect to the Internet and the features of Internet Explorer in myriad ways, and to do most of this you use the Internet Options dialog box, which we looked at in detail in Skill 11. Here we want to touch briefly on a couple of these options again and also look at how you can customize toolbars.

Choosing a Start Page

As we mentioned at the beginning of this skill, when you first install Windows 2000 Professional, your start page is set as www.msn.com. Until you change this setting, this is the page that will open every time you start Internet Explorer. To establish a start page of your choosing, follow these steps:

1.   Open the page you want to use as your start page.

2.   Choose Tools ➢ Internet Options to open the Internet Options dialog box.

3.   If necessary, click the General tab.

4.   In the Home Page section, click the Use Current button.

5.   Click OK.

Changing the Appearance of the Toolbars

To display or hide a toolbar, choose View ➢ Toolbars, and then select a toolbar from the submenu. To add or remove buttons from the Standard toolbar, follow these steps:

1.   Right-click the toolbar, and choose Customize from the shortcut menu to open the Customize Toolbar dialog box:

2.   To add a button, select it from the pane on the left, and click Add.

3.   To delete a button, select it from the pane on the right, and click Remove.

4.   To specify whether or where to display button labels, click the Text Options down arrow and select from the list.

5.   To specify the icon size, click the Icon Options down arrow.

6. To rearrange the order of the buttons, select a button in the pane on the right, and click Move Up or Move Down.

7. When the toolbar is to your liking, click Close.

TIP   To return to the default arrangement of the toolbar, click the Reset button in the Customize Toolbar dialog box.

To move the menu bar or a toolbar up or down, place the cursor over the left vertical bar of the bar you want to move, and drag it to a new position.

Dealing with Cookies and Temporary Internet Files

A cookie is a file that is stored on your computer by the server of a site that you visit. When you revisit the site, Internet Explorer sends the cookie back to the server, perhaps to identify you so that the server can present to you a customized Web page. A cookie is a simple data file that cannot "look" at your hard disk or send any other information back to the server or run other programs on your computer.

A temporary Internet file is a copy of a Web page that you have visited. Both cookies and temporary Internet files are stored in the Temporary Internet Files folder on your computer. To take a look at what's in this folder, follow these steps:

1. In Internet Explorer, choose Tools ➤ Internet Options to open the Internet Options dialog box.

2. If necessary, click the General tab, and then in the Temporary Internet Files section, click the Settings button to open the Settings dialog box.

3. Click the View Files button to open the Temporary Internet Files folder, as shown in Figure 12.12.

4. To take a look at all the information stored for each file, select a file or move the horizontal scroll bar to the right.

When you access a Web page, Internet Explorer first checks to see if the page is in your Temporary Internet Files folder. If it is, it checks to see if the page has been updated since being stored, and if not, it loads the page from the Temporary Internet Files folder (also called the *cache*). This is obviously faster than downloading the page from the server.

If you want to save space on your local disk, however, you can empty the Temporary Internet Files folder, either manually or whenever you exit Internet Explorer. To empty the folder manually, in the General tab of the Internet Options dialog box, click Delete Files. To empty the folder automatically when you close Internet Explorer, follow these steps:

Skill 12

1. In the Internet Options dialog box, click the Advanced tab.

2. Scroll down to the Security section.

3. Click the Empty Temporary Internet Files Folder When Browser Is Closed check box.

4. Click OK.

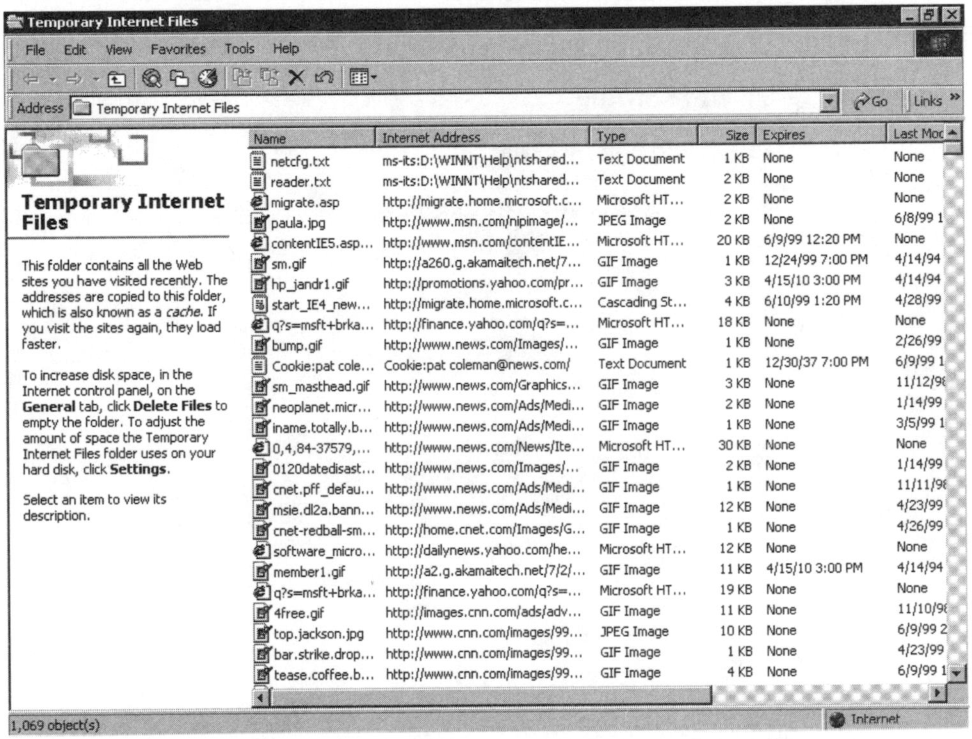

FIGURE 12.12: Cookies and temporary Internet files are stored in the Temporary Internet Files folder.

Are You Up to Speed?

Now you can...

- ☑ start Internet Explorer in a variety of ways
- ☑ use the Address bar to go to specific sites and to search
- ☑ manage links
- ☑ track your favorite sites
- ☑ send links and pages via e-mail
- ☑ tune in a webcast
- ☑ save and print Web pages
- ☑ work offline
- ☑ search the Internet
- ☑ personalize Internet Explorer

SKILL 13

Using Outlook Express for E-mail and News

- **Starting Outlook Express**
- **Touring Outlook Express**
- **Using Outlook Express to read, compose, and send e-mail**
- **Using Outlook Express to read news and post to newsgroups**
- **Customizing Outlook Express**

Of all the features of the Internet, intranets, and local area networks, e-mail is, without question, the most used. Instead of playing phone tag with a colleague at work, you send her e-mail. Millions of extended families stay in touch via e-mail, and an e-mail address has become an expected component of a business card.

Outlook Express is an Internet standards e-mail reader you can use to access an Internet e-mail account. An Internet e-mail account is not the same thing as an account with an online information service. The difference is that an Internet account provides services such as Point-to-Point protocol Internet access and e-mail but does not include services such as chat rooms, access to databases, conferences, and so on. Consequently, you cannot use Outlook Express to access an e-mail account with MS Mail, cc:Mail, CompuServe, America Online, or versions of Microsoft Exchange Server prior to version 5.

TIP   You can use Outlook Express to set up and access a free Hotmail account. To set up a Hotmail account, choose Tools ➤ New Account Signup ➤ Hotmail, and follow the onscreen instructions.

In addition to being an e-mail reader, Outlook Express is also a news reader. In the first part of this skill, we'll look at e-mail features, and in the second part we'll look at how to access and post to newsgroups.

Using Outlook Express As Your Mailreader

The quickest way to start Outlook Express is to click the Launch Outlook Express icon on the Quick Launch taskbar. You can also start it by choosing Start ➤ Programs ➤ Outlook Express or, from within Internet Explorer, by choosing Tools ➤ Mail and News and then selecting an item from the submenu.

NOTE   Before you can open and use Outlook Express to send and receive e-mail, you need to configure Outlook Express to use your Internet connection. You'll find information on how to do this in Skill 11.

A Quick Tour

When you first open Outlook Express, you'll see a screen similar to that shown in Figure 13.1.

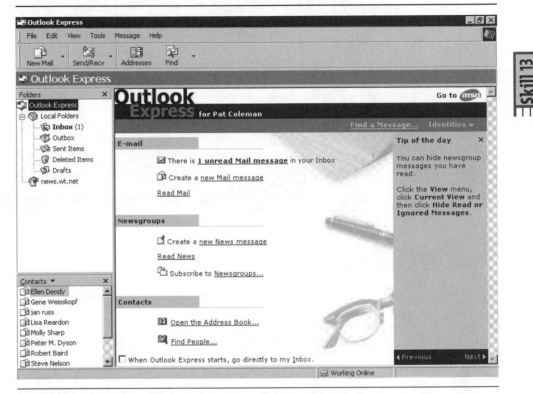

FIGURE 13.1: The opening screen in Outlook Express

To read your mail, click Read Mail, or click Inbox in the Folders list. As you can see in Figure 13.2, initially the Preview Pane is split horizontally; header information is displayed in the upper pane, and the message is displayed in the lower pane.

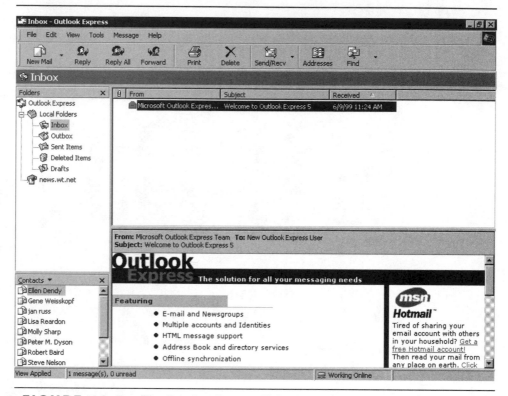

FIGURE 13.2: The Preview Pane, split horizontally

> **TIP**
>
> To change the arrangement of the Preview Pane, choose View ➢ Layout to open the Window Layout Properties dialog box, and select options to show or hide certain parts.

The Folders List

The Folders List is a tool for organizing messages. Initially, it contains the following folders, although you can create additional folders, as you'll see later in this skill:

- Inbox contains both newly received messages and messages that you have not yet disposed of in some way.

- Outbox contains messages that are ready to be sent.

- Sent Items contains copies of messages that you have sent (a handy device if you send lots of e-mail).

- Deleted Items contains copies of messages that you have deleted.

- Drafts contains messages that you are working on but which are not yet ready to be sent.

The Contacts Pane

The Contacts pane contains the names of people in your Address Book (for information on Address Book, see Skill 9). To compose a message to anyone on this list, simply double-click the name.

Retrieving Your Mail

If you are connected to your Internet account, Outlook Express will automatically check the server for new messages and download them when you open Outlook Express. By default, Outlook Express will also check for new mail every 30 minutes, as long as you are connected. To adjust this time interval, follow these steps:

1. Choose Tools ➤ Options to open the Options dialog box:

2. Click the up or down arrow to change the Check for New Message Every *x* Minutes option.

3. Click OK.

You can also check for new mail by choosing Tools ➤ Send and Receive ➤ Receive All or by clicking the Send/Recv button on the toolbar in the main window.

Reading and Processing Messages

If you are working in the split Preview Pane view, simply click a message header to display the message in the lower pane. Otherwise, simply double-click a header to view the message.

Printing Messages

For various reasons, it's often handy to have a paper copy of e-mail messages. You can print in a couple of ways:

- To print a message without opening it, select its header, and click the Print icon on the toolbar in the main window.

- To print an open message, click the Print icon on the toolbar in the message window.

Marking Messages

If you're like us, you don't always handle each message as you receive it or immediately after you read it, and it's easy to forget that you need to take some action or follow up on a message unless it stands out from the others in the header list. One trick that we use is to mark a message as unread even though we have read it (select the header and choose Edit ➤ Mark As Unread). You can also select the header and choose Message ➤ Flag Message to display a red flag to the left of the message header.

In addition, you can mark an individual message as read, and you can mark all messages as read.

Moving Messages

You can easily move a message from one folder to another by dragging and dropping it. For example, if you receive a message that you want to modify and send to some else, select the message header and then drag it to the Drafts folder. Open it, revise it, and then send it on its way.

Saving Messages

You can save messages in folders you create in Windows Explorer, and you can save messages in Outlook Express folders. You can also save attachments as files.

Saving Messages in Windows Explorer Folders   To save messages in a folder in Windows Explorer, follow these steps:

1. Open the message, or select its header.

2. Choose File ➢ Save As to open the Save Message As dialog box:

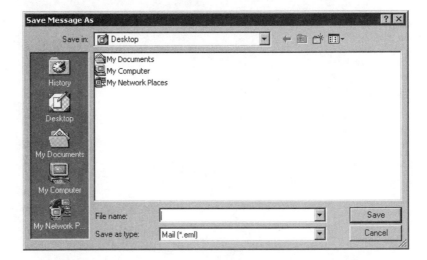

3. Select a folder in which to save the message. Outlook Express places the subject line in the File Name box. You can use this name or type another name.

4. Select a file type, and then click Save.

NOTE   In Windows Explorer, when you click a file that has the .EML extension, it opens in Outlook Express. If you save a message as an HTML file, it opens in Internet Explorer.

Saving Messages in Outlook Express Mail Folders As we've mentioned, you can create your own Outlook Express folders. For example, you might want to create folders for people with whom you regularly correspond, or you might want to create folders for current projects. To create a new folder, follow these steps:

1. Choose File ➢ New ➢ Folder to open the Create Folder dialog box:

2. In the Folder Name box, type a name for your folder.

3. Select a folder in which to place the new folder, and click OK.

You now have a new folder in your Folders List, and you can drag any message to it. You have, however, an even easier and more efficient way to save messages in Outlook Express folders, and we'll look at that in the "Apply Message Rules" section later in this skill.

Saving Attachments An attachment is a file that is appended to an e-mail message. You'll know that a message has an attachment if the header is preceded by the paper clip icon. When you open the message, you'll see the filename of the attachment in the Attach line in the header. To open an attachment, double-click its filename.

To save an attachment, follow these steps:

1. Open the message, and choose File ➢ Save Attachments to open the Save Attachments dialog box.

Save Attachments   ? ✕

Attachments To Be Saved:

ch03_art.zip (391 KB)	Save
	Cancel
	Select All

Save To

D:\Documents and Settings\Pat Coleman\Desktop   Browse...

2.   Select a folder in which to save the file, and click Save.

We'll discuss how to attach a file to a message later in this skill in the "Attaching Files to Your Messages" section.

Replying to Messages

To reply to a message, click the Reply button on the toolbar in the message window. If the message is addressed to multiple recipients and you want to reply to all of them, click the Reply All button.

 TIP   This is a quick and easy way to note the person's e-mail address. By default, Outlook Express automatically places the names of the people you reply to in your Address Book. For more on Address Book, see Skill 9.

By default, Outlook Express includes the text of the original message in your reply. According to Internet tradition, this squanders bandwidth, and it's better not to include the original message unless it's really necessary. When is it necessary?

- When you want to be sure that the recipient understands the nature of your reply and the topic to which it is related

- When your message is part of a series of messages that involve some sort of question-and-answer sequence

- When it's important to keep track of who said what when

An alternative is to include only the relevant portions of the original message in your reply. To do so, follow these steps:

1. Open the message, and click the Reply button.

2. The message is now addressed to the original sender, and the original subject line is preceded by Re:.

3. In the body of the message, edit the contents so that the portions you want are retained, and then enter your response.

4. Click the Send button.

If you don't want to include the original message in your reply, you can simply open the message, click the Reply button, choose Edit ➢ Select All, and press Delete. If you're rather sure that you almost always don't want to include the original message, choose Tools ➢ Options, and in the Options dialog box, click the Send tab. Clear the Include Message in Reply check box.

Forwarding Messages

Forwarding an e-mail message is much easier than forwarding a letter through the U.S. mail, and it actually works. To forward a message, follow these steps:

1. Open the message.

2. Click the Forward button on the toolbar in the message window.

3. Enter an address in the To field.

4. Add your own comments if you want.

5. Click Send.

Deleting Messages

To delete a message, you can select its header and click Delete, or you can open it and then click Delete. The message is not yet really deleted, however; Outlook Express has placed it in the Deleted Items folder. By default, the Deleted Items folder is emptied when you close Outlook Express.

If you want to delete items from the Deleted Items folder yourself, follow these steps:

1. Select the Deleted Items folder.

2. Choose Edit ➤ Empty 'Deleted Items' Folder.

3. When Outlook Express asks if you are sure you want to delete these items, click Yes.

Creating and Sending Messages

In this section, we'll walk through the steps to create and send a simple message. You can, however, create messages in HTML (HyperText Markup Language) and include hyperlinks, pictures, colorful formatting, sounds, and so on. We'll look at that in the next section.

To begin a new message, you can click the New Mail button in the main window to open the New Message window, as shown in Figure 13.3. If the intended recipient is in your Address Book, you can double-click that person's name in the Contacts pane to open the New Message window; the To line will display the recipient's name.

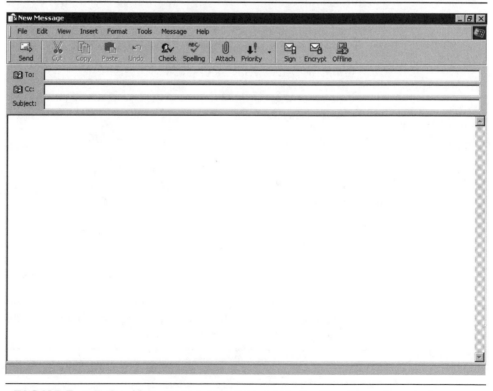

FIGURE 13.3: You create a new message in the New Message window.

If your New Message window includes a Formatting toolbar, the message you compose will be formatted as HTML. For our purposes here, we want only plain text. So, if necessary, choose Format ➢ Plain Text before you begin composing your message. Now, follow these steps:

1. If necessary, enter the address of the primary recipient in the To field. If you are sending a message to multiple primary recipients, separate their addresses with semicolons.

2. Optionally, enter e-mail addresses in the Cc (carbon copy) and Bcc (blind carbon copy) fields. To enter a Bcc recipient, click the Cc icon, enter the name in the Select Recipients dialog box, and click Bcc.

3. Enter a subject line for your message.

NOTE If you don't enter a subject line, Outlook Express will ask if you're sure you don't want a subject line. Unless you have a good reason not to do so, enter some text in the subject line. Your recipient will see this text in the header information for the message and will then have a clue as to the nature of your message.

4. Enter the text of your message.

5. If appropriate, establish a priority for your message. Choose Message ➢ Set Priority, and then choose High, Normal, or Low. The default is Normal.

6. Click Send to start your message on its way.

You can send your message immediately by clicking the Send button, or you can save it in your Outbox to send later by choosing File ➢ Send Later. The message will be sent when you choose Send and Receive All or when you choose Send All.

TIP You can use Copy and Paste in Outlook Express, just as you use those commands in other Windows programs. For example, to include a portion of a Word document in a message, open the document, select the text, and copy it to the Clipboard. In Outlook Express, open the New Message window, place the insertion point where you want to paste the text, and press Ctrl+V. Use this same process to copy portions of e-mail messages to other messages or to documents in other applications.

Creating E-mail Messages with HTML

In the previous section, we created a plain text message, but, as we mentioned, you can also compose messages in HTML and include all sorts of neat effects. Before you send a formatted message, be sure that your recipient's e-mail program can display it effectively. When you open the New Message window and choose Format ➤ Rich Text (HTML), the message you compose is essentially a Web page. Newer e-mail programs such as Netscape Messenger and the commercial version of Eudora, Eudora Pro, can read, compose, and send HTML messages, but many others cannot, including America Online and the freeware version of Eudora. An easy way to find out if your recipient's e-mail program can handle HTML is to send a simple plain text message and ask.

That said, let's look at some bells and whistles you can include in Outlook Express e-mail messages. Click the New Mail icon to open the New Message window, and be sure that the Rich Text (HTML) option is selected. You'll see the screen shown in Figure 13.4. Notice the Formatting toolbar, which contains many of the same tools you see and use in your Windows word processor. You'll also see the Font and Font Size drop-down list boxes that are present in your word processor.

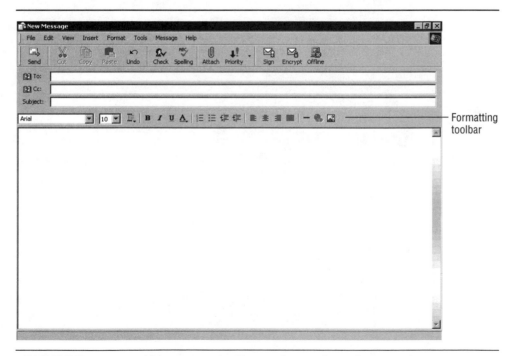

Formatting toolbar

FIGURE 13.4: You can use the Formatting toolbar when creating a message in HTML.

As you create your message, just pretend that you're using a word processor and use the Formatting tools to apply emphasis to your message. All the usual design rules apply, including the following:

- Don't use a lot of different fonts.

- Remember, typing in all capital letters in e-mail is tantamount to shouting.

- Don't place a lot of text in italics. It's hard to read on the screen.

- Save boldface for what's really important.

To insert a horizontal line that spans the message window, choose Insert ➤ Horizontal Line.

To apply HTML styles such as Definition Term or Definition, click the Paragraph Style button on the Formatting toolbar.

Using Stationery

In addition to formatting, you have another way to add some class or some comedy to your e-mail messages: stationery. In the New Message window, choose Message ➤ New Using, and then choose a predesigned format from the list in the submenu, or click Select Stationery to open the Select Stationery dialog box and select from a larger list. Here's one example of what you'll find:

continued ▶

To customize stationery, click Create New in the Select Stationery dialog box to start the Stationery Setup Wizard. Follow the onscreen instructions.

Adding Pictures to Messages

You can insert a picture in a message in two ways:

- As a piece of art
- As a background over which you can type text

To insert a picture as a piece of art that you can size and move, follow these steps:

1. In the New Message window, choose Insert ➤ Picture to open the Picture dialog box.

2. Enter the filename of the picture in the Picture Source text box, or click the Browse button to locate it.

3. Optionally, in the Alternate Text box, enter some text that will display if the recipient's e-mail program cannot display the picture, and specify layout and spacing options if you want. (You can also size and move the picture with the mouse once you place it in the message.)

4. Click OK.

To insert a picture as background, follow these steps:

1. In the New Message window, choose Format ➤ Background ➤ Picture to open the Background Picture dialog box.

2. Enter the filename of the picture, or click Browse to select a predesigned stationery background or locate another file.

3. Click Open, and then click OK to insert the background.

Adding a Background Color or Sound to Messages

To apply a color to the background of your message, choose Format ➤ Background ➤ Color, and select a color from the drop-down list. Now type something. Can you see it on the screen? If not, you have probably chosen a dark background and your font is also a dark color—most likely black if you haven't changed it from the default.

Skill 13

To make your text visible, click the Font Color button, and select a lighter color from the drop-down list.

To add a background sound, follow these steps:

1. In the New Message window, choose Format ➢ Background ➢ Sound to open the Background Sound dialog box.

2. Enter the filename of the sound, or click Browse to locate a sound file.

3. Specify the number of times you want the sound to play or whether you want it to play continuously. (In our opinion, a sound that plays continuously while the recipient is reading the message is far more likely to annoy than to entertain.)

4. Click OK.

Including Hyperlinks in Messages

When you insert a hyperlink in a message, the recipient can go directly to the resource simply by clicking the hyperlink. You can insert a hyperlink in three ways:

- Simply type it in the message body. Be sure to include the entire URL.

- In the New Message window, choose Insert ➢ Hyperlink to open the Hyperlink dialog box, and then enter the URL in the text box.

- In Internet Explorer, choose Tools ➢ Mail and News ➢ Send a Link to open the New Message window. The URL of the current page is automatically inserted in the message body.

Adding a Signature to Messages

We know people who never sign their e-mail messages. After all, their name is in the From line in the message header. We also know people who append elaborate signatures, touting their accomplishments or advertising their businesses. We usually just sign our first name at the bottom of messages, but what you do depends on your personal style or whether you're sending business or personal correspondence.

To create a signature that's automatically added to all your outgoing messages, follow these steps:

1. Choose Tools ➢ Options to open the Options dialog box.

2. Click the Signatures tab.

3. Click New.

4. To create a text signature, enter the content in the box next to the Text option button.

5. If you want to use a file you've already created as your signature, click the File option button, and enter the filename, or click Browse to locate it.

6. If you have multiple e-mail accounts, click the Advanced button to open the Advanced Signature Settings dialog box, and specify which accounts should use this signature.

7. Click the Add Signatures to All Outgoing Messages check box, and click OK.

If you don't want the signature automatically appended to all outgoing messages, leave the Add Signatures to All Outgoing Messages check box unselected. Then, to add this signature to a message, choose Insert ➢ Signature in the New Message window.

Attaching Files to Messages

In Outlook Express, sending a file or multiple files along with your message is painless and simple. Follow these steps:

1. In the New Message window, choose Insert ➤ File Attachment to open the Insert Attachment dialog box:

2. Select a file, and click Attach.

Your message now contains the name of the file in the Attach line.

TIP   If the file is large or if you know that the recipient has a slow connection, you'll want to compress it using a program such as WinZIP. For a list of Web pages from which you can download or purchase such a program, in Internet Explorer search on *compression utilities.* See Skill 12 for information on searching in Internet Explorer.

Applying Message Rules

Using the Rules Editor, you can specify where messages go after they are down-loaded, block unwanted messages, and, in general, manage incoming messages more efficiently—especially if you deal with a lot of e-mail. In this section, we'll give you a couple of examples that illustrate the possibilities, but, as you will see, there are lots of possibilities, and you'll need to apply the options that make the most sense for your situation.

Let's start by establishing a rule that sends all mail from a particular person to that person's Outlook Express folder. Follow these steps:

1. In the main Outlook Express window, choose Tools ➤ Message Rules ➤ Mail to open the New Mail Rule dialog box:

```
┌────────────────────────────────────────────────────────────────┐
│ New Mail Rule                                          ? X       │
├────────────────────────────────────────────────────────────────┤
│ Select your Conditions and Actions first, then specify the       │
│ values in the Description.                                        │
│                                                                  │
│ 1. Select the Conditions for your rule:                          │
│ ┌──────────────────────────────────────────────────────┐ ▲     │
│ │ ☐ Where the From line contains people                 │ ▒     │
│ │ ☐ Where the Subject line contains specific words      │ ▒     │
│ │ ☐ Where the message body contains specific words      │ ▒     │
│ │ ☐ Where the To line contains people                   │ ▼     │
│ └──────────────────────────────────────────────────────┘       │
│ 2. Select the Actions for your rule:                             │
│ ┌──────────────────────────────────────────────────────┐ ▲     │
│ │ ☐ Move it to the specified folder                     │ ▒     │
│ │ ☐ Copy it to the specified folder                     │ ▒     │
│ │ ☐ Delete it                                           │ ▒     │
│ │ ☐ Forward it to people                                │ ▼     │
│ └──────────────────────────────────────────────────────┘       │
│ 3. Rule Description (click on an underlined value to edit it):   │
│ ┌──────────────────────────────────────────────────────┐       │
│ │ Apply this rule after the message arrives             │       │
│ │                                                        │       │
│ │                                                        │       │
│ │                                                        │       │
│ └──────────────────────────────────────────────────────┘       │
│ 4. Name of the rule:                                             │
│ ┌──────────────────────────────────────────────────────┐       │
│ │ New Mail Rule #1                                       │       │
│ └──────────────────────────────────────────────────────┘       │
│                                         ┌──────┐ ┌──────┐        │
│                                         │  OK  │ │Cancel│        │
│                                         └──────┘ └──────┘        │
└────────────────────────────────────────────────────────────────┘
```

2. In the Select the Conditions for Your Rule section, click the Where the From Line Contains People check box.

3. In the Select the Actions for Your Rule section, click the Move It to the Specified Folder check box.

4. In the Rule Description section, click contains people to open the Select People dialog box:

```
┌─────────────────────────────────────────────────────┐
│ Select People                                    X    │
├─────────────────────────────────────────────────────┤
│ Type one name at a time and click Add, or select      │
│ people from the Address Book.                         │
│ ┌─────────────────────────────────┐  ┌──────────┐    │
│ │                                  │  │   Add    │    │
│ └─────────────────────────────────┘  └──────────┘    │
│ People:                                               │
│ ┌─────────────────────────────────┐  ┌────────────┐  │
│ │ Where the From line contains     │  │Address Book│  │
│ │                                  │  └────────────┘  │
│ │                                  │  ┌──────────┐    │
│ │                                  │  │  Remove  │    │
│ │                                  │  └──────────┘    │
│ │                                  │  ┌──────────┐    │
│ │                                  │  │ Options  │    │
│ └─────────────────────────────────┘  └──────────┘    │
│                           ┌──────┐ ┌──────┐           │
│                           │  OK  │ │Cancel│           │
│                           └──────┘ └──────┘           │
└─────────────────────────────────────────────────────┘
```

5. Enter a name, or select a name from your Address Book, and click OK.

6. Click specified to open the Move dialog box.

7. Select the folder where you want this person's messages to go, and click OK. If you need to create a folder, click New Folder.

8. Accept the name of the rule that Outlook Express proposes, or type a new name.

9. Click OK.

Now, when messages arrive from that person, you'll find them in his or her folder rather than in your Inbox.

TIP To delete a rule, select it, and click Remove in the Message Rules dialog box. To modify a rule, select it, and click Modify.

To establish a rule that blocks unwanted messages, follow these steps:

1. In the main Outlook Express window, choose Tools ➢ Message Rules ➢ Blocked Senders List to open the Message Rules dialog box at the Blocked Senders tab.

2. Click Add to open the Add Sender dialog box:

3. Enter the e-mail address that you want to block, specify whether you want to block mail, news, or both from this person, and click OK.

4. Click OK again in the Message Rules dialog box.

Mail from that address will now go immediately to the Deleted Items folder. News from that person will simply not be displayed. (More on news in the last part of this skill.) To change or delete this rule, open the Message Rules box, select the address, and click Modify or Remove.

Adding and Managing Identities

If several people use the same computer either at home, at the office, or elsewhere and thus also use Outlook Express, you'll probably want to take advantage of the Identities feature, which lets each person view his or her own mail and have individualized settings and contacts. Once you set up Identities, you can switch between them without shutting down the computer or disconnecting from and reconnecting to the Internet.

NOTE You can also set up Identities in Address Book by choosing Start ➤ Programs ➤ Accessories ➤ Address Book.

When you install Windows 2000 Professional, you are set up in Outlook Express as the Main Identity. To set up other identities in Outlook Express, follow these steps:

1. In the main Outlook Express window, choose File ➤ Identities ➤ Add New Identity to open the New Identity dialog box:

2. Enter the name of the identity you want to establish. If you want to establish identities for the members of your family, for example, you could simply enter a person's first name.

3. If you want to password protect this identify, click the Require a Password check box. Enter the password twice—once in the New Password box and again in the Confirm New Password box. Click OK twice.

4. Outlook Express asks if you want to switch to this new identity now. If you do, click Yes; otherwise, click No.

5. In the Manage Identities dialog box, click New if you want to set up another identity; otherwise, click Close.

The first time you log on as a new identity, you will be asked for some information about your Internet connection. To switch from one identity to another, choose File ➢ Switch Identity to open the Switch Identities dialog box. Select the identity, and click OK. To log off from an identity, choose File ➢ Identities ➢ Logoff *identity*.

To delete an identity, select the identity in the Manage Identities dialog box, and click Remove.

Using Outlook Express As Your Newsreader

A newsgroup is a collection of articles about a particular subject. A newsgroup is similar to e-mail in that you can reply to what someone else has written (the newsgroup term for this is to *post*), and you can send a question or a response either to the whole group or to individuals within the group.

The primary (but not sole) source of newsgroups is Usenet, which is a worldwide distributed discussion system consisting of newsgroups with names that are classified hierarchically by subject. In a newsgroup name, each component is separated from the next by a period. For example, `rec.crafts.metalworking` is a recreational group devoted to the craft of metalworking. The leftmost portion represents the largest hierarchical category, and the name gets more specific from left to right. Table 13.1 lists the major top-level newsgroup categories and explains the topics each discusses. Currently, there are thousands and thousands of newsgroups on every conceivable topic. For an extensive listing of them, go to `sunsite.unc.edu/usenet-i/hier-s/master.html`.

TABLE 13.1: The Major Newsgroups

Newsgroup	What It Discusses
alt	Newsgroups outside the main structure outlined below
comp	Computer science and related topics, including operating systems, hardware, artificial intelligence, and graphics
misc	Anything that does not fit into one of the other categories
news	Information on Usenet and newsgroups
rec	Recreational activities, such as hobbies, the arts, movies, and books
sci	Scientific topics, such as math, physics, and biology
soc	Social issues and cultures
talk	Controversial subjects, such as gun control, abortion, religion, and politics

You access newsgroups by accessing the server on which they are stored. Not all servers store the same newsgroups. The network administrator or the owner of the site determines what to store. Almost all news servers "expire" articles after a few days or, at most, a few weeks because of the tremendous volume. Although they might be archived at the site, these articles are no longer available to be viewed by users.

> **W WARNING** Newsgroups are uncensored. You can find just about anything at any time anywhere. Nobody has authority over newsgroups as a whole. If you find certain groups, certain articles, or certain people offensive, don't go there, or use the Rules Editor that we talked about earlier to prevent certain articles from even being displayed. But, remember, anarchy reigns in newsgroups, and you never know what you might stumble upon in the least likely places.

Setting Up a Newsgroups Account

Before you can read newsgroups, you must set up a newsgroups account. Before you start, get the name of your news server from your ISP, and then follow these steps:

1. In the main Outlook Express window, select the Outlook Express folder, and, in the pane on the right, click Set Up a Newsgroups Account to start the Internet Connection Wizard.

2. Supply the information that the Wizard requests, and click Finish when you are done.

You'll now see a folder in the Folders list for your news server.

Connecting to Newsgroups

The next task is to download the list of newsgroups from your server. When Outlook Express asks if you want to do this, click Yes. This may take a while if you have a slow connection, but notice the incrementing number of newsgroups in the Downloading Newsgroups dialog box. In the process of writing this section, we downloaded a list of more than 25,000 newsgroups.

TIP   Only the names of the newsgroups are downloaded to your computer; their contents remain on the news server. Periodically, you can update this list by clicking Reset List.

When the list has finished downloading, you'll see the Newsgroup Subscriptions dialog box, as shown in Figure 13.5.

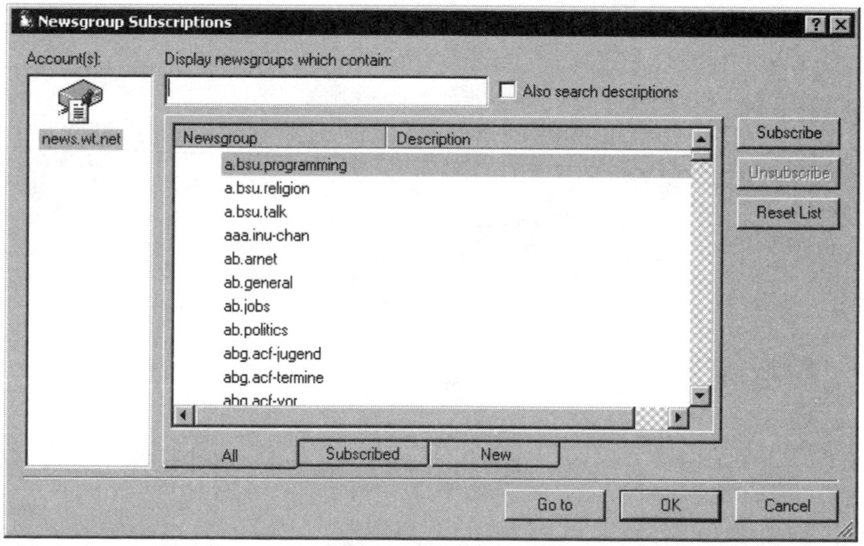

FIGURE 13.5:   Use this dialog box to search for and subscribe to newsgroups.

Finding a Newsgroup of Interest

You can select a newsgroup to read in two ways:

- You can scroll through the list (this will take a lot of time).

- You can search on a term.

Just for the sake of doing it, scroll the list a bit. As you can see, it's in alphabetic order by hierarchical categories. If you don't see anything right away that strikes your fancy, you can perform a search. Enter a term in the Display Newsgroups Which Contain text box, and then don't do anything! In a second, you'll see a list of newsgroups that contain articles about your topic.

Skill 13

Subscribing to a Newsgroup

Subscribing to a newsgroup doesn't involve a fee or any other transaction. Subscribing means simply creating a subfolder for a particular newsgroup in your news folder. Then, instead of selecting it from the Newsgroup Subscriptions dialog box, you can simply click the newsgroup's folder to see the list of articles in it.

Once you've located a newsgroup you want to read, you can select it and click Subscribe and then Go To to open it, or you can simply click Go To. To unsubscribe to a newsgroup, right-click its folder, and choose Unsubscribe.

Reading a Newsgroup

To read an article, simply click its header to display the message in the lower pane.

Outlook Express is a threaded newsreader in that it groups messages that respond to a subject line. If you see a plus sign to the left of a newsgroup header, you can click the plus sign to display a list of related messages. The more up-to-date term for threads is *conversation*. Newsgroup articles are grouped by conversations by default, but you can also organize mail messages by conversations. With your Inbox selected, choose View ➢ Current View ➢ Group Messages by Conversation.

To read the articles from another newsgroup or to search for another newsgroup, double-click your main news folder, and then click Newsgroups to open the Newsgroup Subscriptions dialog box.

Posting to a Newsgroup

Replying to a newsgroup article or sending a message to a newsgroup is known as posting. You post to a newsgroup in much the same way that you compose and send e-mail. To send an original message to a newsgroup, open the newsgroup, and click the New Post button. The New Message window will open with the group's name in the To line.

To reply to an individual article, click the Reply button, and to reply to the entire newsgroup, click the Reply Group button.

Customizing Outlook Express

Throughout this skill, we've mentioned from time to time ways that you can specify how Outlook Express handles certain features, such as signatures. In most cases, you do this through the Options dialog box (shown in Figure 13.6), which you open by choosing Tools ➢ Options. Here's a quick rundown of what to use each tab for in the Options dialog box:

General   Use this tab to specify settings for how Outlook Express starts and for sending and receiving messages.

Read   Use this tab to set options for reading news and mail. For example, you specify a maximum number of news article headers to download at one time.

Receipts   Use this tab if you want to verify that your message has been read by the recipient.

Send   Use this tab to set, among other things, the format (HTML or Plain Text) in which you will send all messages and the format you'll use to reply to messages. You can also specify whether copies of sent messages will be stored and whether you want Outlook Express to put the names and addresses of people you reply to in your Address Book.

Compose   Use this tab to specify the font and font size for mail messages and news articles that you create and to select stationery fonts for HTML messages.

Signatures   For details about how to use this tab, see the section "Adding a Signature to Messages."

Spelling   Checks the spelling of your message. You will have this tab only if you have Microsoft Word, Excel, or PowerPoint 95 or 97 installed.

Security   Use this tab to specify your desired Internet Security zone and to get a digital ID. (For more information on Internet security, see Skill 11.)

Connection   Use this tab to specify how Outlook Express handles your dial-up connection.

Maintenance   Use this tab to specify what Outlook Express does with deleted items and to clean up downloaded messages, as well as to specify that all server commands are stored for troubleshooting purposes.

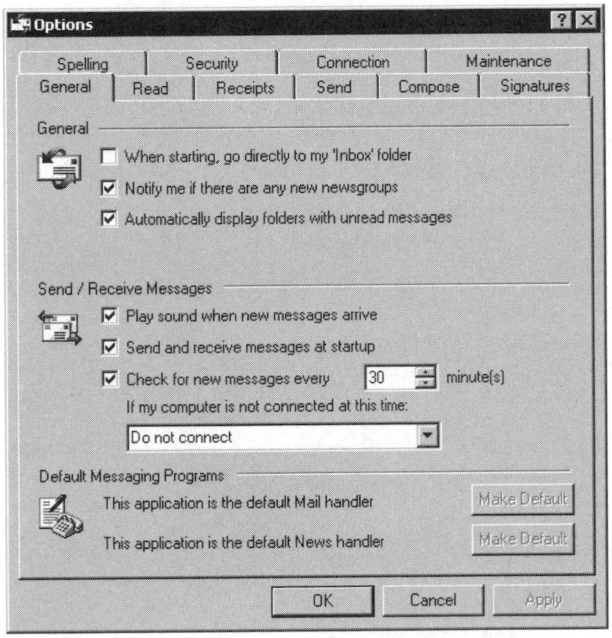

FIGURE 13.6: You use the Options dialog box to customize Outlook Express for the way you work.

Are You Up to Speed?

Now you can...

- ☑ read, compose, and send e-mail messages
- ☑ include pictures, colors, and HTML formatting in messages
- ☑ attach files to messages
- ☑ apply message rules to mail and news
- ☑ locate and read newsgroups that interest you
- ☑ post your own articles to newsgroups
- ☑ customize Outlook Express so that it works the way you do

Getting the Most out of Windows 2000 Professional

- Using Computer Management
- Looking at system information
- Exploring services
- Sharing folders
- Looking at Device Manager
- Optimizing hard-disk performance
- Compressing NTFS volumes
- Adding hardware
- Managing virtual memory

This skill explores several important areas within Windows 2000 Professional, including Computer Management, adding and configuring additional hardware, and optimizing hard-disk performance. We also take a quick look at configuring multimedia and sound and setting up scanners, cameras, and game controllers. Finally, we look at some aspects of managing virtual memory. But we'll begin with Computer Management.

Using Computer Management

One of the criticisms made by system administrators in the past has been that the Windows family of operating systems is difficult and time-consuming to configure. Various initiatives have been suggested to cut down the total cost of ownership (TCO) of Windows systems. Computer Management provides a powerful desktop tool you can use to manage local or networked computers from a single, central location. Computer Management provides several important functions for reporting and diagnosing system conditions. To use Computer Management to the fullest extent, you must be logged on as an administrator of the computer you want to manage.

TIP   Computer Management is a part of a larger Microsoft Management Console (MMC) package, which is used to administer networks, services, computers, and certain system components and is sometimes called a *snap-in*. Describing how Microsoft Management Console works is beyond the scope of this book; for more information see *Mastering Windows 2000 Professional* by Mark Minasi and Todd Phillips, available from Sybex.

To launch Computer Management, choose Start ➤ Settings ➤ Control Panel, open the Administrative Tools folder, and open the Computer Management application. As Figure 14.1 shows, several options are displayed in the main window.

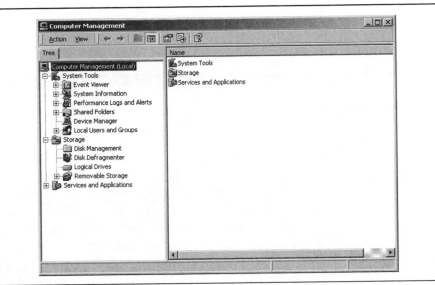

FIGURE 14.1: The main Computer Management window

The main Computer Management window works much like a Windows Explorer window; click the plus sign associated with items in the left pane to expand the list. Initially, there are three entries:

System Tools   Contains tools you can use to look at system configuration, including services and shared folders, and troubleshoot certain aspects of the hardware on your computer.

Storage   Contains tools you can use to look at or change hard-disk configuration and run the Disk Defragmenter.

Services and Applications   Contains tools you can use to look at the services your system runs when it is performing the role of a network server.

Of the items available in System Tools, we'll look at System Information, Shared Folders, and Device Manager in this skill, and, of the items available in Services and Applications, we'll look at Services in this skill and Indexing Service in Skill 4. We'll look at Performance Logs and Alerts in Skill 15 and Local Users and Groups in Skill 16. We'll also look at Disk Management and Disk Defragmenter from the Storage tools later in this skill.

ADMINISTRATIVE TOOLS EXPLAINED

You will see several other tools inside the Administrative Tools folder, including:

Component Services   Manages and configures COM+ applications. COM+ is a Microsoft Windows 2000 specification for building software components that can be assembled into programs or can add functions to existing programs.

Data Sources (ODBC)   Allows access to database systems using SQL (Structured Query Language) via ODBC (Open Database Connectivity).

Event Viewer   Lets you look at the logs of system, security, and program events on your computer; see Skill 15 for details.

Local Security Policy   Lets you look at or change the local security policy, including user rights and audit policies.

Performance   Lets you collect and look at real-time data from your system and presents the results as a graph, bar chart, or report; see Skill 15 for more details.

Services   Allows you to look at the services running on your system, to check their current status, and to start or stop services.

Depending on how your system is configured and which applications and services you are running, you may see additional tools installed in this folder, such as Server Extensions Administrator; this tool allows you to manage any extensions you have installed, such as Microsoft FrontPage.

Looking at System Information

System Information collects together all manner of highly technical information about the hardware, software, and Windows 2000 Professional components that make up your computer system. This is the place to go to get detailed information on all aspects of system configuration.

Click the plus sign next to System Information, and you will see that it contains these options: System Summary, Hardware Resources, Components, Software Environment, and Internet Explorer 5. Click System Summary, and you will see something like the display shown in Figure 14.2; what you actually see, of course, depends on the configuration of your own computer.

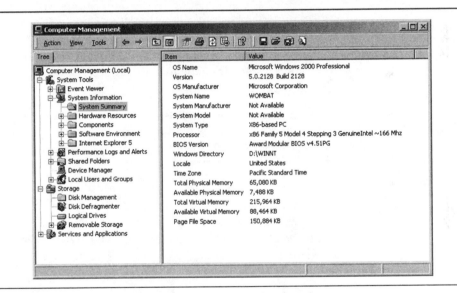

FIGURE 14.2: The System Information System Summary screen

The other options available in System Information are:

Hardware Resources   Contains hardware-specific settings, including memory-address information and information on interrupts, memory access, and interrupt requests.

Components   Displays information about your Windows 2000 Professional system configuration, including currently installed device drivers and changes made to device drivers over time.

Software Environment   Details the system and application software currently loaded into memory.

Internet Explorer 5   Contains information on the options you use with Internet Explorer, including digital certificates and security information as well as a complete listing of all the Internet Explorer filenames and their version numbers.

Applications   Details information about the applications, if any, that are installed on this computer.

The information displayed in the right pane of the System Information window depends on which of these categories you choose. Much of this information is technical and very detailed and is of only minor interest until something goes wrong with your system; then the information can be of vital importance in tracking down and fixing the problem.

> **TIP**   To print a copy of your system information summary, choose Action ➤ Print. You can also save this information as a text file or as a System Information file.

You can choose items from the Tools ➤ Windows menu to run the diagnostic and support tools used by technical support personnel, but don't run them until you are asked to do so by a member of the technical support staff. You can also run the Disk Cleanup, Backup, and Hardware Wizard functions from this same menu.

Exploring Services

Click Services in Computer Management and you will see a display like the one shown in Figure 14.3; this is a list of all the operating system services available on your system. Services perform all the behind-the-scenes tasks needed to keep your system running smoothly, and they rarely need any input from you to do their jobs. You can also open Services from within the Administrative Tools folder and see the same display.

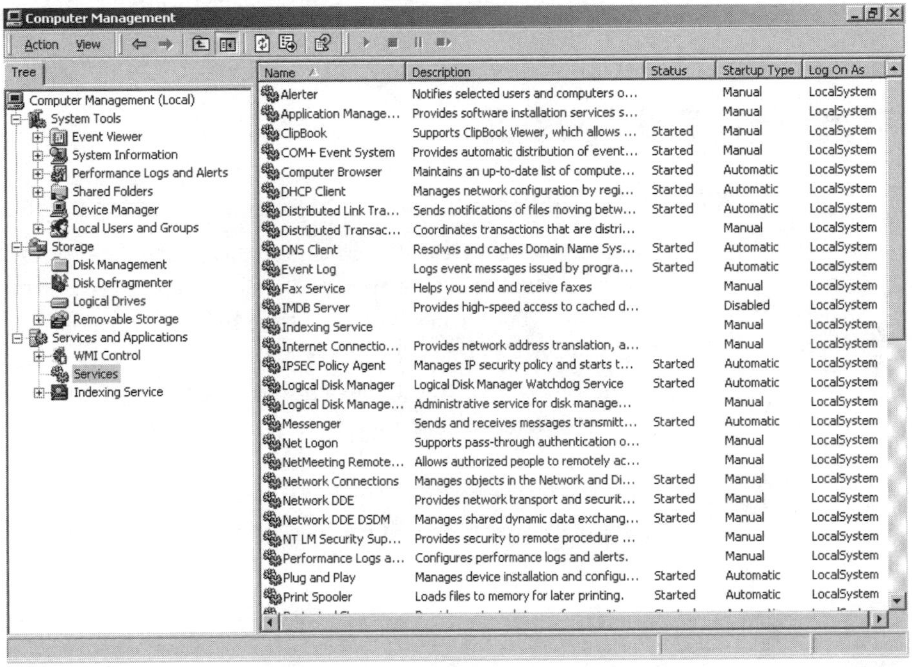

FIGURE 14.3: The Services display

In the right pane, you will see the name of the service followed by a short description of the function it performs. The Status column shows the current operating state of the service; this may be any one of Started, Stopped, Paused, Resumed, or Restarted. The Start Up Type column indicates those services started automatically and those started manually, and the Log On As column shows the account name under which the services are running.

To change the status of a service, right-click the service, and then choose Start, Stop, Pause, Resume, or Restart. Right-click a service, and then choose Properties to find out more about each service, to specify the recovery options to take when a service fails, and to look at which other services depend on this one. Looking at these dependencies can be a useful troubleshooting aid; some services won't run or can't run properly unless other services are also running. For example, if a network interface card fails to initialize as Windows starts up, all the services that depend on the card functioning will also fail to initialize.

Sharing Folders

Click Shared Folders in Computer Management, and you will see three options:

Shares   Lists all the shared directories on your system. Directories in this list with a dollar sign appended to their name are automatically shared by Windows 2000 Professional and are hidden from view in the Explorer or My Network Places. The other directories listed here have been made available by their owners as shared directories. See Figure 14.4 for an example. To stop sharing a folder, right-click the folder, and select Stop Sharing. To see how a folder is shared, right-click, choose Properties, and click the Share Permissions tab to bring it to the front. For more information on sharing files and folders, and for information on how permissions work, see Skill 16.

TIP   If you add a dollar sign to the end of a share name (as in Pat$, for example), that folder will not be visible to other users in the Explorer. People you trust can still access the share by typing its name, including the dollar sign, into the Map Network Drive or Run dialog boxes.

Sessions   Lists all the current sessions and includes user name, computer, the type of network connection, the number of open files, and the connect time and idle time for each user.

Open Files   Lists all the current open files, including the name of the user accessing the file, the network connection they are using, and the permissions granted when the file was opened.

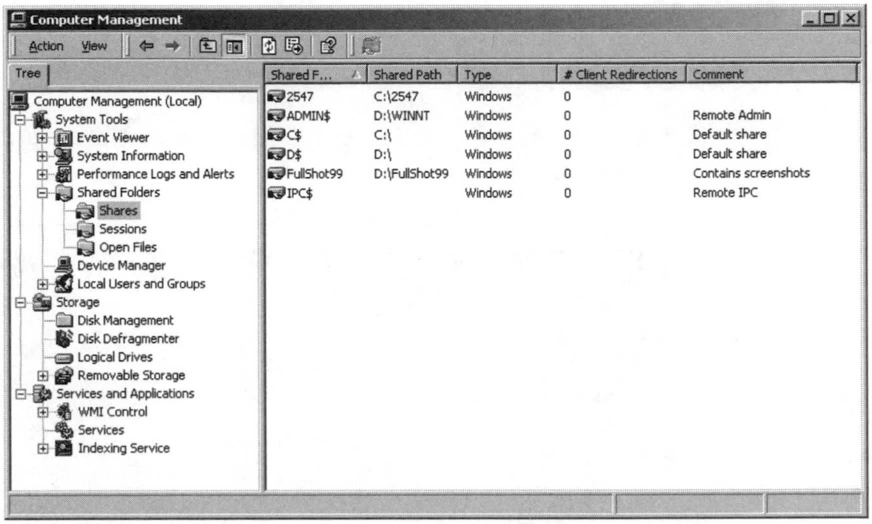

FIGURE 14.4: The Shared Folders Shares window in Computer Management

Looking at Device Manager

In a previous section, we saw how System Information presents detailed information about the hardware and software that make up your system. Device Manager takes that process one stage further for the hardware on your system and allows you to:

- Look at or change hardware configuration settings.
- Enable, disable, or uninstall hardware devices.
- Troubleshoot hardware that is not working properly.
- Identify individual device drivers.
- Identify resource conflicts.

WARNING Changing resource settings without knowing exactly what you are doing can cause your system to operate in unexpected and unpleasant ways. Be careful.

Click Device Manager in Computer Management, and you will see a display like the one shown in Figure 14.5.

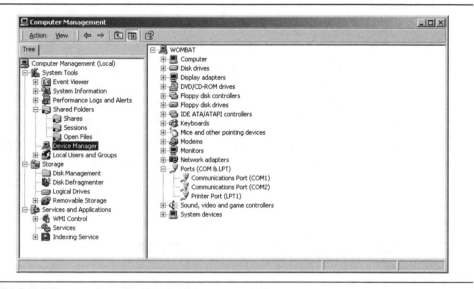

FIGURE 14.5: The Device Manager window

Double-click the device category in the right pane of the Device Manager window, and then right-click the device itself to open the shortcut menu. The options available in this menu depend on the type of device you are working with. Choose Properties to look at the Property dialog boxes for the device. Again, the number of dialog boxes available for a device depends on the type of device you are working with; a CD-ROM might only have a General tab, while a hard-disk controller might have General, Advanced Settings Driver, and Resources tabs.

On the General tab, you will see a Device Status box indicating whether the device is working correctly. If it is working correctly, no further action is required on your part. If it is not, click Troubleshooter, and follow the instructions on the screen to find and fix the problem. We'll be looking at all the Troubleshooters in more detail in Skill 15.

Compressing NTFS Volumes

In Skill 6, we looked at how to compress individual files and folders when using NTFS. Now we can go one step further and look at how to compress an entire hard-disk volume. A volume is a section of a hard disk that behaves as though it were a completely separate disk. When you look at a volume with My Computer or the Windows Explorer, it appears as just another drive letter—just like drives C and D. Windows 2000 Professional automatically uncompresses the volume when you access the files it contains.

To compress a hard-disk volume, follow these steps:

1. Open My Computer on the Desktop, and select the drive you want to compress.

2. Select File ➤ Properties, or right-click the drive and choose Properties.

3. Click the General tab to bring it to the front.

4. Check the Compress Drive to Save Disk Space check box, and click OK. If you are using the FAT32 system, this check box is simply not present.

Remember that compressing an NTFS volume is always a trade-off; on one hand, you gain hard-disk space by compressing the contents, but, on the other, there is always additional overhead in uncompressing the contents for use. Only you can decide which is best for you. But, as a general rule, compressing an NTFS volume makes good sense for a volume you want to keep close at hand but that you don't use every day.

Defragmenting Files

As files on your computer grow, they will not fit back into their original locations on your hard disk, so Windows 2000 Professional divides the files into pieces and spreads the files over several different disk locations. This is how Windows is designed to work and is how the system juggles constantly changing file sizes. An unfortunate side effect is that as a file is divided into more and more pieces, finding and retrieving the whole file when you open an application takes longer and longer. A disk defragmenter keeps your hard-disk performance at its peak by finding fragmented files on your system and rewriting them into contiguous areas of your hard disk.

Disk Defragmenter works behind the scenes; the files on your hard disk are moved from their scattered locations, but you will still find them in their original folders. Follow these steps to use the Disk Defragmenter:

1. Choose Start ➢ Programs ➢ Accessories ➢ System Tools ➢ Disk Defragmenter. Alternatively, right-click the drive, choose Properties, click the Tools tab to bring it to the front, and click Defragment Now.

2. Choose the disk you want to defragment, and click the Analyze button. Disk Defragmenter looks at the drive, prepares a display, and reports on the condition of the files on that drive; the Analysis Display box shows fragmented files, contiguous files, system files, and hard-disk free space as stripes of different colors, as seen in Figure 14.6. Once the analysis is complete, click the View Report button to open the Analysis Report dialog box. At the top of the Analysis Report dialog box, you will see volume information, including the amount of fragmentation, free space, and file and directory fragmentation. In the lower part of this dialog box, you will see detailed information on specific files. Click the heading at the top of the columns to sort the data in that column. On the basis of the data collected, Disk Defragmenter also recommends whether you should continue with the defragmentation.

3. Click Defragment to continue, or click Close to return to the main window.

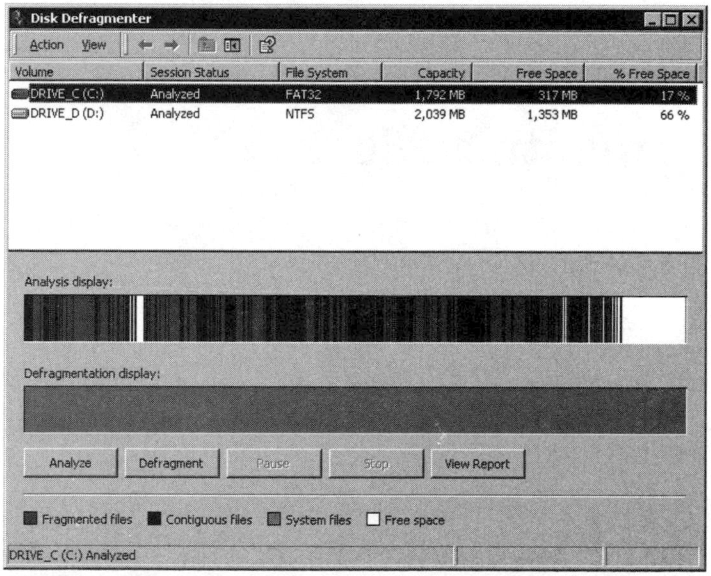

FIGURE 14.6: The Disk Defragmenter Analysis Display for a badly fragmented drive

4. If you click the Defragment button, the Disk Defragmenter starts working. Buttons are available so that you can stop or pause Disk Defragmenter.

You can certainly perform other work on the computer while Disk Defragmenter is running, but the response time will be much slower, and Disk Defragmenter will start over each time you write a file to your hard disk. The best time to run Disk Defragmenter is while you are out for lunch, or you can use the Task Scheduler (see Skill 7 for details) to run the program during the night.

Cleaning Up Disks

Have you ever wished there were some way you could just wave a magic wand and get rid of all the unused or temporary files that take up space on your hard disk? Well, now there is such a tool, and it is called Disk Cleanup. Choose Start ➢ Programs ➢ Accessories ➢ System Tools ➢ Disk Cleanup to open the Select Drive dialog box. Choose the drive you want to work with, and click OK to open the Disk Cleanup dialog box shown in Figure 14.7.

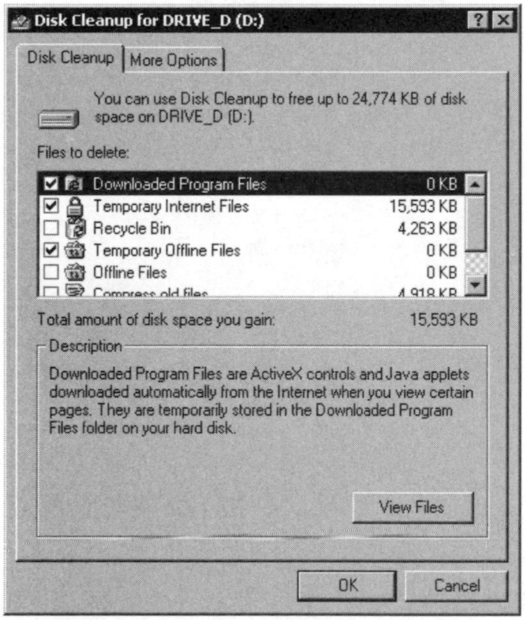

FIGURE 14.7: The Disk Cleanup dialog box

Alternatively, you can open Explorer or My Computer, right-click the disk you want to work with, and then choose Properties from the shortcut menu. On the General tab, click the Disk Cleanup button.

The Disk Cleanup dialog box has these tabs:

Disk Cleanup   Displays the amount of free space that could be recovered by deleting temporary files in certain categories, including Internet files and downloaded program files, or by emptying the Recycle Bin on your Desktop. As you check the boxes to delete files, a running counter tells you how much disk space will be recovered. Click View Files to open an Explorer window so you can check the files a little more closely before you delete them from your hard disk.

More Options   Lets you remove applications or Windows components that you don't use. Click either of the Clean Up buttons to open the Add/Remove Programs applet, and then select the Windows Setup tab to remove Windows components you don't use, or select the Install/Uninstall tab to remove application programs you don't use.

Checking Disks for Errors

Another disk-management task you might have to perform from time to time is to check a hard disk for errors, and Windows 2000 Professional includes a tool for checking FAT32 volumes. All NTFS volumes log file transactions and replace bad clusters automatically. To check out a hard disk, open Explorer or My Computer, right-click the disk you want to work with, and then choose Properties from the shortcut menu. On the Tools tab, click the Check Now button to open the Check Disk dialog box, which contains these two options:

- Automatically Fix File System Errors

- Scan For and Attempt Recovery of Bad Sectors

Check the appropriate boxes, and then click Start to begin scanning the disk. A status bar across the bottom of the Check Disk dialog box indicates the progress of the tests, and you will see a message when the disk check is complete.

Understanding Disk Management

Disk Management is that part of Computer Management used to perform certain disk-related tasks, including:

- Creating partitions

- Deleting partitions

- Upgrading disks

- Changing a drive letter

- Changing a path

- Formatting a disk or partition

- Making a partition active

To start Disk Management, choose Start ➢ Settings ➢ Control Panel ➢ Administrative Tools, and open Computer Management. In the list in the left pane, select Storage, and then open the Disk Management folder. You will see a display similar to the one shown in Figure 14.8, but the disks on your computer will undoubtedly be different.

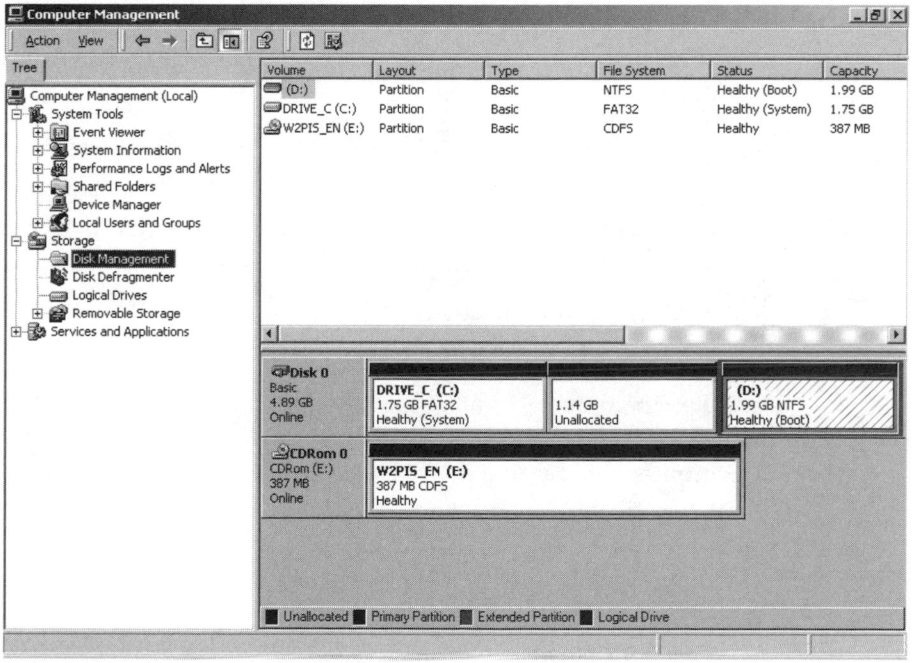

FIGURE 14.8: The Disk Management window

In the top portion of the window, you will see information listed for the logical drives on your system, and in the lower portion, you will see a graphical representation of the disks and partitions available. Right-click any of the items in the graphical portion of the display to open a shortcut menu containing selections specific to that item. A Wizard will walk you through the process you selected; just follow the instructions on the screen.

> **WARNING**   Formatting a hard disk or disk partition erases all of the information that it contained.

Adding New Hardware to Your Computer

There will come the time when you need to add an additional piece of hardware to your system or remove an existing device because you no longer use it. When adding new hardware to your computer, there are three main elements to the process:

- Installing the hardware on your computer, or connecting it to your computer, and turning it on.

- Finding and loading the appropriate device driver. A device driver is a small program used by Windows to control a piece of hardware.

- Configuring the device settings and properties.

Today's hardware conforms to the Plug-and-Play standards, and Windows 2000 Professional can recognize and configure Plug-and-Play hardware automatically. However, you might have some older devices that you want to attach to your computer, devices that might have been built before the Plug-and-Play standards were finalized.

To install a Plug-and-Play device on your system, follow these steps:

1. Turn off your computer.

2. Connect or install the new device according to the manufacturer's instructions.

3. Turn your computer back on to restart Windows 2000 Professional. Windows will locate your new hardware automatically and install the appropriate software for you.

If Windows does not find your new Plug-and-Play device, check that it is installed properly, and, if you can, confirm that the device actually works and is not defective in some way.

> **TIP** You must be logged on as an administrator to configure a device using Add/Remove Hardware.

If the device you want to install is not a Plug-and-Play device, follow these steps instead:

1. Turn off your computer.

2. Connect or install the new device according to the manufacturer's instructions.

3. Turn your computer back on to restart Windows 2000 Professional.

4. Choose Start ➤ Settings ➤ Control Panel, and then click the Add/Remove Hardware icon to open the Add/Remove Hardware Wizard. Click the Next button, and then choose between adding a new device or uninstalling an existing device, as seen in Figure 14.9.

5. Windows then locates the hardware already installed on your system. To add new hardware, select Add a New Device from the Devices list, and click Next. You must next decide whether you want Windows 2000 Professional to automatically detect your hardware or if you want to identify the hardware yourself.

6. Choose Yes if you want Windows to search for your new hardware. You will be warned that Windows may spend several minutes searching and that your machine could quit functioning during the search. Click Next. A status monitor indicates the progress of the search. The duration of the detection process depends on the amount and type of hardware on your system.

   If you don't want Windows to try to detect the device, click No, and then click Next. A dialog box will prompt you to select the new device from a list. Click the hardware type you are installing, and then click Next.

7. From this point on, the dialog boxes you see on the screen depend on the type of hardware you are installing; simply follow the instructions on the screen to complete the installation.

Skill 14

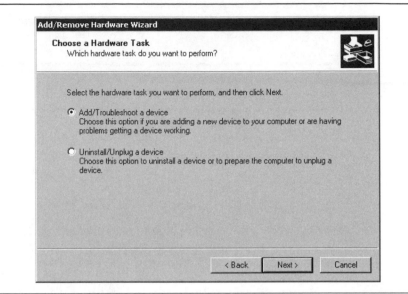

FIGURE 14.9 The Add/Remove Hardware Wizard

TIP   The Add/Remove Hardware Wizard automatically makes the appropriate changes to the Registry and to the configuration files so that Windows can recognize and support your new hardware. Similarly, when you remove hardware, the Wizard tells Windows not to load the device driver and configuration information for that device.

Setting Up Cameras and Scanners

Document scanners and digital cameras are getting cheaper and cheaper while, at the same time, gaining more and more useful features. To set up your scanner or camera, log on as an administrator, and then choose Start ➢ Settings ➢ Control Panel, and open the Scanners and Cameras applet. A Wizard walks you through the steps of setting up the hardware; just follow the instructions on the screen. If your scanner or camera is Plug and Play, Windows 2000 Professional will detect and install it automatically.

To test a scanner or camera, follow these steps:

1.   Choose Start ➢ Settings ➢ Control Panel, and then open the Scanners and Cameras applet.

2.   Select the device you want to test, and click Properties.

3.   Click Test Scanner or Camera. After a moment's pause, a dialog box will open, telling you whether the scanner or camera successfully completed the test.

Setting Up Game Controllers

To configure and test peripherals such as flight yokes, joysticks, gamepads, and the like, you use the Game Controllers dialog box. Choose Start ➢ Settings ➢ Control Panel ➢ Game Controllers to open the Game Controllers dialog box, which has two tabs:

> **General**   Lists the controllers on your system along with their current status. If your controller does not appear in the list, click the Add button to open the Add Game Controller dialog box, and select your controller from the list. Click the Next button to complete the installation.

> **Advanced**   Lists the controllers installed on your system and their corresponding controller ID numbers. If your controller requires assignment to a specific port driver, you can select it from the list at the bottom of this tab.

To calibrate your game controller, follow these steps:

1.   Choose Start ➢ Settings ➢ Control Panel ➢ Game Controllers to open the Game Controllers dialog box.

2.   Select the General tab. If you have more than one game controller installed on your system, select the one you want to work with from the list, and then click the Properties button to open the Game Controller Properties dialog box.

3.   Select the Test tab to run a short test on your game controller; simply follow the instructions on the screen.

4.   If the test is unsuccessful, select the Settings tab to complete a calibration of your controller. If your game controller has a rudder, be sure to check the Rudder/Pedal check box. Then click the Calibrate button, and follow the instructions on the screen.

Configuring Sound and Multimedia on Your Computer

The addition of sound to the personal computer is one of the great steps forward in making the PC a center for entertainment. Not only can you assign certain sounds to specific system events, but you can also collect sounds together to create sound *schemes* for easy reuse and recall. You can play music CDs in your CD-ROM drive (see Skill 10 for more on this) and even customize text-to-speech software.

Assigning Sounds to Windows Events

You can choose sounds and associate them with specific Windows events such as the arrival of new mail or the opening or closing of a window on your Desktop. To do this, choose Start ➢ Settings ➢ Control Panel, and then open the Sounds and Multimedia applet. Click the Sounds tab, which is shown in Figure 14.10, to bring it to the front. This tab contains the following elements:

Sound Events   Lists the Windows events to which you can assign sounds. If an event has a loudspeaker icon to its left, a sound is assigned to it, which you can change.

Name   Lists the names of the sounds that you can assign to an event. This option becomes available when you make a selection in Sound Events. Click the arrow to the right of the Name box to see a list of all the sounds available on your system.

Preview   Plays the sound, if you have a sound card and speakers. When a Name is selected, the Preview button becomes available.

Browse   Searches through the available sounds. Sounds are usually contained in a .WAV file.

Scheme   Lists sets of events with particular sounds assigned to the listed events. Windows Default is the name of the default scheme. You can change the sounds associated with the scheme and then save them under a different name, if you want. Also, you can choose No Sounds from the Schemes list to silence all these sounds when using your laptop in the library, for example.

Sound Volume   Lets you move the horizontal slider to set the playback volume.

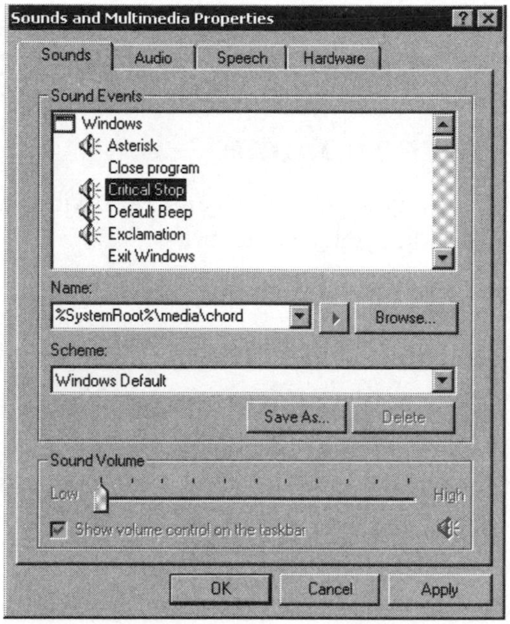

FIGURE 14.10 The Sounds tab in the Sounds and Multimedia Properties dialog box

To assign sounds to certain Windows events, follow these steps:

1. Choose Start ➤ Settings ➤ Control Panel, and then open the Sounds and Multimedia applet.

2. Click the Sounds tab to bring it to the front.

3. In the Sound Events box, choose the event with which you want to associate a sound.

4. In Name, select the sound you want to hear whenever the selected event occurs. If you can't see the sound listed, use Browse to find it.

5. Click Save As, and specify a name for the sound scheme you have just created. Click OK.

You can always go back to the original Windows sounds, if you wish, by selecting Windows Default from the Schemes list box.

T   TIP   Remember, in many settings, silence is golden.

Adjusting the Volume

Click the Audio tab in the Sounds and Multimedia Properties dialog box if you want to adjust the volume for:

- Sound playback
- Multimedia recording devices
- Multimedia playback devices

Click the Volume button, and just drag the slider left or right with your mouse to decrease or increase the volume. For more on adjusting the volume, see Skill 10.

Configuring a Speech Engine

If you like to use the Narrator (see Skill 5 for more information) or other text-to-speech software, you can make configuration changes using Sounds and Multimedia. To do this, click the Speech tab to bring it to the front, select the speech engine you want to work with, and then:

- Click Properties to configure speech-engine–specific options.
- Click Pronunciation to change how the speech engine pronounces words or interprets the words that you speak.
- Click Training to fine-tune a speech engine to your own voice.
- Click Special Handling to specify how a speech engine interprets symbols, abbreviations, numbers, and currencies.
- Click Microphone Settings Wizard to configure microphone input and sound output settings.

If one or more of these buttons are unavailable, the function is not available with the selected speech engine.

Managing Virtual Memory

Windows 2000 Professional uses a part of your hard disk as an extension to the main system memory, moving information out of main memory onto the hard disk when memory becomes full and then restoring it from disk to memory again when it is needed. Information is written into a special file known as a *paging file* or a *swap file*. Using a hard disk in this way is known as *virtual memory*. Careful use of virtual memory means that you can run more programs at the same time than your system's physical memory would normally allow.

Windows 2000 Professional creates the paging file on the drive that contains the Windows system files by default, but if you have another hard disk that is bigger and faster, consider setting up the paging file on that disk instead.

> **TIP**
>
> You must be logged on as a member of the Administrators group to make changes to virtual memory settings.

To look at or change the virtual memory settings on your system, follow these steps:

1. Right-click My Computer, and choose Properties.

2. Click the Advanced tab to bring it to the front, and click Performance Options to open the Performance Options dialog box shown in Figure 14.11.

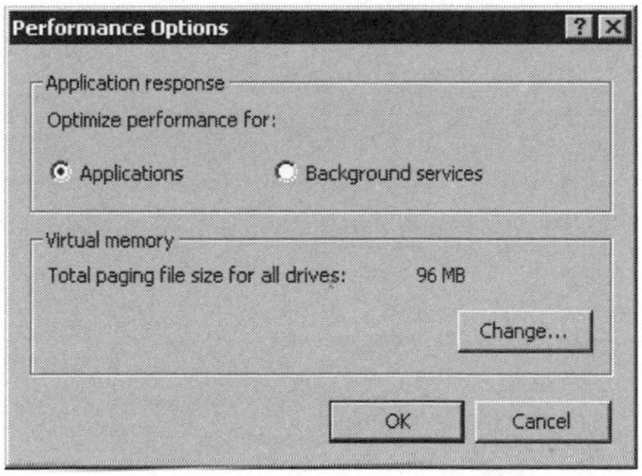

FIGURE 14.11: The Performance Options dialog box

3. In the Application Response box, check Applications if you want to devote system resources to foreground applications rather than background processes, or check Background Services if you want to divide resources equally.

4. In the Virtual Memory box at the bottom of the Performance Options dialog box, you will see the total amount of hard-disk space given over to the paging file on all drives. In this case, 96MB is available.

5. To look at or change the virtual memory settings, click the Change button in the Virtual Memory box, and you will see the Virtual Memory dialog box as shown in Figure 14.12.

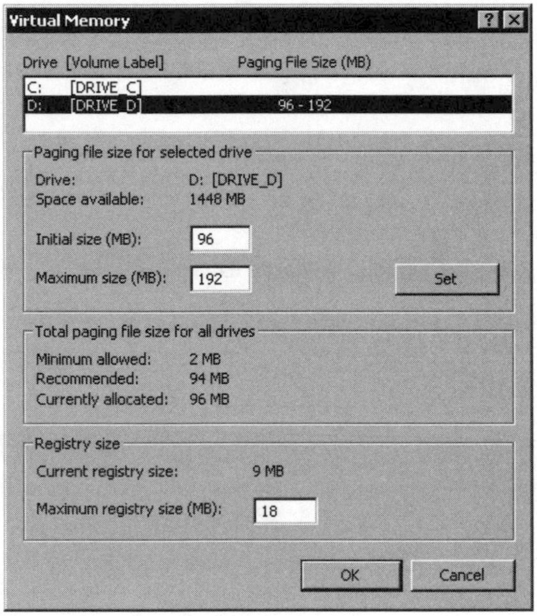

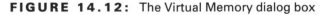

FIGURE 14.12: The Virtual Memory dialog box

6. Select the drive where you want to change settings, enter an initial (or minimum) size and a maximum size for the paging file on this drive, and then click the Set button.

7. Close the System Properties dialog box, and if you have made changes to the virtual memory settings, click Yes to restart your computer so that the changes can take effect.

If you have lots of free disk space, you can definitely get the best performance out of Windows 2000 Professional by specifying a large initial size as well as a large maximum size.

 NOTE The paging file is called pagefile.sys and is located in the root or top-level directory on a drive.

Are You Up to Speed?

Now you can...

- ☑ use Computer Management
- ☑ look at system information
- ☑ explore services
- ☑ share folders
- ☑ work with Device Manager
- ☑ optimize hard-disk performance
- ☑ compress NTFS volumes
- ☑ defragment files
- ☑ clean up disks
- ☑ check for hard-disk errors
- ☑ add additional hardware
- ☑ set up scanners and cameras
- ☑ set up game controllers
- ☑ create sound schemes
- ☑ crank up the volume
- ☑ configure your speech engine
- ☑ manage virtual memory

Skill 14

What to Do When Something Goes Wrong

- Shutting down Windows 2000 Professional
- Making and restoring a backup
- Making an Emergency Repair Disk
- Using the built-in troubleshooters
- Measuring system performance
- Starting Windows 2000 Professional in safe mode
- Starting Windows 2000 Professional using the Last Known Good Configuration
- Starting Windows 2000 Professional from the Setup disks
- Using an Emergency Repair Disk
- Using Recovery Console

The reason you are using Windows 2000 Professional is that you want a robust operating system platform that won't crash upon which to run your applications, right? Of course. But even Windows 2000 Professional crashes sometimes. In this skill, we'll take a look at a couple of things you can do to make life easier for both Windows and yourself, and then we'll look at the tools you can use to see in more detail what is going on inside your system. Finally, we'll look at some of the techniques you can use to rescue a Windows installation in distress.

Shutting Down Windows 2000 Professional

One of the simplest ways of avoiding trouble is to make sure that you *always* shut down Windows 2000 Professional properly. You should choose Start ➢ Shut Down, select Shut Down from the list, and click OK; don't just hit the computer power switch. A message appears on the screen telling you that Windows is saving data to the hard disk, and, after a moment or two, another message appears telling you that it is now safe to turn off your computer. On some of today's computers, especially laptops, the computer will automatically turn itself off at this point.

If you don't go through this short routine every time, you can not only lose data from your applications programs but you may also damage Windows, especially if you are using the FAT32 system; NTFS is much more resilient.

Making a Backup

The next thing you can do to make life easier for yourself is to back up important files. Yes, we know you have heard all this before; everybody's heard about making backups, but why should *you* make a backup?

- To protect against hard disk failure. A hard disk can fail at almost any time, but when it does, it is always at the most inconvenient moment.

- To protect against accidental deletion of a file. If you work on many projects, your chances of accidentally deleting a file are far higher than if you work on only one at a time.

- To create an archive at the end of a project. You can make a backup that contains all the files relating to a single project when the work is done; then if you need to refer to the files again, you know where to find them.

These are the main reasons to make a backup, but there are others. You might back up the files of a terminating employee in case the computer is reassigned within your department or is transferred to another department. In either case, the new user will likely clean up the hard disk—in other words, delete all the most important files. In addition, making a backup is one way to transfer a large number of files from one computer system to another. Finally, you should always back up before making a substantial change to your system such as installing new hardware, upgrading the operating system, or making a major configuration change to your application software.

Once you decide to make a backup, you need to plan your backup strategy and, most important, stick to it. With no plan, you will simply accumulate floppy disks or tapes haphazardly, you will waste tapes, and you will waste time looking for a file when you need to restore a file deleted by accident.

So how often should you make a backup? For an answer that fits the way you work, answer these questions:

- How often do your data files change? Every day? Every week? Every month?

- How important to your day-to-day operations are these files? Can you work without them? How long would it take you to re-create them?

- How much will it cost to replace lost files in terms of time spent and business lost?

In our computerized world, it takes hours to create an HTML page with just the right look or a budget spreadsheet that everyone agrees to, but either can be lost or destroyed in milliseconds. A hard-disk failure, a mistaken delete command, overwriting the file with an earlier version with the same name—these can destroy a file just as surely as fire, flood, or earthquake. You just have to lose one important file to become an instant convert for life to a program of regular, planned backups.

To start the Windows 2000 Professional backup program, choose Start ➤ Programs ➤ Accessories ➤ System Tools ➤ Backup. The first time you start the program, a dialog box welcomes you to the Windows 2000 Backup and Recovery Tools.

Using the Backup Wizard

Using the Backup Wizard is a quick and easy way to learn about backups; it gets you going quickly with the minimum of technical knowledge. If you would rather not use the Wizard, click the Backup tab; you can always restart it from the Tools menu inside the Backup program if you change your mind.

The Wizard walks you through the following sequence:

What to Back Up   You can back up all files and folders on your computer or selected files and folders; you can also back up only those files that have changed since the last time you made a backup.

Where to Store the Backup   Select a destination drive for the backup. You can back up to a network drive, but check with your system administrator before you do so for the first time.

Type of Backup   You can compare the backup against the original copies of your files to ensure that the files are backed up properly, and you can specify whether Backup should compress your files as they are backed up to save space on the destination drive.

Once you have made your selections, click the Start button to begin the backup; a small progress indicator tracks the backup as it proceeds.

A time will come when you want a little more control over your backups, and that is when you stop using the Wizard and take charge of the process yourself. At the Welcome dialog box, rather than invoking the Wizard, click the Backup tab. Using the Backup program involves essentially the same tasks that the Backup Wizard does for you—selecting the files, deciding where to put them, and specifying how the backup should actually be made. Let's take a look.

> **TIP**   You must have the right permissions to make a backup or a restore. Make sure you are logged on as an administrator or as a backup operator if you are backing up files on a local computer. If you are not logged on as an administrator or backup operator, you must be the owner of the file or folders you want to back up, or you must have one or more of the following permissions: Read, Read and Execute, Modify, or Full Control. See Skill 16 for more on these permissions.

Making a Manual Backup

If you have previously specified and saved a backup job, you can select it for use again using Job ➢ Load Selections. That done, all you have to do is click the Start Backup button to begin the backup.

If you don't have a previously saved backup job or if you want to do things a little differently this time, the first task is to decide which files to back up. You can back up all the files and folders selected in the Backup window, shown in Figure 15.1, or you can back up only files that have changed, along with any new files never before backed up.

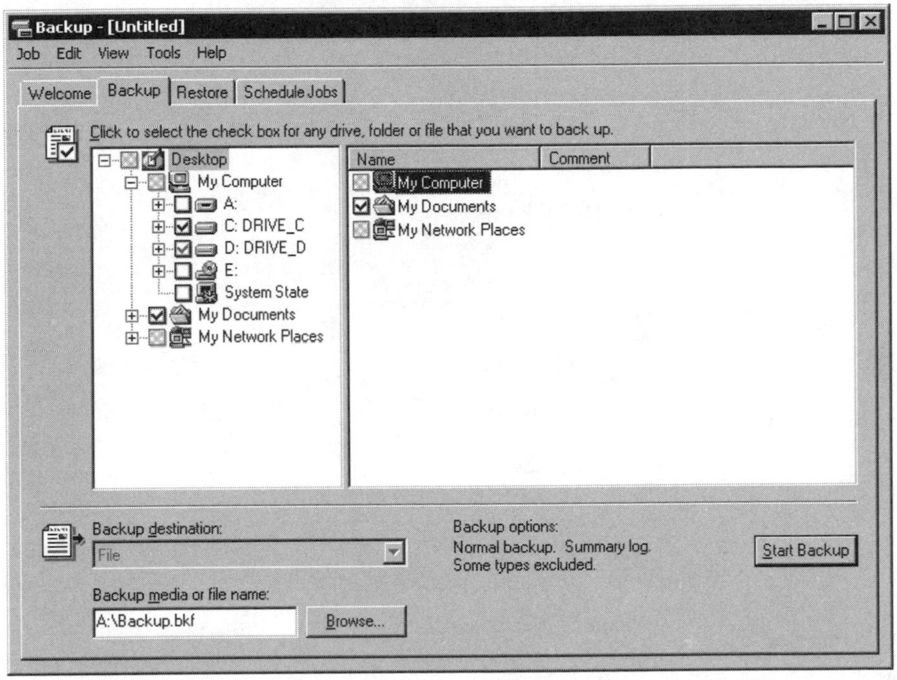

FIGURE 15.1: The main Backup window

In the Backup window, check the box next to the files and folders you want to back up. A blue checkmark indicates that the folder or file is selected for backup; a gray checkmark indicates that some of the files in the folder or on the drive have been selected for backup.

The next task is to select the destination device or drive for the backup and to name the backup file itself. Use the Backup Destination list below the main window to select the destination, and use the Backup Media or File Name box to specify a name for this backup.

The last part of the process is to review the backup configuration settings. Choose Tools ➤ Options to open the Options dialog box shown in Figure 15.2.

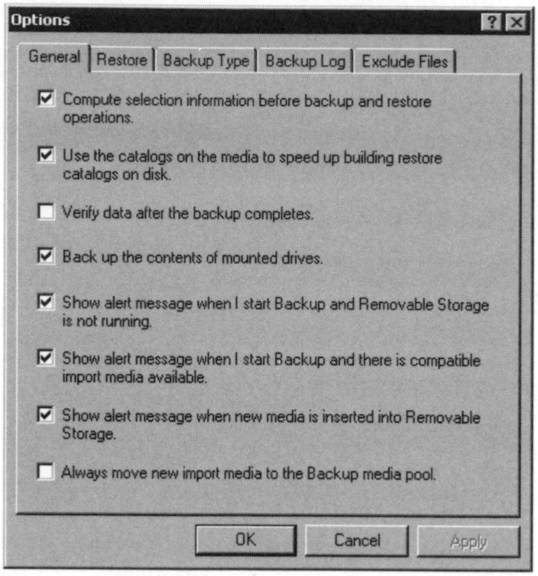

FIGURE 15.2: The Options dialog box

Across the top of the Options dialog box you will see the following tabs:

General Lets you specify that the backed-up data are compared against the original files to ensure the data were properly backed up. You can also specify how data compression is performed and how you want the Backup program to respond if it finds that the medium (tape, disk, or CD) you are using already contains a backup.

Restore Lets you specify what happens when duplicate files are found during a restore operation.

Backup Type Lets you choose how the backup is made:

Normal Backs up all the selected files and clears the archive bit.

Copy Backs up all the selected files but does not clear the archive bit.

Differential Backs up all the selected files that changed since the last Normal or Incremental backup. When the backup is complete, the archive bit for each file is left on.

Incremental Backs up all the selected files that have changed since the last Incremental or Normal backup. When the backup is complete, the archive bit for each file is turned off.

Daily Backs up all the files that have been modified today.

Backup Log   Lets you specify the elements you want to include in the backup log file.

Exclude Files   Lets you specify file types that you want to exclude from this backup; use the Add New and Remove buttons to select files for exclusion.

All that remains is to click the Start Backup button to begin the backup. Keep the backup in a safe place, preferably not next to your computer; if your computer is damaged by the sprinklers going off by accident, there is a very good chance that the backup will be destroyed at the same time.

> **TIP**   Click the Schedule Jobs tab to specify the date for a backup.

Restoring a Backup

Most of the time, making a backup is a simple precaution, and you put it on the shelf along with the other tapes or Zip disks. But there will come a time, after a hard-disk controller failure perhaps, when you will need to restore a backup. Again, as when making the backup, you can use a Wizard, or you can do it manually.

Using the Restore Wizard

Using the Restore Wizard is a quick and easy way to learn about restoring backups; it gets you going quickly with the minimum of technical knowledge. To access this feature, click Restore Wizard. If you would rather not use the Wizard, click the Restore tab, which is described in the next section.

The Wizard walks you through a sequence of dialog boxes that specify the following:

What to Restore   You can restore all files and folders in the backup set, or you can restore selected files and folders.

Restore From   Specify the type and location of the backup you want to restore.

Select Backup Sets   Select a backup set for the restore.

Where to Restore   Specify the target of the restore; most of the time, selecting Original Location to put the file back where it came from makes the most sense.

How to Restore   Specify whether existing files on your hard disk should be overwritten during the restore.

Click the Start Restore button to begin the restore; a small progress indicator tracks the restore as it proceeds.

Using the Restore Tab

Using the Restore tab in the Backup program involves essentially the same tasks that the Restore Wizard does for you: selecting the files, deciding where to put them, and specifying how the restore should actually be made. A checkmark in a gray check box means that only some of the files in a folder have been selected. A checkmark in a white box means that all files in a folder have been selected.

Making an Emergency Repair Disk

Before we leave the Backup program, there is one more thing we must do, and that is to make an Emergency Repair Disk (ERD). As we'll see in later sections in this skill, you can use an ERD to repair and recover a system that can't load and run Windows 2000 Professional.

To create an Emergency Repair Disk, follow these steps:

1. Choose Start ➢ Programs ➢ Accessories ➢ System Tools, and then select Backup.

2. Insert a blank, formatted floppy disk into your floppy-disk drive.

3. When the Backup program starts, click the Emergency Repair Disk button on the Welcome page, or, if the Backup program is already running, choose Tools ➢ Create an Emergency Repair Disk.

4. Check the box in the Emergency Repair Diskette dialog box to copy the current Registry into your repair folder. This copy can then be used to help recover your system if the Registry is subsequently damaged. Click OK.

5. The appropriate files are copied onto the floppy disk, and a message appears telling you the process is complete. Click OK to close the Emergency Repair Diskette dialog box.

WARNING If you have read through this section but haven't made an Emergency Repair Disk, do it now. If you get to the point where you need an Emergency Repair Disk, it's too late to make one.

Label the disk, and put it in a safe place. We'll come back to this Emergency Repair Disk in a later section in this skill.

Using Windows Update

Microsoft has done a great job in blurring the lines that separate your computer from the Internet, and the mechanism you use to get operating system updates is another good example. Windows Update connects to the Microsoft Windows Update Web site at www.windowsupdate.microsoft.com and keeps your system up-to-date by automatically downloading new device drivers and Windows system updates, as they are needed.

Choose Start ➤ Windows Update to open Internet Explorer and connect to the Web site automatically. Once at the Web site, click Product Updates to download the latest updates, or click Support Information to access a list of frequently asked questions. You can also get help online; click Windows 2000 Professional for more information, and follow the instructions on the screen.

You can also uninstall a device driver or system file and restore the previous version by following these steps:

1. Choose Start ➤ Windows Update to connect to the Web site.

2. Click Product Updates.

3. Click Device Drivers.

4. Click Restore, and follow the instructions on the screen.

Alternatively, if you don't have Internet access, you can use these steps:

1. Choose Start ➤ Run, and type **msinfo32** into the Open box.

2. When the System Information program opens, choose Tools ➤ Windows ➤ Update Wizard Uninstall.

3. Follow the instructions on the screen.

Using the Built-in Troubleshooters

In Skill 3, we looked at the Windows Help system and how you can use it to find online information about a task or application. Windows 2000 Professional goes beyond the usual concepts of static help and includes a set of built-in technical support troubleshooters you can use to help diagnose and isolate certain hardware-related problems. There are several methods you can use to find the right troubleshooter and start it running on your system:

- Choose Start ➤ Help to open the Windows Help System. Select the Contents tab, select the Troubleshooting and Maintenance topic, and then open

Windows 2000 Troubleshooters. Choose the appropriate troubleshooter from the list, and follow the directions on the screen.

- Start a troubleshooter directly from a page of Help information. As you read through the information the page contains, you will come across a link to a Hardware Troubleshooter; click the link to start the troubleshooter.

- Choose Start ➤ Settings ➤ Control Panel, and then open Add/Remove Hardware. Click Next, and check Add/Troubleshoot a Device in the Choose Hardware Task dialog box. Click Next. In the Choose a Hardware Device dialog box, select the hardware you want to diagnose, click Next, and follow the instructions on the screen.

- Choose Start ➤ Settings ➤ Control Panel, and then open Computer Management. Select Device Manager from the list of System Tools in the left pane. In the right pane, right-click the hardware you want to work with, select Properties, and, on the General tab, click the Troubleshooter button.

Troubleshooters are available for problems encountered with the following:

- Client Service for NetWare
- Display, video cards, and display adapters
- Hardware, such as digital cameras and CD-ROM drives
- Internet connections
- Modems
- MS-DOS programs
- Multimedia and games
- Printing
- Remote access
- Sound
- System setup
- TCP/IP networking
- Windows 3.x programs

Once the troubleshooter starts, click the Hide button on the Help toolbar to close the left Help pane. Be sure to follow all the steps the troubleshooter suggests, as your answers at each point will help Windows find a solution to your problem.

Tracking Your System with Event Viewer

If you are looking for information on what is actually happening inside your Windows 2000 Professional system, the Event Viewer is one of the most useful management tools available. You can use the Event Viewer to peek behind the scenes and see what Windows is up to, or you can use it to help troubleshoot a computer that is misbehaving. Choose Start ➢ Settings ➢ Control Panel, select Administrative Tools, and open Event Viewer to display the main Event Viewer window, as shown in Figure 15.3.

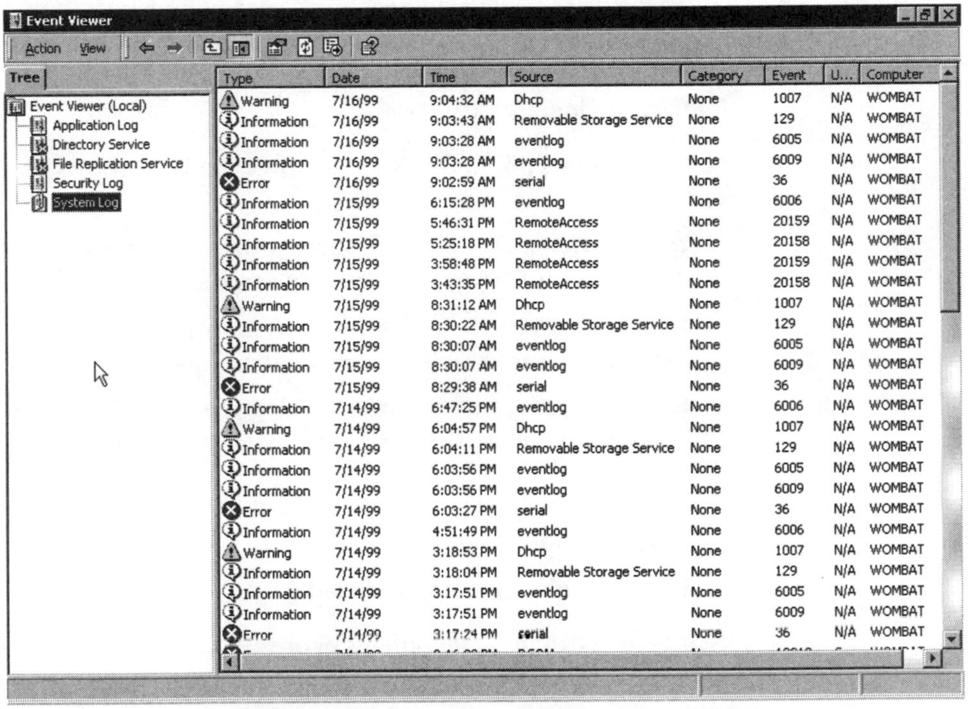

FIGURE 15.3: The main Event Viewer window

The Event Viewer can display the contents of three Windows 2000 Professional event logs (System, Security, and Application), as well as display information on directory services and file replication services if you are connected to a network running Windows 2000 Server. The event log service starts automatically when Windows 2000 starts running. Any user can view the Application and System logs, but only administrators can view the contents of the Security logs. Let's take a look at the three logs:

Application Log   Contains events generated by applications. If one of your programs is behaving oddly or crashes repeatedly, look in the Application log for error messages. The application developers decide which events to log.

System Log   Contains events logged by individual Windows 2000 Professional components. If a device driver fails to load at system startup, an event will be recorded in the System log. Windows 2000 Professional decides which events are logged.

Security Log   Contains security information such as invalid logon attempts as well as events relating to auditing on shared disks, files, and folders. An administrator can specify which events are logged into the Security log.

The Application and System logs use three kinds of events, each with their own icon:

Information   Describes the successful completion of an event, such as a device driver loading or a system service starting

Warning   Describes a condition that may not be significant now but may indicate a future problem, such as a hard disk filling up.

Error   Describes a significant problem, such as a loss of data, a system service that failed to initialize, or even a hardware failure.

And there are two kinds of Security log events:

Success Audit   Indicates a successful event, such as a user logging on.

Failure Audit   Indicates a failed event, such as a log on failure.

Event Viewer displays the contents of one log at a time; for example, Figure 15.3 displays the contents of the System log. Click one of the other logs in the Tree pane to display its contents. To look at a specific event in more detail, right-click the event in the main display, and choose Properties from the shortcut menu. Look in the Description box on the Event Detail tab to see a short description of the event. Use the Next (the down arrow) and Previous (the up arrow) buttons on this tab to move through the events in the log. You can choose View ➢ Find to search for specific events.

Setting Up the Logs

Right-click one of the logs in the Tree display, and select properties to open the log's Properties dialog box. Figure 15.4 shows the Application Log Properties dialog box open at the General tab. Using the settings in this dialog box, you can tweak the maximum log size and specify what you want to happen once the log fills up. Windows 2000 Professional defaults to overwriting events more than seven days old.

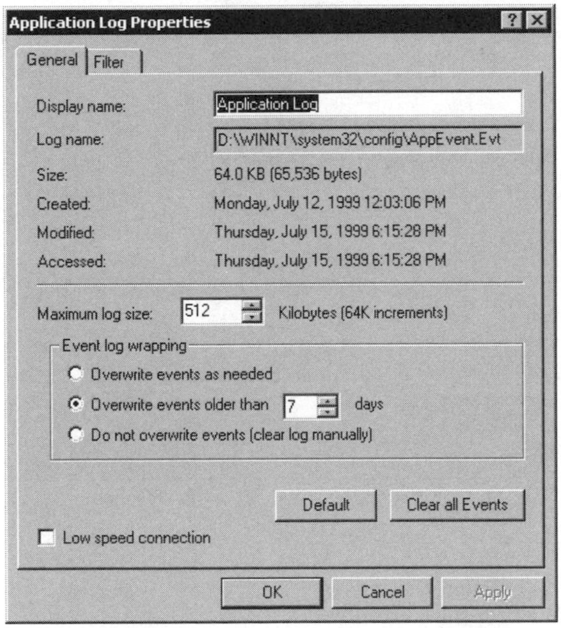

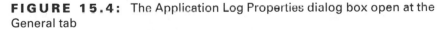

FIGURE 15.4: The Application Log Properties dialog box open at the General tab

Filtering Events

The Event Viewer supports two different viewing modes for all three logs: All Events or Filter Events. All Events, as its name suggests, displays everything, but if you want to focus in on something more specific, use Filter Events. Click the Filter tab in the Properties dialog box to bring it to the front, and you will see the dialog box displayed in Figure 15.5.

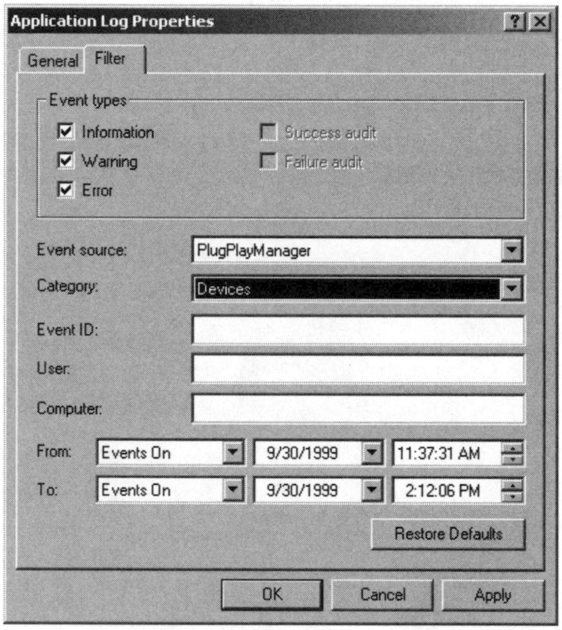

FIGURE 15.5: The Filter tab allows you to focus in on specific types of events.

The settings in this dialog box allow you to display events based on:

- The type of event, such as Information, Warning, or Error

- A specific source, such as the Installer (called Msinstaller in the Event Source list) or the Plug-and-Play Manager (PlugPlayManager)

- A specific category, depending on the option you chose for the source, which might include Disk, Network, Printers, or Services

- An Event ID number

- An event generated by a specific user

- An event generated by a specific computer

- A specific time period

Troubleshooting with Event Logs

So how do you use all this information to find system problems? Here are some suggestions:

- If a particular event seems to trigger system problems, choose View ➤ Find to search for other instances of the same event.

- If you suspect specific hardware is the cause of your system problems, set up a filter to show only those events generated by that piece of hardware.

- Make a note of the Event ID numbers as they directly relate to a text description in a message file. You can use the number when talking to Technical Support people.

- When you archive log data using Action ➤ All Tasks ➤ Save Log File As, save it in log file format with the filename extension of .EVT. This preserves all the binary data associated with the log. Some of this data is discarded if you save the log in text (.TXT) or comma-delimited (.CSV) format.

Looking at Vital Statistics with Task Manager

If you want to take a quick look at what is happening right now in certain parts of your Windows 2000 Professional system, use Task Manager for the job. Right-click an empty portion of the Taskbar at the bottom of the Desktop, and choose Task Manager from the shortcut menu. Alternatively, choose Start ➤ Run, and type **taskmgr** into the Open dialog box.

TIP You can also access Task Manager from the Windows Security dialog box. This is particularly useful if you are having problems on your system that prevent you from using conventional methods. Press Ctrl+Alt+Del (go on, try it) to open the Windows Security dialog box, and choose Task Manager.

Skill 15

The main Task Manager display has three tabs:

Applications   Lists all the programs running on your system, along with the status of each. You can use the information in this window to find out if an application is in trouble, since it will be described in this window as Not Responding rather than bearing the normal description of Running.

Processes   Lists all the processes running on your system by name, process ID number (PID), processor times, and memory usage.

Performance   Displays constantly updated totals for current and historic processor and memory usage. We look at this tab in more detail next.

The Performance tab, shown in Figure 15.6, displays current and historic processor and memory usage in graphical form at the top of the tab. The four boxes in the lower part of the Performance tab show how your system is using memory. The Totals box lists the total number of handles, processes, and threads running on your system now. The Physical Memory box describes how the memory on your system is being used, and the Commit Charge box shows how much memory is allocated to system and application programs. The Kernel Memory box shows the amount of memory being used by Windows 2000 Professional.

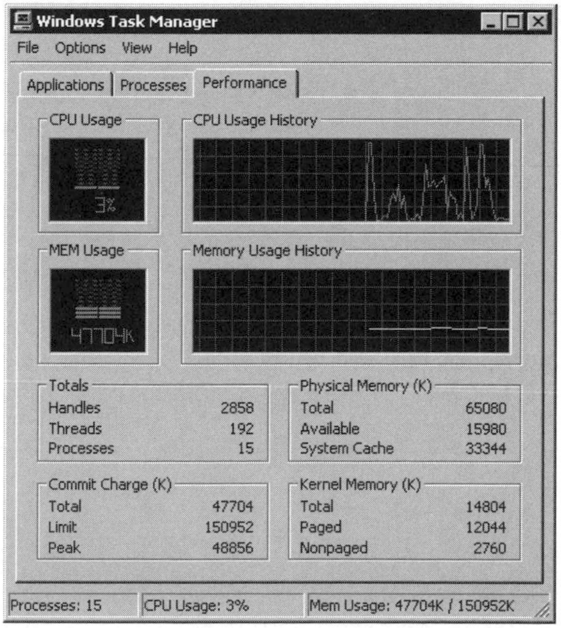

FIGURE 15.6:   Task Manager window open at the Performance tab

TIP   No matter which of the three tabs is open in Task Manager, at the bottom of the dialog box you will always see the total number of processes running, the percentage of processor usage, and how much physical and virtual memory is currently being used. This is a very useful snapshot of current system performance.

Using the Task Manger, you can get a very good idea of what is happening on your system, but if you want more details on specific aspects of system performance, turn to Performance in the Administrative Tools in Control Panel.

Measuring System Performance

One of the benefits of using Windows 2000 Professional is that it is a self-tuning operating system and can make changes by itself to reach optimum performance. But, just to be on the safe side, Windows 2000 also includes tools you can use to find and examine system bottlenecks. You can use Performance to monitor all sorts of system variables, known as *performance counters*, including some odd ones of interest only to developers of very specific sorts of applications.

To open Performance (previously known as Performance Monitor), choose Start ➢ Settings ➢ Control Panel, open Administrative Tools, and then open Performance. You will see a display like the one shown in Figure 15.7.

Performance provides three different displays of real-time data:

View Chart   Displays performance counter information graphically. You can display as many as you like in this view, but more than half a dozen makes for a very hard-to-read chart. Time is shown along the bottom axis, and the performance counter you are interested in is shown on the vertical axis.

View Histogram   Displays performance counter information as a bar chart.

View Report   Displays performance counter information as a text report.

Windows 2000 Professional tracks literally hundreds of performance counters, and as you add certain network-based applications, many more are added automatically. We are not going to list them all here; doing so would turn this book into a huge doorstop. Information on all the counters is available within Performance if you are prepared to search for it.

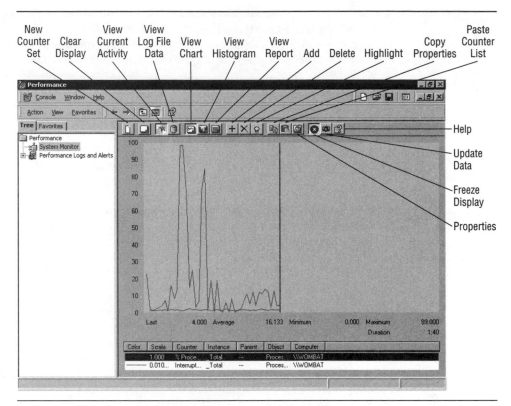

FIGURE 15.7: Performance open in chart mode

To add a performance counter and display it in chart mode, follow these steps:

1. In the Performance window, click the toolbar button that displays the plus sign to open the Add Counters dialog box shown in Figure 15.8.

2. In the Performance Object list, choose the type of object you want to work with. We'll choose Processor.

3. Select the counter you want to display. For example, % Processor Time displays an indicator of how hard your processor is working. Click Explain to see a brief (and sometimes terse) description of your selected counter.

4. Click Add. Select any other objects and counters you want to display, and click Close when you are done.

As the state of your computer changes, the data displayed in the Performance window also changes. A legend at the bottom of the Performance window describes each of the counters you have chosen.

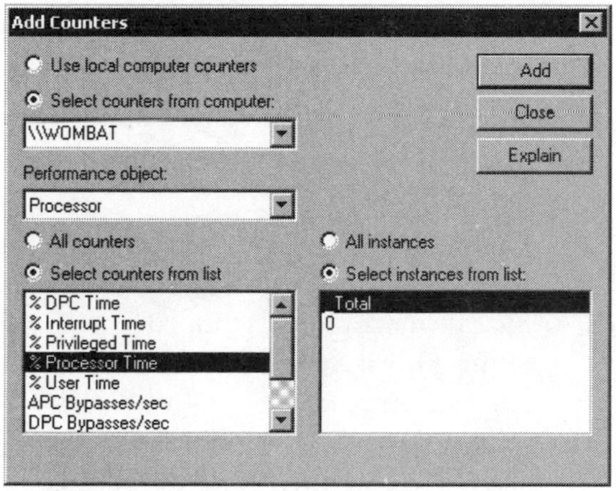

FIGURE 15.8: The Add Counters dialog box

Starting Windows 2000 Professional in Safe Mode

But what if your problem is more fundamental than those solved by the built-in troubleshooters? What if you just installed some new software and now your system won't start? What then? You may be able to start Windows 2000 Professional in a special mode known as *safe mode*. In safe mode, Windows uses the minimum number of default device drivers to get the system running. This minimal safe mode configuration may be sufficient to allow you to remove the software package that is causing the problem. You can also install service packs or even the entire operating system from safe mode if that becomes necessary.

> **TIP** If you can't fix your computer system using safe mode, you may have to use an Emergency Repair Disk to recover your system.

Starting Windows 2000 Professional in safe mode offers the following options:

Safe Mode   Loads only the basic device drivers, including Microsoft mouse, monitor, keyboard, hard and floppy disk storage, basic video, the default system services, and no network connection.

Safe Mode with Networking   Loads the basic device drivers needed to function as in safe mode but also adds network drivers.

Safe Mode with Command Prompt   Loads the basic device drivers needed to function in safe mode and opens a command prompt window rather than the Windows Desktop.

Enable Boot Logging   Saves information on which device drivers were successfully or unsuccessfully loaded onto the system, saving it into a text file called ntbtlog.txt for later analysis. Close examination of the contents of this file can be very useful in determining the exact cause of your system startup problems.

Enable VGA Mode   Starts the system using a basic VGA driver. This mode is especially useful if you have installed a new video driver and the driver is causing problems. You can't unload the driver using conventional methods because the device driver isn't working properly, so you can't see enough information on the screen to perform even basic tasks. This mode can be a lifesaver in these circumstances and can avoid the need to reinstall the entire operating system.

Last Known Good Configuration   Starts Windows using the Registry information saved at the last shut down. We'll look at this option in more detail later in this skill.

Debugging Mode   Starts Windows 2000 Professional and, at the same time, sends debugging information through a serial cable to another computer. This is a rather specialized setup and is only used under very specific circumstances. For example, you might use it when you are tracking down a particularly strange system problem.

 TIP   If you or your system administrator used Remote Install Services to install Windows 2000 Professional on your system, you may also see additional options that relate to Remote Install Services.

To start Windows 2000 Professional in safe mode, follow these steps:

1. Click Start ➢ Shut Down, choose Restart, and click OK.

2. If you have a dual boot system, press F8 when you see the message asking you to select an operating system; otherwise press F8 when you see the bars at the bottom of the screen as Windows 2000 Professional restarts.

3. Use the arrow keys on the keyboard to highlight the safe mode option you want to use, and press Enter.

WARNING Make sure the Num Lock key is off before you use the arrow keys on the numeric keypad.

If the problem disappears when you start the system in safe mode, you can be sure that the basic device drivers and system services are not to blame for the problem. If you think a newly added device driver is to blame, you can remove it using safe mode. But there are circumstances when Windows 2000 Professional system files are damaged and safe mode will not help you. In these circumstances, you should boot your system using an Emergency Repair Disk, as you'll see later in this skill.

Starting Windows 2000 Professional Using the Last Known Good Configuration

When you select the Last Known Good Configuration from the safe mode menu, Windows 2000 Professional restores information in the Registry to the configuration used the last time the system was successfully started. If your computer refuses to start, you don't want to use the current information, so choosing this option lets you go back to a Registry configuration that has worked at least once in the recent past.

WARNING When you use this option, you will, of course, lose any system changes you made since the last successful shut-down.

However, the Last Known Good Configuration can't always save you. You will have to try a different solution if you want to go back to a configuration more than one successful boot ago, if the information you want to change is not saved in the Registry, or if the system boots properly, you log on as a user, and then the system stops.

Skill 15

Starting Windows 2000 Professional from the Setup Disks

You can also restart your Windows 2000 Professional system by using the four original Setup boot disks or by booting from your original Windows 2000 Professional CD (if your CD-ROM drive supports this feature). Here are the steps:

1. Place Setup boot disk 1 in your floppy-disk drive and the Windows 2000 Professional CD in your CD-ROM drive.

2. Choose Start ➢ Shut Down, choose Restart, and click OK.

3. When prompted, insert the next Setup boot disk into the floppy-disk drive.

4. The Setup program starts working in text mode and asks if you want to continue with the installation. Press Enter.

5. Choose the Repair option, not the Installation option.

   You will then have to choose the type of repair you want to make, using either an Emergency Repair Disk or the Recovery Console.

Using an Emergency Repair Disk

The next step in the recovery process is to choose the type of repair you want to make:

Fast Repair   Works quickly and does not require any intervention or input from you. This option will attempt to repair problems associated with the Registry, damaged system files, the boot sector on your boot volume, and the startup environment variables if you have a dual boot or multiboot system. The Fast Repair option uses a copy of the Registry created when the Setup program was run for the first time on your system. Using this option will wipe out any settings or preferences you have changed since Setup was first run. Most of the time, this is a small price to pay for recovering a damaged system. Try the Fast Repair option first; if it doesn't work, you can come back and try another approach later.

Manual Repair   Requires input from you and lets you choose whether you want to selectively repair damaged system files, boot sector problems, and startup environment variables, but does not let you repair problems associated with the Registry. You should only use this option if you are an administrator and are skilled in diagnosing and repairing computer-related problems.

TIP   To repair individual Registry files or replace the entire Registry, use the Recovery Console described in the next section. This is definitely an advanced technique and is not for the faint of heart.

To start the recovery process, you will need the Emergency Repair Disk that you made earlier and your original Windows 2000 Professional CD. Follow the instructions on the screen, and insert the ERD when you are prompted for it.

If you can't find the ERD or didn't make one when we told you to, the emergency repair process will attempt to locate and repair your damaged Windows 2000 Professional system, but it may not be able complete the repairs.

WARNING   The repair process in Windows 2000 Professional relies on information saved in the `systemroot\repair` folder, usually found in `winnt\repair`. Do not change any of the files in this folder, and do not remove the folder.

If the emergency repair process is successful, your computer will restart automatically, and you should be back in business once again with a fully functioning system. If the emergency repair process is not successful, you can use the advanced techniques available in the Recovery Console.

Using Recovery Console

The Recovery Console is a command-line environment you can use to make system changes to a Windows 2000 Professional system that refuses to start. It is useful if you want to repair your system by copying a file from your original CD. You can also use Recovery Console to start or stop system services and to format disks. But, as we've already noted, it is not for the faint hearted; it is intended for use by knowledgeable system administrators who are well versed in system troubleshooting and repair.

Skill 15

There are two ways you can run the Recovery Console on your system:

- If you can't start your computer, you can run the Recovery Console from the Setup disks we described earlier.

- If you can start your computer, you can install Recovery Console as an option in the boot menu.

To install Recovery Console as a start-up option, follow these steps:

1. Log on to the system as an administrator.

2. Insert your original Windows 2000 Professional CD into your CD-ROM drive.

3. If you are prompted to upgrade to Windows 2000, click No.

4. Choose Start ➢ Programs ➢ Accessories, and select Command Prompt. You can choose Start ➢ Run if you prefer.

5. Make your CD-ROM drive the current drive, and type the following:

   `\i386\winnt32.exe /cmdcons`

   Press the Enter key, and follow the instructions that appear on the screen.

To run the Recovery Console, you must restart your computer and select the Recovery Console option when your system restarts. To display a list of the commands available in the Recovery Console, type **help** at the command prompt. You can then make all the required changes to your system. To restart your computer once again, type **exit** at the command prompt.

When All Else Fails

Yes, you guessed it: when all else fails, you will have to reinstall the Windows 2000 Professional operating system over the top of your existing, damaged system. This may seem like a long-winded and time-consuming option, but it certainly works, unless you have a major hardware problem that the Windows failure is just masking.

If you have installed service packs, additional applications, or used Windows Update to download new drivers or applications, you will have to reinstall them also. See Skill 2 for details on installing Windows 2000 Professional.

Are You Up to Speed?

Now you can...

- ☑ shut down Windows 2000 Professional
- ☑ make a backup
- ☑ restore a backup
- ☑ make an Emergency Repair Disk
- ☑ use Windows Update
- ☑ use the built-in troubleshooters
- ☑ work with Event Viewer
- ☑ run Task Manager
- ☑ evaluate system performance
- ☑ start Windows 2000 Professional in safe mode
- ☑ start Windows 2000 Professional using the Last Known Good Configuration
- ☑ start Windows 2000 Professional from the Setup disks
- ☑ use an Emergency Repair Disk
- ☑ use Recovery Console

Skill 15

SKILL 16

Setting Up a Small Network

- Setting up your own peer-to-peer network
- Configuring Windows 2000 Professional networking
- Sharing an Internet connection
- Monitoring network and dial-up connections
- Demystifying and creating new user groups and accounts
- Understanding rights
- Modifying permissions for files, folders, and printers

Are you tired of playing the floppy-disk shuffle? Are you running out of disks to transfer files from computer to computer and running out of patience at the same time? Have you forgotten which important application is installed on which computer? Well, there is a quick and easy answer to all these questions, and that is to network your computers together. The hardware is cheap and readily available, the networking software is fast and reliable, and, best of all, it is included with your Windows 2000 Professional system. A network will save you time and, therefore, save you money. In today's world, access to information is so vital that networking is not a luxury; it's a simple necessity. In this skill, we'll look at how to set up a peer-to-peer network based on Windows 2000 Professional in a couple of hours, and that time estimate includes going to the store to buy the extra hardware you will need.

We'll also look at the classes of users available in Windows 2000 Professional and how to create new users and new groups of users. We'll examine other important security considerations as well, including rights and permissions, and we'll look at how to make two networked computers share one connection to the Internet.

Setting Up Your Peer-to-Peer Network

To compete in today's world, companies must share information not only within the company but with the outside world as well. Networking is a simple and economic way to achieve this goal. In addition, a network can reduce the pressure to buy another printer, add a modem to another computer, or buy a bigger hard disk, because you can share all these resources over your network. Even an outside line connecting to your Internet Service Provider (ISP) can become a shared resource available over the network.

Many of the computer books we have looked at just assume that your network sprang forth completely formed, all connections complete, and ready for you to go to work. Well, that might be the case if you work for a large corporation with a large support staff, but what do you do if you want to set up a network in a small office or home office?

T **TIP**   Networking is one area of technology that is simply riddled with abbreviations, acronyms, and jargon. In this skill, we will have to use some of that jargon because, after all, it is a useful shorthand. But if we use a term that you don't understand and it is not defined in this skill, look in the Glossary at the end of this book for a complete explanation. You will find it there.

In this skill, we'll describe how to set up a network based on well-accepted and easy-to-use standards—a network that can connect from two to hundreds of computers quickly and easily, using hardware that you can buy off the shelf at computer stores, from PC catalog companies, and even at big-box consumer electronics stores. All the software you need is available as a part of the Windows 2000 Professional package. Don't worry, it's as easy as plugging in a toaster.

HOW DOES IT WORK?

The most common networking standard is known as Ethernet, and that standard forms the basis for our network as well as for millions of other networks. Ethernet was devised in 1973 by Xerox and was eventually formalized by Digital Equipment Corporation, Intel, and Xerox. Ethernet transmits data over the network at 10Mbps—that's 10 million bits per second (or close enough that it makes no difference). By way of comparison, the fastest analog modem standard currently available, V.90, operates at a speed of up to 56Kbps, or 56 thousand bits per second. So Ethernet is pretty quick.

There are a couple of variations on the standard that you will hear about:

Fast Ethernet   An advance on the original standard that transmits data at 100Mbps (sometimes called 100BaseT).

Gigabit Ethernet   Another advance on the original standard that transmits data at a phenomenal 1Gbps (or approximately 1,000Mbps) over fiber-optic cable. This is a bit out of our small-network league.

You will find definitions of all these variations in the Glossary at the end of this book.

Skill 16

Despite a growing selection of home and small office networking solutions, including technologies that use existing phone lines, the AC power lines, or even no wires at all (we'll look at infrared technology in Skill 17), Ethernet is definitely a smart choice. It is a longtime standard, is easy to set up, expand, and troubleshoot, and the components are easy to work with and are readily available.

Designing Your Own Network

Network topology is one of those jargon phrases with a simple explanation; it refers to the way the network is designed physically. Three basic network layouts are in common use:

Star Topology A network design in which all the computers are connected to a central hub like the points of a star, and which uses 10BaseT cabling (also called twisted-pair or UTP cable).

Bus Topology A network design in which all the computers are connected to a single cable that connects each computer to the next, and which uses coaxial cable (also called coax or thin Ethernet cable).

Ring Topology A network design in which computers are connected in rings. This type is far less common.

The network that we'll create in this skill will be based on the star topology. At the center of a star network is a *hub* or *switch*, and each computer on the network connects to this hub using thin, flexible 10BaseT cable running between a network interface card (NIC) installed in each computer and the hub, as Figure 16.1 shows. The 10BaseT cable uses industry-standard modular connectors, and installation is simple and inexpensive. The number of ports or connections on the hub determines the number of computers you can connect. The smallest hubs usually allow between five and eight connections, and when you need more capacity, you can either connect several of these smaller hubs together or replace them with larger hubs.

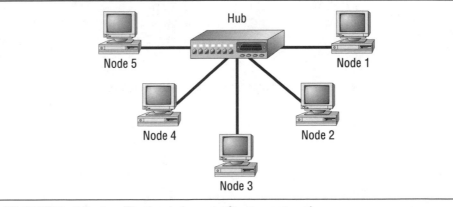

FIGURE 16.1: The basic layout of a star network

The benefits of a star configuration include:

- Uses inexpensive 10BaseT cabling (more on cabling in the next section).

- Allows fast installation with standard modular connectors. RJ-45 connectors are similar to those used in telephone systems but are just a little larger; see Figure 16.2. They snap into the network interface card or the port on the hub, making a quick but very secure connection.

- Provides simple expansion by adding a new hub. When the time comes, you can connect one hub to another using a special cross-over cable.

- Displays network status information. This status information is displayed on the front of the hub to confirm a good connection. If the LED is on, the link is good; if not, there is a problem with the cable. You don't get that with coax cable.

- Allows easy troubleshooting without disrupting the entire network. If a connection fails, only one computer is disabled. The rest of the network continues to function except, of course, no one can access that node until the connection is repaired.

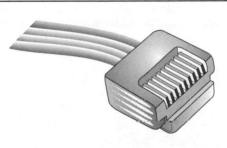

FIGURE 16.2: 10BaseT cabling uses RJ-45 connectors.

If there is a drawback to this kind of network, it is that the maximum cable distance between a computer and the hub is 328 feet (100 meters).

PEER-TO-PEER AND SERVER-BASED NETWORKS: WHAT'S THE DIFFERENCE?

We need to consider two main network configurations:

Peer-to-Peer Networks   A network in which all the connected computers are considered equals. Each computer has its own hard disk and has the ability to talk to all the other computers on the network, sharing resources such as CD-ROMs, printers, modems, and so on. In this skill, we are only considering this kind of network as it works well in a star configuration.

Server-Based Networks   A network in which one or more central computers act as a server, and all the other computers on the network are connected to this server. Management functions are concentrated on the server, which administers applications as well as file and printer sharing. For more information on working in this sort of environment, see Skill 17.

Getting the Cabling Right

Network cabling is the pipeline that holds your network together. It is the physical connection that runs between every computer and hub on your network. Networking standards specify the cable quality and its ability to transmit data; the higher the category, the better the cable.

In 10BaseT networks, two kinds or grades of unshielded twisted-pair (UTP) cable are in common use:

Category 3 UTP   Used in Ethernet networks transmitting data at 10Mbps. Minimum cable length is 8 feet (2.5 meters), and maximum cable length is 328 feet (100 meters). Do not use this cable with 100Mbps Fast Ethernet networks.

Category 5 UTP   Used in Fast Ethernet networks transmitting data at 100Mbps. Computer-to-hub distances must not exceed 165 feet (50 meters). This cable can be used in 10Mbps Ethernet networks.

When you are planning your network, you should always consider cable cost in the light of future expansion because, once you have run the cable, it is likely to be in place for a long time. Category 5 cable costs a little more than Category 3, so if you are planning to expand your network and upgrade to Fast Ethernet, go with Category 5 cable right from the start. After all, the cost of actually running the cable is the same for both grades.

Many of the network starter kits you can buy these days contain everything you need to network two computers together. You will find that the package contains two network interface cards, a hub, a power supply for the hub, and two 10- or 25-feet-long cables. You can buy starter kits made by companies such as Intel (www.intel.com), Linksys (www.linksys.com), 3Com (www.3com.com), and Netgear (www.netgearinc.com)—all for considerably less than $100.

Some Network Devices Defined

It is time for a quick review of some of the components of our network and some of the jargon we have introduced. Once that is done, we can lay out and install our network.

Network Interface Card (NIC)   Each computer connected to the network needs a network interface card. Some of today's computers and certain printers have these cards already built in. The card connects to one of the slots on your computer's motherboard, and several types of NICs are available both for desktop and for laptop computers. The manufacturer assigns every Ethernet card a unique number; this number is known as the *Ethernet address*, or *MAC address*, and it cannot be changed.

Hub   Each network interface card is connected to a hub that allows all the connected computers to communicate. Hubs are easy to install and can be connected together as your network expands. The hub itself does not require any software or configuration, just a power connection for the AC adapter.

Cable Type   Category 3 UTP cable is used in 10Mbps Ethernet networks, and Category 5 UTP cable in Fast Ethernet networks running at 100Mbps. If you plan to start with standard Ethernet and then upgrade to Fast Ethernet, install Category 5 cable.

Network Speed   You will see some network interface cards and certain hubs labeled as 10/100. This is not a new long-distance telephone service but an indication that the hardware can operate at either 10Mbps or 100Mbps. If you plan to start with standard Ethernet and then upgrade to Fast Ethernet, these dual-function cards are the way to go. Each hub port automatically senses the speed that the network interface card is using and then operates at that speed.

WARNING   If you plan on taking your notebook computer home from the office at night and plugging it into your home network, ask your IT support staff for advice on how to do this with the smallest amount of reconfiguration. Depending on which networking system your office uses, this may not be a trivial undertaking.

Just Do It

Most networks begin by connecting two or three computers together, as Figure 16.3 shows, and that's what we'll cover in this section. If you want to set up a larger network, the process is essentially the same; you'll just need a bigger hub. Let's take a look at the steps:

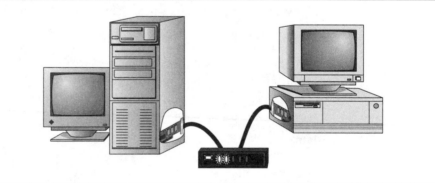

FIGURE 16.3: A basic network connecting two computers via a hub

1. Decide where each piece of equipment—computer, printer, and hub—will be located. Keep an eye on distance to make sure you stay within the Ethernet

specifications. If Internet access is important, be sure to locate one of the computers close to a phone jack or other external connection. Choose between 10Mbps Ethernet and 100Mbps Fast Ethernet.

2. Make a list of all the hardware and cable you will have to buy. Each computer needs a network interface card; be sure to get the right kind for each computer. You can buy the cable in bulk and attach the RJ-45 connectors yourself using a special crimping tool, or if cable runs are more modest, you can buy cables of the right length with the connectors already attached; lengths of 10, 15, 20, 25, and 50 feet are commonly available. Buy Category 3 UTP cable if you plan to use 10Mbps Ethernet, and buy Category 5 UTP cable if you plan to upgrade to or use 100Mbps Fast Ethernet. Buy a basic hub with more ports than you need right now; this will give you some room to expand in the future. Many of the smaller hubs have 5, 8, or 16 ports.

3. Turn off and unplug each computer, open the case, and install a network interface card into an empty slot in each one, according to the manufacturer's instructions. Screw the card bracket into the case so that the card won't work itself loose. Replace the case. Many notebook computers let you insert PC Cards with the power on. Snap one end of the cable (it doesn't matter which end you start with; both ends are the same) into the RJ-45 socket on the network interface card and the other end into the hub, starting with port 1. Plug in the hub power supply, and then plug the power adapter into the hub.

4. Turn on the hub and all the connected computers. On the front of the hub, the numbered indicator light for each connected device should turn on. Depending on the hub manufacturer, a continuously lit light usually indicates a good connection, while a flashing light usually indicates send-and-receive activity on the network. Other lights on the hub may indicate connection speed (either 10 or 100Mbps) and overall network bandwidth use. Some network interface cards also feature activity lights that indicate status, but they can be hard to see as they are only visible from the back of the computer.

Now all we have to do is install and configure the networking software. We'll do that on Windows 2000 Professional next, and then we'll take a look at configuring a Window 98 system on our network.

Skill 16

Setting Up Windows 2000 Networking

To connect to the network, we have to ensure that three essential categories of software are loaded onto each computer on the network:

Client Software   Connects your computer to the network.

Network Protocol   Specifies how communications will take place and be managed over the network.

Service Software   Provides additional functions such as file and print sharing.

As Windows 2000 Professional restarts after you installed the network hardware, the Plug-and-Play management system loads the device drivers you need to connect to the network.

TIP   If Windows 2000 Professional does not detect your network interface card automatically, use Add/Remove Hardware, described in Skill 14, to complete the process manually.

Windows 2000 Professional does not know which one of several possible networking protocols you want to use, so we still have to complete a few more steps:

1. Log on to your Windows 2000 Professional computer as an administrator, and load your Windows 2000 Professional CD into your CD-ROM drive.

2. Choose Start ➢ Settings ➢ Control Panel, and open Network and Dial-up Connections.

3. Right-click Local Area Connection, and choose Properties to open the Local Area Connection Properties dialog box, as shown in Figure 16.4.

4. At the top of the General tab, you will see the make and model of your network interface card, and below this you will see the Ethernet or MAC address that has been read from the card.

5. In the center of this dialog box, we want to see at least three components; others may be present too, but we need to see these three:

   • Client for Microsoft Networks

   • File and Printer Sharing for Microsoft Networks

   • NetBEUI Protocol

6. If these components are not installed, click Install, then select either Client to install Client for Microsoft Networks, Service to install File and Printer Sharing for Microsoft Networks, or Protocol to install NetBEUI Protocol, and click Add. Repeat these steps until these three components are listed in the Local Area Connection Properties dialog box.

7. Click OK, and then click OK again when you are prompted to restart your computer.

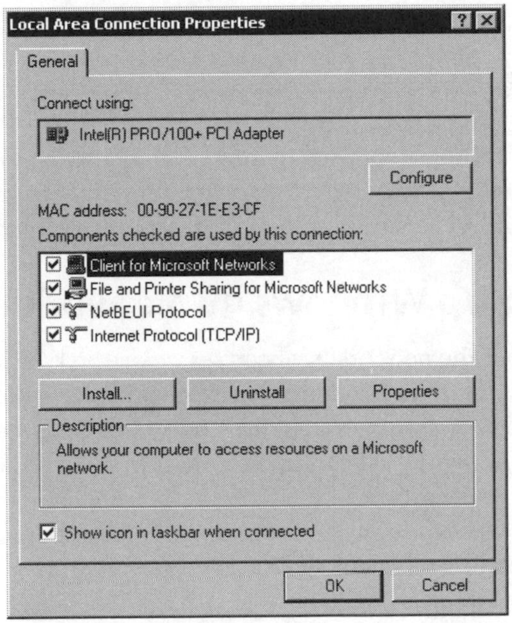

FIGURE 16.4: The Local Area Connection Properties dialog box

Once installation is complete, choose Start ➢ Settings ➢ Control Panel ➢ Administrative Tools ➢ Computer Management, click System Tools in the left pane to expand the menu, and then open Device Manager. Expand Network Adapters in the right pane. If there is no red arrow or yellow exclamation point on the icon for your network interface card, it is installed correctly and is working.

WHAT IS NETBEUI?

NetBEUI, or, to use the full moniker, NetBIOS Extended User Interface, is a networking protocol designed by IBM in 1985. NetBEUI is a very small protocol, ideally suited to small and medium-sized networks due to its speed and ability to tune itself to adapt to changing network circumstances. It is not suitable for large networks, where you would be more likely to use TCP/IP instead.

If you are connecting more than one Windows 2000 Professional system, repeat the preceding steps on each computer. If you want to configure network connections on a Windows 95 or 98 computer, check out the next section.

Setting Up Windows 98 Networking

Once the network has been set up on the Windows 2000 Professional system, you can set up networking on the other connected computers. For this example, we are going to assume that at least one of the other computers is running Windows 95 or Windows 98. The setup is similar in both, but our example will use Windows 98 Second Edition.

We need to install the same software components on Windows 98 that we installed on Windows 2000 Professional:

- Client for Microsoft Networks
- File and Printer Sharing for Microsoft Networks
- NetBEUI Protocol

Here are the steps:

1. Right-click Network Neighborhood, and click Properties.

2. Click the Configuration tab to bring it to the front, and go through a similar set of steps to those described in the preceding section to install these same three networking software elements. You may be prompted to insert your Windows 98 CD into the CD-ROM drive.

3. Click the File and Print Sharing button to open the dialog box shown in Figure 16.5.

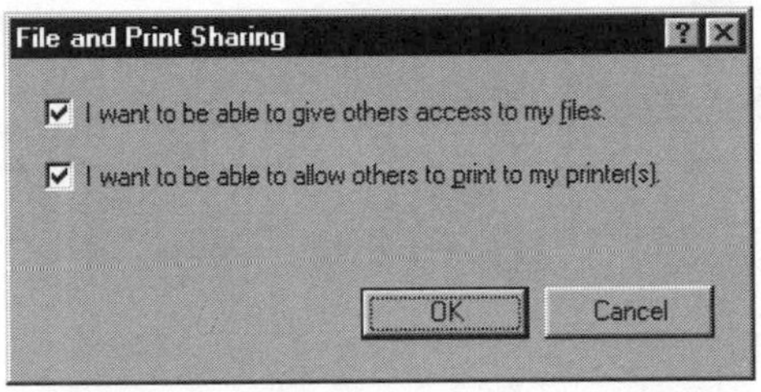

FIGURE 16.5: The Windows 98 File and Print Sharing dialog box

4. Check the appropriate boxes to allow other people on the network to gain access to your files and to allow others to print to the printer connected to your computer. Sharing under Windows 2000 Professional is a little more complex, so we'll look at that in more detail in a later section. Click OK to close the File and Print Sharing dialog box.

5. Click OK to close the Network dialog box, and click OK again when prompted to restart your computer.

The Network Neighborhood icon should appear on the Desktop; if you can't see it, check the "Troubleshooting Your Peer-to-Peer Network" section later in this skill for more information.

Finally, we have to name each computer connected to the network and specify the name of the workgroup we want to belong to. Here are the steps:

1. Right-click Network Neighborhood, and choose Properties. Click the Identification tab to bring it to the front. Enter a name for this computer into the Computer Name box. All the computers on your network must have a *different* name.

2. Enter the name of the workgroup you want to join in the Workgroup box. All the computers that will share files must belong to the *same* workgroup; otherwise, they will not be able to communicate. You don't have to complete the Computer Description field, but it might be handy to add a quick description of this computer.

Skill 16

3. Click OK to close the Network Properties dialog box.

WARNING

Be sure to log on to Windows 98 when you start your computer each day. If you don't specify a password—and you really should—just press Enter to log on. Don't press Escape or click Cancel; otherwise, you may not be able to browse the network in Network Neighborhood.

Now that the basic sharing service is installed, you can begin sharing files, folders, printers, and even complete hard drives. To share a file, folder, drive, or printer, follow these steps:

1. Open My Computer, and browse to the object you want to share.

2. Right-click to open the shortcut menu, and choose Sharing.

3. Choose Share As, and enter a name that is unique on that computer. This is the name that other people on the network will see when they browse your computer, so think for a moment before you call a shared drive simply *DriveC*. Calling the drive *PatsDriveC* is much more helpful.

4. Select the type of access you want to grant users on the network (read-only, full, or password-dependent). In a later section in this skill, we'll look at the special circumstances under which you should *always* use a password to protect a shared resource.

5. Click OK or Apply, and the drive or folder will become available to the other users on your network.

To access documents on the other networked computers, open the Network Neighborhood icon on the Desktop or inside Explorer, where you will see a list of the computers available on the network. Select the computer storing the file you want, and then browse until you locate the file. You can select, open, copy, move, and delete files on shared drives just as though they were on your own computer.

Sharing with Others

Once the network interface cards are installed and you have configured your network software on Windows 2000 Professional, the next step is to select the resources—files, folders, drives, and printers—that you want to share with other network users. Let's start with folders; here are the steps:

1. Open My Computer, and browse to the object you want to share.

2. Right-click to open the shortcut menu, and choose Sharing.

3. Click the Sharing tab to bring it to the front (see Figure 16.6), and choose Share This Folder. Enter a name that is unique on this computer. This is the name that other people on the network will see when they browse your computer, and it is also the name used in the shared folder's network path specification. For example, if the share name is Notes and the computer name is Ferret, the path specification becomes \\Ferret\Notes.

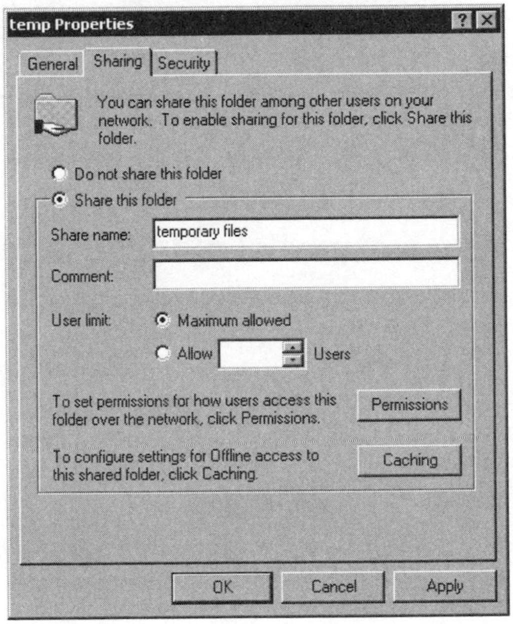

FIGURE 16.6: The folder Properties dialog box open at the Sharing tab

4. In the Comment box, enter a short description of the folder's contents. Other network users can see this comment when they look at the folder's properties in their My Network Places folder.

5. In the User Limit section of this dialog box, you can restrict the number of users who can access this folder simultaneously. On small networks, this is usually left at the default setting of Maximum Allowed.

6. Click the Permissions button to look at or change the default permissions associated with this folder.

7. The default permission associated with a new shared resource is Full Control to Everyone, which means that anyone on the network can do whatever they like with this resource. If the shared folder is on an NTFS volume, individual files can have their own access restrictions. For a complete discussion on how to use permissions on both FAT32 and NTFS volumes, see the "Permissions Explained" section later in this skill.

8. Click OK or Apply, and the drive or folder will become available to the other users on your network.

> **TIP** See Skill 8 for details on how to install and use a network printer.

Mapping a Network Folder to a Drive Letter

When you open Explorer or My Computer, you see a list of the drives available on your computer displayed in the right pane. If you plan to access a specific shared drive on another computer on a regular basis, you can make that shared drive appear just as though it were a drive on your own computer. Here's how:

1. Right-click My Network Places, and choose Map Network Drive to open the Map Network Drive dialog box shown in Figure 16.7.

2. Specify the drive letter that the mapped drive will use on your computer. The default is the next drive letter in sequence, and there is usually no need to change this.

3. Specify the path to the shared folder. For instance, if the drive is called `DriveC` and the computer name is `Ferret`, enter **\\Ferret\DriveC**. You can also use the Browse button to browse the network and find the computer and folder to use.

4. Check the Reconnect at Logon box, and each time you log on to your computer, this drive will automatically be mapped for you.

5. Click Finish, and the Explorer automatically opens on the folder you specified. The next time you open My Computer, you will see this folder and the associated network icon.

> **TIP** Mapped drives become part of My Computer, so, when you choose Start ➢ Search, you can include them in your searches.

To get rid of a mapped drive, open My Computer, right-click the mapped drive, and choose Disconnect. Or, if you are working in Explorer, highlight the drive, and choose Tools ➢ Disconnect Network Drive. Select the correct disk from the list that appears, and click OK. Don't worry, nothing at all happens to the shared drive; it is just removed from the list of drives displayed on your computer; you can always re-map the drive later if you change your mind.

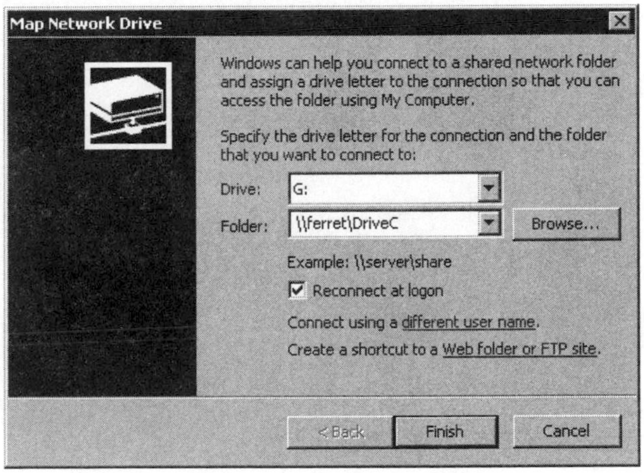

FIGURE 16.7: The Map Network Drive dialog box

Looking Around My Network Places

In this section, we're going to take a quick look at how the various network elements are represented in My Network Places. It's the best place to start when you are looking for network resources, because if you can see another computer or folder in My Network Places that usually means it is shared and you can access it. Click My Network Places, and, depending on how your network is set up, you will see some or all of the following:

Entire Network

Displays all the computers, files, folders, printers, and people on your network

Computers Near Me

Displays the computers in your workgroup

Microsoft Windows Network

Displays the computers connected using Microsoft Windows networking

Marketing

Displays the computers that make up the Marketing workgroup

Wombat

Indicates an individually networked computer

DRIVE C

Indicates a shared drive

A shared printer or folder icon, especially in My Computer or Explorer, will display a hand under it to indicate that it is shared.

Troubleshooting Your Peer-to-Peer Network

Setting up an Ethernet network with Windows 2000 Professional is pretty straight-forward, but before we leave this topic, here are a few troubleshooting hints we have found to be useful:

- Make sure that Client for Microsoft Networks, File and Printer Sharing for Microsoft Networks, and the NetBEUI Protocol are installed on all computers on your network, along with an appropriate device driver for your network interface card.

- If you can't access a specific computer, make sure that the computer has been turned on for a while. It can take a few minutes for all the computers on the network to appear after a shutdown.

- Make sure all the computer-to-hub connections are secure; check the lights on the front panel of the hub.

- If you can't access a computer, folder, or printer, confirm that the resource is actually set up for sharing.

- Keep cable distances within the Ethernet standards, and make sure you are using the correct type and grade of cable.

- If a shared resource requires a password, use the password set on that computer for that shared resource.

- If you are trying to access resources on Windows 2000 Professional from a Windows 95 or 98 computer and you are prompted for a password for a resource called IPC$, log on to the Windows 2000 Professional system as an administrator, and create an account with *exactly* the same user name and password as the user logged on to the Windows 98 system. The Windows 2000 Professional system must have an account for all users on the network. More on creating accounts later in this skill.

Network setup still isn't simple, but if you use the methods detailed here, you won't go wrong. The first network interface card you install may take you an hour or more to set up and configure, but the second one will take half that time, and the rest should be out of your hair in just a few minutes.

Internet Connection Sharing

One of the many benefits of a home or small office is that computers on the network can take advantage of a Windows 2000 Professional feature known as Internet Connection Sharing, which allows more than one computer to access a single connection to your Internet Service Provider (ISP). Here's how to set it up:

1. Log on as an administrator. Choose Start ➤ Settings ➤ Control Panel, and open Network and Dial-up Connections.

2. Right-click the connection you want to share, and select Properties.

3. Click the Sharing tab to bring it to the front, as Figure 16.8 shows.

4. In the Shared Access part of this dialog box, select the Enable Internet Connection Sharing for This Connection check box.

5. If you want to allow other computers on your network to dial out using this connection, check the Enable On-Demand Dialing check box.

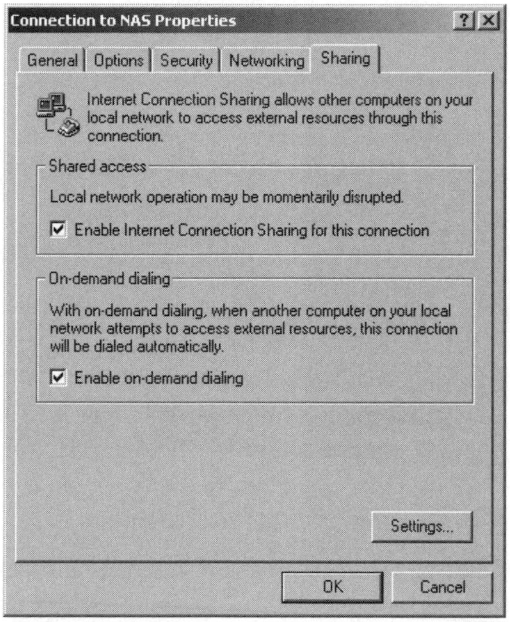

FIGURE 16.8: The Sharing tab

WARNING

When you enable Internet Connection Sharing, new TCP/IP addresses are assigned to the network interface card. So if you are using TCP/IP on your internal network, you may have to reestablish these settings. More on TCP/IP in Skill 17.

DIGITAL SUBSCRIBER LINE AND CABLE MODEMS ARE ALWAYS CONNECTED

Connecting any network to the Internet is fraught with danger, but when you are using a short-duration dial-up connection for Internet access, there is little (but not no) danger that your system security will be compromised. However, things change if you use one of the high-speed, 24-hour, "always on" Internet connections such as a cable modem or one of the newly available Digital Subscriber Line (DSL) services. DSL and cable modems give you an instant and open Internet connection, and there is no dialing involved.

When you connect to the Internet over such a connection with file sharing turned on, there is always the possibility of unauthorized access to your files and other network resources. Once largely a concern of the corporate world, computer security is rapidly becoming an issue in small office and even home networks. If your ISP tells you that you have "security through obscurity," and, believe us, they will, you should not feel reassured.

If your computer is accessible from the Internet, you are just as at risk as any other Internet site. Hackers use automatic probing software to find computers connected to the Internet where security is lax and systems are vulnerable to attack. Make absolutely sure you require passwords to any shared resources, and install firewall software to deflect these probes and subsequent attacks. You can get firewall software from companies such as Sybergen Networks (www.sygate.com) or Signal 9 Solutions (www.signal9.com) for under $30. Do it now.

Skill 16

Monitoring Network and Dial-Up Connections

When you are troubleshooting a network or dial-up connection, or even if you are just curious, it can be very useful to see exactly what is going on at any given time. To monitor a connection, use these steps:

1. Choose Start ➤ Settings ➤ Control Panel, and open the Network and Dial-up Connections applet.

2. Right-click the connection you want information on, and choose Status; you cannot choose Status if the connection is not active.

You will see the Connection Status dialog box shown in Figure 16.9, listing information for that particular connection on the General tab. For a network connection, you will see the connection status, the time since the connection was established, the speed, and the number of packets sent and received. For a dial-up connection, you will see the number of bytes sent and received as well as a count of the number of errors and the compression percentage. The Details tab on a dial-up connection shows client and server IP addresses, the protocol in use, and whether authentication and compression are being used.

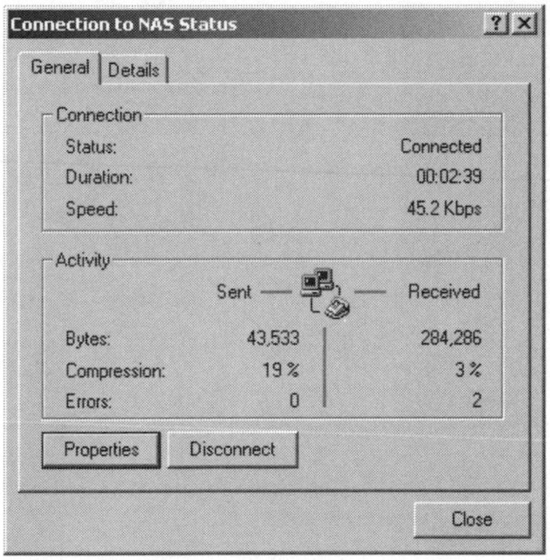

FIGURE 16.9: The Connection Status dialog box open at the General tab

But there is an even faster way to see a quick status report on a connection, and this one is particularly useful if you want to watch your network connections. Follow these steps:

1. Choose Start ➤ Settings ➤ Control Panel, and open the Network and Dial-up Connections applet.

2. Right-click the local area network connection, and choose Properties. At the bottom of the General tab, check the Show Icon in Taskbar When Connected box, and click OK.

When you return to the Desktop, a status monitor of two little screens that flash will display on the Taskbar, indicating network activity. Pretty cool, isn't it? But wait, there's more. Now move your mouse cursor over this status monitor, and you will see something like this:

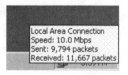

So any time you want to take a quick snapshot of network activity, just run the cursor over to the Taskbar, and you've got it.

Demystifying User Groups and Accounts

In the "Troubleshooting Your Peer-to-Peer Network" section earlier in this skill, and in "Installing and Upgrading to Windows 2000 Professional" in Skill 2, we made reference to creating user accounts. In this section, we are going to go into accounts in more detail to show you how you can tailor Windows 2000 Professional to meet a variety of needs. And then, to close out this skill, we'll take a look at the various file and folder permissions available in both FAT32 and NTFS under Windows 2000 Professional. Knowing about accounts and permissions is important when you use Windows 2000 Professional as a single-user system, but this becomes vital when you use Windows 2000 Professional in support of your network.

Skill 16

User Accounts in Windows 2000 Professional

Unlike some operating systems, Windows 2000 Professional *requires* that you create a user account for yourself before you can access files or print documents. By setting up different accounts for different users, it is possible to create files as one user and make it completely impossible for any other user to access those files. In fact, you can't do *anything* in Windows 2000 Professional unless you have the appropriate permissions. This is all part of the built-in security system.

A user account uniquely identifies a user on the basis of their user name and password, which are entered when a user logs on to the system. Windows 2000 Professional then monitors what that user does and either allows or restricts an activity such as deleting a file based on the rights and permissions assigned by the owner of the resource and the system administrator.

In addition to normal user accounts, Windows 2000 Professional provides two special accounts with a predefined set of capabilities:

Administrator Account   The account you used to create the first user once the Windows 2000 Professional installation was complete. This account has full rights over the entire computer and can go anywhere and do anything on the system. The Administrator account cannot be deleted or removed from the Administrators group, so it is impossible to lock yourself out of your computer by accidentally removing all of the Administrator accounts. Log on as an administrator when you want to create new user accounts or to install software that will be available to all users.

Guest Account   An account for users who do not have a real account on the computer. The Guest account is disabled by default, and it is best left this way. If you want to give a visitor access to some part of the system, create an account for them (we'll see how in a moment), and then delete the account when they no longer need it.

TIP   If you want to install a software package and make it available to only one user, log on as that user, make the installation, and log off again. No one else will ever know it is there.

User Groups in Windows 2000 Professional

Windows 2000 Professional allows you to create user groups, which are accounts that contain other accounts and that share common privileges. By default, a user group called Users is created when you first install the operating system, and every user account is a member of this group except (and there is always one exception, isn't there?) the Guest account. Several other built-in groups are also created, including:

Administrators Group   Has complete control of all aspects of the computer, and automatically has every built-in right available on the system.

Backup Operators Group   Can back up or restore files and folders, regardless of the permissions protecting the files. Users of this group can also shut down the system but cannot change security settings.

Guests Group   Can allow occasional users to access the system. It is much safer and more secure to insist that everyone use regular accounts with proper logon protection than to allow people to use accounts in this group.

Power Users Group   Contains many but not all of the privileges of the Administrators group. Users of this group can create new accounts but can only modify and change accounts they have created themselves. These users cannot load or unload device drivers, manage the security or auditing logs, or back up or restore files and folders.

Replicator Group   A special group associated with functions that are unavailable in Windows 2000 Professional and, therefore, are beyond the scope of this book.

Users Group   Can perform all the common tasks such as running applications, printing to local and network printers, and shutting down the system. Users cannot share directories or create local printers.

Groups are a valuable administrative tool because they allow you to create collections of users very quickly, all with identical privileges.

Skill 16

So Why Not Always Log On as an Administrator?

The Administrator account has all the privileges available within Windows 2000 Professional, so why not just stay logged on as Administrator all the time? Because you or someone else might do something by accident or by design to damage the system, and if you have Administrator privileges, your system can be seriously damaged before you even realize what is happening.

If you access an Internet site that contains a Trojan Horse—a malignant program masquerading as a useful utility program—while you are logged in as Administrator, the Trojan Horse may be able to execute on your system. And because it is running under the Administrator account, it can do anything it likes—delete all your files, reformat the hard disk, you get the picture.

You should add yourself to the Users group or to the Power Users group and log on as a member of that group. If you find you need Administrator capability to perform some task or other, log off, log on as Administrator, do what needs to be done, and immediately log off again. You can then log back on as a member of the Users group or the Power Users group.

Creating a New User Account

To create a new user account, log on as Administrator, and follow these steps:

1. Choose Start ➢ Settings ➢ Control Panel, and open the Users and Passwords applet.

2. In the Users and Passwords dialog box, click the Users tab to bring it to the front, and click Add to open the Add New User Dialog box shown in Figure 16.10.

3. Enter the user name as well as any description you want to attach. Click Next.

4. Enter and then confirm the password you want this user to log on to the computer with, and click Next.

5. Select the access level you want to grant to this new user, as Figure 16.11 shows, and click Finish. Choose from:

Standard User   Power Users Group

Restricted User   Users Group

Other   Administrators Group, Backup Operators Group, Guests Group, Power Users Group, Replicator Group, Users Group

FIGURE 16.10: The Add New User dialog box

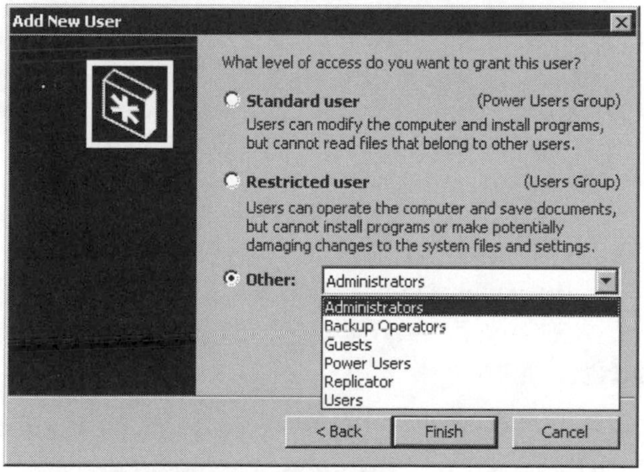

FIGURE 16.11: Select the access level for this new user.

You will see the new user listed in the box at the top of the Users and Passwords dialog box. Click Add to create another new user, or click OK to close this dialog box when you are done.

Modifying an Existing User Account

If you have to modify the password or group membership of an existing user account, log on as Administrator, and follow these steps:

1. Choose Start ➣ Settings ➣ Control Panel, and open the Users and Passwords applet.

2. Click the Advanced tab to bring it to the front, and click the Advanced button to open the Local User Manager window. Click Users.

3. Double-click the user account you want to modify, or right-click and choose Properties from the shortcut menu.

4. On the General tab, you can modify the password attributes or disable the account.

5. On the Member Of tab, you can add or remove the groups to which this user belongs.

6. Click OK to close the Properties dialog box.

Explaining Rights and Permissions

So far so good; we have looked at user accounts and user groups, and we have detailed the various privileges assigned to these different groups. Next, we need to look at two more elements of the Windows 2000 professional security system—rights and permissions—and describe how you can use them to your best advantage.

In the preceding section, we looked at the built-in user groups and described some of the actions each can perform; for example, administrators can create new user accounts, but ordinary users cannot. In Windows 2000 Professional, the ability of a user to perform a particular activity is called a *user right*.

User Rights

The built-in user groups we looked at in the last section already have a set of user rights assigned to them, and this is one of the features that makes using user groups so convenient. User rights are assigned for you; you don't have to do anything unless you want to change them. To look at the user rights and the user groups to which they are assigned, follow these steps:

1. Choose Start ➤ Settings ➤ Control Panel ➤ Administrative Tools, and open the Local Security Policy applet.

2. In the Tree pane on the left, expand Local Policies.

3. In the Tree pane, double-click User Rights Assignment.

You will see the display shown in Figure 16.12, listing the rights and the groups to which they are assigned. To change the assignment, right-click a right, and choose Security, but be very careful, and make sure you understand exactly what you are doing before you make any changes.

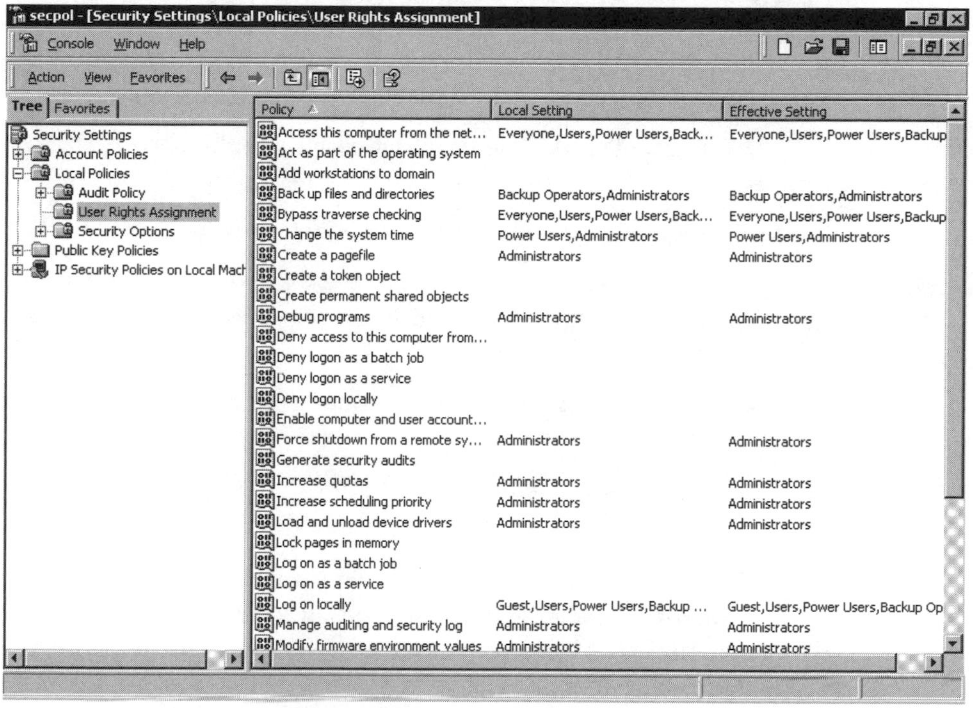

FIGURE 16.12: Looking at user rights in Local Security Policy

File and Folder Permissions on FAT32 Drives

File permissions are another aspect of the Windows 2000 Professional security system. They control what you as a user can do with or to a particular file or folder. The FAT and FAT32 systems have very little security built in to them, so the amount of control we can exert is distinctly limited. NTFS, on the other hand, extends a great deal of control, as we shall see in the next section.

On a FAT32 file or folder, you can look at or change three simple permissions called *attributes*. You can make the file read-only (so it cannot be modified or changed in any way) or hidden (so it is not displayed in Explorer-type windows). Or you can change the archive attribute used to indicate that the file has changed since it was last backed up. Right-click a file or folder, choose Properties, and you will see these three attributes at the bottom of the General tab.

File and Folder Permissions on NTFS Drives

Things change in a big way on an NTFS drive. To look at or change file or folder permissions, follow these steps:

1. Right-click Start, select Explore, and use the Explorer to locate the file or folder you want to work with.

2. Right-click the file or folder, choose Properties, and then click the Security tab.

3. To set up permissions for a new user or group, click Add. Enter the name of the user or group for which you want to set permissions, and click OK to close the dialog box.

4. To change or remove permissions from an existing user or group, click the name.

5. In the Permissions box, click Allow or Deny for the appropriate permission. Click OK to close the dialog box.

When you set permissions in a folder, the new folders and the files you create all inherit the same set of permissions. If the Permissions check boxes are shaded, the permissions have been inherited. If you change the permissions in a parent folder, the changes will cascade down to all the files and folders it contains.

T TIP   NTFS file and folder permissions are effective both on the local computer and over the network.

File permissions are actually made up of groups of special permissions—some that apply just to files, some that apply just to folders, and others that apply to both files and folders. Here is a quick look at some of the more important permissions:

Full Control   Lets you do anything to the file or folder.

Modify   Lets you do anything to the file or folder except delete subfolders and files, change the permissions, or change the ownership of the file.

Read & Execute   Lets you read and execute a file.

List Folder Contents   Lets you list the contents of a folder; not available for files.

Read   Lets you read a file.

Write   Lets you create and change files.

N NOTE   A complete description of how to use all the permissions available for files and for folders is beyond the scope of this book. If you want to know more, please check out *Mastering Windows 2000 Professional* by Mark Minasi and Todd Phillips, available from Sybex.

Shared Folder Permissions

Administrators and members of the Power Users group can share folders on their computer so that the folders and their contents are available to other users on the network. By assigning permissions to a FAT, a FAT32, or an NTFS shared folder, you can control access to that folder

To look at the permissions currently in place on a shared folder, either:

- Right-click the folder, choose Sharing, and, on the Sharing tab, click the Permissions button.

- Right-click the folder, choose Properties, click the Sharing tab to bring it to the front, and then click the Permissions button.

Either way, you'll see the dialog box shown in Figure 16.13, which lists in the upper box the users who have access to this folder (Everyone, in this case) and indicates in the lower box the permissions and their current settings. The permissions include:

Full Control   Lets you do anything to this folder and any files or subfolders it contains.

Change   Lets you do anything to this folder except change the permissions and take ownership of the folder on an NTFS volume.

Read   Lets you read the contents of files and subfolders.

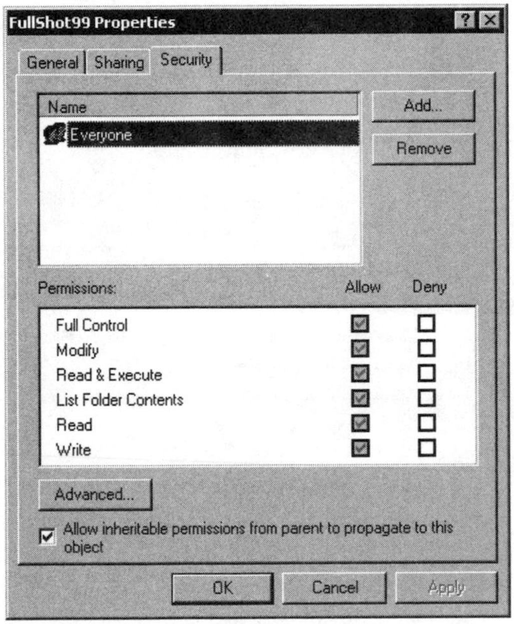

FIGURE 16.13: The folder permissions available for a shared folder

Printer Permissions

And, yes, as you might expect, printers have permissions too. Because network printers are available to everyone on the network, it is useful to limit access for certain users. To look at or change the permissions associated with a specific printer, choose Start ➢ Settings ➢ Printers, right-click the printer you want to work with, and choose Properties. Click the Security tab to bring it to the front, and in the Permissions box you will see the following:

> **Print**　Lets users print to the printer. This permission is assigned to everyone by default.
>
> **Manage Printers**　Gives complete administrative control of the printer to a user, who can pause or restart the printer, share the printer, and change the properties and permissions.
>
> **Manage Documents**　Gives control of documents sent to the printer but not the ability to print. The user can pause, resume, restart, or cancel print jobs submitted by other users.

When you choose Deny for all of these permissions, the user cannot access the printer in any way.

Are You Up to Speed?

Now you can...

- ☑ set up your own peer-to-peer network
- ☑ configure Windows 2000 Professional networking
- ☑ share an Internet connection
- ☑ monitor network and dial-up connections
- ☑ create new users
- ☑ modify permissions for files, folders, and printers

Skill 16

SKILL 17

Connecting to a Corporate Network

- Creating hardware and user profiles
- Managing portable PC power options
- Configuring and customizing network connections
- Connecting to your local area network
- Connecting over a phone line
- Connecting with ISDN
- Connecting through a VPN tunnel
- Connecting directly with a serial or parallel cable
- Accepting incoming calls
- Connecting without wires

In the preceding skill, we looked at some of the most important aspects of setting up your own home or office network. In this skill, we'll look at how to connect to corporate networks, and we'll examine some of the issues facing mobile computer users. Also, we'll look at how to set up hardware and user profiles for different people who use the same computer system but at different times. And in closing, we'll look at some of the wireless connection methods now available using infrared technology.

Windows 2000 Professional and Mobile Computer Users

These days, work is wherever you happen to be at the moment—at home, at the office, on the road, in your client's office. A huge range of portable computing options is available, from tiny mini-notebooks to larger shoulder-numbing desktop replacements, and computers of all shapes and sizes in between. And they all need to connect to the main network back at the office at some point to check e-mail, pick up files, drop off files, and even synchronize files.

Windows 2000 Professional brings some unique benefits to the world of mobile computing, including:

Work Offline   Lets you disconnect your computer from the network and continue to work on your files as though you were still connected. See Skill 4 for more information.

Synchronize Files   Allows you to synchronize any changes you made to your files while you were away from the office with the files on the network when you return.

Encrypt Files   Allows you to encrypt files so that even if your portable computer is stolen no one will be able to access or read your company-confidential information. See Skill 6 for more information.

Connection Options   Lets you connect to the corporate network over standard telephone lines or ISDN connections, and even lets you create a Virtual Private Network (VPN) over the Internet.

Power Management   Allows you to configure power management on your portable for maximum battery life.

User Profiles   Allows you to share portable computers among several people. You can create multiple user profiles on the same computer and protect each user's data from being viewed by anyone else.

Hardware Profiles   Allows you to create different hardware configurations for different environments, such as when a laptop must be used either while away from the office or while connected to a docking station on your desk.

Wireless Connections   Allows you to use wireless infrared technology to connect computers to other computers, to printers, and to networks.

We'll look at all of these Windows 2000 Professional features in this skill and show you how you can use them to get real work done. Throughout this skill, we are going to assume that when you connect to the network back at the office the network operating system in place there is one of the Windows 2000 Server products.

TIP   As in the preceding skill, we may be introducing some unfamiliar network-related terms as we go through the tasks in this skill. If we don't provide a definition in the text for a new term, look in the Glossary at the end of this book; you will find it there.

Using Hardware Profiles

Many people use a portable computer in two different configurations: one when working in the office, with perhaps an external monitor or a docking station, and another for on-the-road use that has none of the "office" equipment attached. Windows 2000 Professional manages these configuration changes with a *hardware profile*. A hardware profile tells Windows 2000 Professional which devices to start when you power up your computer and which settings to use for those devices.

When you first install Windows 2000 Professional, Setup creates a default hardware profile that contains information about every device attached to your computer. If you change your hardware configuration, you don't have to overwrite this default information; you can just create another hardware profile to reflect the changes. And then, whenever you start your computer, Windows 2000 Professional will ask you which hardware profile you want to load.

Skill 17

Creating a New Hardware Profile

The first step in creating a new hardware profile is to duplicate the existing profile. Log on as an Administrator, and follow these steps:

1. Choose Start ➢ Settings ➢ Control Panel, and open the System applet.

2. Click the Hardware tab to bring it to the front, and click Hardware Profiles to open the Hardware Profiles dialog box shown in Figure 17.1.

3. You will see that the current hardware profile is selected from the list of available profiles. Click Copy, give the new profile a name, and click OK.

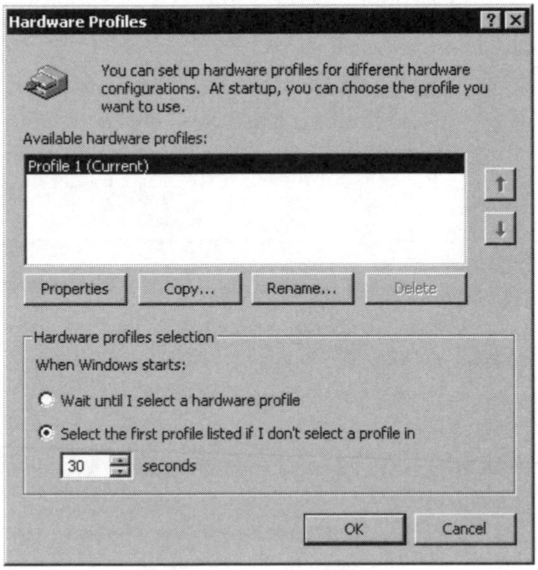

FIGURE 17.1: The Hardware Profiles dialog box

A docking station is a box that you plug your portable computer into when you are working at your desk. You can attach full-sized peripherals to it, such as a full-size monitor and keyboard instead of the smaller ones on the portable computer. The portable computer and the docking station are designed to be two parts of the same system; you cannot swap computers and docking stations from different manufacturers or even different models from the same manufacturer. When you go on the road, you just undock (more on this later in this skill) the portable computer from the docking station, and you are on your way.

When you use a portable computer in this way, it needs to know whether to use the internal monitor and keyboard or those attached to the docking station—a perfect use for hardware profiles.

To look at the docking configuration of the current hardware profile, just click Properties. If Windows 2000 Professional cannot automatically detect the docking status of your system in this profile, check The Docking State Is Unknown on the General tab. You can also specify that it is always docked or always undocked when using this hardware profile.

Managing Hardware Profiles

Now that you have created a new hardware profile, you can specify which profile is loaded when the system starts by following these steps:

1. Choose Start ➢ Settings ➢ Control Panel, and open the System applet.

2. Click the Hardware tab to bring it to the front, and click Hardware Profiles.

3. In the Available Hardware Profiles box, use the up and down arrows to move the hardware profile that you want to use as the new default to the top of the list.

4. In the Hardware Profiles Selection box, use one of the options to select the hardware profile loaded as the system starts. You can specify whether you want Windows 2000 Professional to wait until you select a hardware profile when you start the system or to select one automatically if you don't respond within the specified time period. To load your selected hardware profile without displaying the list at startup, enter **0** in the Seconds spin box as the time period you want Windows to wait. If you change your mind, just press the spacebar as the system starts, and select a hardware profile from the list on the screen.

Configuring Hardware Profiles

Once you have created a new hardware profile, you can enable or disable the hardware devices it contains with the Device Manager, which is covered in Skill 14. When you disable a device in a hardware profile, the device drivers for that hardware are not loaded at startup.

You can also customize the services each hardware profile contains. Each Windows 2000 Professional service (also covered in Skill 14) can be enabled or disabled for each hardware profile. To manage the services you want to load with a hardware profile, follow these steps:

1. Choose Start ➤ Settings ➤ Control Panel, select the Administrative Tools applet, and then open Computer Management.

2. From the left-hand Tree pane, select Services and Applications, and then select Services.

3. Right-click the service you want to manage (for example, Print Spooler), and select Properties to open the Properties dialog box. Click the Log On tab to bring it to the front, as Figure 17.2 shows.

4. At the bottom of the tab, you will see the names of the current hardware profiles listed to the left and their current status on the right. Click Disable to turn this service off for the selected hardware profile.

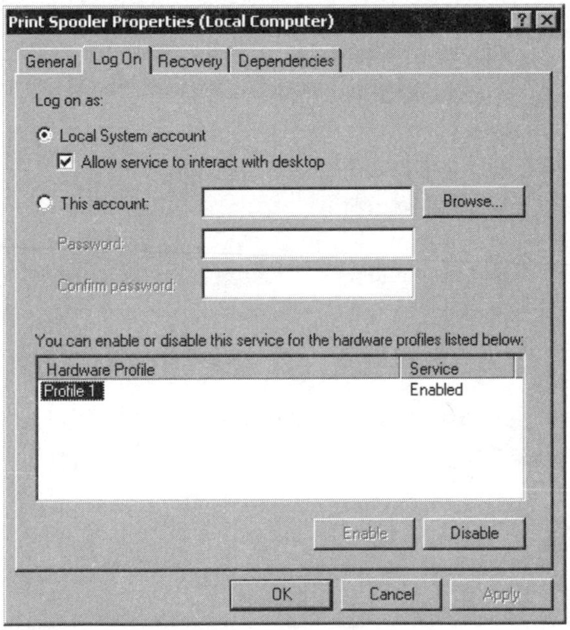

FIGURE 17.2: The Print Spooler Properties dialog box

Creating User Profiles

In the same way that you can customize your computer's changing hardware configuration with hardware profiles, you can do much the same thing for user interface settings with *user profiles*. If you actually like using black and purple as your Desktop colors, you can save these settings into your user profile, and they will be loaded each time you log on to the system. And the other users of the same system can stay with the relatively tame but eminently readable default color settings.

A user profile keeps track of the following:

- Start menu options
- Desktop icons
- Desktop colors
- Wallpaper
- Screen savers
- Mouse cursor
- Accessibility options

User profiles can be of these types:

Local User Profile   Created the first time you log on to the computer, and stored on your local hard disk. Any changes you make to your local user profile are specific to the computer on which you made the changes. This is the most common user profile, particularly on non-networked or peer-to-peer-networked systems.

Roaming User Profile   Created by the network system administrator, and stored on the network file server by Windows 2000 Server. This profile is made available from the server to any computer on the network where you log on. Any changes you make to your roaming user profile are stored on the server.

Mandatory User Profile   Created by the administrator, a special form of the roaming user profile used to specify settings for individual users or for entire groups of users. A mandatory user profile must be loaded success-fully as the user logs on. If the system cannot find the profile for some reason, the user can't log on at all.

To create a new user profile, follow these steps:

1. Choose Start ➤ Settings ➤ Control Panel, and open the System applet.

2. Click the User Profiles tab to bring it to the front, as shown in Figure 17.3.

3. You will see that the current user profile is selected from the list of available profiles. Click Copy To, and enter the location for the new user profile, or click Browse to select the path. Click Change to open the Choose User dialog box, select a new user from the Names list, and click Add. The new user name will appear in Add Name. Click OK to add the user as a new user pro-file on your system.

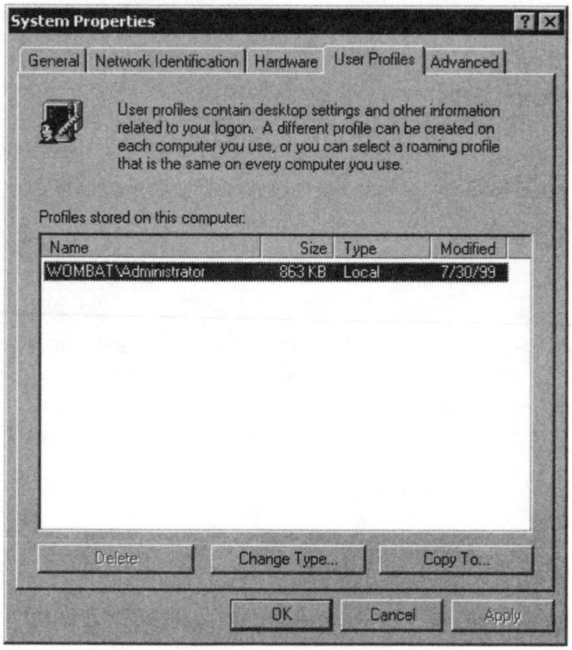

FIGURE 17.3: The User Profiles tab in the System Properties dialog box

> **TIP** You must be logged on as an administrator to create, copy, or change user profiles.

Managing Portable PC Power Options

Recent PC sales statistics indicate that more than half the new computers bought are laptops. Mobile computer users place some unique and demanding requirements on these systems, particularly from the point of view of power management and battery life. The extent to which you can take advantage of power-management features depends entirely on your computer hardware. Some laptop computers have a fully implemented power-saving scheme designed to optimize battery life, and some desktop systems can power down the hard disk and the monitor if they have been inactive for a while. Other computers can even go into hibernation.

Windows 2000 Professional supports the Advanced Configuration and Power Interface (ACPI), an open industry standard that defines how applications and power management work together on a wide range of portable, desktop, and server computers. ACPI is configured using the Power Options applet in Control Panel. Log on as an Administrator, and choose Start ➢ Settings ➢ Control Panel ➢ Power Options to open the Power Options Properties dialog box shown in Figure 17.4. It has several tabs, and depending on your computer hardware, you will see some or all of the following:

Power Schemes   Allows you to set the length of idle time after which you want Windows 2000 Professional to turn off your monitor and your hard disk; time periods extend from After 1 Minute to Never, which effectively disables the power-management features on your computer. Once you have chosen the appropriate settings for your system, you can save them as a named Power Scheme or, in other words, as a group of preset options. Click the Save As button in the top part of the Power Options Properties dialog box for this task.

Alarms   Lets you set a warning alarm for a low or a critical battery condition; specify the settings you want by dragging the slider.

Advanced   Controls additional power management features, including the password you enter when your computer comes out of both hibernation and standby. The options you see on this tab depend on the capabilities of your hardware; if the tab appears to be blank, your computer does not support advanced power-management features. Most of the options available on this tab relate to laptop and other portable computers.

Hibernate   Allows you to specify that your laptop goes into hibernation when you choose Hibernate from the Shut Down menu, when you close the computer, or after it has been idle for the specified period of time. If the Hibernate tab is not available, your computer does not support this feature. When you put your computer into hibernation, everything in memory is saved to the hard disk so that when you turn your computer on again all the applications and documents that were open are reloaded automatically. Hibernate turns off all power to the computer for an indefinite period of time while still maintaining the state of open applications and any connected hardware when the computer went into hibernation. The only catch is that you must have enough free disk space available to accommodate the contents of your computer memory. For example, if you have 128MB of RAM, you need at least 128MB of free hard disk space. For security reasons, the system asks for a password on reactivation, which can take place in as little as 30 seconds—much faster than a typical reboot.

TIP   For even faster access, Windows 2000 Professional also supports a Standby mode that places the computer into a state somewhere between complete hibernation and full operation. Choose Start ➢ Shut Down, and select Standby. Some battery power is used in this mode, and information in memory is not stored on your hard disk, so if there is an interruption in power, the contents of memory will be lost. Always make a point of saving your work before going into Standby mode.

APM   If your computer does not support the latest ACPI standard, you can still take advantage of power management using the older Advanced Power Management (APM) system by checking the box on this tab. Once enabled, APM allows Windows 2000 Professional to place your computer in Standby mode and into hibernation.

UPS   Lets you set various UPS (Uninterruptible Power Supply) alarms. You can use a UPS to provide continuing emergency power when the main supply fails.

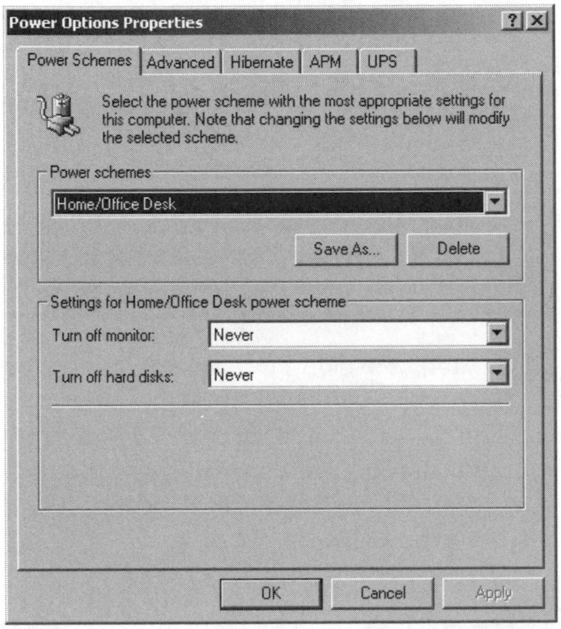

FIGURE 17.4:   The Power Schemes tab in the Power Options Properties dialog box

Docking and Undocking a Portable Computer

Windows 2000 Professional users can plug their portable computers into and out of their docking stations without rebooting. In the preceding section, we mentioned docking and undocking; well, here are the steps to follow:

1.   Choose Start ➢ Eject PC. A message appears telling you that it is safe to continue.

2. Undock your portable computer, or if you have a motorized docking station, the portable will undock automatically.

3. Some portable computers actually have an Eject button on the docking station. Pressing that button also completes the undocking process. Check the manufacturer's instructions for more information.

4. Now that the portable computer is running only on its own internal batteries, don't forget to change the Power Scheme to one that will help you conserve battery life.

TIP If you dock your portable computer into a new docking station—one you have not used before—the start-up process in Windows 2000 Professional will identify and configure new hardware automatically.

If you don't see Eject PC in your Start menu, use the Add/Remove Hardware Wizard in Control Panel the first time you undock your portable computer. If Eject PC still doesn't appear in the Start menu, your portable computer and docking station may not support undocking, or, alternatively, you may not have the appropriate security privileges to undock your portable computer. In that case, talk to your system administrator.

Configuring Your Network Connection

Windows 2000 Professional makes it very easy for remote users to connect to the network back at the office. Earlier operating systems all but required you to have an advanced degree in network protocol tinkering to accomplish this apparently simple task, but with Windows 2000 Professional, that is all behind us now. As we will show in the next few sections, you can connect over a variety of communication channels, including normal analog phone lines, ISDN (Integrated Services Digital Network) connections, direct cable connections, Virtual Private Networks (VPN), and even wireless infrared links. You can also set up your Windows 2000 Professional system so that it accepts incoming calls from other users.

All this is done using the Network Connection Wizard, which is a part of the Network and Dial-Up Connections folder in Control Panel. Choose Start ➢ Settings, and open the Network and Dial-Up Connections folder, where you will see listed any dial-up or networking connections you have already established. To start the Network Connection Wizard, open the Make New Connection icon, and click Next. Figure 17.5 shows the main Network Connection Wizard options:

Dial-Up to Private Network   Allows you to connect to the network using a normal analog phone line or an ISDN connection, and to set dialing properties, including when to use calling cards, PINS, and other connection-specific configuration information.

Dial-Up to the Internet   Lets you create a dial-up connection to the Internet. (We looked at this option in Skill 11.)

Connect to a Private Network through the Internet   Allows you to create a Virtual Private Network connection, sometimes called a tunnel, using the Internet to connect to your network.

Accept Incoming Connections   Lets you accept incoming connections via modem, ISDN, infrared, or directly connected computers.

Connect Directly to Another Computer   Allows you to connect to another computer using a serial or a parallel cable or a wireless infrared port.

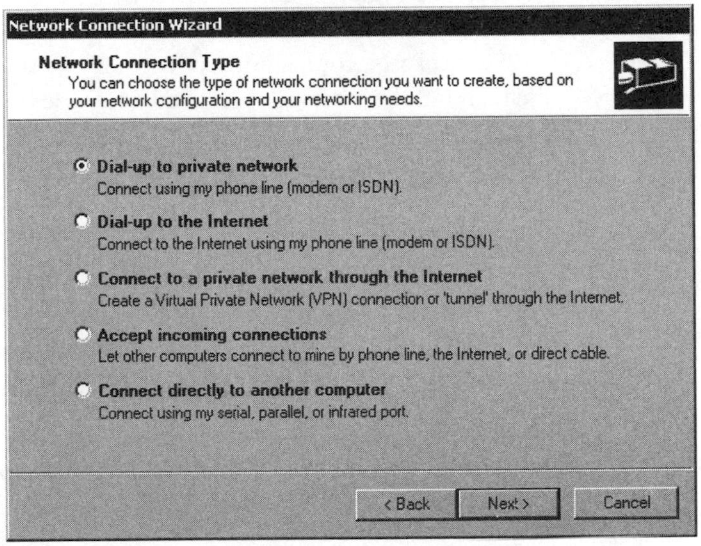

FIGURE 17.5: The Network Connection Wizard

Remove any unused network protocols to increase efficiency; see Skill 16 for information on how to do this. For example, if you always connect to the corporate network using TCP/IP, you probably don't need the NetBEUI protocol installed, and if you never connect to a Novell NetWare server, you don't need the IPX/SPX suite of protocols installed.

Customizing Your Network Connections

Once you have established a connection, you can look at or change the settings associated with that connection. Choose Start ➣ Settings, and open the Network and Dial-Up Connections folder. Right-click the appropriate connection, and choose Properties from the shortcut menu. Depending on the type of connection you are working with, you will see some or all of the following tabs:

General   Allows you to configure phone numbers, host addresses, and country and region codes for a dial-up connection. Also allows you to configure client and communications protocol parameters if you are working with a local area connection. In the case of a local area network connection, the General tab, shown in Figure 17.6, is the only tab you will see.

Options   Lets you look at or change dialing and redialing options, as well as multilink or X.25 settings.

Security   Allows you to configure authentication and encryption information as well as terminal window and scripting options.

Networking   Lets you set client and communications protocol parameters.

Internet Connection Sharing   Allows you to enable or disable Internet connection sharing and on-demand dialing. See Skill 16 for more information.

When you connect to a network from a remote location, or, in other words, from a place outside the office (not necessarily from the middle of the Sahara desert), the server is said to be acting as a *remote access server* and is providing *remote access services*.

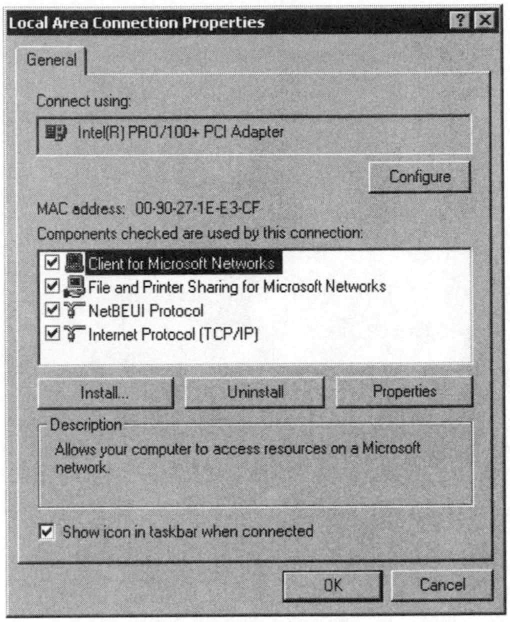

FIGURE 17.6: The Local Area Connection Properties dialog box open at the General tab

Connecting to a Local Area Network

Many users are directly connected to their home or office local area network. When you start your computer, Windows 2000 Professional locates your network interface card and automatically starts the connection to the local area network. Unlike the other types of connections we'll be looking at in the next few sections, you don't have to click on anything to start it running; Windows 2000 professional does it all for you, and you will see its icon in the Network and Dial-Up Connections folder in Control Panel.

As your computer starts, you will see a message on the screen telling you that your computer is establishing communications with the network. When you choose

Start ➤ Shut Down and choose Shut Down, you may see another message telling you that users are logged in to your computer and that if you continue with the shut down they will be logged off and their sessions will be terminated.

USING ACTIVE DIRECTORY

The Active Directory service catalogs information about all the objects on your network, including computers, servers, printers, modems, and users, and makes that information available all across the network. Active Directory performs the following tasks:

- Distributes useful information across the network
- Replicates information to make it available to as many users as possible and make the system resistant to failure
- Partitions the information into multiple units to allow the storage of information on a very large number of objects
- Enforces security to keep information away from the prying eyes of intruders

Active Directory is only available on a Windows 2000 Professional client when one of the Windows 2000 Server products is running on a server on your network.

Connecting Over a Phone Line

One of the most common ways to connect to the network from a remote location is still with a modem and a standard analog telephone line. Windows 2000 Professional supports literally hundreds of modems, and, almost without exception, if a modem supports an industry standard, it can communicate with any other modem that supports the same version of the same standard. Having said that, however, some of the most cryptic and hard-to-find problems we have seen in communications have eventually been traced to incompatible modems. If you want to be sure this won't happen to you, make sure you use the same modem at both ends of the communications channel.

TIP   See Skill 4 for information on Synchronization Manager and how you can keep your files, folders, e-mail, and Web pages updated automatically between your portable system and your desktop computer.

To create a new dial-up connection over a phone line, follow these steps:

1. Choose Start ➤ Settings ➤ Network and Dial-Up Connections.

2. Open Make New Connection, and when the Network Connection Wizard starts, click Next.

3. Select the Dial-Up to Private Network option, and click Next.

4. Enter the phone number to use, and if you want your computer to decide how to dial in from different locations, check the Use Dialing Rules box. Click Next.

5. Specify the connection availability; you can create this connection for use by all users, or you can reserve the connection for just your own use.

6. Enter a name for this connection. This is the name that will be used in the Network and Dial-Up Connections folder, so it makes sense to use a name that you will remember and that relates in some way to the connection you are making.

7. Enter your password, and click Dial if you want to connect now, or click Cancel to return to the Network and Dial-Up Connections folder, where you will see an icon for the connection you just created.

Connecting with ISDN

A standard V.90 analog modem is, in theory, capable of a data rate of 56Kbps, but, in practice, there are several reasons, including FCC rules and the quality of your local telephone circuits, that the maximum data rate you actually achieve is likely to be approximately 50Kbps. And, many times, it will be less than this figure.

A digital connection such as ISDN (Integrated Services Digital Network) is capable of much higher data rates, and because a digital circuit is free from line noise, this data rate will be constant and repeatable. Typical Basic Rate ISDN circuits are capable of 64 or 128Kbps, and Primary Rate ISDN circuits are capable of much higher data rates.

ISDN lines must be available in your area and must be installed by the phone company. You will need special hardware, in place of the usual analog modem, installed at each end of the link. Windows 2000 Professional will use Plug and Play to locate and recognize the ISDN adapter, and you can use Device Manager to tell the ISDN adapter what kind of telephone switch it is connected to. Examples include ATT from AT&T, NI-1 from National ISDN-1, and NT1 from Northern Telecom. If you have an internal ISDN adapter, you will find it listed in Device Manager under the heading of Network Adapters, and if it is an external adapter, you will find it under the heading of Modems. See Skill 14 for more information on how to use Device Manager.

To create a connection using an ISDN adapter, follow the steps outlined in the preceding section for a dial-up connection. To configure the ISDN settings, follow these steps:

1. Choose Start ➢ Settings ➢ Network and Dial-Up Connections.

2. Right-click the connection that uses ISDN, and choose Properties from the shortcut menu.

3. On the General tab in Connect Using, select the ISDN device, and click Configure.

4. In the ISDN Configure dialog box, select the line type you want to use; these are listed from highest to lowest quality.

5. Depending on the type of ISDN adapter you are using, you may see the Modem Settings dialog box.

TIP   When you use any of the techniques we describe in this skill to access your network from a remote location, don't forget that you will first need an account on that network, with a user name and a password, before you will be allowed to log on to the network.

Connecting through a VPN Tunnel

We all know that certain forms of communication using the Internet are inherently not secure, and we also know that connections to the Internet are usually local rather than long distance. What if there were a way to use the Internet to set up a local, secure connection to your network? Well, there is a way to do exactly that with Windows 2000 Professional, and the secure link that you set up is called a Virtual Private Network, or VPN for short.

A VPN is a tunnel through the Internet connecting your computer to the network, and all data that flows through the tunnel is automatically encrypted. When you are away from the office, you can dial up almost any Internet Service Provider (ISP) and set up a VPN session to your network over the Internet. This can significantly reduce your long-distance line charges, and you can stay connected to the network for longer. A VPN also allows your network administrator to add new users and new locations to the corporate network quickly and easily. Windows 2000 Professional supports three popular VPN protocols; look in the Glossary at the end of this book for more on these secure protocols:

- Point-to-Point Tunneling Protocol (PPTP)

- Layer-2 Tunneling Protocol (L-2TP)

- IP Security (IP-Sec)

To create a VPN connection, follow these steps:

1. Choose Start ➢ Settings ➢ Network and Dial-Up Connections.

2. Open Make New Connection, and when the Network Connection Wizard starts, click Next.

3. Select the Connect to a Private Network through the Internet option, and click Next.

4. To establish a connection to your ISP first, before connecting to your network, select Automatically Dial This Connection. Otherwise, click Do Not Dial the Initial Connection. Click Next.

5. Enter the name of the host computer, or enter the IP address. Click Next.

6. Choose between making this connection available to all users or keeping it for your own use. Click Next.

7. To allow other computers to access resources through this connection, select Enable Internet Connection Sharing for This Connection. Click Next.

8. Type a name for this connection, and click Finish.

9. Enter your password, and click Dial if you want to connect now, or click Cancel to return to the Network and Dial-Up Connections folder, where you will see an icon for the connection you just created.

Once you have created a VPN connection in Network and Dial-Up Connections, you can copy it and then modify the connection settings so you can accommodate different hosts, different security options, and so on. Right-click the icon for a VPN in the Network and Dial-Up Connections folder, and choose Create Copy from the shortcut menu.

Connecting Directly

If you don't have a network installed, and your computers are located in the same room, you can connect them directly using one of these mechanisms:

- A serial cable running from a COM port on one computer to a COM port on the other. Due to the way that serial interfaces work, this cable must be a special form of serial cable called a null modem cable; see Figure 17.7 for details of the connections needed for 9- and 25-pin connectors.

- A parallel cable running from a parallel port on one computer to the parallel port on the other. If you can, choose this option over the serial cable option because the parallel port is a lot faster than the serial port. Windows 2000 Professional supports Parallel Technology's Basic or Fast parallel cables; see www.1pt.com for more information.

TIP   To set up a direct connection, both computers must use the same kind of communications port.

To set up a direct connection, follow these steps:

1. Choose Start ➤ Settings ➤ Network and Dial-Up Connections.

2. Open Make New Connection, and when the Network Connection Wizard starts, click Next.

3. Select the Connect Directly to Another Computer option, and click Next.

4. Decide which computer will be the "host" and which will be the "guest." If you are the host computer, the other computer will access information or services on your computer. If you are the guest computer, you will access the other computer for the services or information you need. To create a host, you must be logged on as an Administrator. Click either Host or Guest, and then click Next.

5. Select the port you are using to connect the computers. Both computers must use the same type of port (serial or parallel). Click Next.

6. Select the users you want to allow access to this connection. Click Next.

7. Give the connection a name, and click Finish.

8. Repeat these steps on the second computer.

You'll want to set up the host computer first, and then configure the guest computer. Once you complete the direct cable connection, the guest computer can access any shared resources on the host computer, including hard disks, CD-ROMs, printers, and faxes, as well as any shared resources on the network to which the host computer is attached.

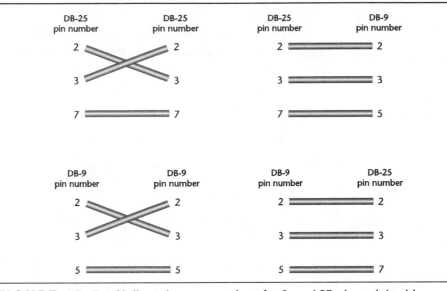

FIGURE 17.7: Null modem connections for 9- and 25-pin serial cables

Accepting Incoming Calls

You can create your own remote access server when you set up Windows 2000 Professional to accept as many as three simultaneous incoming calls. The calls can be one dial-up call, one VPN call, and one direct-connection call. Windows 2000 Professional provides support for the following clients:

- Windows 2000 Professional
- Windows NT 4, 3.51, 3.5, and 3.1
- Windows 98
- Windows 95
- Macintosh

To make an incoming call connection, follow these steps:

1. Choose Start ➢ Settings ➢ Network and Dial-Up Connections.

2. Open Make New Connection, and when the Network Connection Wizard starts, click Next.

3. Select the Accept Incoming Connections option, and click Next.

4. Select the device you want to use with this connection, and click Next.

5. Choose whether or not you will allow VPN connections. Click Next.

6. Specify the users who will be allowed to connect to this computer, and click Next.

7. Select the networking components you want to use with this connection. Click Next.

8. Name the connection, and click Finish.

You will see an icon for the connection you just created in the Network and Dial-Up Connections folder. And just to be as safe as we can be, now that you have created an incoming connection, right-click the icon, choose Properties, and click the Users tab, shown in Figure 17.8, to bring it to the front. Check the Require All Users to Secure Their Passwords and Data check box, which specifies that all users must encrypt all passwords and data.

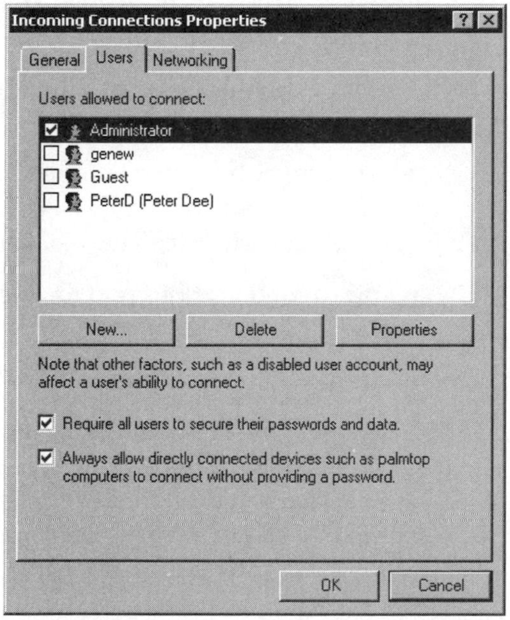

FIGURE 17.8: The Incoming Connections Properties dialog box open at the Users tab

Connecting without Wires

Windows 2000 Professional supports infrared (IR) communications between two computers, between a computer and the network, and between a computer and a printer. All must be equipped with the appropriate infrared hardware.

> **NOTE**   Infrared communication is a method of wireless transmission that uses part of the infrared spectrum to transmit and receive signals. Data can be transmitted between nodes—for example, a computer and a printer—as much as 80 feet apart along an unobstructed path; infrared beams cannot pass through masonry walls.

Many infrared devices are detected automatically by Windows 2000 Professional, using Plug and Play, but if yours was not, or if you want to install a device driver for an infrared device, follow these steps:

1. Choose Start ➢ Settings ➢ Control Panel ➢ Add/Remove Hardware to open the Add/Remove Hardware Wizard.

2. When the Wizard asks if you want to let Windows search for your new hardware, click No, and then click Next.

3. Select Infrared from the list of hardware types, and click Next to open the Add Infrared Device Wizard.

4. Here you specify manufacturer information about your IR device. If the device is built-in, select Standard Infrared Devices; if you have an adapter, choose the name of the manufacturer and the model for your adapter. Click Next.

5. Choose the communications port to which the IR device is physically connected.

6. Accept the default virtual COM and LPT ports, and click Next.

7. When prompted by the Add Infrared Device Wizard, click Finish to complete the installation. If the Wizard did not display New Hardware Found messages in step 4, restart your computer. If the Wizard did display the messages, you need not restart your computer.

8. To activate the IR device, select the Infrared icon in Control Panel. If there is no Infrared icon, choose View ➢ Refresh, or press F5 to force the icon to appear.

To print to an infrared printer, be sure the printer is within range and is assigned to the infrared printer port; then simply print as you normally would. When an infrared device is within range, the infrared connection status icon appears on the Taskbar:

And you will see this Wireless Link icon on the Desktop:

While a program is communicating over the wireless link, the Taskbar icon changes to this icon:

Windows 2000 Professional supports many simultaneous wireless connections, so you can use more than one program at a time over the same link. Now two people traveling with laptop computers can transfer files quickly and easily over the wireless link rather than shuffling floppies or stringing a cable between the two computers.

Disconnecting from a Network

Once your work is done and it is time to disconnect from a network, follow these steps:

1. Choose Start ➤ Settings, and open Network and Dial-Up Connections.

2. Right-click the appropriate connection, and choose Disconnect from the shortcut menu.

This also disables the network interface card associated with that connection until you re-activate the connection.

Are You Up to Speed?

Now you can...

- ☑ use hardware profiles
- ☑ create user profiles
- ☑ manage portable PC power options
- ☑ dock and undock a portable computer
- ☑ configure your network connection
- ☑ connect to your local area network
- ☑ customize your network connections
- ☑ connect over a phone line
- ☑ connect with ISDN
- ☑ connect through a VPN tunnel
- ☑ connect directly
- ☑ accept incoming calls
- ☑ configure a wireless infrared connection
- ☑ disconnect from a network

APPENDIX A

Glossary

In several of the Skills in this book, we have chosen not to clog up the text with technical definitions, but have referred you to this Glossary instead. This was particularly true of the networking skills, Skills 16 and 17, where jargon and abbreviations are used as a form of shorthand. So here you will find a substantial collection of networking terms as well as terms and concepts specific to Windows 2000 Professional. Check here right away if you need more explanation about something you are reading. We'll start with the numeric entries, listed in ascending sequence, followed by the alphabetic listing.

# #

10/100

A term used to indicate that a network interface card or an Ethernet hub can support either the traditional Ethernet standard (at a data rate of 10Mbps) or the Fast Ethernet standard (at a data rate of 100Mbps), or both of them at the same time.

See also Gigabit Ethernet.

10BaseT

A version of the Ethernet networking standard that uses unshielded twisted-pair cable and RJ-45 connectors. Each computer is connected to a central hub in a star topology, with a maximum cable length of 330 feet (100 meters).

See also 10/100, Ethernet, Fast Ethernet, RJ-45 plug, RJ-45 jack, star topology.

10BaseT cable

A popular Ethernet cable that uses twisted-pair wiring and RJ-45 connectors at each end. You should use Category 3 10BaseT cable with 10Mbps Ethernet networks.

See also 10BaseTX, Category 3 cable.

10BaseTX cable

A popular Ethernet cable that uses twisted-pair wiring and RJ-45 connectors at each end. You should use Category 5 10BaseTX cable with 100Mbps Ethernet networks.

See also 10BaseT, Category 5 cable.

10Mbps

An abbreviation for 10 megabits per second. The standard Ethernet network data rate.

See also 100Mbps.

100Mbps

An abbreviation for 100 megabits per second. The standard Fast Ethernet network data rate.

See also 10Mbps.

a

ACPI

See Advanced Configuration and Power Interface.

Active Desktop

A Windows 2000 Professional feature that makes your Desktop look and behave just like a Web page with underlined icons and a hand mouse pointer. Offered as an alternative to the classical Windows user interface. You can use the Active Desktop or the classical interface, or you can swap back and forth between the two; it's up to you.

Active Directory

A directory service available on networks based on Windows 2000 Server. Active Directory stores information about all the objects on the network and makes that information available to network users and to administrators. Active Directory also provides network administrators with a single point of control for all network objects.

active window

The window currently accepting mouse clicks and keyboard input. You can have as many windows open on your Desktop as you like, but only one of them can be active at a time. The active window always has a different color on its title bar from that of the other open windows.

ActiveX

A technology from Microsoft that permits software components to interact within a networked environment.

ActiveX control

The basic building block of ActiveX. An ActiveX control is a software module, written in any language, that cannot run by itself but has to run within an ActiveX container such as Internet Explorer, a word processor, or other application. Each control delivers one specific function and can communicate with other

ActiveX controls, with the ActiveX container, and with the underlying operating system.

administrator

The person or department responsible for designing, implementing, managing, and maintaining all aspects of the network. The administrator sets up user accounts, changes passwords, adds new hardware, performs software upgrades, and answers your questions when you get stuck.

Advanced Configuration and Power Interface (ACPI)

An interface specification developed by Microsoft, Intel, and Toshiba for controlling power consumption on the PC and all peripherals attached to the system, including printers, tape drives, and so on. ACPI is a BIOS-level hardware specification and requires specific hardware that allows Windows 2000 Professional to direct power management and system configuration.

See also Advanced Power Management.

Advanced Power Management (APM)

An interface specification developed by Microsoft and Intel intended to monitor and extend battery life on laptop computers by shutting down certain system components after a period of inactivity. Now superceded by the Advanced Configuration and Power Interface.

See also Advanced Configuration and Power Interface.

American Standard Code for Information Interchange (ASCII)

A standard single-byte numeric code used to represent letters, numbers, punctuation symbols, and a set of special control characters used on computers. In ASCII, each character is assigned a unique number in the range of 0 through 255, which allows ASCII to represent 256 different characters.

See also Unicode.

APM

See Advanced Power Management.

application

A program used to accomplish a specific task, such as a word processor or a spreadsheet.

ASCII

See American Standard Code for Information Interchange.

associate

To use a specific filename extension to connect a type of data file to an application so that when you click the data file the correct application opens the file. Also known as registered file types.

attachment

A file linked to an e-mail message and sent along with the message to all the recipients. An attachment can be a text file, a document created by an application, a graphic, a video clip, or an audio file.

attribute

An indication of the status of a file. Attributes are used to indicate whether a file is read-only, hidden, compressed, encrypted, ready to be backed up, or whether the contents should be indexed for fast searching.

authentication

The process that validates the user's logon information. Authentication compares the user name and password to a list of authorized users. If a match is found, the user can log on and access the system in accordance with the rights or permissions assigned to his or her user account.

See also permissions, rights.

b

B-channel

A single channel in an Integrated Services Digital Network (ISDN) circuit used to carry voice or data. Basic Rate ISDN has two 64Kbps B-channels, and Primary Rate ISDN has 23.

See also D-channel, Integrated Services Digital Network.

backbone

A central network component that connects a number of other networks. The backbone often uses a higher-speed protocol than the individual network segments.

back up

The process of copying and archiving files as an insurance against future accidents or hard-disk failure.

bandwidth

This term has two definitions. In communications, bandwidth is the difference between the highest and the lowest frequencies available for transmissions in any given range. For example, a normal telephone line is said to have a bandwidth of 3,000 hertz (Hz), the difference between the lowest frequency (300Hz) and the highest frequency (3,300Hz) that it can carry.

In networking, bandwidth is the transmission capacity of a network or communications channel, usually expressed in megabits per second (Mbps). For example, Ethernet operates at 10Mbps, and Fast Ethernet at 100Mbps.

Basic Rate ISDN

An Integrated Services Digital Network service that offers two 64Kbps data channels and one 16Kbps channel for control information.

See also Integrated Services Digital Network, Primary Rate ISDN.

bits per second (bps)

The number of binary digits, or bits, transmitted every second during a data-transfer procedure.

BNC

A high-quality locking connector used with coaxial Ethernet cable.

boot

The process of starting or restarting a computer.

bps

See bits per second.

bridge

A hardware device used to connect two or more network segments together to form what appears to be a single network. You can use a bridge to connect networks that use different wiring systems or different network protocols.

See also router.

broadcast

To send a message to all users currently logged on to the network.

broadcast storm

Serious congestion on a network that occurs when a large number of messages are transmitted by many workstations in response to a transmission from one workstation.

browse

To look at a list of computers on a network or a list of files and folders on a disk.

browser

An application used to explore Internet resources. A browser lets you wander from Web site to Web site without regard for the technical details of the links between them or the specific methods used to access them, and presents the information—text, graphics, sound, or video—as a document on the screen.

built-in groups

See user groups.

bus topology

A networking design in which a single cable is used to connect one computer to the next. This allows all network nodes to receive the same message through the network cable at the same time.

See also ring topology, star topology.

byte

In computer storage terms, a single character such as a number, letter, or symbol. A byte usually contains 8 bits, but on some older systems, a byte may contain as few as 7 bits or as many as 11. Because bytes represent such a small unit of storage, they are usually grouped into kilobytes (1,024 bytes), megabytes (1,048,576 bytes), and gigabytes (1,073,741,824 bytes) for convenience, particularly when describing computer memory size or hard-disk capacity.

C

cascading

The technique used when connecting two Ethernet hubs together to expand the network; sometimes called daisy-chaining. Cascading may require a special cable.

See also crossover cable.

Category 3 cable

A 10BaseT unshielded twisted-pair cable commonly used in 10Mbps Ethernet networks.

See also 10BaseT cable, 10BaseTX cable, Category 5 cable.

Category 5 cable

A 10BaseTX unshielded twisted-pair cable commonly used in 100Mbps Ethernet networks.

See also 10BaseT cable, 10BaseTX cable, Category 3 cable.

client

A computer or application requesting services from the network. One of the most familiar clients is the Web browser.

See also server.

client/server

A network computing system in which individual computers acting as clients request services such as file storage, printing, and communications from another computer acting as the server.

coaxial cable

A high-capacity cable used in networking that contains a solid inner copper core surrounded by plastic insulation, and an outer braided copper or foil shield. Depending on the diameter of the cable, it may be known as thinnet (thin Ethernet, used for office installations) or thicknet (thick Ethernet, used for facility-wide applications).

collision

An attempt by two computers on the network to send a message at exactly the same moment; Ethernet automatically resends both messages, but with altered timing so they do not collide and are received properly.

command prompt

A character or group of characters displayed on the screen that lets you know that the operating system is available and ready to receive your input. In Windows 2000 Professional, the command prompt appears in a window on the Desktop.

communications software

Applications software such as e-mail or fax software that allows you to send or receive data to or from a remote system.

computer name

A unique name of as many as 15 characters that identifies a computer on the network.

cookie

A block of data stored by a Web server on a client browser that can be retrieved by the server during a future session. A cookie contains information used to identify the user for administrative purposes or to prepare a custom Web page.

crossover cable

A special cable in which the transmit and receive lines have been reversed. A crossover cable can be used to connect two Ethernet hubs.

See also cascading, null modem.

crosstalk

In communications, any interference from a physically adjacent channel that corrupts the signal and causes transmission errors.

d

D-channel

A channel in an Integrated Services Digital Network (ISDN) circuit used to carry control and signalling information. Basic Rate ISDN has one 16Kbps D-channel, and Primary Rate ISDN has one 64Kbps D-channel.

See also B-channel, Integrated Services Digital Network.

daisy chaining

See cascading.

data transmission speed

The number of bits transmitted per second over a network cable.

decryption

The process of converting encrypted data back into its original form.

See also encryption.

dedicated server

A computer on the network that is assigned to function in a specific role, perhaps as a print server or communications server, and which cannot be used as a client.

See also client/server.

defragmentation

The process of reorganizing and rewriting files on a hard disk so that they occupy one single continuous area on the disk rather than many small, scattered areas. When a file on a hard disk is updated, it may be written into different areas all over the disk, particularly if the file is updated regularly over a long period of time. This fragmentation can lead to a progressive slow-down in loading files, but this effect is reversed by defragmentation.

device

A general term used to refer to any computer peripheral or hardware element that can send and receive data. Some devices require special software known as a device driver to control or manage them; others have built-in intelligence.

device driver

A small program that allows a computer to communicate with and control a device. Windows 2000 Professional contains a standard set of device drivers for the keyboard, mouse, monitor, and so on. When you add a specialized peripheral device such as a network interface card, Windows 2000 Professional uses Plug-and-Play services to install the appropriate device driver automatically.

See also Plug and Play.

digital video disc (DVD)

A compact disc format capable of storing 4.7GB of information. A two-layer standard increases storage capacity to 8.5GB, and eventually double-sided discs are expected to store up to 17GB per disc. DVD drives can also read conventional compact discs.

DLL

See dynamic link library.

document

A data file created by an application. For example, WordPad, included with Windows 2000 Professional, can create and store documents in several formats, including as a Word document, a text file, a rich text file, or Unicode.

See also rich text document, text document, Unicode document.

domain

A description of a single computer, a whole department, or a complete site, used for administrative and naming purposes. Each domain has a unique name.

drive mapping

The technique used to assign a drive letter to represent a complete directory path statement that points to a shared network drive. By mapping a drive, you can refer to the drive by letter as though it were physically attached to your computer, and there is no need to use a long, hard-to-remember path statement.

driver

See device driver.

dual boot

A Windows 2000 Professional configuration that allows you to choose which of two installed operating systems you want to load when the computer starts.

DVD

See digital video disc.

dynamic link library (DLL)

A program module that contains executable code and data that can be used by an application, or even by other DLLs, in performing a specific task. A DLL is only loaded when it is needed by the calling program.

e

e-mail

Short for electronic mail: the use of a network to transmit text messages, memos, reports, graphics, audio, and video. Users can send a message to one or more individuals, to a predefined group, or to all users on the system. When you receive an e-mail message, you can read, print, forward, reply, or delete it.

Emergency Repair Disk (ERD)

A floppy disk, created by the Backup utility, that contains information about your Windows 2000 Professional configuration. You can use an ERD to repair your system if your computer won't start or if some of the essential files are damaged.

encapsulate

The process of inserting a data message from a higher-level communications protocol into the data frame of a lower-level protocol.

See also tunneling.

encryption

The process of encoding information in an attempt to make it secure from unauthorized access, particularly during transmission. The reverse of this process is known as decryption.

ERD

See Emergency Repair Disk.

Ethernet

A computer networking protocol with a data transfer rate of 10Mbps, originally developed by Dr. Robert Metcalf at Xerox in 1970.

Ethernet is the most popular networking protocol in use today.

See also Fast Ethernet, Gigabit Ethernet.

Ethernet address

The address assigned to a network interface card by the original manufacturer. The Ethernet address identifies a computer or other device on the network to the rest of the network and allows messages to reach the correct destination. Also known as the media access control (MAC) or hardware address.

f

Fast Ethernet

A version of the Ethernet networking standard that allows data rates of either 10Mbps or 100Mbps or both.

See also Ethernet, Gigabit Ethernet.

FAT file system

A file allocation table that uses a 16-bit addressing scheme to keep track of files and folders on a disk. FAT can address a hard disk of up to 2.6GB, but is inefficient in disk-space utilization as the default cluster size can be as large as 32KB.

See also FAT32 file system, NTFS file system.

FAT32 file system

A file allocation table that uses a 32-bit addressing scheme to keep track of files and folders on a disk. FAT32 can address a hard disk of larger than 2.6GB as well as a default cluster size of as small as 4KB. FAT32 can support hard disks of up to 2 terabytes in size.

See also FAT file system, NTFS file system.

file server

A dedicated computer on the network used to store files or provide services to client computers. On large networks, the file server runs a special operating system such as Windows 2000 Server. On smaller networks, the file server may run Windows 2000 Professional supporting peer-to-peer networking.

file system

The structure by which files are organized, stored, and named. Windows 2000 Professional supports several different file systems, including NTFS, FAT, and FAT32.

file transfer

The process of moving or copying a file from one computer to another. The file format may also be changed during this transfer.

firewall

A barrier established in hardware or in software, or sometimes in both, that monitors and controls the flow of traffic between two networks, usually a private network and the Internet.

folder

A way to organize or group files and other folders; also called a directory.

full-duplex transmission

Two-way simultaneous transmission on the same communications channel.

See also half-duplex transmission.

g

Gigabit Ethernet

A version of the Ethernet networking standard that supports a data rate of 100Mbps.

See also Ethernet, Fast Ethernet.

global group

User accounts that are granted server and local rights in their own and other domains whose security systems allow access. Global groups are a means of providing rights and permissions to resources inside and outside the domain to a group of users within a single domain.

See also group, local group, permissions, user rights.

group

A collection of users, contacts, other computers, and other groups. Distribution groups are used in Outlook Express for e-mail, while security groups are used to grant access to resources.

guest account

A built-in account available to those users who do not have an account on the Windows 2000 Professional system. Allowing people to use the guest account can breach some corporate security policies.

h

half-duplex transmission

One-way transmission at any one time on the same communications channel.

See also full-duplex transmission.

hardware

All the physical electronic components of a computer system, including peripheral devices, printed-circuit boards, monitors, disk drives, and printers. If you can stub your toe on it, it must be hardware.

hardware address

See Ethernet address.

Hardware Compatibility List (HCL)

A list of all the hardware devices supported by the Windows 2000 family of operating systems. Items on this list have actually been tested and verified to work properly with Windows 2000.

hardware profile

A set of configuration information that defines a specific computer system. For example, if you have a dockable portable computer, you can create a hardware profile called "Docked" for use when you are working in the office and another called "Undocked" for use when you are away from the office.

HCL

See Hardware Compatibility List.

HTML

See HyperText Markup Language.

HTTP

See Hypertext Transfer Protocol.

hub

The central component of an Ethernet network. A hub receives signals from and transmits signals on the network between the computers connected to it. Two hubs can be connected by means of a crossover cable.

hyperlink

See link.

HyperText Markup Language (HTML)

A standard document formatting language used to create Web pages and other hypertext documents. HTML is a subset of Standardized Generalized Markup Language (SGML). HTML defines the appearance and placement on the page of elements such as fonts, graphics, text, and links to other Web sites; it has nothing to do with the actual material presented.

See also Hypertext Transfer Protocol.

Hypertext Transfer Protocol (HTTP)

The command and control protocol used to manage communications between a Web server and a Web browser.

See also HyperText Markup Language.

i

identity

A feature in Outlook Express that allows you to create multiple accounts so you can keep work and home e-mail associated with different identities. You can also use different identities for different users of the same computer.

infrared

A method of wireless transmission that uses part of the infrared spectrum to transmit and receive information.

Internet

The world's largest computer network, consisting of millions of computers supporting tens of millions of users in countries around the world. The Internet is growing at such a phenomenal rate that any size estimates are quickly out-of-date. Most people use the Internet for e-mail and to access the World Wide Web. Internet access can be via a permanent network connection or by dial-up through one of the many Internet Service Providers. The Internet uses the TCP/IP family of networking protocols.

Internet Service Provider (ISP)

A company that provides commercial or residential customers access to the Internet via dedicated or dial-up connections.

internetwork

A large network consisting of at least two network segments that use different networking protocols. The two segments may be connected by means of a router or a bridge. Users on an internetwork can, providing they have appropriate security clearance, access the resources of all the connected segments.

intranet

A private corporate network that uses Internet software and standards, including the TCP/IP family of networking protocols. An intranet may or may not include a permanent connection to the Internet.

Internet Protocol (IP)

That portion of the TCP/IP family of networking protocols responsible for addressing and sending data packets over the network.

See also Transmission Control Protocol, Transmission Control Protocol/Internet Protocol.

IP

See Internet Protocol.

IP address

The unique 32-bit number that identifies a computer on the Internet or other Internet Protocol network.

IP Sec

A suite of communications protocols designed to add security provisions to the Internet Protocol.

IPX/SPX

See Internetwork Packet Exchange/ Sequenced Packet Exchange.

Integrated Services Digital Network (ISDN)

A standard for a worldwide digital communications network originally designed to replace all current systems with a completely digital, synchronous, full-duplex transmission. Computers and other devices connect to the ISDN service via simple, standardized interfaces. They can transmit voice, video, and data all on the same line.

See also Basic Rate ISDN, Primary Rate ISDN.

Internetwork Packet Exchange/ Sequenced Packet Exchange (IPX/SPX)

A communications protocol designed by Novell for use on NetWare-based networks.

ISDN

See Integrated Services Digital Network.

ISP

See Internet Service Provider.

k

kilobit

One thousand bits of data. 56 kilobits per second (Kbps) means 56,000 bits of information are transmitted every second over the network or communications circuit.

See also megabit.

l

LAN

See local area network.

landscape orientation

A horizontal print orientation in which text or images are printed with the width of the image greater than the height.

See also portrait orientation.

link

On a Web page or hypertext document, a connection between one element and another in the same or in a different document.

local area network (LAN)

A group of computers and associated peripheral devices connected by a communications channel, capable of sharing files, services, and other resources among several users.

See also peer-to-peer network, wide area network.

local group

A group granted rights and permissions to only the resources available on the servers of its own domain.

See also global group, group, permissions, user rights.

local user profile

A user profile that is specific to the computer upon which it was created; a local user profile does not follow you if you log on to a different computer on the network.

See also mandatory user profile, roaming user profile, user profile.

log off

To terminate a session on a computer.

log on

To establish a session on the computer by providing a user name and password.

m

megabit

One million bits of data. When an Ethernet network transmits at 10 megabits per second (Mbps), 10 million bits of information are transmitted every second over the network.

See also kilobit.

mail reader

An application used to read e-mail, such as Outlook Express.

mandatory user profile

A user profile created by the Administrator, stored on the server, and downloaded to a workstation when the user logs on to the network. A mandatory user profile is not updated when the user logs off.

See also local user profile, roaming user profile, user profile.

mapped drive

A network disk drive that has been assigned to a drive letter on your computer.

MIME

See Multipurpose Internet Mail Extensions.

Multipurpose Internet Mail Extensions (MIME)

A specification that allows users to send multiple-part and multimedia e-mail messages rather than just simple text messages.

modem

A hardware device that allows you to transmit and receive data to and from other computers using a standard telephone line. A modem translates the digital signals that the computer uses into analog signals suitable for transmission over telephone lines, and another modem then performs the opposite transformation at the other end of the line.

multitasking

The simultaneous execution of two or more programs in the same computer.

n

NetBEUI

A compact and fast networking protocol suitable for use on small networks.

NetBIOS

A networking protocol originally developed in 1984 by IBM and Sytek.

network

A group of computers and associated peripheral devices connected by a communications channel, capable of sharing files and other resources among several users. A network can range from a peer-to-peer network connecting a small number of users in an office or department, to a local area network connecting hundreds of users over permanently installed cables and dial-up connections, to a wide area network connecting users on several networks spread over a wide geographical area.

network adapter

See network interface card.

network interface card (NIC)

An expansion card that plugs into a PC and connects it to a network. Also known as a network adapter.

network protocol

The formal specification that defines the procedures to follow when transmitting and receiving data over a network. Protocols define the format, timing, sequence, and error checking used on a network. TCP/IP, NetBEUI, and IPX/SPX are three of the most common network protocols in use.

newsgroup

An e-mail discussion group devoted to a single topic. Subscribers to a newsgroup post articles that can be read by all the other subscribers.

See also post.

newsreader

An application used to read the contents of newsgroups. Outlook Express is a newsreader as well as an e-mail application.

NIC

See network interface card.

node

Any device connected to the network that is capable of communicating with other devices on the network.

NTFS file system

The high-performance file system designed for use with Windows 2000 Professional.

See also FAT file system, FAT32 file system.

null modem

A short serial cable that connects two personal computers so they can communicate without needing modems. Certain wires within the cable are crossed over so that the wires used for sending data by one computer are used for receiving data by the other computer.

O

object

Any element of Windows 2000 Professional, such as a file, folder, shared folder, or printer, that can be described in unique terms.

Object Linking and Embedding (OLE)

A mechanism that allows you to share information between different applications by pasting information created in one application into a document created by another.

OLE

See Object Linking and Embedding.

p

paging file

An area of disk space used by Windows 2000 Professional as temporary storage to hold parts of applications and data files that do not currently fit into main memory. The paging file, along with the physical memory available in the computer, are managed by Windows 2000 Professional as virtual memory. Also known as a swap file.

parallel port

A port on the computer that manages data eight bits at a time and is often connected to a scanner or printer.

See also serial port.

partition

A portion of a hard disk drive that Windows 2000 Professional treats as though it were a separate drive.

password

A string of characters that a user types, along with their user name, when logging in to a computer. The user name and password identify a specific authorized user of the system. In Windows 2000 Professional, your password can be up to 14 characters in length, and don't forget that it is case sensitive. Keep your password a secret, and change it often.

PC Card

An expansion card roughly the size of a credit card that plugs into the PC Card slot on a portable computer.

PCI

See Peripheral Component Interconnect.

Peripheral Component Interconnect (PCI)

The 32- and 64-bit local bus architecture used on the motherboard, designed to accept network interface cards and other adapters.

peer-to-peer network

A network in which all computers communicate directly as equals, without the need for a dedicated file server.

See also client/server, local area network.

permissions

Used to define who can access resources across a network and what kind of access users can have. In Windows 2000 Professional, network shares have Read, Change, and Full Control permissions, and file and folder permissions offer more options, including Modify, Read & Execute, List Folder Contents, and Write.

See also global group, local group, group, user rights.

personalized menu

A feature of Windows 2000 Professional that hides the programs you don't use very often so you can find the ones you do use quickly and easily.

Plug and Play

A specification defined by Intel, Microsoft, Compaq, and others that allows a computer to identify newly added components quickly and easily and to configure them for use automatically.

Point-to-Point Protocol (PPP)

A member of the TCP/IP family of networking protocols used to transmit data over serial lines and point-to-point dial-up telephone connections.

Point-to-Point Tunneling Protocol (PPTP)

A networking protocol that tunnels or encapsulates another protocol, usually IP, IPX, or Net-BEUI. PPTP is used to set up a Virtual Private Network (VPN) or a secure connection over the Internet.

See also Virtual Private Network.

port

A connector on your computer used to attach a cable. A port may be a serial, parallel, keyboard, or mouse port or a connection to a network.

post

To send an article or e-mail message to a newsgroup.

See also newsgroup.

portrait orientation

A vertical print orientation in which text or images are printed with the height of the image greater than the width. The typical print mode used for most letters, memos, and reports.

See also landscape orientation.

PPP

See Point-to-Point Protocol.

PPTP

See Point-to-Point Tunneling Protocol.

Primary Rate ISDN

An Integrated Services Digital Network service that offers 23 64Kbps data channels and one 64Kbps channel for control information.

See also Basic Rate ISDN, Integrated Services Digital Network.

protocol

See network protocol.

r

Registry

A Windows 2000 Professional database that contains extensive configuration information, including a list of users, a list of the applications currently installed and the types of documents they can create, information about the computer's hardware and which ports are in use, as well as settings for folders and icons.

remote access

A connection to the network made using a modem and telephone line that allows data to be sent and received over large distances.

See also Virtual Private Network.

remote access server

Software that allows users to connect via modem and access network resources. Users can connect using a dial-up telephone connection, an ISDN, or an X.25 network.

rich text document

A document stored in a special format that is used for transferring formatted documents between different applications and even between different computer platforms.

rights

See user rights.

RJ-45 plug

A modular connector on the end of a 10BaseT or 10BaseTX twisted-pair cable; looks much like a standard telephone plug but is just a little larger.

RJ-45 jack

A modular connector on your network interface card that accepts an RJ-45 plug; looks much like a standard telephone jack but is just a little larger.

roaming user profile

A user profile created by the Administrator, stored on the server, and downloaded to a workstation when the user logs on to the network. A roaming user profile is always updated on the server and on the local computer when the user logs off.

See also local user profile, mandatory user profile, user profile.

router

A network device used to connect two or more network segments.

S

Secure Multipurpose Internet Mail Extensions (S/MIME)

An extension to the Multipurpose Internet Mail Extension (MIME) e-mail standard that adds security in the form of data encryption.

Secure Sockets Layer (SSL)

An interface developed by Netscape that provides encrypted data transfers between a Web server and a Web browser over the Internet.

security zone

A mechanism used in Internet Explorer to divide Internet content into a collection of zones.

serial port

A port on the computer that manages data one bit at a time and is often connected to a mouse or modem.

See also parallel port.

server

A computer on the network that provides services such as file storage, communications, or printing to client computers.

See also client, client/server.

server-based network

A network in which all the client computers use a dedicated central server for functions such as file storage, communications, and printing.

See also peer-to-peer network.

service pack

A CD containing a set of upgrades to Windows 2000 Professional. Service packs are numbered in sequence, and each service pack contains all the changes and modifications present in previous service packs as well as the new changes.

shared folder

A folder on another computer that has been shared and made available to other network users.

shared printer

A printer on another computer that has been shared and made available to other network users. A shared printer will receive input from several different computers.

sharing

The process of making a network resource such as a file, folder, or printer available to other network users.

shielded twisted-pair cable

Shielded cable that comprises two or more pairs of insulated wires, twisted together at six twists per inch.

shortcut

A link to an item such as a file, a folder, or an application. You can create as many shortcuts as you like, and you can place them on the Desktop, on the Start menu, or in a particular folder.

S/MIME

See Secure Multipurpose Internet Mail Extensions.

SSL

See Secure Sockets Layer

star topology

A network configuration in the form of a star with a hub at the center. Commonly used with 10BaseT and 10BaseTX Ethernet networks.

subscribe

To join a newsgroup or a mailing list. This is not a subscription in the sense of a magazine subscription; no money ever changes hands.

subnet

A network segment connected to another segment by a router. Subnets can stand alone or can be connected to other subnets to form a small local area network.

swap file

See paging file.

system administrator

The person or department who is responsible for managing the computer system or network.

See also administrator.

t

TCO

See Total Cost of Ownership.

TCP

See Transmission Control Protocol.

TCP/IP

See Transmission Control Protocol/Internet Protocol.

text document

A file that only contains characters from the ASCII character set. A text file includes letters, numbers, symbols, and punctuation but does not include any formatting information.

See also rich text document, Unicode document.

topology

A map of the network; networks are usually configured in bus, ring, or star topologies.

Total Cost of Ownership (TCO)

A term first used by the GartnerGroup in an attempt to quantify the real costs of a particular computer solution. TCO encompasses the direct costs of the hardware and software, and then adds in costs for maintenance and support, costs for the users performing their own technical support rather than their official job, and system productivity costs.

Transmission Control Protocol (TCP)

That portion of the TCP/IP family of networking protocols responsible for reliable data delivery over the network.

See also Internet Protocol, Transmission Control Protocol/Internet Protocol.

Transmission Control Protocol/Internet Protocol (TCP/IP)

A widely available set of networking protocols developed in the 1970s. TCP/IP is an open standard, completely independent of any single hardware or software company. It is supported by a huge number of vendors and is available on many different computers ranging from PCs to mainframes, running many different operating systems. TCP/IP is used by many corporations, universities, and government agencies, and it is also the protocol used on the Internet.

See also Internet Protocol, Transmission Control Protocol.

tunneling

The encapsulation of one protocol within another, often used to transport a local area network protocol across a network that does not support that particular protocol. Tunneling is also used to create a pseudo connection across a network such as the Internet, which is then known as a Virtual Private Network.

See encapsulate, Virtual Private Network.

twisted-pair cable

Cable that comprises two or more pairs of insulated wires, twisted together at six twists per inch. The cable may be shielded or unshielded.

u

Unicode

A 16-bit character code that supports up to 65,536 unique characters rather than the 256 characters available in the ASCII character set. By using two bytes to represent each character, Unicode allows almost all the world's written languages to be represented in a single character set.

See also American Standard Code for Information Exchange.

Unicode document

A document that contains characters from the Unicode character set.

See also rich text document, text document.

UPS

See Uninterruptible Power Supply.

Uninterruptible Power Supply (UPS)

A power source, usually consisting of a large set of batteries, used to power a computer system if the normal supply is interrupted or falls below an acceptable level.

Uniform Resource Locator (URL)

An address for a resource on the Internet.

URL

See Uniform Resource Locator.

user account

The configuration information that describes a single user, including user name, password, the groups the user account belongs to, and the rights and permissions the user has for access to computer and network resources.

user groups

A set of default groups provided with Windows 2000 Professional that defines a collection of rights and permissions for members. Using these built-in groups is an easy way of providing access to commonly used network resources.

user name

A unique name that identifies an account to Windows 2000 Professional.

user profile

A set of configuration information that defines the Windows 2000 Professional environment when a user logs on to the system, including program items, screen colors, wallpaper, network connections, mouse settings, and window size and position.

See also local user profile, mandatory user profile, roaming user profile.

user rights

The ability to perform a particular function such as backing up files and folders, adding new users, or shutting down the computer.

See also global group, local group, group, permissions.

unshielded twisted-pair cable

Unshielded cable that comprises two or more pairs of insulated wires, twisted together at six twists per inch.

V

V.90

The latest standard for analog modems. V.90 describes an asymmetric connection, with theoretical speeds of up to 56Kbps downstream and an upstream rate of 33.6Kbps. To reduce crosstalk between adjacent lines, the FCC has restricted maximum signal levels, which in turn reduced the maximum theoretical data rate to

54Kbps. Whether you can actually achieve these rates depends on the quality of the phone line, and if the other end of the connection is not a digital connection, the modem switches into full analog mode at 28.8 or 33.6Kbps.

virtual memory

A memory-management technique that allows information in physical memory to be swapped out to a file on a hard disk if necessary, providing applications with more memory space than is actually available in the computer.

See also paging file.

Virtual Private Network (VPN)

An encrypted and authenticated private tunnel across the Internet.

See encapsulate, tunneling.

virus

A program intended to damage a computer system without the user's knowledge or permission.

volume

A portion of a hard disk that functions as though it were a separate disk.

VPN

See Virtual Private Network.

W

WAN

See wide area network.

Web browser

An application used to explore Internet resources. A browser lets you wander from Web site to Web site without regard for the technical details of the links between them or the specific methods used to access them, and presents the information—text, graphics, sound, or video—as a document on the screen.

Web server

A hardware and software package that provides services to client computers running Web browsers.

wide area network (WAN)

A network that connects users across large distances, often crossing the geographical boundaries of cities and states.

See also local area network.

workgroup

A group of individuals who work together and share the same files and databases on the network. In Windows 2000 Professional, computers that belong to a workgroup must all have the same workgroup name.

World Wide Web (WWW)

A huge collection of hypertext information available on the Internet. World Wide Web traffic is growing faster than any other Internet service, and the reason for this becomes obvious once you try a capable Web browser; it is very easy and a lot of fun to access the World Wide Web.

WWW

See World Wide Web.

Index

Note to Reader: In this index, **boldfaced** page numbers refer to primary discussions of the topic; *italics* page numbers refer to figures.

ASCII (American Standard Code for Information
    Interchange), 421–422
.ASF files, 196
associate, 422
asterisk (*), as Search command wildcard character,
    69
.ASX files, 196
AT command, 133
attachment, 422
  creating, **296**
  saving, 286–287
attribute, 388, 422
.AU files, 196
audio CDs, **188–190**
  automatic play, 188–189
  recording sound from, 192
authentication, 422
AutoComplete, in Internet Explorer, 245, 256
.AVI files, 196

B

B-channel, 422
Back button, in Internet Explorer, 258
back up, **334–339**, 422
  with Backup Wizard, **335–336**
  excluding files from, 339
  manual process, **336–339**, *337*
  before partition formatting, 24
  restoring, **339–340**
    from Windows 98, 19
  before Windows upgrade, **18–19**
backbone, 422
background
  of Desktop, customizing, **92**
  of Outlook Express message, **293–294**
  of Web page, printing, 269
background processing, 114
Backup Operators group, 383
bandwidth, 422–423
Basic Rate ISDN, 410, 423
bits per second (bps), 423
blocking e-mail messages, 298

BNC, 423
bold type
  in e-mail, 292
  in WordPad, 213
bookmarks. *See* Favorite Sites in Internet Explorer
boot, 423
boot logging, safe mode startup with, 352
boot sector, 9
bootable CD-ROM drive, 20
bottlenecks, locating, 349–351
bps (bits per second), 423
bridge, 423
broadcast, 423
broadcast storm, 423
browse, 423
browser, 423
browsing, mouse pointer design options, 90
bus topology, 362, 423
Business Card format, for Address Book printing,
    202
byte, 424

C

cable modems, **379**
cabling for network, **364–365**
  maximum distance for star topology, 363
  setup, 367
  troubleshooting, 377
cache, 276
Calculator, **204–208**
  keys on, 205
  Scientific view, *206*, **206–208**
  Standard view, *205*, **206**
calendar, default program for, 246
Call menu (NetMeeting), ➣ Directory, 181
camera
  Imaging application and, 217–218
  setup, **324–325**
  for video calls, 233
canceling, printing, 148
capitalization, in e-mail, 292
Caps Lock key
  and passwords, 35

E

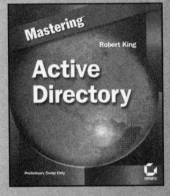